SCHOOL PSYCHOLOGY
Perspectives and Issues

EDUCATIONAL PSYCHOLOGY

Allen J. Edwards, Series Editor
Department of Psychology
Southwest Missouri State University
Springfield, Missouri

Published

Gary D. Phye and Daniel J. Reschly (eds.). School Psychology: Perspectives and Issues

Norman Steinaker and M. Robert Bell. The Experiential Taxonomy: A New Approach to Teaching and Learning

J. P. Das, John R. Kirby, and Ronald F. Jarman. Simultaneous and Successive Cognitive Processes

Herbert J. Klausmeier and Patricia S. Allen. Cognitive Development of Children and Youth: A Longitudinal Study

Victor M. Agruso, Jr. Learning in the Later Years: Principles of Educational Gerontology

Thomas R. Kratochwill (ed.). Single Subject Research: Strategies for Evaluating Change

Kay Pomerance Torshen. The Mastery Approach to Competency-Based Education

Harvey Lesser. Television and the Preschool Child: A Psychological Theory of Instruction and Curriculum Development

Donald J. Treffinger, J. Kent Davis, and Richard E. Ripple (eds.). Handbook on Teaching Educational Psychology

Harry L. Hom, Jr. and Paul A. Robinson (eds.). Psychological Processes in Early Education

J. Nina Lieberman. Playfulness: Its Relationship to Imagination and Creativity

Samuel Ball (ed.). Motivation in Education

Erness Bright Brody and Nathan Brody. Intelligence: Nature, Determinants, and Consequences

The list of titles in this series continues on the last page of this volume

SCHOOL PSYCHOLOGY
Perspectives and Issues

Edited by

GARY D. PHYE
DANIEL J. RESCHLY
Department of Psychology
Iowa State University
Ames, Iowa

ACADEMIC PRESS   New York   San Francisco   London   1979
A Subsidiary of Harcourt Brace Jovanovich, Publishers

ACADEMIC PRESS, INC.
111 Fifth Avenue, New York, New York 10003

United Kingdom Edition published by
ACADEMIC PRESS, INC. (LONDON) LTD.
24/28 Oval Road, London NW1 7DX

Library of Congress Cataloging in Publication Data
 Main entry under title:

 School psychology.

 (Educational Psychology series)
 Includes bibliographies and index.
 1. Educational psychology——Addresses, essays,
lectures. 2. School psychologists——Addresses, essays,
lectures. 3. Educational tests and measurements——
Addresses, essays, lectures. 4. Exceptional children——
Addresses, essays, lectures. I. Phye, Gary D.
II. Reschly, Daniel J.
 LB1055.S42   370.15   78–22531
 ISBN 0–12–554250–X

PRINTED IN THE UNITED STATES OF AMERICA

79 80 81 82   9 8 7 6 5 4 3 2 1

Contents

▯

SCHOOL PSYCHOLOGY: AN OVERVIEW

1

2

v

II

ASSESSMENT AND INTERVENTIONS
WITH SPECIAL POPULATIONS

III

INDIRECT SERVICES OF SCHOOL PSYCHOLOGISTS

List of Contributors

Numbers in parentheses indicate the pages on which the authors' contributions begin.

DOUGLAS T. BROWN (49), Department of Psychology, James Madison University, Harrisonburg, Virginia 22807

HARVEY F. CLARIZIO (309), Department of Educational Psychology, Michigan State University, East Lansing, Michigan 48823

RONALD A. DAVIS (281), Psychology Department, Tempe Elementary Schools, Tempe, Arizona 85282

KATHRYN CLARK GERKEN (157), Division of Special Education, College of Education, The University of Iowa, Iowa City, Iowa 52240

D. L. GOLDWATER (123), Department of Educational Psychology, The University of Texas at Austin, Austin, Texas 78712

M. MADON HAWK (191), Department of Educational Psychology and Research, University of Kansas, Lawrence, Kansas 66044

ELWOOD D. HOUSEMAN (191), Department of Educational Psychology and Research, University of Kansas, Lawrence, Kansas 66044

VIRGINIA MONROE (25), School of Education, University of South Dakota, Vermillion, South Dakota 57069

THOMAS OAKLAND (123), Department of Educational Psychology, The University of Texas at Austin, Austin, Texas 78712

GARY D. PHYE (257), Department of Psychology, Iowa State University, Ames, Iowa 50011

MICHAEL C. PYRYT (191), Department of Educational Psychology and Research, University of Kansas, Lawrence, Kansas 66044

DANIEL J. RESCHLY (215), Department of Psychology, Iowa State University, Ames, Iowa 50011

RALPH H. TINDALL (3), Department of Psychology, University of South Carolina, Columbia, South Carolina 29208

MARTIN TOMBARI (281), Department of Educational Psychology, The University of Texas at Austin, Austin, Texas 78712

DONALD J. TREFFINGER* (191), Department of Educational Psychology and Research, University of Kansas, Lawrence, Kansas 66044

JAMES E. YSSELDYKE (87), Psychology in the Schools Training Program, University of Minnesota, Minneapolis, Minnesota 55455

* *Present Address:* Creative Education Foundation, State University College, Buffalo, New York 14222

Preface

This book has its origins in the many conversations we have had with colleagues at other universities, practicing school psychologists, and our own graduate students. The basic question raised in these conversations was, "Where do you go to find a scholarly, up-to-date, and critical review of topics in school psychology?" We decided to edit a book that would answer this need.

All the chapters in the book were written by persons who have both established credentials as scholars as well as practical experience in school psychology. We requested each author to provide a well-referenced treatment of a topic that would provide the foundation for consideration of practical issues. We believe readers will find the treatment of topics to be thorough, critical, and relevant to practical concerns of training and practice in school psychology.

The book is divided into three parts. The first, School Psychology: An Overview, is devoted to historical perspectives, current influences on roles, and contemporary issues in school psychology. The second part, Assessment and Interventions with Special Populations, includes five chapters on issues in assessment and interventions with exceptional persons. The three chapters in Part III, Indirect Services of School Psychologists, discuss services such as research, evaluation, and consultation. The organization of the book and selection of content was designed to meet the needs of beginning graduate students in school psychology, university faculty in school and educational psychology, and practitioners in the field. Other professional personnel who work with exceptional children will also find much of the content, especially Parts II and III, valuable in developing an understanding of current research on assessment and interventions for exceptional persons.

The historical roots and current trends in school psychology reflect considerable diversity, as illustrated in Part I. In Chapter 1 Ralph H. Tindall describes the historical trends that led to the development of school psychology, trends that continue to influence current developments. Tindall's description of historical context provides the background for Virginia Monroe's consideration in Chapter 2 of the current roles, contemporary influences, and research on school psychologists. In Chapter 3 Douglas T. Brown discusses critical issues in accreditation of training programs, certification, and licensure. Brown advances the argument that school psychology should be regarded as an independent profession with ties to both education and psychology. The detailed information provided by Brown on state certification and licensure standards should be particularly useful to students in school psychology training programs and to practitioners in the field.

In Part II the chapters are organized around research and issues in assessment and interventions for exceptional children. James E. Ysseldyke (Chapter 4) discusses the critical assumptions and implicit models in psychoeducational assessment. Ysseldyke then suggests that many of the current assessment instruments and practices fall short of meeting reasonable standards. Reforms in assessment are advocated. Tom Oakland and D. L. Goldwater (Chapter 5) analyze a number of concerns regarding assessment and interventions with the mildly handicapped. Their discussion of recent developments in measurement of adaptive behavior and psychoneurological assessment are particularly timely. In Chapter 6 Kathryn Clark Gerken provides a comprehensive review of the problems associated with providing school psychological services to preschoolers and persons with low incident handicaps. The references provided for information on instruments and research with special populations such as the visually handicapped, hearing handicapped, severely retarded, etc. should be particularly useful to all professionals who work with exceptional children. In Chapter 7 Donald J. Treffinger, Michael C. Pyryt, M. Madon Hawk, and Elwood D. Houseman provide a much needed review of the literature on gifted and talented including suggestions for increased involvement of school psychologists with this population. A thorough review of the controversial issue of bias in assessment is provided by Daniel J. Reschly in Chapter 8. Reschly contends that the critical issue is *not* the use of standardized tests with minorities, but rather the usefulness and fairness of assessment practices in terms of the educational interventions available to minority children and youth.

The major indirect services provided by school psychologists are discussed in Part III. Gary D. Phye (Chapter 9) describes the use of cognitive instructional objectives in the development of Individualized Educational Plans (IEP). Phye suggests that school psychologists should assume an active role in evaluating the IEPs as well as other special projects. Martin Tombari and Ronald A. Davis (Chapter 10) discuss consultation as a process for delivering psychological services with special emphasis on behavioral approaches. Recent advances in behavior modification and research on variables in consultation are also discussed. In the final chapter Harvey F. Clarizio provides an overview of approaches to improving the mental health climate of the school. The concepts of primary, secondary, and tertiary prevention are used by Clarizio to organize a review of mental health programs and research results.

The contributors to this volume deserve a special expression of gratitude. We not only found all of these persons to be cooperative, but also stimulating and dedicated scholars. We also appreciate the advice and support of colleagues and students at Iowa State University. The editorial staff at Academic Press deserves special mention for their willingness to support the development of this book. Finally, our wives and children, Connie and Julie Phye, and Jane, Blake, and Amy Reschly made valuable contributions to our mental health throughout our preoccupation with the preparation of the book.

The order of editorship was difficult to decide since we shared the editorial responsibilities equally. Since we both come from strong empirical backgrounds, we decided a random process was best. We flipped a coin. The luck of the Irish again prevailed. Our results replicated those of Hallahan and Kauffman,[1] it appears that the score is now Irish Catholics 2, German Mennonites 0.

---

[1]Hallahan, D., & Kauffman, J. *Exceptional Children*. Englewood Cliffs, New Jersey: Prentice Hall, 1978.

SCHOOL PSYCHOLOGY: AN OVERVIEW

The three chapters in Part I are designed to provide an overview of the development of the profession (subdiscipline) of school psychology as well as a discussion of current issues. School psychology reflects great diversity in terms of both historical evolution and current trends. The chapters are organized around the general questions of: What are the roots of school psychology? How did school psychology evolve? What kinds of services are provided by school psychologists? What kinds of training do school psychologists receive? What are the major issues in the training and credentialing of school psychologists?

In Chapter 1, Ralph H. Tindall provides an excellent overview of the roots and evolution of school psychology in the twentieth century in the United States. It should be noted that Tindall was an active participant in many of the significant events that shaped this history. His description of the origins of school psychology in concerns about children with school-related learning and/or adjustment problems provides an important perspective on the current status and roles of school psychologists. The basic reason for our existence today is not new and is tied to a long and rich history. Tindall describes the gradual evolution of school psychology with emphasis on the leadership provided by Division 16, The Division of School Psychology, of the American Psychological Association (APA). The leadership of this division, past and present, has been significant to our development. A basic issue, discussed also in Chapter 3, is related to whether the leadership (and character) of school psychology in the future will be dominated primarily by the positions enunciated by the National Association of School Psychologists (NASP)

1

or the American Psychological Association. Tindall sees school psychology as a major subdiscipline of generic psychology, which leads him to the recommendations that NASP and APA find ways to resolve current disputes, and that school psychology continue to develop within the overall umbrella of American psychology. More information on the debate concerning the positions of APA and NASP is given in Chapter 3 of this volume and is also available in the spring 1979 issue of the School Psychology Digest.

The concerns expressed by Tindall regarding roles and services in school psychology are expanded by Virginia Monroe in Chapter 2. Discussions about appropriate roles and efforts to expand the roles of school psychologists have been a frequent theme in the professional literature throughout the history of school psychology. The continuum of directness of influence on children is suggested by Monroe as a means for organizing the discussion of roles and services. Within this model Monroe describes five major roles and discusses evidence concerning the effectiveness of these roles. Her discussion of the need for accountability and procedures for evaluating school psychological services is valuable and timely. Sources of current and continuing influence on school psychology, particularly recent court and legislative action, are also discussed in Chapter 2.

Perhaps the most intense current debate in school psychology involves the question of standards for training, certification, and licensure. Douglas T. Brown discusses each of these issues in detail in Chapter 3. Training programs are analyzed in terms of content and emphasis. Certification and licensure standards are discussed along with information on specific requirements in each state. Students in training programs and school psychologists in the field will undoubtedly find this information useful when contemplating a change in location, or simply as a means to gain insight regarding the current trends in certification and licensure. Brown advances a strong argument for regarding school psychology as an independent profession with roots in both education and psychology. This point of view is in sharp contrast with the position of Tindall in Chapter 1. Our own uncertainty regarding the issue is reflected in the first sentence of this introduction where we hesitated, and then equivocated, over the use of the nouns profession and subdiscipline. The words profession (independent) and subdiscipline (of professional psychology) are becoming code words in the debate over entry level requirements and standards for certification and licensure. Brown cites trends that he believes will lead to recognition of the sixth year or masters plus (rather than doctorate) as the basic standard in school psychology. The debate over entry level is only one of a number of current issues being discussed in relation to school psychology. School psychologists, whether in training or in practice, need to become informed about and participate in the resolution of these questions. We believe that the chapters in this section will provide a valuable resource for developing a perspective on these issues.

RALPH H. TINDALL

1 School Psychology: The Development of a Profession

School psychology has often been thought of as a relative newcomer in the field of psychology. In reality, school psychology is just about as old as formal psychology in this country.

Many of the early and well-known American psychologists were interested in the learning and development of school-age persons. G. Stanley Hall, the first president of the American Psychological Association, was interested in the adolescent. William James, who was not a psychologist but a biologist and physician turned philosopher, gave psychology a boost in the educational field with his books *The Principles of Psychology* (1890) and *Talks to Teachers on Psychology* (1900). Lightner Witmer is credited with establishing the first psychological clinic in 1896. The first case in this clinic was a classical school problem concerning the reading deficiency of an adolescent. Goddard used the Binet Scale at the Vineland Training School as early as 1908. Thorndike spent time developing a variety of tests for school children. The illustrations are numerous and even the term school psychologist appeared by 1915 (Cutts, 1955). It is improper to refer to school psychology as a relatively new specialty unless in the same breath we look at the relatively youthful age of psychology as a discipline and as a profession.

The purpose of this chapter is to organize and discuss the many diverse events from the past eight decades that influenced the development of school psychology. Definitions of school psychology will be reviewed and clarified. The

3

SCHOOL PSYCHOLOGY
Perspectives and Issues

origins of school psychology will be identified. The influence of important trends, such as the testing movement, the development of special education, the mental health movement, and learning theory including behaviorism, will be discussed.

School psychology, at first slowly and now at an increasing pace, has developed an identity as a profession. The development of the Division of School Psychology (Division 16) within the American Psychological Association (APA) and the formation of the National Association of School Psychologists (NASP) were major events in the development of the profession. An historical perspective on several professional issues will be provided. Issues such as appropriate roles, certification standards, appropriate training programs, and accreditation of training programs will be discussed.

Much of the material to be summarized in this chapter is found in various references in the literature. Some of the history is undoubtedly buried in the Archives of the History of American Psychology at the University of Akron. No one has yet gone through the vast amounts of material being collected in these archives. A complete history of school psychology could be written from study of the papers in these archives if time permitted.

What Is School Psychology?

School psychology, its content, and the limits of its practice have been difficult to define. School personnel may view the school psychologist in a number of roles that are different from what the psychologist perceives as his or her role. Some of the misperception of roles arises from the varied history of the school psychologist. There have been times when this person has been portrayed as a test giver, at other times he or she has been seen as a mental health specialist, one who intervenes in a crisis, an administrator, a specialist in classroom management, a researcher, and in other roles too numerous to mention.

There is no reason why well-trained school psychologists cannot fill specific roles at various periods nor why they should not fulfill a variety of roles. Graduates of broadly conceived training programs should have had experience in multiple roles. As schools evolve there are different demands placed upon the psychologist who is a part of that evolution. School systems differ in their complexities and in their services to children. A wealthy school district with a high tax base can afford more school psychologists and use them differently than a poor, rural school district that is spread over a wide area and has a relatively low tax base.

There have been different emphases at different times in public education that have called for differences in the use of school psychologists. For example, the era of "catch-up" after the launching of sputnik by the Soviet Union in 1957 emphasized identification of gifted students and the development of programs for them. In the 1960s, the period of using the schools to bring about assimilation of minority groups emphasized human relations skills. The current period of emphasis on education for all handicapped children is bringing about other pressures. The list could be very long if we were to examine all of the local and national influences that have had an effect upon the way the school psychologist carries out daily tasks.

School psychologists have come from a variety of training programs that are not at all standardized in their offerings. Some are located in colleges of education, some in departments of educational psychology, some in departments of psychology, and still others are interdepartmental (Brown & Lindstrom, 1977). The diversification of training programs and models ordains different role emphasis in the field.

It has to be concluded that there is no universal agreement as to what a school psychologist is or what such a person does. A review of several definitions of school psychology is necessary to answer the question of what is school psychology. A chronological sample of definitions will provide a perspective on how basic concepts have both changed and remained the same over the years.

The Ontogeny of a Definition

Even prior to the mention of school psychology in the literature, James (1900), in his talks to teachers, was engaged in an inservice function concerned with the school as an institution and with school learning in particular. There are school psychologists today who are concerned with the broad question of the psychology of schooling (White & Harris, 1961).

In the early decades of the twentieth century, the school psychologist was a person engaged in group and individual testing (Walter, 1925). Also included among the psychologists' duties were the diagnosis and therapy of the educationally maladjusted and working with problem children. Walter saw the school psychologist as involved with both the retarded and the gifted. Research, in order to bring a psychological point of view to education, was also included in his definition. The broad roles suggested by Walter are similar to contemporary analyses of school psychologists' roles (see Monroe, Chapter 2 of this volume).

At a later date, Symonds (1942) described the school psychologist by virtue of location. The school was emphasized as the most appropriate setting for psychologists to apply their skills to the benefit of pupils, teachers, and administrators.

In summarizing the Thayer Conference, Cutts (1955) reported a definition that was utilized by members of the conference. The Thayer Conference definition stressed the necessity of training in both psychology and education. School psychologists were seen as using specialized knowledge in areas such as assessment, learning, and human relationships to facilitate, through school personnel, the learning and growth of all children, including the exceptional.

In the following decade, Valett (1963) saw the school psychologist as a highly trained professional psychologist with skills in the clinical, counseling and educational psychology areas. He expected this person to have had extensive experience in the public school, including teaching experience. Valett advocated training at the doctoral level as the minimum for use of the title school psychologist.

More recently, Bardon and Bennett (1974) suggested a somewhat broader definition of school psychology. School psychologists were seen as persons who studied and assisted in solving the problems in the total school system. In addition to the traditional roles included in previous definitions, they suggested that school psychologists might also be involved in such matters as school policy, curricular decisions, and so on.

A common feature of all of these definitions is the emphasis on training in the discipline of psychology and professional employment in the school setting. Increasingly, the definitions stress the importance of understanding the system so that adequate modifications may be made in the interest of all of the personnel bound to the system, which operates within and in the service of the larger community. It becomes quite evident that the skills and techniques of the psychologist, from systematic data gathering to the complex manipulation of that data and the timing of the presentation of that data, as applied to a school system, result in multiskilled roles that cannot be compressed into a simple definition.

Such considerations support the observation that the narrow role of a specialist, as once envisioned by Tindall (1964), can only exist in the largest systems with hierarchies of psychological specialists or in the smaller systems that have so few psychologists that roles have to be unduly limited. In such instances there will be psychologists who concern themselves with research only or with the placement of exceptional children only.

Perhaps the unique characteristic of the school psychologist in comparison with other specialists within the field of psychology is knowledge of schools. The school psychologist is oriented toward solution of common problems of children in school settings, and increasingly, is concerned with analysis and solution of problems at a systems level. By contrast, the clinical psychologist has more training and experience in lengthy therapy in areas of psychopathology but much less training and experience with educational problems and remediation techniques.

The Origins of School Psychology

Since school psychology is currently a multifaceted profession, it is not surprising that its origins are many and diverse. As we trace the origins of school psychology, some of the reasons for the current diversity of the field will become more apparent.

Pre-Twentieth Century Developments

The roots of school psychology, like those of nearly every other profession and discipline, can be traced back to the ancient Greek philosophers. The work of

Aristotle and others in attempting to develop universal laws of behavior were very early precursors of modern psychological theory and research (Heidbreder, 1933).

The contributions of several French scholars and educators in the eighteenth and nineteenth centuries have more direct relevance to modern school psychology. Itard's classic work with a moderately retarded boy known as the "wild boy of Aveyon," Seguin's educational methods for the mentally defective, and Esquirol's descriptions of different levels of mental retardation were important milestones that provided the basis for advances in the early twentieth century (Doll, 1967). Other important nineteenth-century influences include the exposition of psychological methodology (Wundt, 1873), the beginnings of developmental psychology in the work of Preyer (1888) and Hall (1911), and the recognition of individual differences, which was greatly advanced by Galton (1869). The contributions of these early pioneers formed the basis for several major trends in the twentieth century which, in turn, provided the basis for the development of school psychology.

The Testing Movement

The testing movement began with research on psychophysical skills in the laboratories of Weber in 1834, Fechner in 1860, and Wundt in 1879. Galton contributed as a eugenicist and an anthropologist with a variety of measurements of the individual (Wallin & Ferguson, 1972). One of the early tests was weight discrimination, which later became a part of the Ontario School Ability Examination. Few of the psychophysical tests actually related to school achievement or prediction of that achievement. James McKeen Cattell was the first psychologist to actually use the term "mental test" (Wallin & Ferguson, 1972). The testing movement, which originally intended to elaborate on the individual differences demonstrated in the physiologically oriented laboratory of Wundt, was established early in America. Cattell was the first appointed professor of psychology at Columbia, where his interest in testing continued (Heidbreder, 1933). Shortly thereafter, Jastrow was appointed professor of psychology at the University of Wisconsin, where he became interested in a variety of group tests (Greene, 1941). Testing as an experimental method to demonstrate individual dfferences dates from the introduction of psychology to America.

Mental Testing

At the turn of the century, Alfred Binet and V. Henri were critical of the type of psychophysiological test then in use; Cattell was considered to be a chief offender. In 1904, Binet and Simone came up with a scale based on a series of developmental tasks with more of a cognitive bent than a psychophysiological approach. Binet and Simone revised the scales in 1908 and 1911. These scales were normalized for various ages. Henry H. Goddard translated and used the Binet scale in 1908 at the Vineland Training School where he was the director of research (Edwards, 1971).

With the growth of special classes and a beginning interest in classifying students, Terman revised the Binet–Simone Scale in 1916, resulting in the Stanford–Binet. Subsequent revisions of the Stanford–Binet in 1937 and 1960 established a tool that could be used in individual assessment by school psychologists. Misuse of the results of such a tool by inadequately trained persons stimulated early demands for school psychologists. The use of the term IQ as the ratio of mental age to chronological age is credited to Stern (Edwards, 1971). The other basic tool for measuring intellectual ability appeared in 1939 when Wechsler published his Wechsler–Bellevue Scale (Wechsler, 1944). Wechsler scales for all age groups and revisions of those scales have been developed in the years since.

In addition to the influence of the development of individual tests, there were group approaches to measurement in many areas that added to the heritage of the school psychologist. During World War I, in an attempt to classify a large number of men, Arthur S. Otis and a team of eminent psychologists developed the first Army Classification Tests, which have since gone through many revisions. These tests have had their civilian counterparts in the large numbers of group intelligence tests used widely in the schools and colleges.

Achievement Tests

Included in the testing background of the school psychologist is the development of achievement tests. Binet and Varney are credited with developing one of the first achievement scales in France. This scale dealt with arithmetic, reading, and spelling at primary and intermediate grade levels in five different stages (Wallin & Ferguson, 1972).

In the United States, Stone (1908) was one of the first to use standardized achievement tests in arithmetic. Shortly thereafter, Courtis (1909) also devised standardized tests in arithmetic that were used widely. These were survey-type tests that sampled arithmetical skills from the third grade through the high school level. In this same period, E. L. Thorndike (1910) was experimenting with his famous handwriting scales. Probably the first real achievement test battery to provide standardized scores in the areas of arithmetic, reading, spelling, sentence meaning, and vocabulary was developed by Pressey (1920). This battery was the forerunner of the many achievement test batteries now being used in the schools.

Personality Assessment

The measurement of personality is another area that intrigued some of the early psychologists. One of the earliest questionnaires was the Personal Data

Sheet designed by Woodworth in 1919 (Greene, 1941). It was an inventory-type instrument meant to separate the neurotic from the able soldier. At the same time, Thurstone (1919) was making one of the first attempts to use tests in the selection of employees.

Again, it was Pressey who along with his wife Luella, devised the rather famous cross-out technique. This technique was an attempt to clarify personality characteristics by having an individual mark descriptive words or statements as true or untrue about themselves (Pressey & Pressey, 1919). Variations of this technique are incorporated into several personality and interest tests today.

The testing movement has been one of the most important influences on the development of school psychology. The influence of the testing movement has not been entirely positive, however. In many instances test results alone have been the basis for complex diagnostic and classification decisions. Criticisms of an excessive reliance on tests have been made by Reger (1971), who suggested that tests and test interpretation should not be the primary technological base for school psychologists. Tests are useful and valuable tools that must be placed in proper perspective (see Ysseldyke, Chapter 4 of this volume).

Special Education

The development of special education for students who were atypical in one way or another was another factor that had far-reaching effects on the development of school psychology. Earlier in this chapter I cited the case of Itard working with the "wild boy of Averon" (Sarason & Doris, 1969). This experience, though a failure in the eyes of Itard, was an early example of an effort on behalf of the mentally handicapped. From 1896 to 1953, the numbers of classes for the handicapped expanded from one class in one city to classes in 1244 cities in 48 states (Cutts, 1955). Today with Public Law 94-142, even the smallest school district must make provisions for its handicapped children.

Another early influence on the direction of school psychology was the establishment by Witmer in 1896 of his clinic at the University of Pennsylvania. Brotemarkle (1931) on the 35th anniversary of the founding of this clinic, described the early cases in detail. The first two cases were an adolescent with a reading problem and an adolescent with a spelling problem. Witmer discussed the role of the psychologist in assisting teachers with programs for students with achievement problems.

In the following decade, two other important events occurred that were to have profound effects on the direction that school psychology would take. In 1896 the Providence, Rhode Island public schools established the first public school classes for slow-learning students. In 1899 the Chicago Public School System established a Department of Child Study with Dr. Fred W. Smedley as director.

He and his staff surveyed the schools during the week, and on Saturdays principals brought children who were having problems to the Department for treatment (Cutts, 1955).

The first school psychologist, Arnold Gessell, was hired by the state of Connecticut in 1915 to travel about the state diagnosing children who needed special class placement (Cutts, 1955). This action set a precedent for a close relationship between special education and school psychology. This relationship was further strengthened when the Bureau of Child Study, established in Chicago, became aligned administratively with school psychology (Mullen, 1972). This development, which involved persons like Francis Mullen, who administered both special education and school psychology, helped to establish a model for many school systems that still prevails in the United States.

Special education needed psychologists to aid in the diagnosis and classification of children. This role and the relationship of school psychology to special education continues today. In fact, in most states school psychologists' salaries are at least partially funded from special education reimbursement monies; and in some states school psychologists are defined formally as specialists within special education programs. This relationship was one of the most important early bases for the development of school psychology, and it might be regarded as having both positive and negative features today. On one hand, the relationship with special education has provided a secure funding base and clear responsibilities to children who are having learning and adjustment problems. On the other hand, this relationship has frequently been the reason for an excessively narrow testing role that allows insufficient opportunity for involvement with interventions or broader mental health work with both handicapped and nonhandicapped children.

The Mental Health Movement

Near the beginning of the twentieth century increased interest in the emotional well being of people was brought into focus by Beers (1908), who wrote the book *A Mind That Found Itself*. As a former mental patient, Beers became interested in both the treatment of mental illness and its prevention. Also at the beginning of the twentieth century Freud's basic writings attracted increasing attention in America. Freud, Beers, and many others emphasized the importance of experiences during childhood. These events began to have an effect upon the way schools looked at children. More attention began to be paid to the affective or emotional side of childrens' lives and to the interactions between children and adults.

The Bureau of Child Study in Chicago, with its referrals of many children to the Chicago courts, led Dr. William Healy and Dr. Augusta Bronner to form the first mental health clinic in conjunction with a juvenile court. The Chicago Juvenile Psychopathic Institute was established in 1909. Later Healy and Bronner laid the foundation for the Judge Baker Guidance Center in Boston and still later established the Yale Institute of Human Relations (Healy, 1917).

Even though many school personnel have given lip service to mental health concepts, schools have rarely led the way in creating sound mental health programs. Preventive practices have more often been discussed than carried out in any tangible fashion. The emergencies of the moment always seem to establish priority.

Attention to mental health was accelerated with the establishment of child guidance clinics in about 1922 in many urban areas (Wallin & Ferguson, 1972). The school psychologist was frequently the person who made the referral to the child guidance clinic and often sat in on the case conferences. In many communities the link between the child guidance clinics and the schools left a great deal to be desired. There were problems of communication. Often there would be an administrator, a social worker, a psychologist, a guidance worker, or some other person between those who were treating the child and the teacher who was trying to teach the child in the classroom. There were accusations on the part of clinic personnel that school personnel did not understand or were unwilling to understand the child's needs. There were counteraccusations on the part of school personnel that clinic personnel had no idea how schools were operated as institutions. Each community had to resolve these issues as the child guidance clinics began to evolve into community clinics. Later, they became mental health centers with a much broader range of capabilities and service. Unfortunately, many of the problems of communication between institutions established to alleviate mental health problems and the schools are yet to be resolved. In some areas school psychologists have been hired as community mental health center personnel in order to improve communication problems with the schools.

Related to the mental health movement, and of considerable influence on the schools, was the guidance movement. According to Brewer (1942), the major pioneer in the guidance movement was Frank Parsons. Parsons was interested in helping the underprivileged select a vocation as indicated in his book *Choosing a Vocation,* written in 1909.

Historically, school psychology has been closely linked to guidance and to the counseling movement in many training programs. As guidance evolved into the broader domain of counseling psychology, school psychologists and guidance counselors often found considerable overlap in roles. In training programs today there are varying amounts of duplication in the course work and practica for all three of the subprofessions of psychology that deal with mental health: clinical, counseling, and school psychology.

Unfortunately, the mental health movement in this country has not been able to keep pace with the complexity of our civilization. School psychologists have been involved in crisis intervention too frequently rather than in planning for long-term prevention of unwarranted emotional stresses built into the system. The mental health movement has impinged on the direction of school psychology, but we have yet to realize the day when psychologists will really play the strong child advocate role delineated by Hyman and Schreiber (1975). The development of other professionals in the fields of guidance, social work, psychiatry, and clinical psychology has affected the training of school psychologists. Too frequently there have been territorial disputes involving school children where joined forces would have had more effect. A further barrier to more effective mental health services is the lack of agreement concerning goals and means of promoting mental health (see Clarizio, Chapter 11 of this volume). However, the problem is not merely one of inadequate knowledge and techniques. There is much that is available that has not been implemented.

Learning Theory Influences

Another major influence on school psychology has been the development of learning theory. By the very nature of the setting, school people are devoted to helping students learn new facts about their environment, perform new skills, and perfect the tools that will unlock the elements of the culture that the civilization has created. The efforts of Ebbinghaus, who wrote a classical work in the area of memory in 1885, probably marked the beginning of systematized experiments in learning (McGeoch, 1942). Certainly the work of E. L. Thorndike, in his early experiments with animal learning and in his work with the development of psychological tests, was another early influence on school practices in learning (Wallin & Ferguson, 1972).

No one can really measure the far-reaching effects that the efforts of John Dewey (1916) have had since he began to suggest that learning was not a passive activity for the learner and that the learner needed to be actively involved. Dewey's followers, who established the so-called Progressive Education movement of the 1930s and 1940s, quite often misinterpreted Dewey, and perhaps created situations that were more chaotic than desirable in the facilitation of learning. However, anyone who looks closely at modern education will recognize that much of John Dewey lives on in the daily approaches of the school today.

The University of Chicago awarded J. B. Watson the university's first doctorate in psychology in 1903. Although it might not have been apparent at the time, this event probably had an enormously far-reaching effect on modern learning theory (Heidbreder, 1933). Watson was a forerunner of Skinner and the modern social learning theorists (Bandura, 1969). It is impossible in this chapter to detail all of the contributors to modern learning theory, but certainly those mentioned are prominent influences on the skills of the modern school psychologist. For example, the school psychologist who has become skilled in classroom management draws heavily on the principles outlined by the early and modern behaviorists and social learning theorists (see Tombari & Davis, Chapter 10 of this volume).

Professional Development in the Past Four Decades

It is no wonder that role confusion in school psychology exists when one considers the diverse historical influences on the schools and the variety of movements that have involved the schools. It is not uncommon to see the school psychologist as an assessor, a prescriber of learning patterns, a mental health consultant, an intervener in crisis situations, a researcher, a child advocate, as well as an instrument of social change. No school psychologist will fill all of these roles well or even at the same time. Some will try at various times to fill several of these roles, others will be able to specialize so that they may fill only one role and fill it very well. With some exceptions, the school psychologist in the field must still be a generalist. Therefore, school psychologists must be educated broadly in order to perform a variety of professional roles.

Certification and Training

At first there was little regulation of the psychologist who worked in school systems. Training was varied and often involved not much more than a few courses in psychology during a couple of summer school sessions. State departments of education soon began to develop certification standards for school psychologists because there was concern about appropriate training.

According to Wallin and Ferguson (1972), Delaware was the first state to provide for individual psychological and andiometric examinations on a state-wide basis. The qualifications required of the examiners are obscure. In a study of the first survey of state certification practices, Horrocks (1946) indicated that seven states—Connecticut, Indiana, Maine, Nebraska, New York, Ohio, and Pennsylvania—had certification standards for school psychologists. Of those seven, New York, Pennsylvania, Connecticut, and Ohio had the most comprehensive requirements. Other surveys have shown a continuous rise in the number of states that certify or approve the credentials of school psychologists (Brown, Sewall, & Lindstrom, 1977). The various surveys, including the most up-to-date in the area of certification, show great variability in state requirements. This situation makes it difficult for school psychologists trained in one state to be certified in other states. Reciprocity is still to be accomplished.

In the late 1950s, Division 16 of APA became increasingly concerned about the absence of minimum standards to govern the practice of school psychology. In 1962 the executive committee of Division 16 finally agreed upon a document that set out certain basic guidelines for the certification and training of school psychologists. These were reported by Bardon (1963) in the *American Psychologist*. These guidelines were sent to all state boards of education. Initially, many certification departments took action to adopt at least parts of the guidelines. Unfortunately, some of the areas of training were interpreted as course titles and became frozen in some of the state certification standards. Since that time there have been many revisions in state standards, influenced in part by state organizations. These standards have sometimes resulted in quite rigid certification procedures that range from being very lenient to very restrictive. Appropriate standards for certification continue to be a major concern in school psychology (see Brown, Chapter 3 of this volume).

The Thayer Conference

The growing pains of a quarter of a century ago made it necessary to convene the Thayer Conference in August 1954 at West Point, New York. This conference represented a major milestone in the development of school psychology as a profession. It was organized at the request of Division 16 of the APA, which had approached the Educational and Training Board of that organization with the idea. The conference was financed by a grant from the Public Health Service. The entire conference is reported on in detail by Cutts (1955). The purpose of the conference was to establish a definite statement in regard to the roles and the training of school psychologists.

The steering committee for the conference was composed of Edward S. Borden, University of Michigan; Dale B. Harris, Institute of Child Welfare, University of Minnesota; Nicholas Hobbs, George Peabody College; Noble H. Kelley, Southern Illinois University; Samuel A. Kirk, University of Illinois; Beatrice Lantz, Los Angeles public schools; Bertha M. Luckey, Cleveland public schools; Bruce V. Moore, APA Education and Training Board; Frances Mullen, Chicago public schools; and T. Ernest Newland, University of Illinois. This group was composed of leaders in the field at the time.

At the time of the conference only 20 states had certification regulations. There were approximately 75 titles being used by persons doing psychological work in the schools. There were 18 known training programs with 10 of those offered jointly by departments of psychology and schools of education; 7 programs were in psychology departments and 1 in a department of education.

The Thayer Conference represented a broad spectrum of the professionals who were concerned with a developing phenomenon, the school psychologist. The conference resulted in specific recommendations concerning roles of school psychologists; these are summarized as follows:

1. Assessing and interpreting the intellectual, social, and emotional development of children
2. Helping to identify exceptional children and collaborate with other professionals in developing individual educational programs
3. Developing ways to facilitate the learning and adjustment of all children
4. Encouraging and initiating research and interpreting research findings applicable to the solution of school problems

5. Diagnosing educational and personal problems and recommending remediation programs

These functions, reiterated in language not very different from the original, represent job descriptions that would not be far from what many psychologists do in the schools today.

With respect to training, the conference recommended a 2-year graduate program with a half-year internship as the entering level of the profession. The 4-year doctoral program with a 1-year internship was recommended as the second and highest level of training. A perusal of Brown *et al.* (1977) indicates that at present many states have not yet adopted the minimum standards from the Thayer Conference in their certification guidelines.

The Thayer Conference emphasized the training and the function of the school psychologist. It brought together some of the most influential persons in the fields of psychology and education to focus on school psychology. No conference since has been as comprehensive nor has any conference dealt with school psychology in as much depth as did the Thayer Conference. Members of the developing profession, for the first time, had a document that represented some consensus as to what the major functions of the school psychologist were with definite implications for training.

In 1964 a conference known as the Bethesda Conference was convened to analyze problems and issues in school psychology. This conference described four types of school psychologists: the traditional clinical psychologist, the psychologist with a variety of specialties, the human factor engineer, and the school psychologist who is a specialist in counseling and behavior change techniques. According to Bardon (1964–1965), the conference generated much discussion but did not get the nationwide attention generated by the Thayer Conference.

Up until the mid-1950s training programs for school psychologists had been largely patch quilt affairs. Not until the guidelines for certification, reported by Bardon (1963), did the skeleton of a training program take shape. These guidelines—which had been worked on for approximately 5 years by a committee with changing personnel in Division 16—suggested that the areas of psychological foundations, psychological methods and techniques, and educational foundations be required. The approximate number of minimum training hours in each area was also established. Training programs were then able to round out this skeleton and attempt to develop a balanced experience in several areas.

In the 1960s training programs began to develop all across the country. The number of 18 programs reported at the time of the Thayer Conference was soon doubled and redoubled. As nearly as this author can be certain, the period of greatest growth in training programs appeared in the mid-1960s. According to Brown and Lindstrom (1977), there are now 203 programs in some 40 states and the District of Columbia. Of this group there are 70 master's programs, 151 sixth-year programs, and 66 doctoral programs. These programs involve over 7000 students in training and almost 1800 primary faculties. School psychology training has become a major subspecialty within graduate education in psychology.

Brown and Lindstrom (1977) in their current directory of training programs indicate that the requirements of the programs vary greatly. Indeed, a prospective student in school psychology would do well to study this directory carefully and then study the programs that the student intends to apply to for admission, since the emphases and requirements differ. Hartlage (1971) suggested that training programs fall along a continuum from those stressing the academic or basic training in psychology, to those stressing service or methods and techniques. Prospective students should be aware of the purposes and goals of the chosen program.

In the early training programs there was some emphasis on supervision in applied areas, but the experience was usually in connection with course work in testing, counseling, or educational remediation. Seldom was there a true internship experience, although the name might have been attached. Too frequently, the internship experience meant facing service problems with a little help from a harried school psychologist who knew little about supervising others. There was only occasional contact between university faculty and the supervisor in the school. An apprentice-type experience in whatever facilities could be found, either close to the university or within the university, was often the vehicle for internship, whether or not it fitted the needs of the student. Required and systematized periods of internship were not comparable to the development of such experiences in the fields of clinical or counseling psychology. In fact, there are still no lists of approved internship sites for school psychology. Each program has had to devise its own system and requirements.

Recognition of the need for guidelines for practica, externship, and internship experiences culminated in the Peabody Conference (Gray, 1963a). This conference included trainers, school administrators, employers of school psychologists, educators, and representatives of the APA. The conference, sponsored by a grant from the National Institute of Mental Health, drew up standards for practica and internships. Unquestionably, this conference has had an effect upon the development of internship experiences in training programs. The recommendations are still found to be sound, though they must be updated and perhaps modified in accord with the financial abilities of schools and local needs (Tindall, 1973).

As another mark of developing professionalism, school psychologists in the field were expressing the need to upgrade skills and meet with school psychologists from other parts of the country. T. Ernest Newland, a pioneer in the training of school psychologists, had previously chaired a postdoctoral institute for Division 12 of APA. He suggested something analogous for Division 16. As nearly as the date can be fixed, the first professional institute was organized in 1955 and met at Northwestern University (T. E. Newland, personal communication, October 1977). This institute, led by Julian Rotter, Marie Skodak, and Emmett Betts, was an immediate success. These institutes continue to this day. The institutes are

necessary to consider alternatives to current practices that could have a bearing on the direction that the profession takes in the next decade.

The implementation of the Education for All Handicapped Children Act of 1975 appears to have placed increased emphasis on psychoeducational assessment activities with children exhibiting learning or adjustment problems in schools. Leaders in school psychology have continuously emphasized the need for thorough and high-quality assessment, and school psychology training has also emphasized this area. The current emphasis is on multifactored assessment, an idea that is not new (Newland, 1963). Although the needs of special education programs should not completely dominate the role of school psychologists, the provision of high-quality assessment with atypical children will undoubtedly continue to be a challenging role. A crucial development in the future is to broaden the concept of testing to include a wide variety of methods of gathering information (see Ysseldyke, Chapter 4 of this volume) and to place the use of standardized tests into proper perspective.

The training programs with the most prestige have not always emphasized the skills and service needs of the consumer. For various reasons the emphasis placed upon research skills by Gray (1963b), White and Harris (1961), and others have never been implemented widely by school psychologists. Research and evaluation skills, particularly in combination with an applied focus, appear to have great promise for school psychology in the future (see Phye, Chapter 9 of this volume). A healthy future development in school psychology would be greater activity along the lines of empirical evaluation of the effects of interventions or special programs.

Licensure and Training

The *APA Monitor* (1977) carried a report of the action of the Education and Training Board, in agreement with the Board of Professional Affairs and the Board of Scientific Affairs, which resolved that the title "professional psychologist" was to be limited to those persons who hold the doctorate from an institution that is APA accredited or is accredited by a regional agency. Only persons meeting these criteria would be able to offer their services to the public and use the title professional psychologist or its variations, including clinical, counseling, school, and industrial psychologist. A relatively short delay in the date on which the resolution would become effective was passed for school psychology along with a resolution calling for more opportunities for doctoral training in school psychology. The APA resolutions concerning minimum levels of training will have considerable influence on the future of training in all areas of psychology, but perhaps the greatest influence will be in the area of school psychology.

For years there have been arguments that school psychologists should operate at several levels. Trow (1969) suggested a technician level to perform the routine assessment and other chores and a doctoral level to lend leadership, interpretation, and supervision. Gray (1963b) recognized the need for some psychologists to function at various levels. At one time Bardon (1963) suggested two levels of preparation, doctoral and subdoctoral. The issue has been partially an economic one, in that schools appear to need quantities of services that exceed their ability to pay highly trained persons to perform. The situation is not unique to school psychology but is common to almost all areas of public support for educational personnel. O'Shea (1960) was clearly ahead of her time in stating that all school psychologists should have the doctoral level training that would include adequate training in both psychology and education.

There are alternative courses of action that might be taken regarding the minimum level of training. For example, Division 16 and NASP might come out with strong and contradictory positions concerning minimum levels of training, licensure requirements, and use of titles. The profession would then be faced with the unfortunate fact of mutually competing organizations. The two organizations might reach a compromise on the minimum degree requirements, or APA might be convinced to allow a significantly longer time for school psychology departments to implement the APA minimum standards. If no compromises are reached, and NASP and APA compete over these issues, several dangers should be recognized. One danger is that school psychology may develop apart from the mainstream of psychology (Bardon, 1978). The majority of school psychologists currently in practice or currently in training do not possess and are not pursuing doctoral degrees. Virtually all of the states have certification standards that do *not* require the doctoral degree. The majority of the training programs in school psychology are nondoctoral, and many, perhaps most, are at institutions that do not even offer the doctoral degree. There is, therefore, a tremendous vested interest in continuing the nondoctoral pattern of training and practice in school psychology. Predictably, NASP will probably serve as the major vehicle through which nondoctoral school psychologists will advance their concerns over patterns and levels of training. The issues concerning accreditation of training programs, state departments of education certification standards, and state licensure standards for private practice are far from resolved (see Brown, Chapter 3 of this volume). The APA resolution creates many problems for school psychology, problems that will undoubtedly demand the attention of national and state associations of school psychologists over the next decade.

Specialization

Within the present state of knowledge there is room for far more specialization on the part of the school psychologist than is currently possible in most school systems. Michael (1965), in an excellent critique, destroys the myth that all school psychologists must perform similar tasks. The problems arise in channeling psychologists into the areas where they do the best and into areas of greatest need. There have been limited opportunities in the past, owing to the inadequate ratio of school psychologists to the school population, although in some states the current ratio of psychologists to students is at a level that would allow considerable specialization (see Monroe, Chapter 2 of this volume). If the present trend of improved ratios of school psychologists to students continues, we might anticipate greater opportunities for specialization. Obviously, increased specialization is needed in the attention to low-incidence handicaps and preschoolers (see Gerken, Chapter 6 of this volume) and various intervention approaches.

Accountability

In whatever direction school psychology develops as a profession, it will of necessity depend upon the excellent performance of individuals, regardless of level of training or titles. It would be unrealistic to ignore that there have been and are incompetent individuals in school psychology. The profession, in order to survive, as well as fulfill its responsibilities to the public, must establish and uphold the highest standards possible. The current efforts of NASP and APA Division 16 in the areas of ethical standards, training guidelines, and continuing education are important steps toward improving the performance of school psychologists.

Past Predictions Revisited

Prior to concluding our discussion of future directions for the development of school psychology, it would be informative to review past predictions and how they have fared. In 1961 Trachtman forecast that school psychologists would increasingly devote most of their time to preventive mental health activities, to the evaluation of educational programs and research, and to the improvement of the mental health atmosphere of the entire school. He felt that the remaining time would be spent with individual case studies. Although it is difficult to evaluate all aspects of Trachtman's predictions, current data suggest that the typical school psychologist, with a few exceptions, is intervening in crises and spending a great deal of time assessing and planning remedial steps for individuals. Ames and Ilg (1969) also expected the school psychologist to spend less time dealing with problems and more time preventing them.

The most elaborate and specific predictions for the future of school psychology were made by Magary (1972). These can be summarized in abbreviated form as follows: (a) serve all children; (b) work more frequently with small groups than individuals; (c) serve as a consultant on more aspects of the school program; (d) increase the inservice training provided by school psychologists; (e) stress the importance of physical and developmental findings; (f) increase the importance of the team approach; (g) decrease responsibility for special education program administration; (h) increase responsibility to classroom teachers for working out programs; (i) provide individual therapy rather than depend on outside agencies; (j) provide clearer definitions of the roles of other specialists; (k) attempt to clarify the nomenclature; (*l*) change the delivery system for psychological services; (*m*) de-emphasize the role of testor; and (*n*) become increasingly data oriented in fostering cognitive growth. Unquestionably, there have been advances in several of these areas. For example, there has been an increase in team efforts, as well as attempts to clarify nomenclature. However, most of these predictions await further development at this time. Many of these predictions, such as the prediction of an increase in preventive services, deserve much more attention in the profession.

Current Challenges

If school psychology is to continue to grow as a viable subspecialty of psychology, it must find ways to improve the quality of our work and of the national educational product (Mok, 1962). Furthermore, school psychology as a profession must begin to take a strong child advocacy stand if changes are to be brought about in the system so that all children are provided with maximum opportunities (Hyman & Schreiber, 1975). Also, school psychology as a profession needs to contribute more in the areas of research and evaluation (Wrightstone, 1960). Too much of the educational practices and school psychological practices are based on authority or custom rather than on empirical data. Evaluation of the effectiveness of our services and the effectiveness of programs in which we participate is a necessary step in improving school psychology.

If standards of training are upgraded and we can decide within the profession and within the schools just what we expect of the well-trained school psychologist, the future appears bright. If we continue to engage in territorial disputes, argue over the importance of tasks, and proliferate poor-quality training programs, alienation from the larger profession of psychology is inevitable. The school psychologist will be left with a meaningless title and a bag of techniques. In the interest of school children everywhere, this must not occur. Psychology as a science based on careful collection and analysis of data has important contributions to make in educational settings.

References

APA Monitor, June, 1977, **8,** 14. Washington, D.C.: American Psychological Association.

Ames, L. B., & Ilg, F. L. Developmental readiness for learning. In M. G. Gottsegen & G. B. Gottsegen (Eds.), *Professional school psychology,* (Vol. III). New York: Grune & Stratton, 1969.

Bandura, A. *Principles of behavior modification.* New York: Holt, 1969.

Bardon, J. I. Proposals for state department of education certification of school psychologists. *American Psychologist,* 1963, **18,** 711–714.

Bardon, J. I. (Ed.). Problems and issues in school psychology—1964; proceedings of a conference on "new directions in school psychology" sponsored by the National Institute of Mental Health. *Journal of School Psychology,* 1964–1965, **3,** 1–44.

Bardon, J. I. *How to best establish the identity of professional school psychology.* Paper presented at the meeting of the National Association of School Psychologists, New York, March 1978.

Bardon, J. I., & Bennett, V. C. *School psychology*. Englewood Cliffs: Prentice-Hall, 1974.

Beers, C. W. *A mind that found itself*. New York: Longmans, Green, 1908.

Brewer, J. M. *History of vocational guidance*. New York: Harper, 1942.

Brotemarkle, R. A. (Ed.). *Clinical psychology; Studies in honor of Lightner Witmer to commemorate the thirty-fifth anniversary of the founding of the first psychological clinic*. Philadelphia: University of Pennsylvania Press, 1931.

Brown, D. T., & Lindstrom, J. P. *Director of school psychology training programs in the United States and Canada*. Washington, D.C.: National Association of School Psychologists, 1977.

Brown, D. T., Sewall, T. J., & Lindstrom, J. P. *The handbook of certification/licensure requirements for school psychologists*. (Rev. ed.). Washington, D.C.: National Association of School Psychologists, 1977.

Courtis, S. A. Measurement of growth and efficiency in arithmetic. *Elementary School Teacher*, 1909, **10,** 58–74; 177–179.

Cutts, N. E. (Ed.). *School psychologists at mid-century*. Washington, D.C.: American Psychological Association, 1955.

Dewey, J. *Democracy and education*. New York: MacMillan, 1916.

Division of School Psychology. *Memo from the President*. Washington, D.C.: American Psychological Association, 1977.

Doll, E. E. Trends and problems in the education of the mentally retarded: 1800–1940. *American Journal Mental Deficiency*, 1967, **72,** 175–183.

Edwards, A. J. *Individual mental testing: Part I history and theories*. Scranton, Pennsylvania: Intext, 1971.

Galton, F. *Hereditary genius: An inquiry into its laws and consequences* London: MacMillan, 1869.

Gray, S. W. (Ed.). *The internship in school psychology: Proceedings of the Peabody Conference*. Nashville: Department of Psychology, George Peabody College for Teachers, 1963. (a)

Gray, S. W. *The psychologist in the schools*. New York: Holt, 1963. (b)

Greene, E. B. *Measurements of human behavior*. New York: Odyssey Press, 1941.

Hall, G. S. *Adolescence* (2 vols.). New York: D. Appelton, 1911.

Hartlage, L. C. A look at models for training of school psychologists. *Psychology in the Schools*, 1971, **8,** 304–306.

Healy, W. *The individual delinquent*. Boston: Little, Brown, 1917.

Heidbreder, E. *Seven psychologies*. New York: D. Appleton Century, 1933.

Herron, W. G., Green, M., Guild, M., Smith, A., & Kantor, R. E. *Contemporary school psychology*. Scranton, Pennsylvania: Intext, 1970.

Horrocks, J. E. State certification requirements for school psychologist. *American Psychologist*, 1946, **1,** 399–401.

Hyman, I., & Schreiber, K. Selected concepts and practices of child advocacy in school psychology. *Psychology in the Schools*, 1975, **12,** 50–57.

James, W. *The principles of psychology*. New York: Holt, 1890.

James, W. *Talks to teachers on psychology*. New York: Holt, 1900.

Magary, J. F. (Ed.). *School psychological services*. Los Angeles: Gramercy Press, 1972.

McGeoch, J. A. *The psychology of human learning*. New York: Longmans, Green, 1942.

Michael, D. C. The training of school psychologists. *Psychology in the Schools*, 1965, **2,** 345–349.

Mok, P. P. *A view from within*. New York: Carlton Press, 1962.

Mullen, F. A. The role of the school psychologist in the urban school system. In J. Magary (Ed.), *School psychological service*. Los Angeles: Gramercy Press, 1972.

Newland, T. E. Psychological assessment of exceptional children and youth. In William M. Cruickshank (Ed.), *Psychology of exceptional children and youth* (2nd ed.). Englewood Cliffs, New Jersey: Prentice-Hall, 1963.

O'Shea, H. E. The future of school psychology. In M. G. Gottsegen & G. B. Gottsegen (Eds.), *Professional school psychology* (Vol. 1). New York: Grune & Stratton, 1960.

Parsons, F. *Choosing a vocation*. New York: Agathon Press, 1909.

Pressey, S. L. Scale of attainment no. 1: An examination of achievement in the second grade. *Journal of Educational Research*, 1920, **1**, 572–581.

Pressey, S. L., & Pressey, L. C. Cross-out tests with suggestion as to a group scale of emotions. *Journal of Applied Psychology*, 1919, **3**, 138–150.

Preyer, W. *The mind of the child*. New York: D. Appleton, 1888.

Reger, R. The technology of school psychology. In Fred D. Holt & Richard Kicklighter (Eds.), *Psychological services in the schools*. Dubuque, Iowa: Brown, 1971.

Sarason, S. G., & Doris, J. *Psychological problems in mental deficiency*. New York: Harper & Row, 1969.

Stone, C. W. *Arithmetical abilities and some factors determining them*. New York: Teachers College Contributions to Education, 1908.

Symonds, P. J. The school psychologist—1942. *Journal of Consulting Psychology*, 1942, **6**, 173–176.

Thorndike, E. L. Handwriting. *Teachers College Record*, 1910, **11**, 1–81.

Thurstone, L. L. Mental tests for prospective telegraphers. *Journal of Applied Psychology*, 1919, **3**, 110–117.

Tindall, R. H. Trends in the development of psychological services in the schools. *Journal of School Psychology*, 1964, **3**, 1–12.

Tindall, R. H. The internship in school psychology: A contiguous model. *Journal of School Psychology*, 1973, **11**, 258–262.

Trachtman, G. M. New directions for school psychology. *Exceptional Children*, 1961, **28**, 159–164.

Trow, C. What should be expected of psychologists in education reform. *Journal of School Psychology*, 1969, **7**, 64–69.

Valett, R. E. *The practice of school psychology; Professional problems*. New York: Wiley, 1963.

Wallin, J. E., & Ferguson, D. G. The development of school psychological services. In J. Magary (Ed.), *School psychological service*. Los Angeles: Gramercy Press, 1972.

Walter, R. The functions of the school psychologist. *American Education*, 1925, **29**, 167–170.

Wechsler, D. *The measurement of adult intelligence*. Baltimore: Williams & Wilkins, 1944.

White, M. A., & Harris, M. W. *The school psychologist*. New York: Harper and Brothers, 1961.

Wrightstone, J. W. Research in school psychology. In M. G. Gottsegen & G. B. Gottsegen (Eds.), *Professional school psychology* (Vol. I). New York: Grune & Stratton, 1960.

Wundt, W. *Principles of physiological psychology*. London: MacMillan, 1873.

VIRGINIA MONROE

2 Roles and Status of School Psychology

This chapter is a review of research and opinion concerning the roles and status of school psychology. The information covered will provide beginning students with a clearer idea of what school psychology is all about as well as provide current practitioners with an opportunity to view their profession from a national perspective. The current roles and influences within school psychology are remarkably diverse, a situation that stems at least in part from historical trends (see Tindall, Chapter 1 of this volume). Nevertheless, a number of crucial questions are considered here, including: Who are school psychologists, and who are their clients? What are school psychologists doing, and how well are they doing it? What forces are affecting the future of school psychology, and where are they leading?

Demography of the Profession

To gather together information on training and experience of persons currently functioning as school psychologists would be an important contribution, since much can be learned about a profession by looking at the practitioners. In terms of training and experience, the "typical" school psychologist not only does not exist, but such a person almost defies conceptualization. This is true in part

25

SCHOOL PSYCHOLOGY
Perspectives and Issues

because of the diversity of training programs, degree levels, theoretical orientations, and experiential backgrounds that exists among practicing school psychologists. Also, the data on which the idea of "typical" can be based is frequently contradictory. For example, Farling and Hoedt (1971) reported that 59% of the school psychologists who responded to a questionnaire they sent out were *male*, whereas in another study (Keogh, Kukic, Becker, McLoughlin, & Kukic, 1975), 62% of the psychologists responding were *female*. The discrepancies in the data regarding the characteristics of school psychologists are probably due to the techniques used to gather this information. Usually such information is based on the analysis of the characteristics of respondents to questionnaires or applicants to specific training programs. Such approaches do not yield representative samples and therefore the literature contains much confounded information.

The variety of training backgrounds among persons who have been granted school psychological certification led Bennett (1970) to regretfully state that many persons called "school psychologists" would not be considered psychologists by some psychologists. Bennett developed four categories of school psychologists on the basis of their training background: (1) doctoral level school psychologists from school psychology training programs; (2) "subdoctoral" psychologists who are eligible for associate membership in the American Psychological Association (APA); (3) school psychologists who would not be considered psychologists because they could not qualify for associate membership in APA; and (4) psychologists who work in schools but who know very little about schools, regardless of degree level, since their training and continued professional orientation is toward a clinical setting.

According to a number of surveys (Barclay, 1971; Farling & Hoedt, 1971; Keogh *et al.*, 1975), the majority of school psychologists meet the requirements for APA associate membership since most have obtained a master's degree plus 30 semester hours of graduate credit. What percentage of these fall into Bennett's fourth category is impossible to determine. One study addressing training and resultant professional orientation found that counseling and guidance, school psychology, and psychology training programs are about equally represented (Keogh *et al.*, 1975). Also, more than 50% of school psychologists hold a teaching certificate and have worked for 3 or 4 years in public schools (females typically teaching at the elementary level, males typically at the secondary level or in administrative positions). Many also hold counseling credentials (Barclay, 1971; Farling & Hoedt, 1971). All of this information is 5 to 10 years old and there are a number of indications that if similar surveys were conducted today, more formal training and less teaching experience would be reported.

In reviewing information on the diversity of backgrounds, the common denominator in professional preparation appears to be training in standardized testing and report writing. The impact that this commonality must have on the role that psychologists assume in the schools will be discussed later in this chapter.

Employment and Clientele

Other important demographic information concerns employment settings and clientele. According to a national survey conducted by Farling and Hoedt (1971), the vast majority of school psychologists are under a 10-month contract with a public school system. About 5% are employed by mental health institutions, and less than 2% are in private practice or are self-employed.

Kicklighter (1976) surveyed state departments of education regarding the provision of psychological services in their schools. From the 32 states that responded, it was apparent that the availability of psychological services varied greatly from state to state, with a tendency for the more sparsely populated and southern states to provide the fewest services. During the 9-year interval from 1966 to 1974, a dramatic increase in the employment of school psychologists was noted; Kicklighter concluded that the number of school psychologists in the United States had doubled during that time.

School psychologist's clients are predominantly (75%) elementary-aged children (Tomlinson, 1974). Of these children, the largest number of referrals come from the first grade. Consonant with the male–female ratio of most developmental problems, more boys are referred for psychological services than girls (Tomlinson, Acker, Canter, & Lindborg, 1977).

Tomlinson (1973) attempted to describe the kinds of problems exhibited by children who are referred for psychological services. In a metropolitan setting, 67% of the "target behaviors" were academic, either involving skill or ability; 22% were management problems, and the remaining 11% were classified as social problems involving such things as rejection by peers or situational anxiety.

Psychologist–Pupil Ratio

The psychologist–pupil ratio has a significant bearing on the practice of school psychology. Both the APA and NASP guidelines suggest 1 : 2500 as an appropriate ratio. However, the median ratio reported by Kicklighter (1976) was 1 : 4800 with a range of 1 : 1000 in Connecticut to 1 : 47,400 in Wyoming. Projections 5 to 10 years hence indicated that most of the states were aiming for a 1 : 2000 or 1 : 3000 ratio.

It may not be appropriate to set an ideal ratio from a national perspective, as a workable ratio of pupils to psychological personnel would seem to be dependent upon many factors, including the characteristics of the population served, the density of the population, and the availability of other professional staff. All other things being equal, the ideal ratio should be lower in a rural setting than in a metropolitan setting where distances between clients and services are not so great. But in practice, the situation is just the opposite. Many small, rural school districts cannot afford to employ school psychologists or the setting does not attract them. These districts must either purchase the services on a per diem or per case basis or enter into a cooperative arrangement with other districts. Several predominantly rural states, for example, Iowa and Nebraska, have met this problem by providing psychological services through agencies that serve a prescribed area of the state.

Roles of School Psychologists

> *Is the school psychologist a task analyzer, behavior describer, diagnostic and management specialist, consultant to teachers, technologist of cognitive styles . . . modifier of the conditions of learning, test expert, program evaluator, behavior modifier, any of these, some of these, or all of these* [Bardon, 1972, p. 208]?

This quotation exemplifies the concern in the profession with the role it plays in the public schools. In a 1969 survey by Farling and Hoedt (1971), one of the major concerns of practicing school psychologists was the need for role clarification. What brought about this role diffusion and confusion? The variety of training and experiential backgrounds of school psychologists already discussed interacts with the variety of school settings and administrative expectations to produce significant role diversity. Perhaps this diversity is something the profession must always live with. According to Bardon (1964–65), the science of psychology is too broad and the function of schools too varied to enable any one kind of psychologist to bring to the schools all relevant techniques and principles. Nonetheless, the profession of school psychology does reflect some unifying threads and commonalities.

All employees of a public school system must have as their ultimate raison d'etre the well-being and development of children. From this perspective, it is possible to view the various roles in a school system along a continuum of directness-of-influence on children, from the classroom teacher to the superintendent and school board members. The uniqueness of the school psychologist's role from this vantage point is that the profession, as such, does not determine where one falls on the continuum. Rather, the determining factors are each individual within the profession and the unique setting in which each practices. School psychologists provide the full spectrum of services, from the extreme of very direct influence on children in the form of individual counseling or therapy, to the other extreme of very indirect influence on children in the form of research activities. Somewhere in-between these two extremes lie such services as psychoeducational assessments, consultation with teachers and parents, and in-service with groups of teachers and parents.

In Figure 2.1, five primary roles of school psychologists are outlined along a directness-of-influence continuum. This perspective on psychologists' roles oversimplifies reality, but it does provide a structure for the discussion of the multi-

FIGURE 2.1. *Influences of school psychological as a series of child*

plicity of roles that have been suggested in the literature. Each of the five roles are presented separately along with examples of services.

Counseling/Therapy

The most direct services provided to children by school psychologists are in the form of counseling or therapy. This service is provided either individually or in small group settings and has as its purpose the enhancement of adjustment or development through the child's relationship with the psychologist or other children.

Counseling or therapy is the most controversial of the services provided by school psychologists (see Clarizio, Chapter 11 of this volume). While Kaplan, Clancy, and Chrin (1977) reported that superintendents in Ohio were supportive of this role, Lesiak and Lounsbury (1977) did not report such support. The controversial nature of this service is best exemplified by the study of supervisors of school psychologists in which 50% viewed therapy as important while 20% not only viewed it as unimportant, but also saw it as undesirable (Kirschner, 1971).

Psychoeducational Assessment

Psychoeducational assessment activities have been the most prominent of the services provided by school psychologists. The testing movement and developments in the field of special education greatly influenced the profession of school psychology and defined its initial realm of expertise. School psychologists were the standardized test experts who categorized children according to their performance on the tests and recommended appropriate (for the times) educational placements.

on the results of the assessments. The report usually contains: (*a*) a description of the child's behavior in the testing setting; (*b*) a description of the test results and how they compare with those of other children of the same age; (*c*) some inferences that draw relationships between the test results and problems in school; and (*d*) broad recommendations regarding the educational program for the child.

In this role, the school psychologist functions primarily in a refer–test–report–recommend cycle. The emphasis is on the use of standardized tests, identifying and describing deficits, and, where appropriate, explaining how identified deficits may be related to present behaviors. Recommendations are centered around educational placements but also may include some very general intervention suggestions. Recommendations are frequently of an automatic nature—certain findings always lead to certain recommendations.

As can be seen, these services rely heavily upon written communication and frequently require large inferential leaps from the child's behavior in the testing setting to the causes of the child's problems in the classroom. The psychologist is usually called upon to say a lot about a child on the basis of a little information. Furthermore, a few instruments are used for a multitude of purposes. This practice encourages the abuse of assessment instruments, namely, using them for purposes for which they have not been validated.

The broader psychoeducational assessment role is more oriented toward the specific referral problem. For example, not all children referred are given an intellectual assessment; assessment techniques are determined by the referral problem and include many more criterion-referenced instruments and behavioral assessment techniques. This orientation can yield more specific recommendations regarding what the parents and teachers can do to remediate the problem (see Ysseldyke, Chapter 4 of this volume).

The traditional testing role preserves professional role boundaries by placing narrow limits around each professional's area of expertise. Teachers preserve their areas of expertise, which include curriculum, educational planning, and classroom management. The psychologists preserve their area of expertise, which in essence is differential diagnoses for educational purposes. Overlap between the professionals is kept to a minimum, since where the work of the psychologist ends, the responsibility of the teacher begins. Interaction or communication relies primarily on the written report, and therefore the potential influence of that report becomes critical (Mertens, 1976).

Consultative Child Study

The consultative child study role is neither a new nor a revolutionary idea; this becomes clear after only a cursory reading of the recent school psychology literature. Following a conference on "New Directions in School Psychology", held in the early 1960s, Bardon (1964–65) reported that a shift in focus was seen in the profession; a shift in focus from working with individual children to working more with those who influence children. The fact that the consultation model is not revolutionary is pointed out by Reschly (1976), who states, "The innovation is a matter of degree, not kind, since various types of consultation services have been provided by school psychologists over the years [p. 112]."

At the same 1964 conference, considerable differences among psychologists regarding the meaning of "consultation" were noted (Bardon, 1964–65). Over the past decade or so, the confusion has continued. Unfortunately, consultation has been used to describe any and all activities of a school psychologist. For example, Fairchild (1976) presented a restricted, content-oriented view of consultation, suggesting that it was most consonant with the use of behavioral management interventions. By contrast, Gallessich (1974) suggested a broad view in which consultation was categorized into six different types, depending upon the purpose.

Although there is no consensus regarding the use of the term *consultation,* for the purposes of this chapter, it will refer to a process that seeks to modify the behaviors of significant adults in the child's environment in order to produce a change in the child's behavior. The fact that consultation is an *indirect* form of service distinguishes it from the psychoeducational assessment role that has as its major focus the collection of information through direct contact with the child. It should be noted that several consultation models have been proposed that differ on a number of key variables (Reschly, 1976; Tombari & Davis, Chapter 10 of this volume).

Characteristics of the consultative model of child study include more face-to-face contact between the psychologist and the adults in the child's environment. There is less emphasis on written communications, such as formal reports or referral forms. Assessment procedures are oriented more specifically toward the referral problem and interventions rather than toward classification (Gallessich, 1974). These features usually lead to a reduction in the use of standardized, norm-referenced measures and an increase in the use of informal, nonstandarized measures or analyses of situational factors. Meyers (1973) described important characteristics of the interaction between the consultant (e.g., school psychologist) and consultees (e.g., parents or teachers). The relationship in consultation should be on the basis of colleague to colleague rather than on the basis of expert to novice. Accordingly, the consultant's contribution is de-emphasized, and the consultee is free to accept or reject any suggestions. Furthermore, there is a joint responsibility for the success or failure of the instituted interventions.

Inservice

The inservice role represents a major change regarding the school psychologist's influence on children. Attention is no longer focused on individual children and their development but is expanded to specific groups of children or children in general. The school psychologist works with a group of school personnel to produce a broad effect on children rather than through one or two adults or directly with the child.

The inservice role is characterized by the school psychologist providing expertise based on research or theory in such a way as to produce an attitude change or to increase pertinent knowledge or skills in others that in turn enables them to function more effectively in their professions. Kaplan et al. (1977) found that superintendents viewed the inservice role of the school psychologist as being fairly important. Classroom teachers, on the other hand, placed it in the least important category when they ranked the services they wanted from a psychologist (Grubb et al., 1976).

Although the relative merit of inservice may be viewed differently by those involved, that is, by the school psychologist, classroom teachers, and administrators, it still remains an active role in many school systems. Who determines the topics to be covered through inservice depends on the school system and particularly the administration. Some systems allow for the input of ideas from all levels. For instance, administrators may see the need for inservice on the writing of individual educational plans (IEP); teachers may desire inservice on learning disabilities; and school psychologists could request group time to deal with the classroom management of disruptive behaviors. Who perceives the need for the inservice undoubtedly affects its success, and the success of the inservice undoubtedly affects the teachers' perceptions of the psychologist.

Research

The last of the five roles of the school psychologist to be discussed is that of research, which is the most indirect service on the influence continuum detailed in Figure 2.1. In the mid-1960s, at the "New Directions Conference," school psychologists were encouraged to take on greater responsibility for carrying out applied research in the school (Bardon, 1964–65). The research role is best characterized by the systematic collection and analysis of information relevant to decision making regarding children and their educational programs (see Phye, Chapter 9 of this volume).

A survey of superintendents revealed that they placed a rather low priority on research activities conducted by school psychologists (Kaplan *et al.*, 1977). The only activities ranked lower were legislative efforts and the selection of curriculum materials. Lesiak and Lounsbury (1977) reported that supervisors of school psychologists placed greater emphasis on the importance of the research role than did principals. The push for involvement in research seems to be coming from university faculty in training programs (Bennett, 1976). This then would appear to be a controversial role for the school psychologist.

In summary, if the roles of the school psychologist are viewed along a continuum of working directly and primarily with children to working primarily with adults and only indirectly with children, then five roles can be differentiated. These were specified as counseling/therapy, psychoeducational assessment, consultative child study, inservice, and research. Few school psychologists provide all of these services to the public schools; some provide only one, while most offer the services contained in two or three of the roles.

From a 1969 national survey, Farling and Hoedt (1971) concluded that most school psychologists were primarily evaluating children and reporting test results to parents and teachers; both the planning of educational programs based on evaluations and follow-up activities were minimal. More recently, Keogh *et al.* (1975) reported that school psychologists spent the bulk of their time testing with a limited scope and depth of instruments, for example, Stanford–Binet, WISC-R, WRAT, and Bender; there was little use of educationally focused instruments. They further reported minimal communication between school psychologists and other school personnel, particularly teachers. Still more recently, Medway (1977) analyzed daily logs maintained by master's and doctoral candidates in school psychology while they were interning as school psychologists. Most of their time was spent in test administration and report writing. The least time was spent gathering information from school personnel and consulting with teachers on ways to remediate problems. Apparently the activities associated with the traditional testing or diagnostic role have dominated the profession, and other roles have been considerably less prominent.

Hopefully, school psychologists are sufficiently flexible and knowledgeable to seek creative ways to expand and modify current roles in the direction of meeting critical needs of school-age children (Bennett, 1970). How psychologists function within the schools is dependent upon many variables, including the expectations of their employers, characteristics of the employment settings, and their own unique expertise. Another very important source of information that *should* influence roles of school psychologists is the accumulation of information on the effectiveness of various roles.

Effectiveness of Roles

> *There is increasing evidence today that school psychology practice*
> *has been weighed in the balance and found wanting* [Barclay,
> *1971, p. 257*].

Barclay's statement is certainly a strong one to make about any profession. However, the statement needs to be analyzed and placed in perspective. Of the variety of roles in school psychology, which ones or how many have been "weighed in the balance"? In this section, the efficacy data on each of the five roles discussed earlier is presented. This is followed by a discussion of some of the accountability problems facing school psychologists and solutions that have been proposed.

Counseling/Therapy

As discussed previously, the counselor/therapist role is controversial among school psychology supervisors, with some viewing it as important, while others frankly find it undesirable (Kirschner, 1971). Classroom teachers, on the other hand, have strongly supported this role. Roberts (1970) found that 50% of the teachers wanted much more therapy conducted. These findings were further supported by Grubb *et al.* (1976) when they found that teachers chose counselor/therapist activities as one of their top preferences for services from a school psychologist. However, Styles (1965) found that teachers had an unrealistic idea regarding the training emphasis of school psychologists—they credited them with having more knowledge and skill in psychotherapy than their training background would justify. These factors must be kept in mind when interpreting and responding to teacher preferences for school psychologists' roles.

The controversial nature of this role has not stimulated the collection of much data. There are few if any studies that have attempted to measure the effects of school psychologists' therapy with children. If it can be assumed that the efficacy studies involving relationship-based therapy with adults in a clinical setting can be generalized to children in a school setting, then results would certainly not be encouraging (see Clarizio, Chapter 11 of this volume). Admittedly, this may be a tenuous supposition and as such should not preclude research studies in the area.

Psychoeducational Assessment

Few have been particularly pleased with the traditional testing role, including the profession itself. Even though nationally there has been much role consistency, that being the traditional testing role, nonetheless psychologists have expressed much concern about the definition of their role (Farling & Hoedt, 1971).

This may indicate that there is more dissatisfaction with the role than confusion about it. School psychologists are perhaps not so concerned about a role definition as they are about a role *re*definition. This interpretation is also supported by Roberts (1970), who found that psychologists felt they should be spending less time in test administration and diagnosis and more time in consultative activities.

Dissatisfaction with the traditional testing role is understandable in light of the predominantly negative feedback this role has received from teachers. Perhaps the most devastating findings come from a study conducted in New York City in the late 1960s. The United Federation of Teachers conducted a survey in which 6.5% of the teachers responding found psychologists helpful or very helpful; 7% said they were slightly helpful; 18% said they were of no help; 52% felt they were not relevant to teaching; and 1.6% actually saw psychologists as detrimental (Barclay, 1971). More recently Grubb *et al.* (1976) reported that 78% of, the teachers stated that the traditional services did not provide them with what they wanted, and 50% of the teachers found the recommendations of school psychologists to be largely or totally irrelevant. Gilmore and Chandy (1973) reported that teachers in Texas who had never worked with school psychologists had great expectations of their services; with use, the teachers' confidence in them declined.

The following are some of the specific complaints voiced by teachers regarding the traditional testing role. Teachers wanted much more follow-up (Grubb *et al.,* 1976); they wanted to be included more often, both prior to and after the evaluations (Baker, 1965); and they wanted more relevant and expanded recommendations (Grubb *et al.,* 1976; Mussman, 1964). Baker (1965) concluded that the largest single weakness was the relatively poor communication existing between the classroom teacher and the school psychologist. This, then, brings us to the consultative child study role, since face-to-face communication is emphasized in the delivery of these services.

Consultative Child Study

Several studies investigating the effectiveness of school psychological services have used a "before and after" approach—they have evaluated the services before changing to a consultative model and again after the model has been in effect for some time.

Fairchild (1976) conducted such a comparative study and found that when teachers were asked if the recommendations of the school psychologist were effective, 67% of those who received some type of consultative service answered affirmatively, compared to 55% of those who obtained traditional child study services. He further reported that with the consultative model, the teachers received more immediate feedback because of the reduction in the number of time-consuming tests that were administered. Although these results are tantalizing, they cannot be generalized because Fairchild used only one school psychologist in the study— himself.

Grubb *et al.* (1976) made a similar comparison by first evaluating the services provided by two school psychologists under what they called the refer–test–report–recommend model. The feedback from the teachers using this model was predominantly negative. A high percentage found fault with the time lag between referral and services (3 to 4 months), found the recommendations either largely or totally irrelevant, complained of the lengthy referral form, and complained about the lack of time spent with students and teachers, particularly on follow-up. The school then instituted a new system for providing psychological services. Although it was not called consultative child study, the services described fit the definitions used herein, such as, closer communication with teachers, less formal testing and report writing, and more follow-up activities. The feedback from both teachers and administrators regarding the new service system was not reported quantitatively, but it was described by Grubb *et al.* (1976) as being "extremely positive [p. 44]." Teachers particularly liked the personal and continued contact with the school psychologist.

Another comparative study looked at the effects of intensive consultation versus limited consultation (Tyler & Fine, 1974). Consultation was defined as professional encounters between a psychologist and a teacher regarding the resolution of a problem. Intensive consultation involved 45 to 65 minutes of face-to-face contact with the teacher with a report of at least three pages in length. Limited consultation involved only 15 to 25 minutes of contact and included a much shorter report. It was found that under the intensive consultation conditions, the teachers were more apt to internalize the psychologist's view of the child, they underwent greater changes in their understanding of the child's problem, and they reported more satisfaction with psychological services. The only item on which there was not a significant difference between ratings of satisfaction concerned the helpfulness of the report. It may be that the time spent writing the much longer report could have been used more effectively. The difference between the two groups on the implementation of recommendations, though not statistically significant, favored the intensive experience.

Tomlinson (1973) had teachers rate the behavioral changes in children following psychological services. Although the services were not labeled as such, from the description, they would appear to be most consonant with the consultative role. For example, only 55% of the children were given some type of test, and a significant amount of time was spent observing children in the classroom. On follow-up, it was found that in 85% of the case recommendations were implemented and, when implemented, the teachers reported a significant change in behavior 80% of the time.

As with teacher effectiveness research (Yamamoto, 1963), there is no single or simple profile of a successful school psychologist. In addition, not all school psychologists will be equally effective in the consultative child study role. The critical skills required of this role have yet to be determined. However, good interpersonal skills in relating to others are likely to be crucial to successful consultations. Also, some preliminary research is available regarding the consultant's skills in interviewing (Bergan & Tombari, 1976; Tombari & Davis, Chapter 10 of this volume).

Although it is unlikely that school psychologists will be able to focus all or even most of their efforts on the consultation role, there is mounting evidence that teacher satisfaction and change in children's behaviors is significantly increased when consultative, rather than traditional, child study services are offered.

Inservice and Research

The inservice and research roles are treated together because there is no published data regarding the effectiveness of inservice provided by school psychologists and little regarding the effectiveness of the research role.

Inservice has not generated the kind of controversy within the profession that it would logically seem to warrant. The compatibility of inservice and consultative child study is questionable. The expert–journeyman relationship and the one-way communication that might dominate inservice would seem to be counterproductive to the formation of the consultative relationship outlined by Meyers (1973). Furthermore, inservice topics would need to be carefully selected to assure that the possible benefits to be gained by the inservice outweigh the possible detriments.

The effectiveness of research activities is a difficult question to address, which probably explains why few attempts have been made to objectively justify this role for the school psychologist. Bennett (1976) described one instance of applied research in which the psychologist gathered and analyzed data to address a question about the effectiveness of various prekindergarten programs. Although the research admittedly had many shortcomings, she reported that the results were nonetheless useful to the school administrators when they had to make a decision regarding the local prekindergarten program. On the basis of this positive experience, Bennett encouraged psychologists to engage in more "applied" research activities. However, the fact that the results of the local research did not contradict the accumulated literature on the topic was surely advantageous. Would or should the decision makers have relied on the local research—even with its admitted statistical and design weaknesses—if it had been at variance with other studies? If not, then the "applied" research would have served no practical function, since the decision would have been the same regardless of the locally gathered findings.

To summarize the effectiveness data on school psychological services, it would appear that only the traditional testing role has been "weighed in the balance and found wanting," as Barclay (1971) put it. The counseling/therapy role with children in the school setting has not been sufficiently weighed, but it has been found rather wanting with adults in other settings. Neither the inservice nor the research role has been adequately weighed to support an evaluative statement. However, the consultation role has been placed on the scales and the initial results are very encouraging.

Accountability—Problems and Solutions

Few people will argue against the need for school psychologists to be accountable for the services they provide. Instead, the major discourse revolves around how to approach the accountability question. Many have addressed this problem and have offered suggestions (Clair & Kiraly, 1971; Conti & Bardon, 1974; Fairchild, 1974; Tomlinson, 1973). There appear to be basically two approaches to accountability in school psychology: descriptive and evaluative. The descriptive approach is used to describe the services offered, whereas the evaluative approach looks at the effects of those services.

The descriptive view of psychological services typically uses both frequency counts and time measures. Examples of frequency counts are the number of tests administered, number of students counseled, or number of contacts with teachers. Measures of time as a technique to provide evidence of the type of services offered would include amount or percentage of time spent in various activities and time-lapse information, such as, time from referral to initiation of services and time from initiation to recommendations. With this data, a fair description of the services provided by the psychologist can be made available, making psychologists accountable for their time (but not necessarily for the quality of their work).

The evaluative approach to accountability involves many more measurement problems but relates more closely to the ultimate justification for psychological services. The literature contains many suggestions regarding *what* to measure, but it offers few ideas regarding *how* to measure. Following is a list of four "what to measure" suggestions:

1. Implementation of recommendations
2. Consumer (parent, teacher, administrater) satisfaction
3. Changes in the child's behavior
4. Ability of teachers to deal with future problems

The ultimate in the evaluative approach to accountability for psychological services was offered by Barclay (1971) when he suggested calculating the ratio of "successes" to the total number of cases handled.

When responding to the need for accountability of psychological services, there is a danger that the accountability measures will determine the services. For example, if the number of tests administered is calculated, it may foster traditional testing services and discourage consultative child study. A careful job description with general goals and appropriate behavioral objectives would help ensure that this would not happen. Another caution regarding accountability measures is that they should not interfere with the delivery of services. Measurements should not be so time consuming as to significantly reduce the amount of time available for providing the services for which one is being held accountable.

Fairchild (1975) outlined six tools of accountability centered around child study services. The tools he suggested, which are summarized in the following list, gather both descriptive and evaluative information and should be used simultaneously.

1. Daily log: Maintain a daily account of activities and record of time to determine the type of services dominating the psychologist's time.
2. Time-lapsed information: Calculate the time between referral and initial contact and between initial contact and conference with the referral source to encourage efficient services.
3. Accountability interview: Interview the building principal after he/she has talked with the teachers to uncover problems and obtain suggestions for altering service delivery.
4. Follow-up questionnaire: Administer a questionnaire to the teachers regarding their perceptions of the usefulness of the psychological services.
5. Telephone follow-up: Telephone the parents of children served at least once during the year to determine if the recommendations were implemented and if the results were satisfactory.
6. Behavioral consultation: Collect baseline data, determine intervention strategies, and establish criteria of success.

These tools appear cumbersome at first, and some elements, specifically numbers 3 and 5, do not yield readily quantifiable information. However, as an accountability procedure it is admirable for its thorough coverage. If implemented, Fairchild's system should encourage the development of effective school psychological services.

Influences on Roles

The profession of school psychology originated from a variety of influences. Among these influences, the testing movement and the need to identify children for categorical special education services were extremely important elements. These two forces—testing and special education—still have the greatest impact on psychological services in the schools. Over the past 10 years, both special education and school psychology have been profoundly influenced by litigation and legislation dealing with special children. For example, the "mainstreaming movement" away from categorical, self-contained special education classes, which may reduce the need for traditional testing services (Meyers, Sundstrom, & Yoshida, 1974), has now become a legislated requirement.

Forces also arise from within the profession that exert great influence on the practice of school psychology. Responses to feedback regarding services provided, changes in training requirements, and the inevitable evolution of ethical guidelines are all examples of internal forces that serve to shape the profession.

In this section, the current influences on the practice of school psychology arising out of litigation and legislation are covered. Also considered are the ethical concerns of psychologists currently practicing in the schools and some speculations as to where these concerns might lead.

Litigation and Legislation

Since the late 1960s many court decisions have affected special education services in the public schools (Theimer & Rupiper, 1975). Abeson and Bolick (1974) categorized the court cases into two general areas: (a) those establishing the right of all handicapped children to an education, for example, *Pennsylvania Association for Retarded Children* v. *Commonwealth of Pennsylvania* (Note 1) and *Mills* v. *Board of Education* (Note 2); and (b) those concerned with the procedures followed when placing a child in a special education program, for example, *Hobson* v. *Hansen* (Note 3), *Diana* v. *Board of Education* (Note 4), and *Larry P.* v. *Riles* (Note 5).

The rights of handicapped children, which were gained bit by bit through the courts, were incorporated into landmark legislation in 1975 through the enactment of the Education of All Handicapped Children Act (Public Law 94-142). This law has changed special education for all time and has had, and will continue to have, a profound effect on the role of school psychologists. There are basically six principles contained in the law, each of which will affect psychological services in the public schools.

RIGHT TO AN EDUCATION

All children, between the ages of 3 and 21, regardless of handicapping condition, have a right to a free and appropriate education at public expense. This expansion of services to the previously unserved has a number of implications for school psychologists. They must become knowledgeable in the assessment of preschool children and aware of all of the pitfalls inherent in this assessment process (Bersoff, 1977). Early identification can be a blessing or a curse, depending on how wisely it is used. It can allow for earlier intervention and therefore enhance development, or it can result in erroneous, prejudicial labeling at an early age and thereby interfere with optimal development. Moving into the preschool arena cannot be approached casually by school psychologists.

Services will also need to be expanded at the other end of the spectrum. Psychological services have been primarily provided to elementary school children; secondary and postsecondary persons have received little or no attention (Hohenshil, 1975). Vocational education and the provision of psychological services at the secondary level will need to assume a higher priority with psychologists if the requirements of Public Law 94-142 are to be met.

Finally, services to the multiply handicapped and to the severely and profoundly handicapped will need to be expanded. This will require expertise with a wider range and variety of both formal and informal assessment techniques (see Gerken, Chapter 6 of this volume).

PLACEMENT PROCEDURES

P.L. 94-142 makes placement decisions the responsibility of a group of persons, including the parents and others who are knowledgeable about the child, about the techniques used in the evaluation procedures, and about the educational program options. If the placement committee determines that the child is in need of special education services, an individualized educational plan (IEP) is written specifying the services needed and the objectives and duration of such services. The individualized educational plan is to be reviewed yearly.

This aspect of the law has had pronounced effects on the practice of school psychology. In the past, school psychologists were frequently called upon to make unilateral placement decisions. It is perhaps surprising that psychologists accepted this untenable role for as long as they did. Apparently the assumption was that standardized instruments in standardized settings provided the best information for determining the most appropriate educational program for children. Unfortunately, a child's behavior in a test situation could be an atypical sample of his/her behavior. Now, because of parental involvement, placement committees, IEPs, and follow-up requirements specified in P.L. 94-142, the school psychologist is "better protected from legal and moral liability [Kabler, 1977, p. 28]."

However, it may be that as one responsibility declines, another responsibility will develop. The functioning of the placement committee is of paramount importance if the spirit as well as the letter of the law is to be followed. A provocative study on the functioning of placement committees (Yoshida, Fenton, Maxwell, & Kaufman, 1976) found a strong positive relationship between staff role and participation in the placement committee process. School psychologists were highest in participation and highest in satisfaction with the process. In general, Yoshida *et al.*, found that regardless of the role, the higher the participation in the process, the higher the satisfaction with it.

Who will assume the responsibility of eliciting the full participation of all committee members and thereby ensuring the optimal functioning of the placement committee? From the study conducted by Yoshida *et al.* (1976), it would appear that psychologists in some settings have either been given or have assumed that responsibility. The colleague relationship with other school personnel, which is essential to consultative child study services, would seem to foster participation. Therefore, the interpersonal skills required for consultation may become essential in carrying out the spirit of P.L. 94-142.

The requirement of an individualized educational plan for each child receiving special services may also have an effect on school psychologists. The IEP requires the specification of intervention procedures, which may motivate school psychologists to use assessment procedures that are more directly related to intervention strategies.

DUE PROCESS

P.L. 94-142 requires that due process procedures be followed when providing special services to children. Procedural due process specifies that if an individual is to be treated differently, a specific, proper procedure must be followed to ensure fairness to parents and children (Lambert & Cole, 1977). Included in this is the right to appeal, and the procedures for appeal are specified. Part of the requirements of due process are that appropriate assessment procedures be used that are rationally related to the resultant treatment.

The concept of informed consent is crucial to due process. Informed consent means that there must be sufficient communication with parents regarding the intent and nature of all evaluations and the potential treatments or interventions to assure that their consent is based on accurate and adequate information. Informed consent is an ideal that perhaps cannot be attained (Bersoff, 1975), but as a minimum, it requires that all communication with parents and children be in terms and language they understand.

CONFIDENTIALITY

This aspect of the law controls how and to whom psychological information can be transmitted. Written consent must be obtained before releasing information to another person outside the school if the student's identity is not concealed. This law also has considerable effect on the content of psychological reports, since when they become part of the student's educational record, the parent has access to them. Turnbull (1977) related confidentiality requirements to accountability by pointing out that consumer access to educational records would hold psychologists accountable for the accuracy and defensibility of the contents of their reports.

What constitutes an educational record becomes very important under the confidentiality requirements. According to Bersoff (1975), parents do not have access to records that the psychologist keeps for strictly private use, to which others may not have access, and which will not be shown to other persons. However, there is some question as to whether such material is protected if it is the basis for placing a child in a special class. In such a case, the parent *may* have the right to review such material to determine its accuracy.

NONDISCRIMINATORY ASSESSMENT

P.L. 94-142 stipulates that tests and other evaluative materials be administered in the child's primary language by trained personnel familiar with the local cultural and social patterns and practices. The tests must have been validated for the purpose for which they are used. In addition, the law stipulates that instruments shall be used that yield more information than a single IQ score and that no one test result shall determine placement. The impact of the nondiscriminatory assessment requirements on the practice of school psychology is far reaching and will be dealt with later (see Reschly, Chapter 8 of this volume).

LEAST RESTRICTIVE ENVIRONMENT

The "mainstreaming" or normalization trend in special education was strongly supported in this part of the law. It requires that handicapped children, in both public and private institutions, be educated with nonhandicapped children to the maximum extent deemed appropriate. Obviously this leaves wide latitude within which the placement committee must exercise judgment. In many settings where there is not a wide variety of support services, the school psychologist will need to have a broad knowledge of the continuum of services for all handicapped conditions.

The Education of all Handicapped Children Act will have far-reaching effects on the practice of school psychology. Of the five roles addressed in this chapter, the impact of this legislation may be greatest on the psychoeducational assessment services provided. It might be possible for school psychologists to meet the minimal requirements of this law through the traditional testing or the refer–test–report–recommend form of services. However, to the extent that psychologists respond to the emphasis on intervention, the intent of the placement committee process, and the de-emphasis of the sanctity of standardized, norm-referenced tests, to that extent the legislation will influence a movement toward a broader assessment and consultative role.

Ethics

A code of ethics is the hallmark of a profession. It is through a code of ethics that the profession controls the quality of the services provided by its members. Along with state legislation, certification, and licensure requirements, a code of ethics is designed to protect the public, which cannot judge the adequacy or competency of those offering services (Trachtman, 1974).

Both NASP and APA have established a code of ethics that covers such issues as professional responsibility and competency, relationship to students, schools, parents, and other professionals, use of assessment techniques, and pursuit of research activities.

The requirements of such codes should be used by each professional to monitor his/her own behavior. In addition, it is explicit in the codes that each school psychologist has the responsibility to confront and report a colleague who may be engaging in unethical activities. However, as Trachtman (1974) points out, this is often perceived as informing or tattling and contrary to some more basic ethical prompting. Nonetheless, ethical violations must not go unchecked, since ethical behavior is the basis for public trust.

One issue that is essentially an ethical question is not covered by the code of ethics; that is the issue surrounding the question, "Who is the school psychologist's client?" Is it the parent, the school, or the child? This is the essence of the dilemma surrounding the child advocacy movement. This movement was anticipated at the Thayer Conference when it was recommended that the welfare of children, staff members, and the school as an educational organization must all be taken into account, yet the welfare of the child must be kept as the main consideration (Trachtman, 1974).

The tone of some of the writings of the proponents of the child-as-client perspective (Hyman & Schreiber, 1977) would suggest that being the child's advocate is synonymous with being the system's adversary. An assumption that seems to underlie this position is that the child's advocate will of course be supporting what is right against what is wrong. Such an assumption is obvious in the statement, "Surely, older youth would appreciate the opportunity to be heard and understood by a student advocate who they believed to be sufficiently independent from the system to offer support when the student was *right* [Catterall & Hinds, 1972, p. 21; emphasis added]."

Although most school psychologists would probably agree with Trachtman (1974) when he states that the child-as-client is a "more satisfying moral commitment [p. 9]," the parent-as-client is certainly a logically viable position as well. The authority of public schools comes from the public and therefore the public (parent) is the contractual client.

The essence of this ethical question is, How would the practicing school psychologist behave when his/her opinion regarding the welfare of a child is at variance with that of either parents or school personnel? The response can range from the extremes of confrontation to acquiescence, and in any given situation the response will be the result of many considerations, for example, parental receptivity or resistance, professional rapport, etc. In the following statement, Trachtman (1974) recognized the fine judgment that must be exercised by the school psychologist when differences of opinion arise:

> Information is useful or advice valuable when the recipient is ready and receptive. It is best withheld, at least temporarily, when it will provoke resistence or denial, or stiffen defenses, and when the development of a relationship and the establishment of trust are necessary preconditions to effective intervention [p. 7]."

The issue of client determination will not be easily resolved. Other ethical considerations include: (*a*) confidentiality, or when and how should one communicate what to whom? (The APA was not able to resolve differences of opinion on this topic during the recent revision of the code of ethics.); (*b*) behavior management interventions, or when is what type of punishment or reinforcement warranted to achieve what goals? and (c) drug intervention for educational purposes, or what is the psychologist's relationship to the medical profession on this issue? These are but a few of the ethical concerns facing practicing school psychologists.

Summary

Never have school districts needed good school psychologists so much [*Kabler, 1977, p. 29*].

School psychologists are gradually molding their own profession out of all the forces that have created and affected it. With greater emphasis on the consultation role and expertise in behavior management, the current trend is toward modification of the child's environment to enhance his/her development and away from working individually with the child to enhance his/her adjustment to that environment. The challenges inherent in the current practice of school psychology are evident. The school setting has and will continue to provide a unique arena, offering opportunities to the psychologist that do not exist in any other setting. Thus, school psychology is potentially one of the most dynamic of the applied psychologies.

ACKNOWLEDGMENTS

Appreciation is due to Don Monroe and Maureen Stanton for their extensive help in the preparation of this manuscript.

Reference Notes

1. *Pennsylvania Association for Retarded Children* v. *Commonwealth of Pennsylvania*, Civil Action No. 71-42 (E.D.Pa., 1971).
2. *Mills* v. *Board of Education of the District of Columbia*, Civil Action No. 1939-71 (Dist. of Columbia, 1971).
3. *Hobson* v. *Hansen*, II, 320 F. Supp. 720 (D.D.C., 1971).
4. *Diana* v. *Board of Education*, Civil Action No. C-70-37 (N.D. Cal., 1970).
5. *Larry P.* v. *Riles*. 41 U.S.L.W. 2033 (U.S., June 21, 1972).

References

Abeson, A., & Bolick, N. (Eds.) *A continuing summary of pending and completed litigation regarding the education of handicapped children.* Washington, D.C.: Council for Exceptional Children, 1974.
Baker, H. Psychological services: From the school staff's point of view. *Journal of School Psychology,* 1965, **3**, 36–42.
Barclay, J. R. Descriptive, theoretical and behavioral characteristics of subdoctoral school psychologists. *American Psychologist,* 1971, **26**, 257–280.

Bardon, J. I. Problems and issues in school psychology—1964 proceedings of a conference on "New Directions in School Psychology." *Journal of School Psychology*, 1964–65, **3**, 6–14.

Bardon, J. I. Overview of issue—implications for future trends in school psychology. *Journal of School Psychology*, 1972, **10**, 207–211.

Bennett, V. Who is a school psychologist? (And what does he do?) *Journal of School Psychology*, 1970, **8**, 166–171.

Bennett, V. 'Applied' research can be useful: An example. *Journal of School Psychology*, 1976, **14**, 67–73.

Bergan, J. R., & Tombari, M. L. Consultant skill and efficiency and the implementation and outcomes of consultation. *Journal of School Psychology*, 1976, **14**, 3–14.

Bersoff, D. N. Professional ethics and legal responsibilities: On the horns of a dilemma. *Journal of School Psychology*, 1975, **13**, 359–376.

Bersoff, D. N. Special education for preschoolers: Impact of the Education for all Handicapped Children Act of 1975. *Journal of School Psychology*, 1977, **15**, 190–191.

Catterall, C. D., & Hinds, R. Child advocate—emerging role for the school psychologist. *The School Psychology Digest*, 1972, **1**, 14–22.

Clair, T. N., & Kiraly, J. Accountability for the school psychologist. *Psychology in the Schools*, 1971, **8**, 318–321.

Conti, A., & Bardon, J. I. A proposal for evaluating the effectiveness of psychologists in the schools. *Psychology in the Schools*, 1974, **11**, 32–39.

Fairchild, T. N. An analysis of the services performed by a school psychologist in an urban area: Implications for training programs. *Psychology in the Schools*, 1974, **11**, 275–281.

Fairchild, T. N. Accountability: Practical suggestions for school psychologists. *Journal of School Psychology*, 1975, **13**, 149–159.

Fairchild, T. N. School psychological services: An empirical comparison of two models. *Psychology in the Schools*, 1976, **13**, 156–162.

Farling, W. H., & Hoedt, K. C. *National, regional and state survey of school psychologists.* Washington, D.C.: U.S. Department of Health, Education and Welfare, 1971.

Gallessich, J. Training the school psychologist for consultation. *Journal of School Psychology*, 1974, **12**, 138–149.

Gilmore, G. E., & Chandy, J. Teachers' perceptions of school psychological services. *Journal of School Psychology*, 1973, **11**, 139–147.

Grubb, R. D., Petty, S. Z., & Flynn, D. L. A strategy for the delivery of accountable school psychological services. *Psychology in the Schools*, 1976, **13**, 39–44.

Hohenshil, T. H. Call for redirection: A vocational educator views school psychological services. *Journal of School Psychology*, 1975, **13**, 58–62.

Hyman, I. A., & Schreiber, K. Some personal reflections on the changing role of the school psychologist as child advocate. *The School Psychology Digest*, 1977, **6**, 6–10.

Kabler, M. L. Public Law 94-142 and school psychology: Challenges and opportunities. *The School Psychology Digest*, 1977, **6**, 19–30.

Kaplan, M. S., Clancy, B., & Chrin, M. Priority roles for school psychologists as seen by superintendents. *Journal of School Psychology*, 1977, **15**, 75–80.

Keogh, B. K., Kukic, S. J., Becker, L. D., McLoughlin, R. L., & Kukic, M. B. School psychologists' services in special education programs. *Journal of School Psychology*, 1975, **13**, 142–148.

Kicklighter, R. H. School psychology in the U.S.: A quantitative survey. *Journal of School Psychology*, 1976, **14**, 151–156.

Kirschner, F. E. School psychology as viewed by the supervisors of school psychological services. *Journal of School Psychology*, 1971, **9**, 343–346.

Lambert, N. M., & Cole, L. Equal protection and due process consideration in the new special education legislation. *The School Psychology Digest*, 1977, **6**, 11–21.

Lesiak, W. J., & Lounsbury, E. Views of school psychology services: A comparative study. *Psychology in the Schools*, 1977, **14**, 185–188.

Medway, F. J. Teachers' knowledge of school psychologists' responsibilities. *Journal of School Psychology*, 1977, **15**, 301–307.

Mertens, D. M. Expectations of teachers-in-training: The influence of a student's sex and a behavioral vs. descriptive approach in a biased psychological report. *Journal of School Psychology*, 1976, **14**, 222–229.

Meyers, J. A consultation model for school psychological services. *Journal of School Psychology*, 1973, **11**, 5–15.

Meyers, C. E., Sundstrom, P. E., & Yoshida, R. K. The school psychologist and assessment in special education. *School Psychology Monograph*, 1974, **2**, 3–57.

Mussman, M. C. Teacher's evaluations of psychological reports. *Journal of School Psychology*, 1964, **1**, 35–37.

Reschly, D. J. School psychology consultation: "Frenzied, fadish or fundamental?" *Journal of School Psychology*, 1976, **14**, 105–113.

Roberts, R. D. Perceptions of actual and desired role functions of school psychologists by psychologists and teachers. *Psychology in the Schools*, 1970, **7**, 175–178.

Styles, W. A. Teachers' perceptions of the school psychologist's role. *Journal of School Psychology*, 1965, **3**, 23–27.

Theimer, R. K., & Rupiper, O. J. Special education litigation and school psychology. *Journal of School Psychology*, 1975, **13**, 324–334.

Tomlinson, J. R. Accountability procedures for psychological services. *Psychology in the Schools*, 1973, **1**, 42–47.

Tomlinson, J. R. Functional analysis and accountability of psychological services. *Psychology in the Schools*, 1974, **11**, 291–294.

Tomlinson, J. R., Acker, N., Canter, A., & Lindborg, S. Minority status, sex and school psychological services. *Psychology in the Schools*, 1977, **14**, 456–460.

Trachtman, G. M. Ethical issues in school psychology. *The School Psychology Digest*, 1974, **3**, 4–15.

Turnbull, H. R. Accountability: An overview of the impact of litigation on professionals. *The School Psychology Digest*, 1977, **6**, 46–52.

Tyler, M. M., & Fine, M. J. The effects of limited and intensive school psychologist-teacher consultation. *Journal of School Psychology*, 1974, **12**, 8–16.

Yamamoto, K. Evaluating teacher effectiveness: A review of research. *Journal of School Psychology*, 1963–1964, **2**, 60–71.

Yoshida, R. K., Fenton, K. S., Maxwell, J. P., & Kaufman, M. J. *Group decision making in the planning team process: Myth or reality?* Washington, D.C.: U.S. Office of Education, 1976.

DOUGLAS T. BROWN

③ **Issues in Accreditation, Certification, and Licensure**

Introduction

School psychology as an identifiable profession has emerged from a variety of
fields during the past 25 years. To comprehend many of the critical issues that
face the profession today, one must examine a complex array of professional/
political antecedents that have their historical roots in both psychology and education. In its initial stages of development, school psychology emerged as an applied
branch of clinical psychology that utilized clinical psychometric techniques within
educational settings. As such, most practitioners in the field were first trained in
master's level clinical programs that in fact did not have identifiable school psychology components. This psychometric role was clearly reflected in the credentialing patterns for school psychologists during the 1950s and 1960s. Analysis of
trends in school psychology (Brown, Sewall, & Lindstrom, 1977) reveals that most
states have progressed through certification procedures that initially identified the
school psychologist in terms of his/her psychometric or testing skills. Only later in
the evolution of these standards were other skills added.

The historical trend toward greater individualization of instruction within
education placed increased demands on the diagnostic skills of school psychologists. Instruments and techniques long employed in the clinic were seen as inadequate for use in the schools. The rapidly developing field of special education

49

SCHOOL PSYCHOLOGY
Perspectives and Issues

also put pressure on school psychologists to become more literate in the fundamentals of education, including curricular design and program development. Changes in certification requirements were gradually followed by changes in training program content. This process stimulated the development of new training programs. Early research into the number and location of such programs is confusing, however. Ross and Harmon (1964) identified some 40 programs within departments of psychology during the early 1960s but did not examine other programs housed in departments of educational psychology, special education, and counseling. A subsequent survey by Smith (1965) revealed an additional 30 programs located within schools of education. Other studies continued to indicate a rapid increase in the number of programs being developed in both psychology departments and schools of education (Bardon & Walker, 1972; Bardon & Wenger, 1974).

Clearly the new field of school psychology was emerging, but from a number of sources. Some of these sources were within the mainstream of education rather than psychology. In this respect the early literature that chronicles the profession tends to mislead the student of school psychology in that it portrays the field as having its sole roots in mainstream psychology. A more accurate appraisal would perhaps indicate that the field emerged in three somewhat parallel ways. At first it did evolve as a subdiscipline of clinical psychology. Later, joint training programs were formed between clinical psychology, special education, counselor education, and educational psychology. Finally, programs began to develop within departments other than psychology that resulted in the formation of autonomous programs or departments of school psychology.

The credentialing of school psychologists has traditionally been administrated through state departments of teacher certification (Brown *et al.,* 1977). Development of a profession within a given state is generally preceded by enactment of certification legislation. In 1946 only 7 states certified school psychologists. By 1960 that number had grown to 24 and by 1973 to 38. Today, all but 2 states certify school psychologists within their teacher certification division. The rapid growth pattern in training programs has followed that in certification with an approximate lag time of 5 years. Thus, those states that have enacted certification legislation within the last 7 years are experiencing the most rapid growth in training. Regional trends are evident with the Southeast, Midwest, and Southwest expanding most rapidly. With the general public acceptance of school psychology has come increasing pressure for private practice liensure. Recent standards for the provision of school psychological services have been developed by the American Psychological Association (1977a) and by the National Association of School Psychologists (1978a). These standards attempt to define the entry level credentials necessary to gain either certification or private practice licensure. In some instances they attempt to define the basic competencies necessary for obtaining a credential, whereas in others they identify training program characteristics (e.g., degrees awarded, course areas offered) that lead to credentialing.

As the field of school psychology has grown, the number of organizations that purport to partially or totally represent its constituency have increased. Initially only Division 16 of the American Psychological Association (APA) claimed total representation. In 1969 the National Association of School Psychologists (NASP) was formed in order to more broadly represent school psychologists with various levels of training. Other organizations that have attracted school psychologists include the Council for Exceptional Children, National Education Association, and the American Personnel and Guidance Association. It is scarcely surprising that school psychologists should desire to affiliate with such a broad range of organizations given the historic ties of their training programs. The development of a second major national organization that claims to represent the profession does, however, require further investigation. It is this development within school psychology that has proven to be simultaneously the antecedent and consequence of most of the professional issues to be discussed in this chapter. It is therefore critical that the student of school psychology understand the similarities and differences in the goals and actions that characterize the two major national organizations.

Professional Associations

APA Division 16

Division 16 (the Division of School Psychology) represents the profession within the American Psychological Association. While full membership within APA is based on possessing an earned doctorate, this has never been the case in Division 16. All persons holding a master's or higher degree in school psychology or a related area have been granted full membership. Traditionally most of Division 16's membership has been composed of those who hold the doctorate. Currently about 36% hold other degrees. An analysis of the membership reveals that many trainers of school psychologists belong to Division 16 and that the Division has its greatest regional membership within the Northeast, Far West, and other areas of the country where school psychology originally developed from clinical psychology in the 1950s. Division 16 has for many years attempted to promote and develop the scientist/practitioner model as being the best suited for the practice of school psychology. It has also attempted to accept for membership those psychologists trained solely within the applied practitioner model. Hyman (1977) has described Division 16 as representing the scientific and academic interests of school psychology, especially at the doctoral level. He contrasts Division 16 with NASP, which he views as representing practitioner/applied interest.

In 1977 APA adopted a new set of *Standards for the Providers of Psychological Service* (1977a). These standards required that those practicing as "professional psychologists" and holding the title "psychologist" possess an earned doctorate in psychology with emphasis in the appropriate specialty. In effect the parent organization was attempting to restrict the use of the term "professional psychologist." Nondoctoral persons were excluded from the purview of professional psychology. In reaction to the new APA standards, Division 16 argued that school psychology was different from other areas in psychology in that most practitioners were at the nondoctoral level and that this was the appropriate entry level for the professional school psychologist. APA agreed to exclude school psychology temporarily from the standards by allowing all school psychologists certified by September 1974 to be grand-personed as professional psychologists. This deadline was later extended to December 1977. APA did not modify its basic position, however, and Division 16 now supports the doctoral degree in school psychology as the minimum level for full entry into the profession. Its membership policy remains the same with regard to nondoctoral professionals, however.

National Association of School Psychologists

The National Association of School Psychologists (NASP) was formed initially to represent the interests of nondoctoral practitioners in school psychology. Membership is based upon certification as a school psychologist rather than degree level. In contrast to Division 16, NASP views school psychology as a blend of psychology and education rather than as a subdiscipline of either one. Therefore school psychology is seen as neither psychology nor education, but a third profession spanning both areas. Predictably, membership patterns within NASP have been the inverse of those of Division 16, with a majority of members being practitioners. Recent data indicates an increase in general membership and substantial increases in doctoral membership. NASP has attempted to present itself as the most comprehensive representative of the profession in attracting new membership.

In 1977 and 1978 NASP published new guidelines for the training and credentialing of school psychologists. These guidelines were a revision of the 1972 standards in which NASP recognized a continuum of practice in school psychology that extends from the premaster's level through the doctorate. Central to the revised NASP guidelines was the notion that the practice of school psychology should be viewed in relation to competency levels rather than degree levels. The NASP standards asserted that competency is not adequately reflected by the acquisition of a degree. Another basic principle contained within the NASP standards suggested that optimal training for school psychologists can be accomplished within a 3-year graduate program. Finally, NASP proposed national standards for service provision in both the public and private sector that were in direct conflict with those of APA. Specifically, NASP challenged the legal and ethical authority of the APA parent organization to claim exclusive control of the term "professional psychologist" and particularly the term "professional school psychologist." NASP had in effect taken the stance that *it* was the most competent representative of school psychology at the national level.

It can be argued that the growth and maturity of a profession is reflected by the actions of its national organizations. Conversely, the vitality and stability of a profession is, to some extent, influenced by the policies developed by these organizations. Under optimum conditions this process operates to bring continued growth in professional competence. Both NASP and APA have proposed standards that set minimum levels for entrance into the profession. It has been suggested that the very existence of two national organizations and therefore the promulgation of two sets of standards would be expected, given the history of the profession. Since Division 16 must interface its actions with general APA policy, standards that are degree related would be expected. Conversely, NASP would be expected to produce competence in the provision of services. One of the purposes of this discussion will be to examine the basic professional issues that have always existed within the profession but that require constructive resolution in the near future. The reader will be provided with comprehensive data regarding the present status of school psychology, particularly in its training and credentialing dimensions. It is only through complete understanding of these processes that insight into the future development of the profession can be gained.

In reading what follows, one should be mindful of the basic professional issues that will require eventual resolution. These are briefly discussed in the following section and will be further discussed at the end of the chapter.

Professional Issues

Basic Entry Level

The issue of who is competent to practice as a school psychologist is one that sparks instantaneous and heated debate at all levels of the profession. At the core of the debate are several interrelated questions. First, is it possible to distinguish the quality of service provided by school psychologists on the basis of any criteria that can be extrapolated from their training? Specifically, can we examine degree level, course content, program accreditation, or any other academic variable and distinguish those who are qualified to enter the field from those who are not? Second, which organizations will act as the "gate keepers" for the profession? At present, five national organizations influence the current entry levels in school psychology. These include NASP, APA, Division 16, the National Council for Accreditation of Teacher Education (NCATE), and the National Association of State Directors of Teacher Education and Certification (NASDTEC). Countless other state agencies that deal with certification and private practice licensure also have influence. Other groups such as the Trainers of School Psychology (TSP) and their various state organizations also have impact. An understanding of the relationships among these groups would certainly be instructive in resolving the basic question as to which organizations will oversee the profession. The third question raised is, Is it possible to construct a viable network of criteria that define the profession we call school psychology?

In examining the third question, it is disturbing to find that little evidence exists to support the use of current training methods as a means of guaranteeing quality control (McDermott, 1978). Examination of current training procedures (Brown & Lindstrom, 1978a) reveals that much programming is being performed under the same rubrics nationally but that wide discrepancies exist with regard to specific course content. While many institutions offer the doctorate, the variance in the amount and type of course content is staggering. Similar conditions exist in other degree programs. If we review current certification and licensure standards we find surprising similarity in the number of semester hours required but minimal overlap in course content. In fact, licensure boards often do not specify the course content required but only degree level. No national organization has yet advanced a model that would provide a solution to the problem of measuring competencies. In order to be accepted and useful to various constituencies within the profession, such a model would need to relate training to credentialing and practice. The facets this model would contain is another professional issue that will be of interest to school psychology for years to come.

Is School Psychology an Independent Profession?

The issue of school psychology as an independent profession has its origin in the historical beginnings of school psychology (see Tindall, Chapter 1 of this volume). The existence of two parallel but interacting groups within psychology and education has gradually increased the pressure to autonomize the profession. The casual observer may feel that this issue is merely organizational in nature, with APA maintaining that school psychology is a subdivision of generic psychology and NASP advocating independence. This is a gross oversimplification. First, overlap in membership between the two organizations is about 30%. Therefore, they are not discrete entities. Second, one issue, that of entry level into the profession, is forcing school psychologists to consider the advantages of autonomy and separation from mainstream psychology. Third, pressures from within education have been growing for years to encourage school psychologists to form closer alliances with other groups such as the National Educational Association, the Council for Exceptional Children, and the American Association of Colleges of Teacher Education (the academic branch of generic education). Finally, the rapid growth of the profession from approximately 13,000 practitioners in 1977 (Leppaluoto, 1978) to a projected 30,000 in 1985 has tended to militate for autonomy.

Those who advocate that school psychology is properly a subdivision of generic psychology point to the academic and professional advantages of remaining within the stable structure that has been developed by the American Psychological

Association. Comparisons between school psychology and other disciplines within generic psychology are often made (e.g., industrial psychology, social psychology, and educational psychology). Tindall argues in Chapter 1 that the major leaders in school psychology have come from other fields within generic psychology. The implicit assumption underlying this observation is that future critical decisions within the field will flow primarily from generic psychology. Tindall further articulates the position held by many that school psychology is most properly defined as psychology practiced in the schools. Fundamental to this premise is the assumption that only persons highly trained in psychology are competent to apply various psychological techniques to school settings.

The fundamental philosophical issue requiring resolution can be stated in two parts. First, can we identify historical trends which, when examined critically, lead us to the conclusion that school psychology is *more* than its principle components? Second, is there evidence that an independent science of school psychology is evolving? A tertiary issue is political in nature: What impact will the numerous professional organizations influencing school psychology have on its future professional identity? Possible resolutions to these questions will be explored later in this chapter.

Future Representation of School Psychologists

As has been stated previously, both NASP and APA currently seek to represent school psychology nationally. The future of these organizations may well depend upon how the autonomy issue is resolved. If conditions are such that the majority of school psychologists are able to agree that the entry level for the profession lies at the specialist level, or sixth year of training, then greater autonomy would result. Under these circumstances it is difficult to envision APA, with its current opposition to nondoctoral practice, as the major representative of the profession. It is reasonable to conclude that if the profession becomes more autonomous it will seek autonomous leadership.

Another possible, albeit unfortunate, result of the dispute over entry level could be the splintering of the profession. Doctoral practitioners might affiliate with APA and nondoctoral practitioners with NASP. On the surface, it would appear that the recent actions taken by APA have in fact forced the issue. This can only be the case, however, if the public schools are willing to accept the doctoral level of training as paramount in school psychology. The general trend toward sixth-year certification standards would tend to predict the opposite. Therefore, if polarization of the profession were to occur, it would undoubtedly result in a difficult position for Division 16. This is supported by the fact that nondoctoral practitioners outnumber their doctoral counterparts in a ratio of 5:1.

On the basis of current statistics one would have to conclude that a shift in national representation may be in process. NASP membership continues to grow at an increasing rate while that of Division 16 has remained constant. NASP involvement in education and related disciplines has increased while Division 16 has tended to be relatively uninvolved with educators. Finally, the recent NASP entry into the process of training program accreditation has challenged the basic APA program approval mechanism. It is likely that the professional body that is able to accurately define the basic training and role characteristics of school psychology will ultimately be the primary representative.

Other issues that relate to those previously discussed include the following:

1. Who will have the legal right to use the term "professional school psychologist" in the future? The present APA standards would limit the use of the term to doctoral persons who hold certification and/or licensure. The question of whether any professional organization has the legal right to control a specific professional title is central to this issue.
2. How will market demand for school psychologists change over the next 20 years? What level(s) of training will be necessary to meet needs as expressed by those who hire school psychologists?
3. What changes in graduate training for school psychologists will be necessary to assure both competence and marketability of school psychologists for the future?

While it is difficult to predict future trends in the profession, an attempt will be made to present data that will aid the reader in drawing some tentative conclusions.

Training of School Psychologists

Historical information on the characteristics of graduate training programs in school psychology is sketchy. Most early studies tended to concentrate on demographic variables such as geographic location, degrees offered, departmental affiliation, and financial information. Thus little is known about the specific program content of school psychology programs as they emerged in the 1950s.

Surveys of Training Programs

The first comprehensive survey of training programs was done by Smith (1964–1965). Smith noted that the APA annual list of programs included only those in departments of psychology. He attempted to identify those that were housed in other university administrative units. In total he identified 79 programs; 37 were in departments of psychology and 30 were in schools of education. French, Smith, and Cardon identified 87 graduate training programs in 1968. Their data indicated an approximately even distribution of programs between psychology departments and schools of education. By the 1970s other studies were showing a rapid increase in the number of developing programs. Bardon, Cos-

TABLE 3.1

School Psychology Training Program Characteristics by State, Degree Level, Student Enrollment, and Faculty Number

State	Number of programs	Degree program/student enrollment					Number of primary faculty
		Master's	Sixth year	Doctoral	Total enrollment	Student graduates 1976–1977	
Arizona	3	17	45	56	118	24	12
Arkansas	1	n.a.	28	n.a.	28	8	1
California	26(19)[a]	42	757	120	919	242	92
Colorado	3	26	50	52	128	24	10
Connecticut	5	60	219	7	286	105	17
District of Columbia	2	9	25	14	48	15	7
Florida	9	46	146	45	237	69	33
Georgia	3	70	75	34	179	100	12
Idaho	1	8	4	n.a.	12	4	1
Illinois	8	104	52	n.a.	156	92	33
Indiana	3	60	36	68	164	36	22
Iowa	4	32	28	19	79	21	14
Kansas	5	15	141	14	170	50	23
Kentucky	3	15	5	7	27	6	6
Louisiana	1	n.a.	4	n.a.	4	2	1
Maryland	2	118	21	15	154	19	4
Massachusetts	8	37	33	1	71	48	24
Michigan	6	40	160	58	258	90	37
Minnesota	2	n.a.	24	44	68	18	8
Mississippi	3	10	10	21	41	12	6
Missouri	1	n.a.	n.a.	15	15	1	7
Nebraska	3	4	68	19	91	21	14
Nevada	1	n.a.	n.a.	n.a.	n.a.	3	3
New Jersey	7	61	207	40	308	88	38
New York	18(17)	203	653	521	1377	345	95
North Carolina	7	30	54	50	134	48	43
Ohio	12(11)	79	248	41	368	145	34
Oklahoma	3	28	33	18	79	43	9
Oregon	1	n.a.	18	5	23	5	4
Pennsylvania	13	350	212	137	699	135	43
Rhode Island	2	70	13	18	101	37	9
South Carolina	2	12	25	40	77	28	10
South Dakota	1	n.a.	4	10	14	5	2
Tennessee	8(7)	31	35	93	159	44	29
Texas	5	n.a.	107	62	169	63	22
Utah	3	25	45	37	107	44	14
Virginia	4	28	77	25	130	47	17
Washington	4	49	30	n.a.	79	33	22
West Virginia	1	5	25	n.a.	30	3	5
Wisconsin	9	90	219	34	343	141	39
Totals	203	1744	3936	1740	7450	2263	822

[a]Numbers in parentheses indicate those programs that were able to provide complete data.

tanza, and Walker (1971) were able to locate 112 programs in 1971. By 1972 Patros, Gross, and Bjorn (1972) had located 131 institutions offering training in school psychology. Bardon and Wenger (1974) again did a comprehensive survey and were able to locate 146 programs. Recent studies (Brown & Lindstrom, 1977, 1978a) reveal the existence of at least 203 programs within the United States. School psychology training has indeed expanded at an ever-increasing rate. Table 3.1 presents recent data with regard to the distribution of programs by state. These data show the distribution of degree programs, the approximate number of students in training by degree level, student graduation for 1976–1977, and the number of faculty involved in training. Table 3.2 presents the same data from a different vantage point. Here the number of training programs at each degree level is shown together with information on faculty, departmental affiliation, accredita-

TABLE 3.2

General Information Summary of School Psychology Training Programs in the United States

Program descriptors	Number	Program response level[a]
States training school psychologists	40[b]	
Training programs (total)	203	
Master's	70	
Sixth year	151	
Doctoral	66	
Students in training (total)	7450	195
Master's	1774	63
Sixth Year	3936	143
Doctoral	1740	64
Primary faculty	787	193
Secondary faculty	1165	152
Accreditation/programs		
NCATE	104	196
APA	12	196
State department of education	47	196
Other	8	196
None	25	196
Programs with the following departmental affiliation:		
Psychology	80	198
Education	83	198
Special education	5	198
Counseling/guidance	8	198
Interdepartmental	22	198
Total student graduation		
1975–1976	2112	173
1976–1977	2263	180

[a]This column contains the number of programs providing data in a given category.
[b]Includes District of Columbia.

tion, and student graduation as reported by program directors. A comparison of these data with the most comprehensive previous study (Bardon & Wenger, 1974) reveals some interesting trends. The total number of programs has increased by 57 (37%). This figure is misleading, however, since the number of doctoral programs has increased by only 7 (12%) while sixth-year programs have advanced from 78 to 151 (94%). The number of master's level programs has *decreased* from 115 to 70 (39%). Clearly the trend would appear to be away from master's level programs toward sixth-year or specialist degree programs. Although interest in doctoral level training remains high, sixth-year programs are the norm. The traditional notion that master's level programs are proliferating at an increasing rate is simply not supported by these data.

Several other comparisons between the two sets of data are warranted. First, the number of students in training has increased by 1477 (25%). The greatest increase in enrollments has been at the sixth-year level with 2744 additional students in training. The number of master's level students in training has decreased from 3410 in 1974 to 1774 in 1977. The number of doctoral students in training has increased slightly from 1371 to 1774. Bardon and Wenger (1974) also examined the departmental affiliation of programs and found that approximately 51% were in psychology departments while 38% were in schools of education. The present data indicates that in 1977, 40% of the programs reported affiliation with a psychology department, 48% were in schools of education, and 11% were interdepartmental. It is the opinion of the author, however, that such distinctions are not easily made in today's universities. It is not uncommon to find psychology departments attached to schools of education rather than to schools of arts and sciences. Also, an increase in interdisciplinary programming among psychology, school psychology, counseling, and educational psychology programs has added another dimension to the character of school psychology programs.

Bardon and Wenger (1974) also studied the number of programs accredited or seeking accreditation by APA. In 1974, 5 programs were accredited at the doctoral level by APA. In the present data 12 programs indicated that they were either accredited by or were seeking APA accreditation. In addition, 112 programs indicated that they were either accredited by or were seeking accreditation from NCATE. Forty-seven were accredited solely by their state department of education. The distinctions among national, regional, and state accreditation agencies will be discussed later in this section.

As has been suggested, school psychology programs initially trained practitioners within the clinical/diagnostic model. The development of new training models during the 1950s and 1960s is difficult to chronicle, since few national surveys addressed the issue of program content. It is therefore impossible to trace definitive trends during that period. Nevertheless, the literature is replete with theoretical suggestions for the training of school psychologists. As Hartlage (1971) has indicated, a continuum exists along which various models may be placed. At one extreme lies the service/practitioner model and at the other the academic model. If the research and scientific knowledge generated by the academic model is suited to social application, applied training programs tend to emerge. Since service-oriented programs generally enjoy wide public support and visibility, they tend to proliferate at a greater rate than their scientific/research counterparts. There is some evidence that school psychology has moved rapidly toward the service/practitioner model during recent years. Certainly the sharp increase in sixth-year programs that are service oriented would tend to support this notion. However, it must be noted (Brown & Lindstrom, 1978a) that an increasing number of specialist level programs have research components within their required curricular sequence. Conversely, there is evidence that some doctoral programs are moving toward greater emphasis on the service/practitioner model. The recent interest in the applied doctorate (Psy.D.) in psychology is evidence for this trend.

Training Models

Although Monroe in Chapter 2 of this volume reviews in detail the numerous role functions ascribed to the school psychologist, it is appropriate to review in this chapter several basic training models advanced during the past 15 years.

The psychometric model has dominated much of school psychology training and practice over the years. However, little support for this model is to be found in the literature. One finds most authors suggesting alternatives that partially remove the school psychologist from the traditional diagnostic function.

THE MULTIDISCIPLINARY TRAINING TEAMS MODEL

Buktenica (1970) has advanced the notion of training school psychologists within multidisciplinary teams composed of a variety of professionals (e.g., physicians, teachers, special educators, and speech pathologists). Central to this training concept is the need to provide service to children, teachers, and others within their natural environment. This is in sharp contrast to the traditional diagnostic model in which those to whom the school psychologist provides service are removed from the normal environment. Smith and DiBacco (1974) have described some of the strengths and weaknesses of training within multidisciplinary training teams (MDTT).

The MDTT has the advantage of acquainting the school psychologist with other collateral professionals. It promotes integrated decision making with regard to service provision to exceptional children. It mininizes formal role conflict among the various professions represented on the team. However, certain recurring complexities have been shown to be associated with such teams. First, the team must be attached permanently to a school or other identifiable social system within a school administrative unit. Second, the MDTT must be able, within itself, to identify the array of possible professional resources represented and to utilize them effectively. Also, the team must be able to make successful entry into the school environment. Finally, if entry into the situation is achieved, the MDTT is faced with the constantly changing roles, relationships, and goals associated with various parts of the system. Generally the MDTT model speaks to the environment in which the school psychologist is trained. Specific services to be provided (i.e., skill areas) would vary among individuals trained through this approach. (The MDTT approach clearly attempts to move the school psychologist into a more direct involvement with the schools.)

The Professional Child Psychology Model

Carboy and Curley (1976) have recently advocated a model for training that is not institutionally related. The professional child psychology (PCP) training model attempts to train practitioners in a specific set of skills that are assumed to be applicable to an array of institutional settings. The training model stresses the child as the primary recipient of services. Training areas within this model include physiological processes, child development, motivational patterns, sensory processes, learning, adjustment, atypical behavior, socialization, and research. Carboy and Curley articulate the position that school psychology is in reality a subdiscipline of child psychology. They advocate that all school psychology programs be expanded to subsume the more general role of the child psychologist. Stress on the medical aspects of child development is seen as critical. It is assumed that anyone trained in the PCP model will be competent to practice in all environments containing children. They conclude that the current concept of school psychology as a profession should be scrapped in favor of more generic training methods. They further advocate the removal of school psychology from the teacher certification system, which is seen as restrictive in terms of role and function.

The Consultation Model

During the past several years an emerging emphasis in the training of school psychologists has been in the area of consultation (Dinkmeyer, 1973). It is argued that the school psychologist should provide service to all school personnel employing a general consultative methodology or service delivery framework. Gallessich (1974) has identified several variables that influence consultation techniques. These include the value system in which the school psychologist works, the target group to receive services, the system to be changed, the specific method(s) to be employed, and the role of the consultant. Thus the consultant may be seen as either authoritarian or nonauthoritarian, as working with individual children or with entire schools, and as bringing varying skills to the consultant situation. Several major types of consultation have been identified by Gallessich. They range from consultation that merely transmits information to social system intervention. Other roles include clinical diagnosis and recommendation, mental health consultation with individuals and groups, program planning and implementation, and group process consultation.

Advocates of the consultation model of training suggest that it broadens the perceived role of school psychologist to include much more than diagnosis and recommendation. The consultation model allows practice to occur at all levels within the system and with virtually any group or individual within the school system. Obviously the consultation model allows great versatility in the training of school psychologists. However, it is a vehicle for service delivery and does not specify the service to be delivered.

We have discussed three quite different perceptions of the training in school psychology. The first viewed the school psychologist as part of a professional team, the second viewed him/her as an autonomous child clinical psychologist, and the third as a provider of virtually any service. Gilmore (1974) described five traditional approaches to the practice of school psychology: (*a*) the preventive mental health model (Bower, 1965); (*b*) the clinical model (Bardon, 1965); (*c*) the psychoeducational model (Vallett, 1963); (*d*) the educational programmer model (Reger, 1965); and (*e*) the data-oriented problem solver model (Gray, 1963a). Gilmore concluded that school psychology is fixated at an adolescent stage of development in that no agreement has been reached with regard to the viability of these approaches. Each approach tends to be treated with reverence by its advocates and does little to examine the scientific and applied validity of the others. Gilmore indicates that more comprehensive analysis of the training procedures employed in such programs must be forthcoming before school psychology can advance to an independent identity.

Content of Training Programs

The trend toward more diversified models of training is evidenced by an examination of training program content recently performed by Goh (1977). Data on 99 training institutions were collected in 1975. The curricular content of each program was coded and subsequently factor analyzed. A total of nine significant factors were extracted from 38 school psychology curricular components identified across the entire sample of programs. Goh labeled the first extracted factor "School-Based Consultation" and described the training activities associated with it as being related to the identification of exceptional children and the development of specialized counselor programs. He labeled the second factor "Educational Assessment and Remediation" techniques. Factor three was labeled "Behavior Modification Technology" and related primarily to classroom management activities. Factor four was "Psychological Evaluation," which was concerned solely with assessment of individual differences among children. The remaining factors accounted for a relatively small proportion of the variance and included "Psychotherapeutic Procedures," "Quantitative Methods," "Community Involvement and Consultation," "Professional Roles and Issues," and "Psychological Foundation."

Goh also performed comparative analyses among master's, specialist, and doctoral programs with regard to the nine factors listed in the preceding paragraph. He found significant differences between doctoral and master's programs on such factors as "School-Based Consultation" and "Quantitative Methods," with doctoral programs stressing these areas more. No differences were found between specialist programs and the other two levels on any factor. Goh concluded that a shift in curricular priority is gradually taking place within school psychology programs with increased intensity of training. Generally programs have maintained their psychoeducational component but have made it secondary to school consultation activities. Few "clinically oriented" master's programs were in evidence; rather, the consultant/specialist appeared to be the role being adapted by most programs. No distinction was found among programs on the basis of departmental affiliation.

In order to further clarify the nature and content of training programs, Brown and Lindstrom (1978b) analyzed the structure of 203 graduate school psychology programs in the United States. Their data tended to partially support that of Goh in that a strong emphasis on teacher consultation was evident. Virtually all programs identified had a psychoeducational component. Eighty percent required behavior modification training and 89% required subspecialization in counseling, special education, or administration. Only seven master's level programs were producing terminal students at the 30-semester-hour level. The majority of master's programs (63) were intermediate steps within program sequences leading to the specialist or doctoral degree. The remaining master's programs required from 45 to 60 graduate semester hours. In examining doctoral level programs, Brown and Lindstrom found a tendency toward requiring a strong research component. However, a surprising number of specialist programs also contain research components. Of particular interest was the fact that a number of doctoral programs examined had adopted the "diagnostic/therapeutic model" for functioning in the school. A number of doctoral programs in the Northeast indicated that they had extensive training components in traditional child/clinical methodology.

Brown and Lindstrom also examined the type of field experience required by programs. Ninety-eight percent of the programs identified required either a practicum, internship, or externship of some type. Practicum experiences ranged from 3 semester hours to 15 semester hours and included from 90 to 2000 clock hours of supervised experience. Most practica were integrated in the training program course sequence. However, internships were most often designed to be either half-time or full-time supervised field experiences of relatively long duration (from 1 semester to 2 years). An increase in required field experience was observed in comparison to previous studies. Models for the implementation of this component of a program have been comprehensively reviewed in the literature (Cortes, 1969; Pryzwansky, 1971; Catterall, 1973; Fagan, 1977). As will be discussed in detail later, new standards for the field training of school psychologists have been developed by a number of state certification agencies and by two national accreditors. These standards are being adopted by many programs. It might also be observed by reading literature produced by training programs that a new "field-oriented" training philosophy is now developing.

In summary, a review of the current training literature reveals greater similarity among programs than had been the case during the 1960s. A number of identifiable training components are common to most programs. Emphasis is toward teacher, child, and parent consultation in the schools. Although diagnostic/ prescriptive expertise is seen as a critical component by almost all programs, this area does not occupy the position of preeminence that it once did. Programs are tending to express more desire to train school psychologists who are competent to deal with a wide variety of situations in the schools (Brown & Lindstrom, 1978b). As such, they draw curricular content from a variety of collateral professions in an effort to meet the changing demands of the school setting. If current trends continue, further diversification of program curriculum could be expected in the coming years with new subspecialty areas being added as field demand dictates. It is clear from all research data presented that the most common training level is at the specialist level, or sixth year. Since very few new doctoral programs have been developed during the past 5 years, one would expect this trend to continue for the immediate future. However, program concepts such as the professional doctorate seem to be one possible direction for future development. At present, approximately five Doctor of Psychology (Psy.D.) programs exist nationally with an emphasis in school psychology. These programs are highly applied in nature and partially or totally omit the research component required in traditional Ed.D. or Ph.D. programs. It is not known at the present time if the concept of the professional doctorate can be made more acceptable to certification and licensure boards. The question of national accreditation of such programs is also critical to their future.

Accreditation of Training Programs

The accreditation of school psychology training programs by state and national agencies is a topic that has profound impact on the profession. It is through this mechanism that training programs are identified in terms of various quality dimensions. Accreditation, as it is presently practiced, is a process in which training programs are objectively evaluated with reference to a standard set of criteria (Brown, 1977a, 1977b). This evaluation has several purposes. First, it seeks to provide the training program with information and feedback that will stimulate growth and improvement. Second, it provides the basis for quality control, in that the results of accreditation evaluations are made public. Thus prospective students often seek out accredited programs in preference to nonaccredited programs. Third, accreditation often provides the basis for reciprocity among states and other jurisdictions in the licensing and certification of school psychologists. Finally, accreditation functions to stimulate the formation of a uniform set of standards for the entry level of training into the profession.

At the present time two types of accreditation agencies predominate in school psychology. Most state departments of education approve programs within their state. Such approval is primarily based upon the program meeting state certification requirements rather than some regional or national criteria. However, certain states subscribe to the criteria established by the National Association of State Directors of Teacher Education and Certification (NASDTEC). These criteria are an extrapolation of the *Training Standards* developed by NASP (1972).

With the exception of state agencies, all other accreditors within the United States are private, nongovernmental and nonprofit professional bodies. More than 25 groups are accredited by the Council of Post-Secondary Accreditation (COPA), which is itself a private, nonprofit organization. COPA also accredits the six regional accreditors responsible for more generic approval of colleges and universities. Two national organizations currently have responsibility for school psychology accreditation, the National Council for Accreditation of Teacher Education (NCATE) and APA. NCATE was the first organization sanctioned to accredit school psychology programs. NCATE was given this sanction in 1953 by the National Commission on Accrediting (NCA), which was the predecessor of COPA. NCATE has authority to accredit all programs within schools of education that lead to practice in the public schools. It also accredits programs in other university administrative units that produce public school personnel. NCATE engages in both generic and program-specific accreditation (NCATE, 1977). Thus it evaluates the general quality of a given school of education and determines its accreditability prior to individual program evaluation. Individual program evaluation is performed in the areas of elementary and secondary education, school administration, special education, counseling and guidance, and school psychology. In the past, school psychology programs have been accredited at the master's, sixth-year, and doctoral levels.

NASP has traditionally supported NCATE's efforts to accredit programs in school psychology. In 1972 NCATE adopted NASP's guidelines for competency-based training. In 1976 NASP became an associate member of NCATE. In 1978 NASP constitutionally affiliated with NCATE for the purpose of gaining further involvement in the accreditation of all pupil services programs. At the same time NASP released its revised standards for *Training Programs, Field Placements, Service Provision, and Credentialing* (NASP, 1978a, 1978b). With this action, NASP was projecting a new and more extensive role for itself in the accreditation, training, and credentialing processes.

The American Psychological Association has been sanctioned to accredit doctoral programs in clinical and counseling psychology since 1948. In 1970 it applied to the National Commission on Accrediting (NCA, now COPA) for the authority to accredit doctoral programs in school psychology. After some controversy with NCATE, the traditional accreditor of school psychology programs, APA was granted the authority to accredit only doctoral level programs. NCATE retained its authority to accredit both doctoral and nondoctoral programs in school psychology. Kurz (1974) has carefully reviewed the historical conflict between NCATE and APA. By allowing APA to accredit doctoral programs in school psychology, NCA violated one of its major standards, which prohibits proliferation and overlap of accrediting bodies. If COPA were to remove NCATE's authority to accredit doctoral programs, however, two separate agencies would have primary responsibility for school psychology: one at the doctoral level and the other at the nondoctoral level. Kurz suggested that APA seek sanction to become the sole accreditor of school psychology programs at all levels. However, Kurz was unable to predict that APA would limit the practice of school psychology to the doctoral level in its *Standards for Providers of Psychological Services* (APA, 1977a). These standards were followed by the revised *Criteria for the Accreditation of Doctoral Training Programs and Internships in Professional Psychology* (APA, 1977b). Thus APA, by restricting the entry level to the profession within its standards, has also severely restricted the number of programs that it could potentially accredit. As we have seen before, the core of this issue for APA is the view that school psychology is a subdiscipline of generic professional psychology. NCATE has always viewed school psychology as an autonomous profession that practices within the public schools. NASP became a constituent of NCATE on this basis and monitors school psychology accreditation within this framework. As of 1978, NCATE was accrediting on a continuing basis some 108 school psychology programs at the doctoral and sixth-year levels. APA currently accredits seven doctoral programs. Accreditation for five other programs will be sought in the near future. At the present time NCATE accredits programs that lead to certification. APA defines its accreditation procedure as one that approves professional programs in psychology.

APA Accreditation Standards

In order to understand the function of accreditation more clearly, it may be helpful to review the basic aspects of APA standards. (NASP standards are discussed in the section that follows this.) The current APA *Criteria for Accreditation* (1977b) are in the process of revision and therefore would be expected to change somewhat over the next 2 years. These criteria are generic in nature in that they attempt to provide general guidelines for all doctoral training programs in professional psychology. The criteria are divided into the following areas:

1. Institutional settings: This standard describes the type of institutional structure necessary to house a psychology program. The program must be clearly labeled a "psychology program" and be recognizable as an independent administrative unit. The program must have an identifiable psychology core including a

practicum, internship, and other supervised experience and must award a doctoral degree (Psy.D. or Ph.D.).

2. Cultural and individual differences: Selection of faculty, design of curriculum, and provision for field placement sites must reflect a program commitment to understand the cultural and social milieu in which the student will practice. Discrimination on the basis of sex, race, religion, or ethnic background is prohibited.

3. Training models and curricula: Each program must specify a detailed training model and goals associated with that model. The program's training model must be relevant to local and regional service needs. Theory, research, and practice must be combined within the program. Courses are required in history and systems of psychology, human development, individual differences, learning motivation, organizational and community psychology, perception, personality, physiological psychology, psychopathology, social psychology, statistics, and research design. Training in assessment, intervention, and consultation is also required. In designing programs, faculty are required to be aware of regulations published by state psychological associations.

4. Faculty: Faculty should have a full-time commitment to the program and should be experienced practitioners. The person with major responsibility for the program should show evidence of high faculty rank and professional recognition, such as APA fellowship or American Board of Professional Psychologists diploma status. The general faculty should be large enough to ensure adequate attention to individual student program needs. At least one faculty person should be assigned full-time to coordinate practicum facilities.

5. Students: Students who are recruited to programs should have access to precise statements of program goals and objectives. Students should be admitted employing objective criteria and should be completely informed with regard to the types and extent of professional practice that they can expect to engage in after graduation.

6. Facilities: The program should provide adequate facilities to students and faculty that include practicum sites, work space, office space, research tools (e.g., calculators, computers), library materials, audio-video equipment, and basic research equipment.

7. Practicum and internship training: The program should contain a minimum of 300 clock hours of practicum experience. Practicum facilities should be diverse and relevant to program goals. Internship settings must provide full-time experience that is program relevant. Internships are supervised by psychologists who meet the criteria for *Providers of Psychological Services* and are normally 1 year or 2000 clock hours in length.

Currently, Division 16 of APA is developing a set of specialty area standards for school psychology. Until these standards are complete, doctoral school psychology programs will be evaluated using the more generic framework specified in the preceding list.

NASP Accreditation Standards

The *Standards for Training Programs in School Psychology* developed by NASP (1978b) are similar in structure to those of APA. They are, however, specific to the profession of school psychology. They contain the following provisions:

1. Structure of training programs in school psychology: Training programs in school psychology shall lead to a recognized degree at the doctoral or sixth-year (specialist) level. In each case there shall be a planned, supervised, and integrated program of graduate study. Programs shall be titled "School Psychology" and shall be clearly identifiable as organizational units.
   a. Doctoral programs shall consist of a minimum of 4 years of academic study including at least 90 graduate semester hours of credit and 1 year of predoctoral supervised experience.
   b. Sixth-year programs shall consist of a minimum of 3 years of academic study including at least 60 graduate semester hours of credit and 1 year of supervised experience.
   Both sixth-year and doctoral programs shall culminate in the awarding of an appropriate degree.
2. Program content: Training of the school psychologists shall include foundations in both psychology and education together with psychoeducational methods and professional school psychology. The program must have explicitly stated objectives and/or competency training in the following areas:
   a. Psychological foundations, which includes human learning, child and adolescent development, human exceptionality, and cultural diversity
   b. Educational foundations, including organization and operation of the schools, instructional and remedial techniques, and special education
   c. Psychoeducational methods, including psychoeducational assessment, research design and statistics, consultation, behavior modification, counseling, and organization and administration of pupil services
   d. Professional school psychology, including professional issues, standards, and ethics in school psychology
3. Orientation of the school psychologist to the educational process: The program demonstrates that school psychologists in training are effectively exposed to all operational aspects of elementary and secondary schools.
4. Practica and internship experience: The program provides planned supervised experience in accordance with NASP *Standards for Field Placement in School Psychology*. This experience includes a supervised practicum that is related to the required core content areas.
5. Credentialing standards: The program shall meet the NASP *Standards for the Credentialing of School Psychologists* (1978b) and the approval standards as

established by the state department of education in whose jurisdiction the program is located.

6. Criteria for program faculty: Both doctoral and sixth-year programs are directed by persons who hold the doctorate with specialization in school psychology. The faculty for each degree program will include at least three full-time positions including at least two full-time persons who hold the doctorate with specialization and experience in school psychology. The faculty are sufficient to assure an average faculty–student ratio not in excess of 1:10.

7. Faculty responsibilities: Faculty responsibilities shall include teaching, research, and university community service. Faculty members who teach applied courses or supervise field work shall have continuing association and involvement with the schools. These faculty shall have at least 2 years of full-time experience as practicing school psychologists.

8. Criteria for students: The program applies specific published multiple criteria for admission. The program also applies specific criteria for the evaluation of students to ensure that they possess the personal characteristics and academic/ professional competencies necessary for their role as practicing school psychologists.

9. Institutional resources and facilities: The program shall provide adequate office, clinical, laboratory, and research facilities, as well as observation rooms, teaching laboratories, and other areas suitable for work with children, parents, and teachers.

10. Evaluation of program: The program carries out a well-defined plan for the evaluation of its graduates and uses the results for the development and improvement of its program. The program has representative student, faculty, and consumer participation in the evaluation and development of the school psychology program. Long-range development of the school psychology program is done with knowledge of trends in professional school psychology.

11. Human resources: As part of its overall program design, the training program in school psychology shall provide a plan to recruit, maintain, and promote the professional development of students and faculty with minority characteristics in terms of sex, race, ethnic origin, and handicapping conditions representative of the population they hope to serve.

In addition to the basic provisions cited in the preceding lists of standards, both the APA and NASP documents require that the training program provide continuing professional development (CPD) experiences for graduates. Walker (1977) has delineated three areas in which CPD can take place. These include the broad areas of assessment and evaluation, intervention and remediation, and program planning, development, and research. Almost all states require that school psychologists demonstrate continued professional training in order to renew their certification or licensure. Since accreditation agencies have now stipulated similar requirements, it is likely that all school psychologists can expect to be renewing their training periodically throughout their careers. A review of the various strategies employed to provide CPD in nonuniversity settings has been presented by Lesiak, Petty, and Braccio (1975).

It is to be expected that further refinements will be made in APA and NASP standards. Both sets of standards speak mainly to program structure rather than to specific training procedures. The development of a number of model training concepts that are objectifiable would be the next logical step in order to implement the intent of the standards. From this process it would be expected that several primary models of training would emerge over the next 10 years.

Credentialing of School Psychologists

The term "credentialing" refers to the process of legally sanctioning the practice of school psychology. This process is carried out in two major forms. State departments of teacher education usually certify school psychologists for practice in the schools. However, in some states this process is called licensure. Also, it is common for state boards of psychological examiners to license either the generic area of psychology or in certain instances the specialty of school psychology. The license is primarily for private practice. In some states where no legal basis for credentialing exists, state psychological associations may develop a registry of psychologists who meet certain criteria. Since two quite different processes for credentialing exist, they will be discussed separately in some detail.

Certification of School Psychologists

Periodic studies of trends in certification have been conducted since 1946 (Horrocks, 1946; Hall, 1949; Clayton, 1950; Newland, 1956; Hodges, 1960; Gray, 1963b; Nelson, 1963; Gross, Bonham, & Bluestein, 1966; Traxler, 1967; Graff & Clair, 1973; Sewall & Brown, 1976; Brown *et al.*, 1977). Only 7 states certified school psychologists in 1946. By 1960 this number had grown to 24 states and by 1967, to 38. In 1977 all but 2 states were certifying some form of school psychologists. As has been indicated, the growth rate in certification preceded that in training, since certification is often linked to the funding mechanisms in public school systems.

Four basic types of certification systems have developed nationally. These may be categorized as course based, area based, competency based and program based. Course-based certification simply requires that the applicant show evidence of having completed certain specific courses (either graduate or undergraduate) in order to be certified. This model was the earliest form of certification employed. Area-based certification requires that the candidate show evidence of training in certain broad course areas (e.g., intellectual assessment, consultation) in order to be certified. Most states currently use some form of this system. Competency-based certification requires that the candidate show evidence of being able to perform certain highly defined tasks that are described in the state certification standards, usually in the form of a role statement. Currently, eight states employ competency-based standards. Program-based certification requires that the applicant complete a school psychology program that has been approved or accredited by a state or national agency. A number of states utilize this method in combination with one of the other three methods cited.

States differentiate types of certification on a number of other parameters. Two states certify four levels of school psychologists. Ten states certify at three levels, while 12 states have bilevel certification. Twenty-six states specify one level of certification. Thirteen states accept some undergraduate credit toward certification. Six states require the candidate to be eligible for teacher certification or to have had experience as a teacher in order to be certified. Twenty-nine states require graduation from a sixth-year program in order for the candidate to be fully certified under the title of school psychologist. One state requires the doctorate in order to gain certification at the entry level.

Table 3.3 presents current data on certification requirements within the United States. A comparison of these data with that collected by other researchers cited in the text reveals some interesting trends. Nine states have developed new standards during the past 4 years. Six of the 9 states have instituted single-level systems. Previous studies have indicated a trend toward multilevel certification. This trend would appear to be reversing. Approximately half of the states currently certify at one level for school psychology. Of the 22 states that have recently modified their requirements, the trend is toward single-level, competency-based standards. This is especially true for states that have had certification requirements for a number of years. Two other trends seem to be apparent in the data. First, most states have adopted some form of field experience requirement (i.e., practica, externship, or internship). Presently, only 9 states lack this requirement. Second, the overall level of training and experience required for certification is increasing. Only 4 states allow certification at the submaster's level. Eighteen states are currently in the process of revising requirements.

Data over the past several years suggest that states that employ the course-based method of evaluation report the greater difficulty in evaluating credentials. States that have adopted the competency-based model report difficulty in verifying the specified competencies. Consequently, the program-approval approach appears to be gaining support. However, this approach is highly dependent upon reciprocity mechanisms. Three national agreements currently form the basis for reciprocity among states. These include the Interstate Reciprocity Project (ICP), the NASDTEC agreement, and the NCATE network. The NCATE agreement provides the most comprehensive reciprocity, with 18 states represented in school psychology. If current NCATE teacher education agreements were expanded to school psychology, the number of states would increase to approximately 38. The NCATE process probably has the best potential to eventually provide national reciprocity in school psychology through program approval (accreditation). This

TABLE 3.3
Summary of Certification Requirements for School Psychologists by State

State	Levels and titles	Certification requirements					Licensure requirements		
		Degree	Hours required	Areas/ courses	Field experience	Teaching experience	Statute	Level[a]	Type[b]
Alabama	Psychometrist	MA	n.a.	Courses	Yes	No	Yes	D	G
	School psychologist, Class A	MA	27	Areas	No	Yes	Yes	D	G
	School psychologist, Class AA	Sixth year	MA+30	Areas	No	Yes			
Alaska	School psychologist	BA	n.a.	None	No	No	Yes	N	G
Arizona	School psychometrist	MA	30	Areas	Yes	No			
	Assistant school psychologist	MA	50	Areas	Yes	No	Yes	D	G
	School psychologist	MA	70	Areas	Yes	No			
Arkansas	Educational examiner	MA	MA+18	Areas	Yes	No	Yes	N	
California	School psychologist	MA	n.a.	Competency	Yes	No	Yes	N	S
Colorado	K–12 school psychologist								
	Type A or B certificate	MA	60	Areas	Yes	No	Yes	D	G
	Type E certificate	MA	60	Areas	Yes	No	Yes	D	G
Connecticut	School psychologist								
	Provisional certificate	MA	45	Areas	Yes	No	Yes	D	G
	Standard certificate	MA	60	Areas	Yes	No	Yes	D	G
Delaware	School psychometrist	BA	30	Areas	Yes	No	Yes	D	G
	School psychologist	MA	66	Areas	Yes	No	Yes	D	G
District of Columbia	School psychologist	MA	30(20)	Areas	Yes	No	Yes	D	G
Florida	Specialist in school psychology	MA	n.a.	Competency	Yes	No	Yes	D	G
Georgia	School psychometrist	MA	40 qt.	Areas	Yes	No			
	Associate school psychologist	Sixth year	MA+45 qt.	Areas	Yes	No	Yes	D	G
	School psychologist	Ph.D.	n.a.	Areas	Yes	No	Yes	D	G
Hawaii	Psychological examiner	MA	30	Areas	Yes	No	Yes	D	G
Idaho	Psychological examiner	MA	33(12)	Areas	Yes	No	Yes	D	G
	School psychologist	MA	48(21)	Areas	Yes	No	Yes	D	G

State	Certificate	Degree	Hours						
Illinois	School psychologist	MA	56	Areas	Yes	No	Yes	D	G
Indiana	School psychometrist	MA	n.a.	None	Yes	No	Yes	D	G
	School psychologist	Ph.D.	n.a.	None	Yes	No	Yes	D	G
Iowa	School psychologist	MA	n.a.	None	No	Yes	Yes	N	S
Kansas	School psychologist I	MA	60	Areas	Yes	No	Yes	D	G
	School psychologist II	MA	90	Areas	Yes	No	Yes	D	G
Kentucky	School psychometrist	MA	n.a.	Areas	Yes	No	Yes	N	S
Louisiana	School psychologist, Type C	MA	18	Areas	Yes	No	Yes	D	G
	School psychologist, Type B	MA	24	Areas	Yes	No	Yes	D	G
	School psychologist, Type A	MA	MA+30	Areas	Yes	No	Yes	D	G
Maine	School psychologist								
	Provisional certificate	MA	60	Areas	Yes	No	Yes	N	G
	Professional certificate	Ph.D.	n.a.	Areas	Yes	No	Yes	N	G
Maryland	School psychologist I	MA	45(34)	Areas	Yes	No	Yes	D	G
	School psychologist II	MA	60(36)	Areas	Yes	No	Yes	D	G
	Consultant psychologist	Ph.D.	60(36)	Areas	Yes	No			
	Supervisor of psychological services	Ph.D.	60	Areas	Yes	No	Yes	D	G
Massachusetts	School psychologist	MA	60	Areas	Yes	No	Yes	D	G
Michigan	School psychologist								
	Minimal temporary approval	BA	30	Areas	Yes	No	Yes	N	G
	Minimal full approval	MA	45	Areas	Yes	No	Yes	N	G
Minnesota	School psychologist I	MA	n.a.	None	No	No	Yes	N	G
	School psychologist II	Sixth year	n.a.	None	No	No	Yes	N	G
Mississippi	School psychologist, Class AAA	MA	60	Areas	Yes	No	Yes	D	G
	School psychologist, Class AAAA	Ph.D.	n.a.	Areas	Yes	No	Yes	D	G
Montana	School psychologist	MA	65(23)	Areas	Yes	No	Yes	D	G
Nebraska	School psychologist	MA	MA+30	None	Yes	Meet requirements	Yes	N	G

Continued

TABLE 3.3 (continued)

				Certification requirements				Licensure requirements		
State	Levels and titles	Degree	Hours required	Areas/ courses	Field experience	Teaching experience	Statute	Level[a]	Type[b]
Nevada	School psychologist	MA	50(36)	Areas	Yes	No	Yes	D	G
New Hampshire	School psychologist	Ph.D.	n.a.	None	No	No	Yes	N	G
New Jersey	School psychologist	BA	60	Areas	Yes	No	Yes	D	G
New York	School psychologist	MA	60	Competency	Yes	No	Yes	D	G
North Carolina	School psychologist I	MA	30	Competency	Yes	No	Yes	N	G
	School psychologist II	MA	60	Competency	Yes	No	Yes	N	G
	School psychologist III	Ph.D.	n.a.	Competency	Yes	No	Yes	D	G
North Dakota	School psychologist	Ph.D.	n.a.	None	No	No	Yes	D	G
Ohio	School psychologist								
	Provisional certificate	MA	24	Areas	Yes	No	Yes	N	S
	Professional certificate	MA	32	Areas	Yes	No	Yes	N	S
	Permanent certificate	MA	40	Areas	Yes	No	Yes	N	S
Oklahoma	School psychometrist	MA	30	Areas	Yes	No	Yes	D	G
	School psychologist	MA	60	Areas	Yes	No	Yes	D	G
Oregon	School psychologist	MA	96 quarters	Areas	Yes	Yes	Yes	N	G
Pennsylvania	K–12 school psychologist	MA	n.a.	Competency	No	No	Yes	N	G
Rhode Island	School psychologist								
	Provisional certificate	MA	42(36)	Areas	Yes	No	Yes	D	G
	Professional certificate	MA	42(36)	Areas	Yes	No	Yes	D	G
South Carolina	Educational evaluator	BA+	18	Areas	Yes	Pass exam	Yes	N	G
	School psychologist I	MA	36	Areas	Yes	Pass exam	Yes	N	G
	School psychologist II	Sixth year	60	Areas	Yes	Pass exam	Yes	N	G
	School psychologist III	Ph.D.	n.a.	Areas	Yes	Pass exam	Yes	N	G
South Dakota	School psychological examiner	MA	30	Courses	Yes	No	Yes	N	G
	School psychologist	MA	45	Courses	Yes	No	Yes	N	G
Tennessee	School psychologist	MA	n.a.	Competency	Yes	No	Yes	N	G

State		Degree						[a]	[b]
Texas	Educational evaluator	MA	n.a.	n.a.	No	No	Yes	D	S
	Associate school psychologist	MA	30(24)	Areas	Yes	No	Yes	D	S
	School psychologist	Ph.D.	n.a.	Areas	Yes	No	Yes	D	S
Utah	School psychologist								
	Basic professional certificate	MA	n.a.	Competency	Yes	No	Yes	D	G
	Professional certificate	MA	n.a.	Competency	Yes	No	Yes	D	G
Vermont	School psychologist								
	Probationary certificate	MA	n.a.	None	No	No	Yes	N	G
	Standard certificate	MA	n.a.	None	Yes	No	Yes	N	G
	Continuing certificate	MA	n.a.	None	Yes	No	Yes	N	G
Virginia	School psychologist	MA	48	Areas	Yes	No	Yes	N	S
Washington	School psychologist								
	Preparatory certificate	MA	n.a.	Areas	No	No	Yes	D	G
	Initial certificate	MA	n.a.	Areas	No	No	Yes	D	G
	Continuing certificate	MA	n.a.	Areas	No	No	Yes	D	G
West Virginia	Provisional school psychologist	MA	48(30)	Competency	Yes	No	Yes	N	G
	Permanent school psychologist	MA	78(60)	Competency	Yes	No	Yes	N	G
Wisconsin	Provisional school psychologist	BA+	30	Areas	Yes	No	Yes	N	S
	School psychologist I	MA	42	Areas	Yes	No	Yes	N	S
	School psychologist II	MA	60	Areas	Yes	No	Yes	N	S
Wyoming	Psychological technician								
	Initial certificate	MA	30	Courses	No	No	Yes	D	G
	Standard certificate	MA	30	Courses	Yes	No	Yes	D	G
	Professional certificate	MA	30	Courses	Yes	No	Yes	D	G
	Educational diagnostician								
	Initial certificate	MA	30	Courses	No	No	Yes	D	G
	Standard certificate	MA	30	Courses	Yes	No	Yes	D	G
	Professional certificate	MA	30	Courses	Yes	No	Yes	D	G
	School psychologist								
	Initial certificate	Ph.D.	n.a.	Courses	Yes	No	Yes	D	G
	Standard certificate	Ph.D.	n.a.	Courses	Yes	No	Yes	D	G
	Professional certificate	Ph.D.	n.a.	Courses	Yes	No	Yes	D	G

[a] This column indicates the entry level for licensure, with N referring to nondoctoral and D to doctoral.
[b] This column indicates whether the state provides generic (G) or specialty area (S) licensure.

process would substantially streamline the certification of school psychologists. It would also guarantee the recognition of credentials by various states.

Private Practice Licensure

Private practice licensure for the specialty of school psychology is a relatively new phenomenon. In fact, specialty area licensure within generic psychology has only recently been legislated by some states as a result of APA's new standards. Prior to the promulgation of these standards most states licensed the title "psychologist," "psychological examiner," or some associated term. Brown *et al.* (1977) reported that 17 states licensed psychologists at the nondoctoral level. Of the 17, 7 provided for the specialty licensure of school psychology. At least 15 other states are in the process of submitting legislative proposals for specialty licensure at the sixth-year level. Table 3.3 summarizes current licensure standards for 48 states and the District of Columbia. As can be seen by inspecting the information in the table, most states continue to maintain generic licensure for the practice of psychology at the doctoral level. A few states, such as Kentucky and Texas, license school psychologists through the state Board of Examiners for public school practice. Texas performs this activity as a cooperative effort between the state board of examiners and the state department of education.

The question of who should be licensed to practice privately in school psychology is currently being debated in a number of states. Central to the debate is the entry level question. Many school psychologists who hold certification at the sixth-year level seek to offer their professional services for private compensation outside of the schools. In states that restrict the practice of psychology to the doctoral level, such persons are not permitted to practice. As would be expected, NASP and APA have advanced different positions on this issue. APA has adopted the stance that only persons with doctorates should be permitted private practice, which is in accordance with their *Standards for Providers*. Since NASP advocates entry level practice at the sixth-year, or specialist level, it has actively supported legislation for specialty licensure in school psychology. The rationale for this action may be found in the *Standards for the Provision of School Psychological Services* (NASP, 1978a).

Another related issue deals with the administrative structure of school psychology licensure boards. In some states, such as California, these boards are autonomous and therefore not responsible to the board of psychology examiners. In other instances they are merely a subdivision of the psychology board. Those who advocate the independence of school psychology prefer the former arrangement, whereas those who see school psychology as a subdiscipline of generic psychology prefer the latter. Although the traditional separation between certification and licensure boards continues, some exceptions are apparent. In one state, Wisconsin, licensure is granted through reciprocity to those who hold certification at the highest level. In Iowa those who are certified school psychologists may practice privately under this certification.

Unlike certification agencies, licensure boards rarely publish extensive role and function statements for the various specialities they license. With both APA and NASP advocating specialty licensure, increased pressure to define the major areas of clinical, counseling, and school psychology has been building. In those states that have designed standards, however, the use of course-based criteria and degree designation is evident. Licensure boards seem to be evolving their standards in much the same manner that state certification departments did in the 1960s. If this follows, it may be expected that a totally competency-based approach will be attempted by some states in the future. States that are currently exploring this avenue include California, Kansas, Ohio, Virginia, West Virginia, and Wisconsin. The development of service provision criteria and credentialing standards by national organizations should aid in delineating the role functions of each area licensed. This may speed the development of competency standards in other states.

The present debate about licensure in school psychology was recently generalized into the area of certification. In the initial draft of the *Standards for Providers of Psychological Services,* APA addressed the area of licensure only. In January 1978, APA extended the standards to apply to both certification and licensure. Since school psychologists are certified by state departments of education, the impact of this change would be to require the doctorate as the entry level into the schools. The acceptance of APA requirements by state departments of education is doubtful, since they attempt to transfer the authority to certify to licensure boards. The future direction that credentialing in school psychology will take is difficult to predict. On the basis of present trends, however, one would expect the sixth-year, or specialist level, to predominate within certification for some time. Licensure, on the other hand, seems to be a matter of highly individualized forces acting within a given state. In those states with strong school psychology organizations, nondoctoral licensure has often been legislated in the past. Other factors to be considered are how recently school psychology certification was passed within a state, the general legislative climate surrounding licensure in other professions, and private demand for school psychological services. At the core of future licensure may well be the ability of state and national groups to define the profession and differentiate it from others.

Future Trends and Issues

At this point it is appropriate to return to the basic professional issues facing school psychology as presented earlier in the chapter. The growth of the profession has been quite rapid over the past few years. Kicklighter (1976) has presented data that indicate that states are improving their ratio of school psychologists to students. The rapid increase in numbers of training programs and in states certifying school psychologists has been documented. The recent trend toward private practice licensure is further evidence of growth. It must be concluded, however, that the major impetus for this rapid expansion has come from state departments of education and indirectly from the public school system. It is this constituency that will largely determine the type and extent of school psychological services provided in the future.

The ability of the profession to anticipate the specific skills that will be required to meet this demand will strongly influence its viability. It is surprising to note that, to the author's knowledge, no comprehensive study on future market demand characteristics has ever been performed in the area of school psychology. At a time when other groups within psychology and education are experiencing overproliferation of graduates, it would seem incumbent upon school psychology to scrutinize its future carefully. Will school systems and other agencies hire large numbers of doctoral graduates? What specific skills will be required of the practitioner in 1990? How can training programs and credentialing agencies anticipate the ever-changing role required of the school psychologist? How can the profession actively promote acceptance of new roles for school psychologists within the public schools? The answers to these questions will only be forthcoming if we, as a profession, are able to accurately understand the professional/political system in which we are imbedded and actively participate in its change.

The question of entry level into the profession cannot be easily answered at this time. It is clear that most state departments of certification perceive entry level to be at or near the specialist level. As we have seen, this notion is supported by NASP, NASDTEC, and NCATE standards. Employment characteristics of the field also seem to support this view. APA, on the other hand, has taken the position that to be a professional psychologist one must possess the doctorate. Despite this pronouncement, training programs continue to develop most rapidly at the specialist level.

It should be clear to the reader by this time that the processes of training, credentialing, and accreditation are highly interactive and interdependent. To identify a prime mover is difficult. But at the national level, accreditation policies seem to have the greatest long-term impact, since they eventually determine the level of training in the profession. It must be remembered, however, that certification agencies are members of accreditation agencies such as NCATE. Ultimately the question of entry level is decided by those who buy the services of school psychologists. If the consumer of school psychological services were to demand the doctorate or any other criteria in order to reimburse services, the entry level would be defined. In a society that is progressively becoming more competence oriented, public demand for quality service will surely increase.

In Chapter 1 of this volume, Tindall suggests that the separation of school psychology from generic psychology would result in hopeless confusion for the profession. Indeed others (Chartoff & Bardon, 1974; Hyman, 1977) have concluded that autonomy for the profession would bring an end to scientific advances in school psychology. It must be agreed that many advances in school psychology have been derived from generic psychology. It can be equally argued that school psychology's relationship with generic psychology has reduced interaction with educational groups critical to its future. However, for school psychology to in fact degenerate as a result of autonomy, it would have to be devoid of theoretical content. The review of training program content currently being developed, cited earlier, demonstrates that school psychology is perhaps the most diverse profession within psychology or education. The models adopted recently are much more of a blend of knowledge in education, psychology, and social systems theory. Numerous models for training and service provision are advanced each year. More sophisticated models of credentialing are being employed across the country. The great potential once predicted for school psychology may be close to realization. Few other professions are experiencing the growth and professional development currently seen in school psychology. The apparent conflict between APA and NASP with regard to service and training standards may be viewed as one more example of growth for the profession. It is my view that conflict of this nature does not develop from mere territorialism, as Hyman has suggested, but rather reflects basic differences in philosophical orientation. The resolution to these differences should reside in the efficacy of the positions being promulgated. If autonomy comes to school psychology, it will be the result of a philosophical/empirical position that translates into effective service provision in field settings. Any professional thrust that fails to attend to the critical factor of effectiveness of services is not likely to succeed.

Neither NASP nor Division 16 will cease to exist in the near future. However, the current policies of APA could reasonably be expected to reduce Division 16's nondoctoral membership. If membership in either organization were to increase markedly it could influence the autonomy issue. Should NASP reach a membership of 15,000 within the next few years, major changes in professional identity would result. The nature of that identity would probably be psychologist/educator or professional school psychologist rather than subspecialty of psychology. Many of the indicators discussed earlier point to this outcome as probable. The close alliance between NASP and educational professional groups has convinced many educators that school psychology can operate effectively in the schools. NASP, not APA, is seen as the primary representative of school psychology by educators. But Division 16 is seen as the primary representative of school psychology by generic psychology. If Division 16 and NASP were to form a cooperative effort to represent the profession nationally, a number of benefits would be derived. First, such an alliance might encourage APA to modify its stance on service provision. Second, the profession would cease to appear to the public to be divided into factions. This would increase the influence of school psychology in dealing with political issues. Finally, school psychology would remain attached to all aspects of its historical roots, both in psychology and education.

As school psychology has matured, increased independence and clearer identity has resulted. This new identity would appear to be quite attractive to those who utilize school psychological services. It has also begun, for the first time, to attract the attention of generic psychology. What was once the controversial stepchild of psychology and education is now one of the largest areas within psychology and the most complex area within education. The issue of whether school psychology will meet its potential is no longer pertinent. The real issue involves how we will use our expertise and professional prestige to better serve our clients in the future.

References

American Psychological Association. *Standards for providers of psychological services.* Washington, D.C.: Author, 1977. (a)

American Psychological Association. *Criteria for the accreditation of doctoral training programs and internships in professional psychology.* Washington, D.C.: Author, 1977. (b)

Bardon, J. I. Problems and issues in school psychology. *Journal of School Psychology,* 1965, **3**(2), 1–14.

Bardon, J. I., Costanza, L. J., & Walker, N. W. Institutions offering graduate training in school psychology, 1970–1971. *Journal of School Psychology,* 1971, **9,** 252–260.

Bardon, J. I., & Walker, W. Characteristics of graduate training programs in school psychology. *American Psychologist,* 1972, **27,**(7), 652–666.

Bardon, J. I., & Wenger, R. D. Institutions offering graduate training in school psychology, 1973–1974. *Journal of School Psychology,* 1974, **1,** 70–83.

Bower, E. M. Reactions to the conference. *Journal of School Psychology,* 1965, **3**(2), 36–39.

Brown, D. T. Accreditation, certification, and training: An overview of professional school psychology. *School Psychology Digest,* 1977, **6**(2), 8–16. (a)

Brown, Douglas T. *Accreditation procedures for school psychology training programs.* Paper presented at the American Psychological Association convention, 1977. (b)

Brown, D. T., & Lindstrom, J. P. *Directory of school psychology training programs in the United States and Canada.* Washington, D.C.: National Association of School Psychologists, 1977.

Brown, D. T., & Lindstrom, J. P. The training of school psychologists in the United States: An overview. *Psychology in the Schools,* 1978, **15,** 37–45. (a)

Brown, Douglas T., & Lindstrom, John P. *Characteristics of training models in school psychology.* Unpublished manuscript. 1978. (b)

Brown, D. T., Sewall, T. J., & Lindstrom, J. P. *The handbook of certification/licensure requirements for school psychologists* (2nd ed.). Washington, D.C.: National Association of School Psychologists, 1977.

Buktenica, N. A. A multidisciplinary training team in the public schools. *Journal of School Psychology,* 1970, **8,** 220–225.

Carboy, J. J., & Curley, J. F. A new training model: Professional child psychology. *Psychology in the Schools,* 1976, **8,** 152–156.

Catterall, Calvin D. A competency based school psychology internship. *Journal of School Psychology,* 1973, **11**(3), 269–275.

Chartoff, M. B., & Bardon, J. I. Doctoral school psychology program graduates in the United States: The first seventeen years. *Journal of School Psychology,* 1974, **12**(2), 102–113.

Clayton, M. P. State certification requirements for public school psychologists. *Journal of Psychology*, 1950, **29**, 380–396.

Cortes, Carlos F. An internship program in school psychology—a working model. *Psychology in the Schools*, 1969, **6**, 172–177.

Dinkmeyer, D. C. *Consulting: Facilitating human potential and change processes.* Columbus, Ohio: Merrill, 1973.

Fagan, Thomas K. Field placement in school psychology. *School Psychology Digest*, 1977, **6**(2), 34–50.

French, J. L., Smith, D. C., & Cardon, B. W. Institutions offering graduate training and financial assistance in school psychology. *Journal of School Psychology*, 1968, **6**, 261–267.

Gallessich, June. Training the school psychologist for consultation. *Journal of School Psychology*, 1974, **12**(2), 138–149.

Gilmore, George F. Models for school psychology: Dimensions, barriers, and implications. *Journal of School Psychology*, 1974, **12**(2), 95–101.

Goh, David S. Graduate training in school psychology. *Journal of School Psychology*, 1977, **15**, 207–218.

Graff, M. P., & Clair, T. N. Requirements for certification of school psychologists: A survey of recent trends. *American Psychologist*, 1973, **8**, 704–709.

Gray, S. W. *The psychologist in the schools.* New York: Holt, 1963. (a)

Gray, S. W. (Ed.). *The internship in school psychology: Proceedings of the Peabody conference, March 21–22, 1963.* Nashville: Department of Psychology, George Peabody College for Teachers, 1963. (b)

Gross, F. P., Bonham, S. J., & Bluestein, V. W. Entry requirements for state certification of school psychologists: A review of the past nineteen years. *Journal of School Psychology*, 1966, **4**, 43–51.

Hall, M. E. Current employment requirements of school psychologists. *American Psychologist*, 1949, **4**, 519–525.

Hartlage, Lawrence C. A look at models for the training of school psychologists. *Psychology in the Schools*, 1971, **8**, 304–306.

Hodges, W. State certification of school psychologists. *American Psychologist*, 1960, **6**, 346–349.

Horrocks, J. E. State certification requirements for school psychologists. *American Psychologist*, 1946, **1**, 399–401.

Hyman, Irwin. *School psychology in America: A study of jurisdictional imperialism.* Unpublished manuscript, 1977.

Kicklighter, Richard H. School psychology in the United States: A quantitative survey. *Journal of School Psychology*, 1976, **14**(2), 151–156.

Kurz, Ronald B. Emerging issues in accreditation of training programs in school psychology. *Journal of School Psychology*, 1974, **12**(2), 114–120.

Leppaluoto, Jean R. *National survey of school psychologists.* Washington, D.C.: National Association of School Psychologists, 1978.

Lesiak, W. J., Petty, S., & Braccio, H. The multiplier effect: A strategy for the continuing education of school psychologists. *Psychology in the Schools*, 1975, **12**, 393–401.

McDermott, Paul A. Measures of diagnostic data usage as discriminants among training and experience level in school psychology. *Psychology in the Schools*, 1978.

National Association of School Psychologists. *Guidelines for training programs in school psychology.* Washington, D.C.: Author, 1972.

National Association of School Psychologists. *Standards for the provision of school psychological services.* Washington, D.C.: Author, 1978. (a)

National Association of School Psychologists. *Standards for training programs in school psychology. Standards for credentialing of school psychologists. Standards for field placement programs in school psychology.* Washington, D.C.: Author, 1978. (b)

National Council for the Accreditation of Teacher Education. *Standards for the accreditation of teacher education.* Washington, D.C.: Author, 1977.

Nelson, W. H. Variations in patterns of certification for school psychologists. *Journal of School Psychology,* 1963, **2,** 17–33.

Newland, T. E. Formalized psychological services in state education programs. *American Psychologist,* 1956, **11,** 136–140.

Patros, P. G., Gross, F. P., & Bjorn, M. A. *A survey of institutions offering graduate training in the area of school psychology.* (Report No. 401) Washington, D.C.: The National Association of School Psychologists, 1972.

Pryzwansky, Walter B. Practicum training in the school setting. *Psychology in the Schools,* 1971, **8,** 307–313.

Reger, R. *School Psychology.* Springfield, Illinois: Charles C Thomas, 1965.

Ross, S., & Harmon, J. T. Educational facilities and financial assistance for graduate students in psychology: 1964–1965. *American Psychologist,* 1964, **18,** 814–845.

Sewall, T. J., & Brown, D. T. *Handbook of certification/licensure requirements for school psychologists.* Washington, D.C.: National Association of School Psychologists, 1976.

Smith, D. C. Institutions offering graduate training in school psychology. *Journal of School Psychology,* 1964–1965, **3,** 58–66.

Smith, K. E., & DiBacco, J. The multidisciplinary training team: Issues and problems. *Journal of School Psychology,* 1974, **12,** 158–167.

Traxler, A. J. State certification of school psychologists. *American Psychologist,* 1967, **22,** 660–666.

Vallett, R. E. *The practice of school psychology: Professional problems.* New York: Wiley, 1963.

Walker, William N. The NASP program for continuing professional development. *School Psychology Digest,* 1977, **6**(2), 70–83.

ASSESSMENT AND INTERVENTIONS WITH SPECIAL POPULATIONS

Psychoeducational assessment has always been a fundamental role of school psychologists. The school psychologist who does not engage in a significant amount of assessment activities has been and continues to be very rare indeed. In Chapters 1 and 2, respectively, Ralph H. Tindall and Virginia Monroe suggested that training in assessment was the most identifiable commonality in the training of school psychologists. In view of the importance of the assessment role, we decided to devote a significant portion of the book to chapters on this topic.

Although the assessment role is fundamental to school psychology, this role has been the focus of controversy for many years. Occasionally, the controversy seems to focus on narrow questions such as whether school psychologists should use tests at all, particularly individual tests of ability. The criticism that many school psychologists have used a narrow range of instruments (e.g., WISC-R, Bender, WRAT) that were applied to virtually every child, regardless of referral problem(s), is not entirely unfounded (see Monroe, Chapter 2 of this volume). However, our strong impression is that school psychologists are increasingly gathering a broader variety of data that are related to referral problem(s) and interventions. The crucial issue then is not *whether to use tests, but rather* how *we can gather information with formal tests and other data collection procedures that will be useful in making decisions for and with children. The chapters in this section should stimulate additional thought and action along the lines of ensuring better assessment procedures.*

The chapters in this section reflect the influence of a number of external forces as well as trends within the assessment discipline. The strong influence of litigation and legislation is mentioned in several chapters. The external forces of litigation and legislation have provoked closer examination of existing ethical guidelines developed within the disciplines. It is apparent that closer observance of ethical principles, including such basic issues as validity and reliability of tests, would have prevented many of the abuses that have led to court and legislative action. Other trends within psychology and education—such as reduced level of inference in interpreting tests, greater emphasis on situational rather than internal causes (correlates) of behavior, and greater concern for positive outcomes (i.e., accountability) as a result of assessment activities—are also reflected in these chapters. Perhaps the most important theme throughout the chapters in this section is the concern for accurate classification that will result in positive benefits to the individual. Clearly, the concern is for assessment that will result in effective interventions.

James E. Ysseldyke's overview of psychoeducational assessment in Chapter 4 emphasizes purposes and models of assessment. The reader is encouraged to think in terms of both purpose of assessment and model of assessment. This sort of self-reflective process should lead to wiser selections of assessment procedures and more systematic consideration of the many available alternatives for gathering information. Ysseldyke reminds us that we always need to consider the question "What decision do we need to make?" before selecting a data collection procedure. Ysseldyke also provides a review of recent advances in behavioral assessment and a critique of the ability training versus task analysis views in assessment and interventions with learning problems.

In Chapter 5, Thomas Oakland and D. L. Goldwater draw together a number of important issues related to school psychological services for children with mild mental retardation and learning disabilities. Contrary to the information presented in some introductory textbooks on these topics, there are very puzzling discrepancies in the literature regarding definition, prevalence, incidence, etiology, and interventions. Chapter 5 includes an up-to-date examination of these issues. Two somewhat nontraditional areas of assessment—adaptive behavior and psychoneurological assessment—are also reviewed with implications suggested for possible future developments in school psychology.

Perhaps the most difficult chapter assignment was undertaken by Kathryn Clark Gerken in Chapter 6. We saw the need for consideration of high-risk preschoolers and children with low-incidence handicapping conditions, since these children are new populations for many schools, and school psychology training programs have usually not emphasized these areas. In Chapter 6, Gerken organizes the information in a very useful manner by identifying various common characteristics among the diverse groups. These common ties, the challenges they represent, and the extensive references cited by Gerken will provide the foundation for school psychologists to develop the specialized skills required for effective services with these groups. Gerken also discusses the need and rationale for specialization within school psychology, which is likely to be an increasingly prominent trend in the field.

We included a chapter on education for the gifted and talented because of our expectation of considerably more emphasis in this area in the immediate future. Current trends seem to point in the direction of renewed concern for the gifted. One bit of evidence for this trend is the recommendation by the Council for Exceptional Children that the Federal Bureau for the Education of the Handicapped (BEH) be changed to the Bureau of Education for Exceptional Persons (BEEP?). Furthermore, there has been an upsurge of solid research evidence concerning early recognition and nurturance of superior capabilities. In Chapter 7, Donald J. Treffinger and his associates provide a much-needed review of that literature, including suggestions for increased involvement of school psychologists with the gifted and talented.

Chapter 8, the final chapter in this section, is devoted to concerns with the fairness and usefulness of the school psychologist's assessment of minority persons. This area, perhaps more than any other, has provoked intense debate within the profession. The debate has, however, been conducted for too long around the narrow question of test bias, which Daniel J. Reschly argues is impossible to resolve. Recent court cases and legislative mandates are reviewed and analyzed in detail. Contrary to the views expressed by some persons, the recent legislation is viewed as having positive influences on school psychology. The mandate for multifactored assessment and accountability for placement decisions provides further opportunities for school psychologists to move beyond the narrow testing role. Guidelines for special education assessment procedures are included at the end of the chapter.

JAMES E. YSSELDYKE

 Issues in Psychoeducational Assessment

A textbook on school psychology would be incomplete without several major chapters on assessment. The history of school psychology is in many ways synonymous with the history of efforts to assess children; school psychologists were first employed in most states for the purpose of assessing children and assisting educational personnel in making decisions about them. One reason school psychologists are currently maligned as often as they are is that other professional personnel view them as responsible for assessment in school settings, and it is currently fashionable to malign assessment practices with school children. This chapter is an overview of current issues in psychoeducational assessment. Not only are these issues addressed, but also an overview of those factors serving as an impetus for change is included. Finally, the chapter presents some prospects for the future of assessment activities in educational environments.

Assessment should be viewed broadly as the process of collecting data for the purpose of making decisions for or about students. In guidance settings, assessment data are often provided directly to students for the purpose of allowing those students to make decisions about themselves. Assessment is not synonymous with testing; testing is simply one part of assessment. Assessment includes several means of data collection: gathering developmental and medical histories, making formal and informal observations, conducting interviews with significant others in a student's life, and searching of cumulative records.

In educational environments, assessment data are used to make five different kinds of decisions. These were outlined by Salvia and Ysseldyke (1978) as follows:

87

SCHOOL PSYCHOLOGY
Perspectives and Issues

Screening/Identification. Assessment data are collected for the purpose of identifying those who are sufficiently different from others that further attention and/or assessment are believed warranted. Screening, usually consisting of group administration of norm-referenced tests, is designed to identify both those who are significantly ahead of and behind their age-mates in either learning aptitude or academic achievement.

Classification/Placement. Educational personnel often assess children for administrative purposes, to support classification of children as exceptional and to provide accountability for the making of placement decisions. Educational administrators need data to support the classification of a child as handicapped, to specify the nature of the handicap, and to support placement of children in least restrictive educational environments.

Instructional Planning. Assessment data are collected for the purpose of assisting educational personnel to plan instructional programs for students. Emphasis, in this case, is usually placed on ascertaining specifically those skills that students do and do not have. The use of assessment data is an *instructional* use; teachers want and need to know specifically what to teach (content) and how to teach (methodology, technique, methods of feedback to use, etc.).

Pupil Evaluation. Considerable data are collected in educational environments for the purpose of helping professionals evaluate the extent to which individual children are making progress in their educational programs. Parents, teachers, and children themselves have a right and need to know the extent to which progress is being made. Typically, such information is provided in two ways: norm-referenced evaluation of individuals relative to a group of their age-mates, and criterion-referenced evaluation of the extent to which the student is achieving the objectives of the curriculum.

Program Evaluation. Assessment data are also collected for the purpose of facilitating evaluation of educational programs. Examples of such efforts are evidenced by evaluations of specific programs or curricula, such as evaluation of the effectiveness of Title I programs, compensatory and/or remedial education programs, and evaluations of the effectiveness of specific curricular interventions.

Assessment cannot, and should not, be viewed apart from the purposes for which it is engaged in; it plays a critical role in educational decision making.

Current Issues in the Assessment of Children

The Use of Tests for Purposes Other Than Those for Which They Were Designed

Lorenz (1937) and other ethologists have observed captive starlings going through the highly stereotyped aerial acrobatics of their insect-hunting maneuvers without another living thing in their cages. The male of a small feshwater fish, the stickleback, performs a complex dance in an early part of its mating ritual. Ordinarily, this dance does not take place other than in the presence of a pregnant female serving as a releaser. However, ethologists have sometimes observed the elaborate dance without a female or any other fish in the vicinity (Tinbergen, 1951).

Lorenz called the performance of these complex, highly coordinated reactions without the presence of a suitable releaser *Leerlaufreaktion.* According to Lorenz, certain basic, well-integrated responses occur in certain species when two conditions are met: (1) the internal hormonal secretions and the tension system associated with them exceeds a certain minimum level; and (2) a suitable and highly specific releasing stimulus occurs. Rothkopf (1973) noted that when no such specific releaser appears in the immediate environment of the animal, the tension system continues to increase until it finally gets so high that the reaction will take place in essentially complete form even in the absence of a suitable releaser. Such *Leerlauf* reactions do not benefit the species. They are highly elaborate acts for which no suitable occasion exists and which serve no purpose.

I would like to suggest that many of the assessment activities that occur in educational settings, resemble such *Leerlauf* reactions. Educational personnel often engage in assessment for no apparent purpose and with no reasonable outlet for their findings. Much assessment takes place simply because tension exceeds a certain level. Diagnostic personnel are expected to assess children.

Not only does assessment often occur in a vacuum, in the absence of purpose, but assessors also often fail to differentiate their assessment devices, strategies, and activities in light of the kinds of decisions they make. An example of such a failure is readily apparent in the use of intelligence tests. Intelligence tests were originally designed for the purpose of helping professionals classify individuals. Yet, we witness the repeated use of the tests, especially evidenced in profile analyses, for the purpose of planning specific instructional interventions for children. To date, there is no empirical support for such activity (Ysseldyke, 1973).

The Use of Technically Inadequate Tests in Decision Making

Educational decisions made for or about children directly and significantly affect their life opportunities. It is imperative that educational personnel who use norm-referenced tests use the most technically adequate devices available. In evaluating technical adequacy, we must consider three factors: (1) the nature of the reference group to whom children are compared; (2) the reliabilities of the tests used; and (3) the validities of the tests used in decision making.

NORMS

Norm-referenced tests are those in which the pupil's performance is compared to the performance of a reference group. In norm-referenced assessment we assume that the pupil we assess is like those on whom the test was standardized. We do not assume likeness in every respect (i.e., hair color, skin color, etc.), but emphasis is on the extent to which the acculturation of the child assessed is like that of the reference group. Acculturation refers simply to the particular set of background experiences and opportunities that a child has had, both in formal and informal educational environments. When norm-referenced tests provide interpretive tables describing the performance of the reference group, it is imperative that the authors of those tests include in the test manuals a complete and thorough description of the normative sample. In 1972 a joint committee of the American Psychological Association, American Educational Research Association, and National Council on Measurement in Education published the *Standards for Educational and Psychological Tests* (APA, 1972). This document serves as a guide for test developers and publishers, as well as a sourcebook for the users of tests, outlining the necessary technical characteristics that must be present. Based on the recommendations included in this manual, Salvia and Ysseldyke (1978) listed the descriptive information that must be included in a test manual. Data must be included on the ages of those in the reference group, their grade and sex, the acculturation of their parents, the geographic region in which they live, their race, intellectual level, and the extent to which they demonstrate specific handicapping conditions.

Abuse occurs in assessment when children's performance is compared to the performance of those who differ systematically from them. Most school psychologists have learned in their training that if an individual child differs significantly from those on whom a test was standardized, use of the scores the student earned on that test to make important decisions may well be invalid.

As I have spoken individually with practicing school psychologists and conducted workshops with them and for them, I am repeatedly surprised to learn that they are often unaware of the nature of the reference groups for the tests they use daily. For example, the Quick Test, Peabody Picture Vocabulary Test, Slosson Intelligence Test, Gray Oral Reading Test, Wide Range Achievement Test, Gates–McKillop Reading Diagnostic Test, and the Durrell Analysis of Reading Difficulties are important pieces in the armament of most school psychologists. The tests are used daily to make important psychoeducational decisions. However, many of the school psychologists I have encountered are unable to tell me the groups on whom the tests were standardized. A quick overview of the nature of the reference groups will illustrate the tremendous importance of this point.

The Quick Test was standardized on 458 white children and adults from parts of Montana and Louisville, Kentucky. The Peabody Picture Vocabulary Test was standardized on all white children in and around Nashville, Tennessee. The standardization group for the Slosson Intelligence Test (SIT) is described by its author as follows:

> [The SIT was standardized on children and adults who] came from both urban and rural populations in New York State. The referrals came from cooperative nursery schools, public, parochial, and private schools, from junior and senior high schools.

They came from gifted as well as retarded classes—white, negro (*sic*), and some American Indian. Some came from a City Youth Bureau, some from a Home for Boys. The very young children resided in an infant home. The adults came from the general population, from various professional groups, from a university graduate school, from a state school for the retarded, and from a county jail.

Many of these individuals were difficult to test as they were disturbed, negativistic, withdrawn, and many had reading difficulties. Some suffered from neurological disorders or other defects. The only cases which were excluded from this study were individuals who could not speak English [Slosson, 1971, p. IV].

The Wide Range Achievement Test was standardized in seven states; norms for the Gray Oral Reading Test are tentative, based only on the performance of 502 children in Florida and Chicago and its suburbs. Although the Gates–McKillop and Durrell tests include elaborate normative tables in their manuals, neither describes the nature of the group on whom the test was standardized.

Two important points can be noted here. First, many decisions made about children in educational environments are made using data based upon their performance on inadequately standardized norm-referenced devices. Second, and perhaps most important, is the fact that decision-making personnel are unaware of, or fail to consider, the limitations of the devices they use. Salvia and Ysseldyke (1978) gathered data for a table that listed tests with inadequately constructed or inadequately described norms. Those data are reproduced here as Table 4.1 to illustrate how serious and widespread this problem is.

Reliability

Norm-referenced tests used to make important psychoeducational decisions about children must also be reliable. Reliability refers simply to consistency in measurement, to freedom from error. Error is always present in psychoeducational assessment (Newland, 1971). We must be especially concerned, however, with the extent to which error is present. Decision makers can get an index of the error typically present when they use specific tests by referring to the reliability coefficients for those tests. Reliability coefficients range from .00 to .99. Salvia and Ysseldyke (1978) provided interpretation guidelines for the size of reliability coefficients necessary in decision making. They state that:

> When important educational decisions, such as tracking and placement in a special class, are to be made for a student, the minimum standard should be .90. When the decision being made is a screening decision, such as a recommendation that a child receive further assessment, there is still a need for high reliability. For screening devices, we recommend a .80 standard [p. 92].

Table 4.2 lists the reliabilities of tests used routinely to make important decisions about students. Coefficients reported in the table are taken directly from the test manuals. It is readily apparent that, with the exception of most intelli-

TABLE 4.1
Tests with Norms That Are Inadequately Constructed or Described

---

Arthur Adaptation of the Leiter International Performance Scale (13)[a]
Bender Visual Motor Gestalt Test (15)
California Achievement Test (9)
Culture Fair Intelligence Tests (14)
Cognitive Abilities Test (14)
Developmental Test of Visual–Motor Integration (15)[b]
Developmental Test of Visual Perception (15)
Diagnostic Reading Scales (10)[b]
Durrell Analysis of Reading Difficulty (10)[b]
Full-Range Picture Vocabulary Test (13)[b]
Gates–MacGinitie Reading Tests (9)[b]
Gates–McKillop Reading Diagnostic Tests (10)[b]
Gilmore Oral Reading Test (10)
Goodenough–Harris Drawing Test (14)
Gray Oral Reading Test (10)
Henmon–Nelson Tests of Mental Ability (14)
Illinois Test of Psycholinguistic Abilities (17)
Memory for Designs Test (15)
Metropolitan Achievement Test (9)
Peabody Picture Vocabulary Test (13)
Primary Mental Abilities Test (14)
Purdue Perceptual–Motor Survey (15)
Quick Test (13)
Silent Reading Diagnostic Tests (10)
Slosson Intelligence Test (13)
Stanford–Binet Intelligence Scale (13)
Wide Range Achievement Test (9)

Source: Salvia, J., & Ysseldyke, J. E., *Assessment in Special and Remedial Education,* Boston: Houghton-Mifflin, 1978. Reproduced with permission of the authors and the publisher.

[a]Numbers in parentheses refer to chapters in Salvia and Ysseldyke (1978) where the tests are described.

[b]These tests include norms in their manuals but include *no* data about the group on whom the test was standardized.

gence tests and group measures of academic achievement, the majority of norm-referenced tests lack the necessary reliability to be used in decision making. Furthermore, subtest reliabilities are almost always lower than reliabilities for total tests. This principle will be referred to later in the discussion of profile analysis. Finally, no data are reported on specific personality tests. As noted by Walker (1973) and by Salvia and Ysseldyke (1978), nearly all socioemotional measures lack the necessary reliability to be used in decision making.

VALIDITY

Most persons learn a very important rule when they take measurement courses: Reliability is a necessary but not sufficient condition for validity. Given the fact that very many of the tests used in educational environments lack reliability, we must conclude that they do not measure what they purport to measure. To be valid, a test must first be reliable. Evidence of reliability, however, is not enough. Test authors and/or developers must also demonstrate that the test measures what it says it measures. A recurrent problem evidenced far too often in educational environments consists of assigning children to remedial programs based upon test-identified ability deficits with no evidence that the tests measure the abilities they purport to measure.

CONTENT

No discussion of technical adequacy should end without reference to test content. Tests are merely samples of behavior. The first matter of concern in testing, a *part* of assessment, is the kind of behavior to be sampled. Information obtained from technically inadequate tests is of little use in decision making; but even technically adequate information is of little use if it lacks educational relevance.

We observe, then, that a very critical current issue in assessment is the use of technically inadequate data in decision making. Failure to consider the adequacy of test norms, reliability, validity, and content can very quickly lead to abuse in decision making.

Profile Analysis and the Use of Deficit Scores

Current definitions of educational handicaps, specifically the definition of a learning disability, require that we demonstrate that students exhibit a discrepancy, deficit, or difference between current level of performance and the level at which they are capable of working. Diagnostic personnel typically operationalize such definitions by demonstrating significant differences between pupil performance on more than one test. In planning instructional programs for students, we often observe diagnostic personnel engaging in profile analyses of pupil performance on norm-referenced devices, apparently with the good intention of identifying specific learner strengths and weaknesses.

Several problems are relevant to using difference scores in either classification or instructional planning. Primary among these is the fact that difference scores are nearly always less reliable than either of the scores that enter into the calculation of the difference. Salvia and Clark (1973) used statistical formulas for the reliability of difference scores and the standard error of measurement for difference scores to demonstrate that even when reliable tests are used, considerable misclassification (over- and underidentification) can and does occur. I referred earlier to the tremendous lack of reliability for many of the tests currently used to assess children. Clearly, given the state of the art in assessment, the use of deficit scores is a very dangerous and misleading practice.

Ysseldyke and Sabatino (1972) used the Illinois Test of Psycholinguistic Abilities to illustrate the fallacy of using diagnostic "rules of thumb" to interpret pupil performance. Identification of specific diagnostic strengths and weaknesses

TABLE 4.2
Reliabilities of Frequently Used Tests

Measure	Reliability
California Achievement Test (subtest reliabilities)	.76–.97[a]
Iowa Test of Basic Skills (1974 edition)	None
Peabody Individual Achievement Test	.42–.94[b]
Metropolitan Achievement Test	.84–.96[c]
Stanford Achivment Test (1973 edition)	.65–.97[a]
Gates–MacGinitie Reading Test	.88–.96[c]
Wide Range Achievement Test	
Gray Oral Reading Test	.97–.98[d]
Gilmore Oral Reading Test	.53–.94[d]
Gates–McKillop Reading Diagnostic Test	None
Durrell Analysis of Reading Difficulty	None
Stanford Diagnostic Reading Test (1976 edition)	.75–.94[c]
Silent Reading Diagnostic Test	.85–.97[c]
Diagnostic Reading Scales	.87–.96[a]
Woodcock Reading Mastery Tests	.79–.99[c]
Key Math	.39–.90[a]
Stanford Diagnostic Mathematics Test	.84–.97[a]
Stanford–Binet Intelligence Scale	None
Wechsler Intelligence Scale for Children-Revised	
Verbal	.91–.96[c]
Performance	.89–.91[c]
Full scale	.95–.96[c]
Subtests	.62–.92[c]
Wechsler Adult Intelligence Scale	
Verbal	.96[c]
Performance	.93–.94[c]
Full scale	.97[c]
Subtests	.60–.96[c]
Wechsler Preschool and Primary	
Verbal	.93–.95[c]
Performance	.91–.95[c]
Full scale	.96–.97[c]
Subtests	.62–.91[c]
McCarthy Scales of Children's Abilities	
Verbal	.86–.92[c]
Perceptual–performance	.75–.90[c]
General cognitive	.90–.94[c]
Quantitative	.77–.86[c]
Memory	.72–.83[c]
Motor	.60–.84[c]
Full Range Picture Vocabulary Test	None
Quick Test	.60–.96[d]
Peabody Picture Vocabulary Test	.67–.84[d]
Nebraska Test of Learning Aptitude	.92–.95[c]
Blind Learning Aptitude Test	.93[a]

Continued

TABLE 4.2 (*continued*)

Measure	Reliability
Arthur Adaptation of the Leiter International Performance Scale	None
Pictorial Test of Intelligence	.87–.93[a]
Columbia Mental Maturity Scale	.85–.91[a]
Culture Fair Intelligence Scale	
Scale 1 total	.80[b]
Scale 2 total	.71–.81[a]
Scale 3 total	.51–.68[a]
Cognitive Abilities Test (total)	.91–.95[a]
Goodenough–Harris Drawing Test	.60–.70[b]
Henmon–Nelson Intelligence Test (total)	.84–.97[a]
Kuhlmann–Anderson Intelligence Tests (total)	.93–.95[a]
Otis–Lennon Mental Ability Test (total)	.88–.96[a]
Primary Mental Abilities Test (total)	.86–.95[b]
Short Form Test of Academic Aptitude (total)	.90–.96[a]
Bender Visual Motor Gestalt Test (1975 manual)	.50–.90[b]
Developmental Test of Visual Perception (subtests)	.29–.70[b]
Developmental Test of Visual Perception (total)	.69[b]
Memory for Designs Test	.72–.90[b]
Purdue Perceptual–Motor Survey	None
Goldman–Fristoe Test of Articulation	Interater only
Wepman Auditory Discrimination Test	None
Northwestern Syntax Screening Test	None
Illinois Test of Psycholinguistic Abilities	
Subtests	.12–.90[b]
Total	.66–.91[b]

Source: Data are from test manuals and were compiled from data reported earlier by Ysseldyke and Salvia (1974) and Salvia and Ysseldyke (1978).

[a] Internal consistency.
[b] Test–retest.
[c] Split-half.
[d] Alternate form.

was shown to be an especially difficult practice and one in which the diagnostician must always take into account the reliabilities of specific subtests with the specific age level of the student assessed. To date, there is no empirical support for such practices (Ysseldyke, 1973; Salvia & Ysseldyke, 1978).

Bias in Assessment

Public Law 94-142 (Note 1), the Education for All Handicapped Children Act, contains a set of "Protection in Evaluation Procedures" provisions. These provisions (Section 615-5c) specify that states and their localities will develop:

Procedures to assure that testing and evaluation materials and procedures utilized for the purpose of evaluation and placement of handicapped children will be selected and administered so as not to be racially or culturally discriminatory. Such materials or procedures shall be provided and administered in the child's native language or mode of communication, unless it clearly is not feasible to do so, and no single procedure shall be the sole criterion for determining an appropriate educational program for a child.

Local and state education agencies are required to demonstrate compliance with these provisions of the law and are engaging in interesting activities in an effort to do so. We witness state education agencies and local education agencies engaged in the development of lists of tests that are culture fair (or culture free) and insisting that diagnostic personnel use those devices. Educators have not learned from the long history of such efforts in psychology.

Since an entire chapter later in this volume (Chapter 8) addresses nondiscriminatory assessment, only a quick overview is presented here.

Early research on bias in assessment began with the observation that when norm-referenced tests were administered to students from majority and minority groups, the members of the minority group *on the average* earned lower scores. The fact that, in general, average scores earned by *groups* of minority students tend to be lower than those earned by *groups* of nonminority students has led to numerous speculations regarding the reasons for the observed differences. While some investigators have argued that observed differences between groups for the most part reflect genetic differences between groups, still others have argued that observed differences are primarily due to environmental differences. The "position of choice" these days appears to be an "interactionalist position" in which the performance of an individual on a test is viewed as the function of an interaction between genetic and environmental influences. The nature–nurture debate has produced, within the past decade, a plethora of theorizing and a number of empirical investigations. Investigators have debated the concept of "intelligence" (Cattell, 1963, 1971; Guilford, 1967; Humphreys, 1971; Vernon, 1969; Wechsler, 1971) and the relative contributions to intelligence of genetic and environmental variables (Bayley, 1965; Bijou, 1971; Bloom, 1964; Cronbach, 1969; Eells, Davis, Havighurst, Herrick, & Cronbach, 1951; Elkind, 1969; Ginsberg & Laughlin, 1971; Hirsch, 1971; Jensen, 1967, 1968a, 1968b, 1969a, 1969b, 1971). A large number of studies have been designed to investigate the fairness of tests by comparing the performances of groups of students on norm-referenced tests (Boone & Adesso, 1974; Guilliams, 1976; Hoepfner & Strickland, 1972; Jensen, 1974a, 1976; Kallingal, 1971; Matuszek & Oakland, 1972; Mercer, 1972a; Rincon, 1976; Temp, 1971).

Bias in Test Use

Investigations of group differences in performance on psychometric devices led other investigators to examine the fairness of specific items as used with members of minority groups (Breland, 1974; Merz, 1976; Newland, 1973; Pine & Weiss, 1976). Specific subcomponents of the research on the extent to which specific tests and test items are biased against members of minority groups have been observed in research on linguistic bias (Bartell, Grill, & Bryen, 1973; Berry & Lopez, 1977; Matluck & Mace, 1973; Matluck & Mace-Matluck, 1975) and on sex bias (Diamond, 1976; Harmon, 1973; Prediger & Hanson, 1976; Tittle, 1974, 1975).

Research demonstrating differences between groups in performance on tests or test items, along with contentions that bias existed in selection and employment of people, led several psychologists to develop models of evaluating test fairness in their efforts to define the concept of culture fairness. Cole (1973) and Petersen and Novick (1976) have provided a useful conceptualization of six different models of fairness: the Quota Model, the Regression Model, the Subjective Regression Model, the Equal Risk Model, the Constant Ratio Model, and the Conditional Probability Model.

Several investigators have reviewed the models of test fairness (Frazer, Miller, & Epstein, 1975; Hunter & Schmidt, 1976; Linn & Werts, 1971; McNemar, 1975; Petersen & Novick, 1974, 1976) and have concluded that there is little agreement among the several models. It is readily apparent that major measurement experts have been essentially unable to agree on a definition of a fair test, let alone identify a test that is fair for members of different groups. There is little agreement on the *concept* of nondiscriminatory assessment. As Petersen and Novick (1976) note:

> The Regression, the Constant Ratio, the Conditional Probability, the Equal Probability, and Equal Risk and the Culture-Modified Criterion Models are each explications of general concepts of what constitutes the fair use of tests in a selection situation. There seems to be nothing in the literature that clearly indicates when, if ever, one of the models is preferable to the other five models. Thus, the practitioner has no clear guidance in the choice of a culture-fair selection model. Further, we have suggested that the Constant Ratio, the Conditional Probability, the Equal Probability Models and their converses are *internally contradictory* [pp. 23–24].

In addition to analyses of the fairness of specific tests and items, we have witnessed a number of other concerns in the professional literature. There have been several analyses of litigation and legal issues (Sharf, 1977; Weckstein, 1973), calls for culture-specific assessment (Long & Anthony, 1974; Simon & Joiner, 1974; Williams, 1975), and discussions of the social and legal consequences of using tests to classify individuals (Epps, 1973; Hunt, 1972; Kamin, 1973, 1975).

Cronbach (1975, 1976) has provided an excellent analysis of the sociopolitical nature of the arguments regarding testing. The considerable controversy regarding this topic has resulted in the recent publication of numerous position papers (Barnes, 1973; Bersoff & Ysseldyke, 1977; Humphreys, 1973; Jensen, 1974b; McClelland, 1973; McNemar, 1975; Mercer, 1972b; National Association for the Advancement of Colored People, 1976; Scales & Smith, 1974; Southwest Regional Resource Center, 1977).

Clearly, this nation and its researchers have vested considerable effort, time, and financial resources in attempts to develop or identify assessment devices that are not biased against members of racial or cultural groups.

Review of congressional testimony on the "Protection in Evaluation Procedures" provisions indicates a much broader concern than simply that of the fairness of tests and test items as used with members of minority groups. The overall concern is with abuse in the entire decision making process. Abuse is evident in many aspects of assessment and decision making and includes: (*a*) inappropriate and indiscriminate use of tests; (*b*) bias in the assessment of handicapped children and in the identification as handicapped those who are not; (*c*) bias throughout the decision-making process; and (*d*) bias following assessment.

Salvia and Ysseldyke (1978) noted the futility of efforts designed to find *the* fair test. They observed that intelligence tests, for example, like any other tests merely sample behaviors. Any student's performance on an intelligence test is the function of an interaction between the kinds of behaviors sampled by the test and the kinds of background experiences and opportunities that children bring to the assessment setting. Given the tremendous variation in background experience with which children enter a testing situation, and the very large number of different kinds of behaviors sampled by tests, the number of possible interactions is larger than we can even begin to realize (estimated conservatively by Salvia and Ysseldyke at greater than 1.35×10^{32} possible interactions). Educators can, and probably will, argue for a very long time about which of these interactions are "fair." We will make considerably more progress, I believe, by addressing ourselves to something we *can* affect: bias in the entire process of decision making.

Bias in Decision Making

That bias in decision making does occur has been aptly and abundantly illustrated. If we suddenly had *the* fair test, we would still have considerable bias in decision making. Salvia and his colleagues have addressed this issue in a number of investigations (Algozzine, 1975; Ross & Salvia, 1975; Salvia, Algozzine, & Sheare, 1977; Salvia, Sheare, & Algozzine, 1975). They demonstrated that naturally-occurring pupil characteristics act to bias the decisions that teachers make about children. Race, sex, socioeconomic status, and physical attractiveness have been shown to act as biasing factors in placement and treatment decisions made regarding children for whom there are identical objective data.

To facilitate fairness in decision making we need to be ever aware of the nature of the kinds of data we collect on children. Mercer and Ysseldyke (1977) described five current models of assessment: the medical model, the social system (deviance) model, the psychoeducational process model, the task analysis model, and the pluralistic model. The psychoeducational process model and the task analysis model are described at length later in this paper. Table 4.3 analyzes each of the models from a variety of perspectives, looking at the kinds of data afforded

TABLE 4.3
Outline of Different Assessment Models

Elements of the models	Medical model	Social system (deviance) model	Psychoeducational process model	Task analysis model	Pluralistic model
Definition of abnormal	Presence of biological symptoms of pathology.	Behavior that violates social expectations for specific role.	Psychoeducational process and/or ability deficits.	No formal definition of normal or abnormal. Each child is treated relative to himself/herself and not in reference to a norm.	Poor performance when sociocultural bias is controlled.
Assumptions	Symptoms caused by biological condition. Sociocultural background not relevant to diagnosis and treatment.	Multiple definitions of normal are role and system specific. Biological causation not assumed.	Academic difficulties are caused by underlying process and/or ability deficits. Children demonstrate ability strengths and weaknesses. Processes or abilities can be reliably and validity assessed. There are links between children's performance on tests and the relative effectiveness of different instructional programs.	Academic performance is a function of an interaction between enabling behaviors and the characteristics of the task. Children demonstrate skill development strengths and weaknesses. There is no need to deal with presumed causes of academic difficulties. There are skill hierarchies; development of complex skills is dependent upon adequate development of lower-level enabling behaviors.	Learning potential similar in all racial–cultural groups. Tests measure learning and are culturally biased.

Continued

TABLE 4.3 (*continued*)

Elements of the models	Medical model	Social system (deviance) model	Psychoeducational process model	Task analysis model	Pluralistic model
Characteristics	Not culture bound; deficit model.	Social system bound and role bound; deficit and asset model.	Continuous model: degree of deficit. Evaluative: good development of psychoeducational processes necessary to academic success. Deficit model: norm referenced. Disabilities or deficits are within the child. Deficits can exist unrecognized and undiagnosed. Completely culture bound.	Continuous model: degree of skill development. Bipolar with respect to specific skills. Evaluative: high-level skill development better than low-level skill development. Subject-matter referenced. Each child treated individually rather than in comparison with others. Idiographic; based upon task analysis. Skill development influenced by sociocultural background. Completely culture bound.	Socioculturally bound; asset model. Infers beyond test performance.
Characteristics of appropriate measures	Measure biological symptoms. Validity determined by biological correlates.	Measure competence in social roles. Validity determined by correlates with group judgments.	Focus on deficits: measures of ability or psychoeducational process deficits. Norm-referenced assessment. Hypothetical internal determinants.	Focus on assessment of skills. Criterion-referenced assessment. Actual environmental determinants.	Culture-specific tests. Gain measures—test-train–retest. Pluralistic norms.

Interpretation of test scores	Scores interpreted in biological context. No sociocultural information needed.	Scores relate to specific role in specific social system.	Scores norm referenced. Bound to expectations of the educational system.	Scores criterion referenced Skill development strengths and weaknesses. Analysis of skill development hierarchies.	Scores interpreted as estimates of learning potential.
Nature of treatments or interventions	Treat biological organism. ABCD-type constructs.	Teach child socially expected behaviors. BCD- and BD-type constructs.	Compensatory or remedial ability training. BD-type constructs.	Test–teach–test. Teach enabling behaviors. BC(D)-type constructs.	Nonspecific estimate of performance level. ABD- and BD-type constructs.
Extent of racially and culturally discriminatory effect	Nil when testing, interpretation, and treatment confined to biological organism.	Nil when testing, interpretation, and treatment are role and system specific.	Considerable, if the acculturation of the child differs considerably from those on whom the test was standardized.	Nil when racial and cultural characteristics held constant.	Nil when racial and cultural characteristics held constant.
Examples of appropriate measures	Measures physical factors: vision, hearing, nutrition, health, and developmental histories, etc.	Measures social competence in specific roles: student, family, peer group, community, etc.	Measures cognitive, perceptual, psycholinguistic, and psychomotor factors.	Criterion-referenced reading and mathematics tests.	Culture-specific test (BITCH). Learning potential assessment (Budoff). Pluralistic norms for standard measures.
Properties of statistical distributions	Dichotomous data.	Multivariate normal distributions.	Multivariate normal distributions.	Dichotomous data.	Dichotomous data.

Source: Mercer, J., & Ysseldyke, J. E. Designing diagnostic-intervention programs. In T. Oakland (Ed.), *Psychological and Educational Assessment of Minority Children*. New York: Brunner-Mazel, 1977. Reproduced with permission of the authors, editor, and the publisher.

by each. As Mercer and Ysseldyke (1977) concluded: "Each of the five assessment models, viewed separately, provides only a partial view of the child. Attempts to develop a nondiscriminatory diagnostic-intervention program should consider using a multimodel approach in which the child is viewed simultaneously from all five perspectives [p. 121]."

Bias Following Assessment

In addition to the considerable amount of bias that occurs in the making of psychoeducational decisions, bias also occurs following assessment as a function of the label assigned to a child. Foster and Ysseldyke (1976) investigated the effects of deviancy labels on teachers' expectations of child behavior and their ability to evaluate child behavior objectively. One hundred elementary school teachers were randomly assigned to one of four label groups. Each group of teachers dealt with one label (emotionally disturbed, learning disabled, mentally retarded, normal), and each group participated in two separate treatment phases. During phase I, teachers identified behaviors they expected to be displayed by hypothetical children denoted by the labeled condition. During phase II, each group saw the same videotape of a *normal* fourth-grade boy and completed a second checklist based on the behaviors displayed during this presentation. Experimental procedures were identical for the four groups, except that each group was told the child was a member of a different category.

Results indicated that teachers hold negative expectations toward children labeled as deviant and maintain these expectancies even when confronted with normal behavior that is inconsistent with the stated label. Maintenance of this bias is sufficient to cause teachers to *misinterpret* actual child behavior, resulting in a halo effect. Results indicated that the label "educable mentally retarded" generated a greater degree of negative bias than did the labels "learning disabled" or "emotionally disturbed," although all three deviancy labels produced negative expectations and halo effects significantly different from those found under control conditions. Other research (Foster, Ysseldyke, & Reese, 1975; Salvia, Clark, & Ysseldyke, 1973; Ysseldyke & Foster, 1978) supports these findings.

The discrimination occurring in assessment is as much a "people problem" as it is a problem specific to the use of tests. In our efforts to eliminate bias and discrimination in assessment, it is high time we reject the practice of blaming tests and quit trying to find *the* fair test. We can more constructively and profitably address our efforts to the identification of ways to modify or eliminate human bias, both in and following assessment.

Assessment of Abilities versus Assessment of Skills

Assessment is only the first part of the assessment–intervention process. The nature of our assessment activities is pretty well dictated by the nature of the interventions we use with children. In a very real sense, it is imperative that assessment be viewed within the assessment–intervention context.

The ability training debate has been with us for a long time and has been frequently addressed in the professional literature (Hammill & Larsen, 1974; Mann, 1970, 1971; Mann & Phillips, 1967; Minskoff, 1975; Newcomer, Larsen, & Hammill, 1975; Ysseldyke, 1973, 1978a; Ysseldyke & Bagnato, 1976; Ysseldyke & Salvia, 1974). The current debate, while multifaceted, boils down pragmatically to "What should we assess and train?"

There are two fundamentally different approaches to the assessment and treatment of children who experience academic difficulties. Ysseldyke and Salvia (1974) labeled these *task analysis* and *ability training*. These competing approaches differ in the nature of the behaviors assessed and the nature of treatments or interventions used.

Those who espouse an ability or learning process training vewpoint believe that there are specific abilities that underlie the acquisition of academic skills and that for most children failure to acquire academic skills is a direct result of fundamental ability deficits. When children fail academically, batteries of tests are administered to identify the ability deficits that are causing failure. Remedial programs are instituted to alleviate or ameliorate the deficits, with the belief that such remedial instruction is a necessary prerequisite to academic success.

Those who advocate a task analytic viewpoint reject the notion that for most children underlying ability deficits cause academic difficulties. When children fail academically, complex behaviors are task analyzed, and efforts are directed toward identifying those enabling behaviors that children do and do not demonstrate. Within this model, standardized tests are not usually used. Specific assessment strategies (Bijou, Peterson, Harris, Allen, & Johnson, 1969) are designed to ascertain the extent to which children demonstrate specific skill development strengths and weaknesses. Interventions are directed toward the teaching of specific skills.

Ysseldyke and Salvia (1974) identified four critical assumptions in diagnostic–prescriptive teaching and examined the extent to which the ability training and task analysis models meet those assumptions. The assumptions are listed in Table 4.4. First, it is assumed that children enter a teaching situation with identifiable strengths and weaknesses. Those who espouse an ability training

TABLE 4.4
Assumptions in Diagnostic–Prescriptive Teaching

1. Children enter a teaching situation with strengths and weaknesses.
2. Strengths and weaknesses are causally relevant to academic success.
3. Strengths and weaknesses can be reliably and validly assessed.
4. Pupil performance on diagnostic devices interacts with intervention methodology to produce differential instructional gains.

viewpoint talk about and seek to identify ability strengths and weaknesses. Task analysts speak of skill development strengths and weaknesses.

A fundamental assumption in diagnostic–prescriptive teaching is that the strengths and weaknesses assessed are causally related to academic success. Within the ability training model, *correlates* of academic success and failure have been identified and have been presumed to *cause* failure. Within the task analysis model, there is no search for underlying causes; skill development hierarchies are emphasized.

A third assumption is that the child's strengths and weaknesses can be reliably and validly assessed. We have seen earlier that current measures of processes and abilities lack both reliability and validity. The ability training model fails to meet this vital assumption. Within the task analytic model, skill development strengths and weaknesses are not assessed using traditional norm-referenced testing. Rather, procedures with demonstrated reliability are used to assess skill development strengths and weaknesses.

Finally, it is assumed that pupil performance on tests tells us how to teach. Evidence for this assumption within the ability training model requires evidence for aptitude–treatment interactions. In an extensive review of the literature on diagnostic–prescriptive teaching (Ysseldyke, 1973), I found no evidence for aptitude–treatment interactions.

Historically, intervention efforts have been ability-training efforts: An attempt is made to identify those process or ability deficiencies that presumably cause academic difficulties. The ability deficiencies are test-identified constructs (e.g., "figure–ground difficulties," "form perception difficulties"), and interventions are designed to alleviate or ameliorate these underlying causes of academic difficulty. Yet, to date, there is little evidence that we are able to assess ability strengths and deficits either reliably or validly. There is even less empirical evidence to support the contention that specific interventions or treatments lead to desirable academic outcomes.

The task analysis model considers the identification of hypothetical constructs that are presumed to cause academic difficulties to be unnecessary; instead, the focus is on assessment of current child characteristics (usually skills) and on prescription of specific interventions based on a child's current level of academic skill development. The model is a test–teach–test model in which specific treatments have empirically demonstrated outcomes. The primary assumption in the task analysis model is that academic success or failure is due to an interaction between the child's mastery of the skills that are prerequisite to successful completion of an academic task and the characteristics of that task. The task analysis model meets the assumptions listed in Table 4.4.

As a profession, school psychologists need to address more effectively than we have in the past the extent to which assessment of learning disabled students should focus on ability assessment. The issues relevant to assessment that must be addressed are as follows:

1. Is there support for the contention that ability deficits underlie the failure of students to acquire academic skills?
2. Do efforts designed to alleviate or ameliorate test-identified ability deficits actually improve students' chances to succeed academically?
3. Can we continue to support the practice of identifying pupil strengths and weaknesses and assigning instructional interventions based on performance on nonreliable norm-referenced tests?
4. Can we continue to assign students to instructional interventions with little if any empirical support for the efficacy of those interventions?

Who Is to Test and Decide?

Closely related to the other issues raised in this chapter is the issue of who is responsible for assessing children and who is to make decisions regarding the placement of and intervention for these children. Currently, school psychologists, special education teachers, resource teachers, speech therapists, counselors, occupational therapists, and remedial reading teachers engage in some aspects of assessment with children. Furthermore, most states now require that teams of professionals participate in decision making.

Cognitive assessment is the turf of school psychologists in most states. Yet training required to be certified as a school psychologist varies from state to state (see Brown, Chapter 3 of this volume). Clearly, requirements for certification or licensure to test are not consistent throughout the nation.

Most state education agencies require that assessment data obtained by a credentialed person be used in making important educational decisions for handicapped children. Yet it is well known, though not clearly documented, that many school personnel commonly administer and interpret individual tests with neither the training nor the statutory authority to perform such tasks. Clearly, the potential for abuse in assessment is considerable. To the extent that those who engage in assessment lack the necessary training and expertise to administer, score, and interpret pupil performance correctly, we stand a very good chance of making many inappropriate decisions regarding children, which directly and profoundly affect their life opportunities.

The Impetus for Change in Assessment Strategies and Activities

During the past decade, and certainly during the past few years, several forces, singly and in combination, have produced an impetus for change in the assessment strategies and activities used with school-aged children. The following specific factors are impelling change.

1. *Increased disillusionment on the part of classroom teachers with the kinds and quality of assessment.* Classroom teachers have become increasingly vocal regarding what they perceive as limitations in the kinds and quality of current assessment activities. Study after study has shown (see Monroe, Chapter 2 of this volume), and my own contacts with teachers support this finding, that classroom teachers, in general, view the school psychologist as a psychometric robot, a number getter whose sole usefulness is his or her authority to remove a deviant youngster from a classroom.

Teachers want and need to know specifically what to do for and with children, both academically and behaviorally. Rather than getting specifics, they report that they typically receive generalities couched in impressive arrays of subtest scaled scores, grade equivalents, and psychological jargon. Rather than getting clear psychoeducational pictures of children and precise statements of specific skills that youngsters do and do not have, they report that they have received statements describing causes of a child's difficulties ranging from unfulfilled needs and unresolved conflicts to specific ability deficits.

2. *Increased emphasis on the rights of children.* The recent and significant revisions in public policy on the education of handicapped children are reflected in Public Law 94-142. Recent judicial and legislative rulings have mandated zero exclusion within educational settings, appropriate educational programming of all children in least restrictive educational environments, and maintenance of an educational plan for each handicapped pupil. Courts have acted in a number of cases to ensure equal protection of students. Specific cases have addressed the provision of services to handicapped pupils. We must note with special attention the fact that the substantive issue in nearly all court cases relevant to the education of handicapped students—*Hobson* v. *Hansen,* 1967 (Note 2); *Mills* v. *Bd. of Educ.,* 1972 (Note 3); *P.* v. *Riles,* 1972 (Note 4); *Pennsylvania Association for Retarded Children* v. *Commonwealth of Pennsylvania,* 1972 (Note 5); *Washington* v. *Davis* 1976 (Note 6)—has been abuse in assessment. Bersoff and Ysseldyke (1977) noted that:

> Courts develop rules of conduct in piecemeal fashion and only when litigants present legally cognizable issues. Rule-making bodies, on the other hand, such as legislatures and government agencies, need not wait for complaining parents or children to sue school systems. When lawmakers determine that certain problems need a broader reach than courts can provide, when problems begin to affect a great many people, or for other good reasons, they begin to enact statutes and regulations which have comprehensive effect. This process is in full swing in special education. If we have just passed through the era of litigation, the mid-1970s are clearly the era of legislation. It is in this legislation proclaiming the rights of handicapped persons (and those misclassified as handicapped) that assessment practices... are most affected [pp. 6–7].

3. *Mandated nondiscriminatory assessment.* I noted earlier that Public Law 94-142 mandates nondiscriminatory assessment. The mandate is having, and will

continue to have, an impact on the kinds of assessment procedures and activities in which educational personnel engage.

4. *Increased activity in mainstreaming handicapped children.* Educational personnel are increasingly required to make recommendations on the "least restrictive" placement of students classified as handicapped. Most have had training in distinguishing only between pupils who need self-contained placement and those who should remain in regular classes. As the number of possible placements increases and the boundary lines between them shift, training and retraining of those who must make placement decisions is necessary.

5. *Increased movement toward individualization of instruction for increasing numbers of children.* Public Law 94-142 mandates development of individualized educational programs for all handicapped youngsters. A written statement is to be developed for each child. It is to specify: (*a*) the child's present levels of educational performance; (*b*) the goals for the child, including short-term instructional objectives; (*c*) the educational services to be provided to the child, including the extent to which the child will be able to participate in regular educational programs; and (*d*) the projected date for initiation and anticipated duration of services, and the criteria, procedures, and schedules for evaluating whether instructional objectives are being achieved.

The mandate for individual educational plans for handicapped children will be implemented in most schools by teams of regular and special educators and school psychologosts. Few professionals are currently able to apply their knowledge of assessment to program planning. Empirical evidence for assessment–intervention links is missing (Ysseldyke, 1973).

6. *Due process.* Parents are becoming increasingly involved in educational planning for their children. Court mandates have enunciated the right of children and their parents to due process hearings when changes in educational programs are proposed. Current assessment procedures will be challenged; diagnostic personnel must be willing and able to back up their decisions with data.

Clearly, there are many forces serving as an impetus for change in current assessment practices. It is imperative that professionals carefully consider the future of assessment activities and plot a course for appropriate assessment of all handicapped children.

Alternatives to Current Practices

I firmly believe that it is incumbent on those who raise issues and address problems to propose mechanisms for dealing with those issues and problems. I also believe that no one person is able to address effectively the complex set of issues so apparent in the assessment of handicapped children. Many professionals and professional organizations have articulated their positions on the issues I have described, and the one thing most obvious is that there is considerable disagreement among those most concerned about the current state of affairs.

Assessment is a critical component in the assessment–intervention process. Assessment data are used to make educational decisions, and we must consider ways in which the assessment data we collect interface with the kinds of decisions we make. One of the primary problems in the assessment of handicapped children has been the failure of assessors to differentiate their strategies and tools in light of the kinds of decisions to be made. We witness today considerable global thinking regarding assessment; tests are viewed as either "good" or "bad"; there are calls for moratoria on testing activity, and statements are made that norm-referenced tests should *never* be used and that criterion-referenced assessment is a panacea for all our testing ills.

Differentiated Assessment

It is time we engage in, and facilitate, differentiated assessment. No test is universally good for all purposes, and only a few tests are universally bad for all purposes. The extent to which specific assessment activities are appropriate is a function of an interaction between the kinds of data provided by those activities and the kinds of decisions we are required to make. Norm-referenced tests were designed for the purpose of helping professionals make decisions requiring comparisons of individuals to groups (screening, placement, evaluation of individual pupil progress); they do a reasonably effective job and generally are technically adequate for that purpose. However, information on pupil performance on norm-referenced tests is relatively useless in planning instructional interventions. Interventions can best be planned on the basis of the extent to which students demonstrate specific skills, information characteristically obtained from criterion-referenced tests. Those who assess children often use identical tools and procedures regardless of the decision to be made. Assessors must be trained or retrained to engage in differentiated assessment.

Selection of Appropriate Tests

A second, and obviously related, need is to view tests as samples of behavior. Preservice training has typically consisted of education in the use of specific tests, and assessors too often approach the assessment of a pupil by asking, "What tests should I (or can I) give to this child?" The appropriate question in assessment is, "What behaviors do I want to sample?" This distinction is important in that it results in the use of specific tests or subtests that will yield the data needed to help make decisions, rather than simply yielding a set of test or subtest scores. Viewing tests and test items as samples of behavior should keep us from making unwarranted inferences based on test or subtest names.

Technical Adequacy

The third pressing need is to use technically adequate assessment devices with children. It is a fact that many of the norm-referenced tests currently used to collect data on children have been inappropriately standardized. Assessors must continuously consider the extent to which the children they assess have acculturation comparable to those on whom the test was standardized. Many tests do not report the nature of the group on whom they were standardized; others were inappropriately standardized. We should discourage use of such devices for screening, classification, and placement decisions.

Earlier in this chapter I described the problem of using unreliable tests. There are two ways to proceed in efforts to correct this practice. We could restrict assessment to the use of only those tests with sufficient reliability to be used in decision making. Obviously, this would limit considerably the number of tests we could use. A second, and less restrictive, way of dealing with the reliability issue would be to recommend the use of estimated true scores rather than obtained scores in interpreting pupil performance on norm-referenced tests. Salvia and Ysseldyke (1978) describe in detail the reasons for using estimated true scores and the steps in computing these scores. Briefly, estimated true scores compensate, to a certain extent, for limited reliability by incorporating information about the test mean and the test reliability. Typically, diagnostic personnel report obtained scores. I am suggesting that we compute estimated true scores for all obtained scores, construct confidence intervals around estimated true scores, and interpret assessment information in light of these considerations. Such practices should help eliminate some of the error in assessment and contribute to more accurate decision making.

I also addressed earlier the issue of using difference scores to identify learning disabled children. Clearly such a practice is fraught with problems and is at best questionable. I want to go beyond simply recommending that assessment personnel compute the reliabilities and standard errors of measurement for difference scores. I believe we should abolish the practice of using such scores to identify learning disabled children.

The issue of limited validity for many currently used assessment devices can be addressed best by endorsing two of the regulations proposed by the Office of Civil Rights (*Federal Register,* July 16, 1976) relative to implementation of the Rehabilitation Act of 1973 (Note 7—Public Law 93-112 as amended by Public Law 93-516). The Office of Civil Rights proposed that:

1. All evaluation devices must be properly and professionally validated for the specific purpose for which the school proposes to use them; and
2. All evaluation devices must be recommended by their producer for the specific purpose for which the school proposes to use them and administered only by trained personnel

Full compliance with the legal requirement of nondiscriminatory assessment is going to be exceedingly difficult to achieve. The requirement is obviously closely entwined with the decision-making process in special education. The real issue is nondiscriminatory decision making.

Assessment–Intervention Links

Educators have long debated and heatedly discussed the question of which instructional approach is "best" for children. Joyce and Weil (1972) effectively summarize the evidence on this question.

> The research evidence dealing with this question is remarkably ambiguous. There have been several hundred studies comparing one general teaching method to another, and the overwhelming portion of these studies, whether curriculums are compared, specific methods for teaching specific subjects are contrasted, or different approaches to counseling are analyzed, show few if any differences between approaches. Although the results are very difficult to interpret, the evidence to date gives no encouragement to those who would hope that we have identified a single reliable, multipurpose teaching strategy that we can use with confidence that it is the best approach [p. 4].

No one broad method of instruction is universally effective. Nevertheless, we *have* continued to assume that different methods are effective with different kinds of children. For over a decade we have been assigning children to specific instructional interventions with little or no empirical evidence to support the contention that they will profit from such intervention. Hallahan and Cruickshank (1975) have noted some interesting distinctions between programs for learning disabled children and programs for those who are in other ways handicapped. They note that instructional programs for the mentally retarded were instituted only after considerable research on learning in mentally retarded persons. Programs for learning disabled children were established prior to the presence of empirical evidence on ways of teaching such children. The assumption that different children learn best when instruction is tailored to their individual differences brings us back to the assessment–intervention link. In practice we have administered batteries of norm-referenced tests to children and have assigned them to instructional programs on the basis of their test performance. Again, we have little empirical support for doing so. We have not demonstrated that ability deficits *cause* academic difficulties, that ability strengths and weaknesses can be reliably and validly assessed, or that there are interactions between children's performance on tests and the extent to which they profit from differential instruction.

Research on the assessment–intervention process is desperately needed. We must strive to develop reliable and valid measures of specific processes or abilities. We must, using an aptitude–treatment interaction methodology, attempt to identify interactions between test performance and instructional treatments. A science of instructional intervention can be developed only after such research has been done.

In practice, it is time to call a halt to current diagnostic–prescriptive efforts characterized by assignment of children to ineffective instructional programs based on their performance on unreliable norm-referenced devices. Instead, we need to shift our assessment–intervention efforts to strategies for which we do have support. We should restrict our assessment to the assessment of specific skill development strengths and weaknesses, and our instructional interventions should be limited to the teaching of *skills* (Kazdin, 1975; Kazdin & Straw, 1978). Hunt (1975) states:

> Psychological assessment should guide teaching. It should tell a teacher what kinds of assignments and curricular materials a given child can utilize profitably to foster his psychological development and pick up the knowledge and skills which he must acquire in order to adapt to his culture. The form of psychological assessment now most prevalent in education fails utterly to do this [p. 545].

When planning instructional programs for children, it is imperative that we shift away from the currently dominant prediction orientation to one that will facilitate instructional planning. As Reynolds (1975) has observed:

> We are in a zero-demission era; consequently, schools require a decision orientation other than simple prediction; they need one that is oriented to individual rather than institutional payoff. In today's context, the measurement technologies ought to become integral parts of instruction, designed to make a *difference in* the lives of children and not just a *prediction about* their lives [p. 15].

Behavioral Assessment

The methodology of behavioral or *in situ* assessment is growing in popularity and has considerable promise for use in all five major educational decisions, particularly those of instructional planning and program and pupil evaluations. Generally, the procedures involve the observation of the subject by an assessment agent, usually the teacher, psychologist, or social worker. This observation may be systematic, where the assessment agent formally records the extent to which predetermined behaviors or categories of behaviors are demonstrated (Ysseldyke, 1978b). This observation may also be informal or nonsystematic, where there is no predetermined set of behaviors of concern and only those events believed to be significant are recorded.

Behavioral assessment procedures offer a number of advantages. Their foremost advantage is their directness. According to Goldfried and Kent (1972), "Recorded observations accurately reflect the occurrence of some specific event rather than using the observable performance as indicative of an unobservable construct [p. 415]." Within a norm-referenced paradigm, aggressiveness is typically measured by using tests like the Edwards Personal Preference Inventory or the Thematic Apperception Test. Pupil responses to items are observed and degree of aggressiveness is inferred. In behavioral assessment, the assessor formally records the number of aggressive acts in which the pupil engages, or in some instances the actual number of aggressive thoughts or "feelings" the student reports. Cronbach (1956) has argued that norm-referenced assessment encounters trouble because it involves hazardous inferences. By using directness, behavioral assessment procedures keep inferences to a minimum. Behavioral assessment is also more "ecologically valid," since it attempts to assess the subject in the natural environment in which the behavior of concern occurs (Bronfenbrenner, 1976).

Behavioral assessment procedures usually involve the collection of data *across time*. One of the most cogent arguments against "traditional" achievement testing has been that the subject may do particularly poorly or well at a given point in time, or the subject's performance may be influenced by a number of temporal factors. By collecting data across time, that is, collecting repeated samples, one can get a more accurate estimation of a subject's performance as well as notice trends and variability. This data collection across time allows the same data collected to make identification decisions to be used in program planning and evaluation decisions. This is very useful, since simply by looking at a record of the subject's performance, the assessor can evaluate the effectiveness of the decisions made about the child. Assessment data can then be used to make further decisions about the subject. Lovitt (1977) has argued that this process prevents overteaching and underteaching.

Two major approaches to behavioral assessment have been identified as *person-centered* and *situation-centered* assessments (Deno, Mirkin, & Shinn, 1978) and are categorized by different assumptions regarding the locus of the problem. In a person-centered approach, the problem is thought to be in the behavioral repertoire of the subject. It is therefore common to remove the subject from his/her typical environment to conduct assessment. For example, a person-centered approach to a child having difficulty with reading could remove that child from the classroom and ask him or her to read words from a list. According to this approach, a change in environment would not affect the child's performance. In a *situation-centered* approach, the locus of the problem is seen as the discrepancy between an individual's behavior and the behavior desired from that individual by someone else. The problem, therefore, does not reside in the behavioral repertoire of the individual. For example, a child can get along with peers (he or she has the skills to do so) but for some reason, because of the situation, the child does not behave in such a manner as to get along with peers. According to this approach, behavioral assessment *must* involve assessment in the environment in which the problem occurs. By removing the child and assessing his or her behavior, the assessor may not receive reliable or valid information about the problem.

There are a number of generally accepted steps in behavioral analysis. Bijou, Peterson, and Ault (1968) include the following:

1. Define the target behavior(s) in a way suitable for measurement
2. Develop a measuring device
3. Decide when the data are to be collected
4. Determine the context of observations
5. Assess reliability and observer bias

The importance of the first step, defining the target behavior, cannot be overemphasized. Through a concise statement of the problem, the specific observable behaviors to be recorded are determined. The definition of the target behavior should be one agreed upon by all parties involved and should be so defined as to result in high interobserver agreement. A precise definition, including examples of what the target behavior is and what it is not, increases reliability and decreases observer bias.

A number of behavioral data collection systems are described in the sections that follow.

RATING SCALES

Rating scales are actually a quasi-behavioral assessment device. Though they are systematic data collection instruments, they are subject to differences in the interpretation of those behaviors to be rated and may not therefore provide the assessor with a reliable and valid measure of the child's performance. Rating scales are lists of predetermined behaviors that raters usually complete in terms of frequency of occurrence ("often," "seldom") or in terms of whether the behavior occurs at all ("swears," "wets pants"). Rating scales are probably the most frequently used device to assess children's social behavior. There has been considerable controversy about the use and accuracy of the data collection system, both pro (Haring & Ridgway, 1967; Keogh & Smith, 1970; Ohlson, 1978) and con (Blunden, Spring, & Greenberg, 1974; Forness, & Esveldt, 1975; Bryan, & McGrady, 1972). If one adopts a situation-centered approach to assessment, this argument is moot (Deno *et al.,* 1978). If one of the parties involved believes there is a problem, a problem exists. Rating scales can then be used as screening devices, although to the extent that the behaviors to be rated are stated in nonobservable or inferential terms (i.e., "nervous," "hyperactive," "jittery," "depressed"), there is considerable confusion in rating, resulting in low reliability. When rating scales are used, particularly in person-centered assessment, it is recommended that scales be selected and used that include observable descriptions of the behavior to be cited (i.e., "raises hand," "solves a single-digit addition problem," "assists another pupil with a task").

FORMAL BEHAVIORAL RECORDING

Formal behavioral recording consists of observation and recording of the extent to which specific, predetermined, or target behaviors occur *and* the functional relationships that those behaviors have for the subject. We have witnessed a rapid increase in the use of formal behavioral recording procedures, both in instructional planning and in evaluation by the direct and continuous monitoring of instructional progress (Deno & Mirkin, 1977; Kazdin, 1975). Kazdin, Hall, and others have provided detailed descriptions of such techniques (i.e., frequency or event recording, interval or time sampling recording, duration and latency recordings), yet too often the important aspect of discovering controlling variables in the environment has been ignored. Such an analysis, together with rates of behavior, can lead directly to specific instructional planning intervention techniques.

Measurement of permanent products provides educators with a method of collecting data that are useful and highly reliable, and this method does not consume much time. In this method, permanent products, the results of a particular behavior, are counted and recorded over time. Examples of permanent products include completed homework assignments, completed worksheets, clean work areas, locked doors, and so on.

Frequency counting or event recording involves the observer tallying the occurrence of the predetermined and defined target behavior. In other words, the observer records on a piece of paper, a blackboard, a recording bracelet, or golf counter, each time the behavior occurs. This system works best when recording discrete behaviors, those that are of short duration and have an exact beginning and end (e.g., number of times a student participates in class, hits another student, gets out of his or her seat, etc.).

Interval recording or time sampling is an assessment procedure based on units of time rather than on absolute frequency (Kazdin & Straw, 1978) and is used when the target behavior is more continuous than discrete (e.g., when the behavior has no exact beginning or end, or when 8 minutes of a behavior is not equal to 2 minutes of the same behavior). Interval recording is also used when less exact and time-consuming data are required. In interval recording, a period of time (e.g., 2 hours) is divided into intervals (e.g., 10-minute intervals), and the observer simply records whether or not the target behavior occurred during the interval. A teacher might, for example, want data on the number of times a child asks for help. Rather than record the absolute frequency of occurrence, the teacher might just check whether or not the behavior occurred during a 10-minute interval. The product of such a procedure requires less time on the teacher's part and does not result in an actual rate of the target behavior but an estimate.

A third formal behavior recording system involves actual units of time, how long until a behavior occurs, latency, and how long the behavior actually occurs. Latency recording is just recording the time between when a behavior should occur and when it finally does. For example, a teacher may want to record the amount of time between the giving of a direction and the following of that direction. Duration recording is especially useful when one wants data on the length of a response such as how long a child daydreams or can work without bothering others.

Behavior recording procedures and *in situ* assessment offer exciting alternatives or supplements to norm-referenced assessment (see Tombari & Davis, Chapter 10 of this volume).

Competencies of Assessment Personnel

Finally, we must decide *who* tests. Once again, this must be considered in light of the kinds of decisions made using assessment data. Hopefully, this question will not be answered by simply asserting that only those who hold the necessary credentials should assess children, for it is readily apparent that credentials and competence are too often unrelated. Those who assess children must have the necessary training and expertise to do so. They must be skilled in establishing rapport with children, in correct test administration, in scoring, and in interpretation. They must be able to evaluate the technical adequacy of the tests they use, to ascertain the behaviors sampled by tests, and to differentiate strategies and tools in light of the kinds of decisions they are charged with making. Assuring that this will occur is extremely difficult, and the obvious problems now apparent in the system must be addressed at several levels.

First, preservice training of educational personnel must include more training in the intelligent use of tests and assessment information. Second, considerable retraining of assessors must be done. Most professionals have been inadequately prepared to meet the complex set of demands now placed on them. Third, we must work with state departments of education in an effort to ensure that only competent persons are credentialed and that there is a system of continuing education for personnel charged with the task of gathering assessment information and using it to make important decisions that directly and significantly affect the lives of children.

The state of the art in assessing children is not good. I have described the many reasons why I believe this is so. We are aware of the many complex problems and issues that must be addressed, and awareness, hopefully, will lead to action. We need to strive to improve current assessment and decision-making practices to the end that, someday, the *only* effect of assessment will be the enhancement of children's life opportunities.

Reference Notes

1. Public Law 94-142 (Education for All Handicapped Children Act of 1975).
2. *Hobson* v. *Hansen*, 269 F. Supp. 401 (D.D.C., 1967) *aff'd en banc sub nom, Smuck* v. *Hobson*, 408 F. 2d 175 (D.C. Cir., 1969).
3. *Mills* v. *Bd. of Educ.*, 348 F. Supp. 866 (D.D. Cir., 1972).
4. *P.* v. *Riles*, 343 F. Supp. 1306 (N.D. Cal., 1972).

5. *Pennsylvania Association for Retarded Children* v. *Commonwealth of Pennsylvania*, 334 F. Supp. 1257 (E.D. Pa., 1971); 343 F. Supp. 279 (E.D. Pa., 1972).
6. *Washington* v. *Davis*, 96 S. Ct. 2040 (1976).
7. Public Law 93-112 as amended by Public Law 93-516 (Rehabilitation Act of 1973).

References

Algozzine, R. A. *Attractiveness as a biasing factor in teacher–pupil interactions.* Unpublished doctoral dissertation, State University, Pennsylvania State University, 1975.

American Psychological Association. *Standards for educational and psychological tests.* Washington, D.C.: Author, 1972.

Barnes, E. *IQ testing and minority school children: Imperatives for change.* Storrs, Connecticut: Connecticut University, Leadership Institute-Teacher Education/Early Childhood, 1973. (ERIC Document Reproduction Service No. ED 078 006)

Bartel, N. R., Grill, J. J., & Bryen, D. N. Language characteristics of Black children: Implications for assessment. *Journal of School Psychology,* 1973, **11**(4), 351–364.

Bayley, N. Comparisons of mental and motor test scores for ages 1–15 months by sex, birth order, race, geographical locations, and education of parents. *Child Development,* 1965, **36,** 379–411.

Berry, G. L., & Lopez, C. A. Testing programs and the Spanish-speaking child: Assessment guidelines for school counselors. *School Counselor,* 1977, **24**(4), 261–269.

Bersoff, D. N., & Ysseldyke, J. E. *Nondiscriminatory assessment: The law, litigation, and implications for the assessment of learning disabled children.* Paper presented at the annual convention of the Association for Children with Learning Disabilities, Washington, D. C., March 1977.

Bijou, S. W. Environment and intelligence: A behavioral analysis. In R. Cancro (Ed.), *Intelligence: Genetic and environmental contributions.* New York: Grune & Stratton, 1971.

Bijou, S. W., Peterson, R. F., Harris, F. R., Allen, K. E., & Johnson, M. S. Methodology for the experimental studies of young children in natural settings. *Psychological Record,* 1969, **19,** 177–210.

Bijou, S. W., Peterson, R. F., & Ault, M. H. A method to integrate descriptive and experimental field studies at the level of data and empirical concepts. *Journal of Applied Behavior Analysis,* 1968, **1,** 175–191.

Bloom, B. S. *Stability and change in human characteristics.* New York: Wiley, 1964.

Blunden, D., Spring, C., & Greenburg, L. Validation of the classroom behavior inventory. *Journal of Consulting and Clinical Psychology,* 1974, **42,** 84–88.

Boone, J. A., & Adesso, V. J. Racial differences on a black intelligence test. *Journal of Negro Education,* 1974, **63**(4), 429–436.

Breland, H. M. *An investigation of cross-cultural stability in mental test items.* Paper presented at the annual meeting of the American Educational Research Association, Chicago, April, 1974.

Bronfenbrenner, U. The experimental ecology of education. *Teacher's College Record,* 1976, **78,** 157–204.

Bryan, T. S., & McGrady, H. J. Use of a teacher rating scale. *Journal of Learning Disabilities,* 1972, **5,** 199–206.

Cattell, R. B. The structure of intelligence in relation to the nature-nuture controversy. In R. Cancro (Ed.), *Intelligence: Genetic and environmental influences.* New York: Grune & Stratton, 1971.

Cattell, R. B. Theory of fluid and crystallized intelligence: A critical experiment. *Journal of Educational Psychology,* 1963, **54,** 1–22.

Cole, N. S. Bias in selection. *Journal of Educational Measurement,* 1973, **10,** 237–255.

Cronbach, L. J. Assessment of individual differences. *Annual Review of Psychology,* 1956, **7,** 173–196.

Cronbach, L. J. Heredity, environment, and educational policy. *Harvard Educational Review,* 1969, **39,** 190–199.

Cronbach, L. J. Five decades of public controversy over mental testing. *American Psychologist,* 1975, **30**(1), 1–14.

Cronbach, L. J. Equity in selection: Where psychometrics and political philosophy meet. *Journal of Educational Measurement,* 1976, **13**(1), 31–41.

Deno, S. L., & Mirkin, P. K. *Data-based program modification: A manual.* Minneapolis: Leadership Training Institute/Special Education, 1977.

Deno, S., Mirkin, P., & Shinn, M. Behavioral perspectives on the assessment of learning disabled children. In J. Ysseldyke (Ed.), *Synthesis of the knowledge base: Identification and assessment of learning disabled children (Monograph No. 2).* Minneapolis: University of Minnesota, Institute for Research on Learning Disabilities, 1978.

Diamond, E. E. Minimizing sex bias in testing. *Measurement and Evaluation in Guidance,* 1976, **9**(1), 28–33.

Eells, K., Davis, A., Havighurst, R. J., Herrick, R., & Cronbach, L. J. *Intelligence and cultural differences.* Chicago: University of Chicago Press, 1951.

Elkind, D. Piagetian and psychometric conceptions of intelligence. *Harvard Educational Review,* 1969, **39, 39,** 171–189.

Epps, E. G. Race, intelligence, and learning: Some consequences of the misuse of test results. *Phylon,* 1973, **34**(2), 153–159.

Forness, S., & Esveldt, K. Classroom observation of children with learning and behavior problems. *Journal of Learning Disabilities,* 1975, **8,** 382–385.

Foster, G. G., & Ysseldyke, J. E. Expectancy and halo effects as a result of artificially induced teacher bias. *Contemporary Educational Psychology,* 1976, **1,** 37–45.

Foster, G. G., Ysseldyke, J. E., & Reese, J. I wouldn't have seen it if I hadn't believed it. *Exceptional Children,* 1975, **41,** 469–473.

Frazer, W. G., Miller, T. L., & Epstein, L. Bias in prediction: A test of three models with elementary school children. *Journal of Educational Psychology,* 1975, **67**(4), 490–494.

Ginsberg, B. E., & Laughlin, W. S. Race and intelligence: What do we really know? In R. Cancro (Ed.), *Intelligence: Genetic and environmental contributions.* New York: Grune & Stratton, 1971.

Goldfried, M. R., & Kent, R. N. Traditional versus behavioral personality assessment: A comparison of methodological and theoretical assumptions. *Psychological Bulletin,* 1972, **77,** 409–420.

Guilford, J. P. *The nature of human abilities.* New York: McGraw-Hill, 1967.

Guilliams, C. I. *Item analyses of American Indian and Chicano responses on the vocabulary scales of the Stanford-Binet LM and Wechsler batteries* (Final report). Washington, D.C.: National Institute of Education, 1976. (ERIC Document Reproduction Service No. ED 111 878)

Hallahan, D. P., & Cruickshank, W. M. *Psychoeducational foundations of learning disabilities.* Englewood Cliffs, N. J.: Prentice-Hall, 1975.

Hammill, D. D., & Larsen, S. C. The effectiveness of psycholinguistic training. *Exceptional Children,* 1974, **41,** 5–14.

Haring, N. G., & Ridgway, R. W. Early identification of children with learning disabilities. *Exceptional Children,* 1967, **33,** 387–395.

Harmon, L. W. Sexual bias in interest measurement. *Measurement and Evaluation in Guidance,* 1973, **5**(4), 496–501.

Hirsch, J. Behavior-genetic analysis and its biosocial consequences. In R. Cancro (Ed.), *Intelligence: Genetic and environmental contributions.* New York: Grune & Stratton, 1971.

Hoepfner, R., & Strickland, G. P. *Investigating test bias.* Los Angeles: California University, Center for the Study of Evaluation, 1972. (ERIC Document Reproduction Service No. ED 066 443)

Humphreys, L. G. Theory of intelligence. In R. Cancro (Ed.), *Intelligence: Genetic and environmental influences.* New York: Grune & Stratton, 1971.

Humphreys, L. G. *Fairness for individuals and fairness for selection: Some basic considerations.* Paper presented at the annual meeting of the American Educational Research Association, New Orleans, 1973.

Hunt, J. McV. *Psychological assessment in education and social class.* Paper presented at the annual Missouri Conference on the Legal and Educational Consequences of the Intelligence Testing Movement: Handicapped Children and Minority Group Children, University of Missouri—Columbia, April 1972. (ERIC Document Reproduction Service No. ED 077 943)

Hunt, J. M. Psychological assessment in education and social class. In B. Z. Friedlander, G. M. Sterritt, & G. Kirk (Eds.), *Exceptional infant* (Vol. 3). New York: Brunner-Mazel, 1975.

Hunter, J. E., & Schmidt, F. L. Critical analysis of the statistical and ethical implications of various definitions of test bias. *Psychological Bulletin,* 1976, **83**(6), 1053–1071.

Jensen, A. R. Estimation of the limits of heritability of traits by comparison of monozygotic and dizygotic twins. *Proceedings of the National Academy of Sciences,* 1967, **58,** 149–156.

Jensen, A. R. Social class, race and genetics: Implications for education. *American Educational Research Journal,* 1968, **5,** 1–42. (a)

Jensen, A. R. Patterns of mental ability and socio-economic status. *Proceedings of the National Academy of Sciences,* 1968, **60,** 1330–1337. (b)

Jensen, A. R. How much can we boost I.Q. and scholastic achievement? *Harvard Educational Review,* 1969, **39,** 1–123. (a)

Jensen, A. R. Reducing the heredity-environment uncertainty. *Harvard Educational Review,* 1969, **39,** 209–243. (b)

Jensen, A. R. The race × sex × ability interaction. In R. Cancro (Ed.), *Intelligence: Genetic and environmental contributions.* New York: Grune & Stratton, 1971.

Jensen, A. R. Race and intelligence: The case for genetics. *Times Educational Supplement* (London), September 20, 1974, p. 3095. (a)

Jensen, A. R. How biased are culture-loaded tests? *Genetic Psychology Monographs,* 1974, **90**(2), 185–244. (b)

Jensen, A. R. Test bias and construct validity. *Phi Delta Kappan,* 1976, **58**(4), 340–346.

Joyce, B., & Weil, M. *Models of teaching.* Englewood Cliffs, New Jersey: Prentice-Hall, 1972.

Kallingal, A. The prediction of grades for black and white students at Michigan State University. *Journal of Educational Measurement,* 1971, **8**(4), 263–265.

Kamin, L. J. IQ tests as instruments of oppression—from immigration quotas to welfare. *South Today,* 1973, **4**(9), 6–10.

Kamin, L. J. Social and legal consequences of IQ tests as classification instruments: Some warnings from our past. *Journal of School Psychology,* 1975, **13**(4), 317–322.

Kazdin, A. E. *Behavior modification in applied settings.* Homewood, Illinois: Dorsey Press, 1975.

Kazdin, A. E., & Straw, M. K. Assessment of behaviors of the mentally retarded. In M. Hersen & A. S. Bellack (Eds.), *Behavioral assessment: A Practical handbook.* New York: Pergamon Press, 1978.

Keogh, B. K., & Smith, C. E. Early identification of educationally high potential and high risk children. *Journal of School Psychology,* 1970, **8,** 285–290.

Linn, R., & Werts, C. Considerations for studies of test bias. *Journal of Educational Measurement,* 1971, **8,** 1–4.

Long, P. A., & Anthony, J. J. The measurement of mental retardation by a culture-specific test. *Psychology in the Schools,* 1974, **11**(3), 310–312.

Lorenz, K. Über den bergriff der instinkthandlung. *Folia Biotheoretica,* 1937, **2,** 18–50.

Lovitt, T. C. *In spite of my resistance, I've learned from children.* Columbis, Ohio: Merrill, 1977.

Mann, L. Perceptual training: Misdirections and redirections. *American Journal of Orthopsychiatry,* 1970, **40,** 30–38.

Mann, L. Psychometric phrenology and the new faculty psychology: The case against ability assessment and training. *Journal of Special Education,* 1971, **5,** 3–14.

Mann, L., & Phillips, W. A. Practional practices in special education: A critique. *Exceptional Children*, 1967, **33**, 311–319.

Matluck, J. H., & Mace, B. J. Language characteristics of Mexican-American children: Implications for assessment. *Journal of School Psychology*, 1973, **11**(4), 365–386.

Matluck, J. H., & Mace-Matluck, B. J. Language and culture in the multiethnic community: Spoken-language assessment. *Modern Language Journal*, 1975, **59**(5–6), 250–255.

Matuszek, P. A., & Oakland, T. D. *A factor analysis of several reading readiness measures for different socioeconomic and ethnic groups.* Paper presented at the annual meeting of the American Educational Research Association, Chicago, April 1972.

McClelland, D. C. Testing for competence rather than for intelligence. *American Psychologist*, 1973, **28**(1), 1–14.

McNemar, Q. On so-called test bias. *American Psychologist*, 1975, **30**(8), 848–851.

Mercer, J. R. *Sociocultural factors in the educational evaluation of Black and Chicano children.* Paper presented at the tenth annual conference on civil rights educators and students, NEA, Washington, D.C., February 1972. (a) (ERIC Document Reproduction Service No. ED 062 462)

Mercer, J. R. *The origins and development of the pluralistic assessment project.* Sacramento: California State Department of Mental Hygiene, Bureau of Research, 1972. (b) (ERIC Document Reproduction Service No. ED 062 461)

Mercer, J., & Ysseldyke, J. Designing diagnostic-intervention programs. In T. Oakland (Ed.), *Psychological and educational assessment of minority children.* New York: Brunner-Mazel, 1977.

Merz, W. R. *Estimating bias in test items utilizing principal components analysis and the general linear solution.* Paper presented at the annual meeting of the American Educational Research Association, San Francisco, April 1976.

Minskoff, E. H. Research on psycholinguistic training: Critique and guidelines. *Exceptional Children*, 1975, **42**, 136–144.

National Association for the Advancement of Colored People. *NAACP report on minority testing.* New York College Entrance Examination Board, May 1976. (ERIC Document Reproduction Service No. ED 128 535)

Newcomer, P., Larsen, S., & Hammill, D. A response. *Exceptional Children*, 1975, **42**, 144–151.

Newland, T. E. Psychological assessment of exceptional children and youth. In W. Cruickshank (Ed.), *Psychology of exceptional children and youth.* Englewood Cliffs, New Jersey: Prentice-Hall, 1971.

Newland, T. E. Assumptions underlying psychological testing. *Journal of School Psychology*, 1973, **11**(4), 316–322.

Ohlson, E. L. *Identification of specific learning disabilities.* Champaign, Illinois: Research Press, 1978.

Petersen, N. S., & Novick, M. R. *An evaluation of some models for test bias* (Technical Bulletin No. 23). Iowa City: American College Testing Program, Research and Development Division, September 1974. (ERIC Document Reproduction Service No. ED 128 372)

Petersen, N. S., & Novick, M. R. An evaluation of some models for culture-fair selection. *Journal of Educational Measurement*, 1976, **13**(1), 3–29.

Pine, S. M., & Weiss, D. J. Effects of item characteristics on test fairness (Research Report No. 76–5). Minneapolis: University of Minnesota, Department of Psychology, December 1976. (ERIC Document Reproduction Service No. ED 134 612)

Prediger, D. J., & Hanson, C. R. *Evidence related to issues of sex bias in interest inventories.* Paper presented at the annual convention of the American Psychological Association, Washington, D.C., September, 1976.

Reynolds, M. Trends in special education: Implications for measurement. In M. Reynolds & W. Hively (Eds.), *Domain-referenced testing in special education.* Minneapolis: Leadership Training Institute/Special Education, University of Minnesota, 1975.

Rincon, E. L. Comparison of the cultural bias of the KIT: EXP with the WISC using Spanish surname children differing in language spoken. *Educational and Psychological Measurement*, 1976, **36**(4), 1037–1041.

Ross, M., & Salvia, J. Attractiveness as a biasing factor in teacher judgments. *American Journal of Mental Deficiency*, 1975, **80**, 96–98.

Rothkopf, E. Z. What are we trying to understand and improve? *Educational Psychologist*, 1973, **10**, 58–66.

Salvia, J., Algozzine, R., & Sheare, J. Attractiveness and school achievement. *Journal of School Psychology*, 1977, **15**, 60–67.

Salvia, J., Clark, G., & Ysseldyke, J. E. Teacher retention of stereotypes of exceptionality. *Exceptional Children*, 1973, **40**, 651–652.

Salvia, J., & Clark, J. Use of deficits to identify the learning disabled. *Exceptional Children*, 1973, **39**, 305–308.

Salvia, J., Sheare, J., & Algozzine, R. Facial attractiveness and personal–social adjustment. *Journal of Abnormal Child Psychology*, 1975, **3**, 171–178.

Salvia, J., & Ysseldyke, J. E. *Assessment in special and remedial education.* Boston: Houghton-Mifflin, 1978.

Scales, A. M., & Smith, G. S. Strategies for humanizing the testing of minorities. *Negro Educational Review*, 1974, **25**(4), 174–180.

Sharf, J. C. Fair employment implication for HRD: The case of Washington vs. Davis. *Training and Development Journal*, 1977, **31**(2), 16–18, 20–21.

Slosson, R. *Slosson intelligence test.* East Aurora, New York: Slosson Educational Publications, 1971.

Simon, A. J., & Joiner, L. M. *Adapting the Peabody Picture Vocabulary Test for use with Mexican children.* Paper presented at the annual meeting of the American Educational Research Association, Chicago, April 1974.

Southwest Regional Resource Center. *Unbiased assessment: Guidelines, procedures, and forms for the SEA's implementation of Public Law 94-142.* Salt Lake City, Utah: Southwest Regional Resource Center, January 1977. (ERIC Document Reproduction Service No. ED 138 024)

Temp, G. Validity of the SAT for blacks and whites in thirteen integrated institutions. *Journal of Educational Measurement*, 1971, **8**(4), 245–251.

Tinbergen, N. *The study of instinct.* Oxford: Clarendon Press, 1951.

Tittle, C. K. Sex bias in educational measurement: Fact or fiction. *Measurement and Evaluation in Guidance*, 1974, **6**(4), 219–225.

Tittle, C. K. Fairness in educational achievement testing. *Education and Urban Society*, 1975, **8**(1), 86–103.

Vernon, P. E. *Intelligence and cultural environment.* London: Methuen, 1969.

Walker, D. K. *Socioemotional measures for preschool and kindergarten children.* San Francisco: Jossey-Bass, 1973.

Weckstein, P. Legal challenges to educational testing practices. *Inequality in Education*, 1973, **15**, 92–101.

Wechsler, D. Intelligence: Definition, theory, and the I.Q. In R. Cancro (Ed.), *Intelligence: Genetic and environmental influences.* New York: Grune & Stratton, 1971.

Williams, R. L. The Bitch-100: A culture-specific test. *Journal of Afro-American Issues*, 1975, **3**(1), 103–116.

Ysseldyke, J. E. Diagnostic–prescriptive teaching: The search for aptitude–treatment interactions. In L. Mann & D. Sabatino (Eds.), *The first review of special education.* Philadelphia: Journal of Special Education Press, 1973.

Ysseldyke, J. E. Remediation of ability deficits in adolescents: Some major questions. In L. Mann, L. Goodman, & J. L. Wiederholt (Eds.), *The learning disabled adolescent.* Boston: Houghton-Mifflin, 1978. (1)

Ysseldyke, J. E. Assessment of retardation. In J. Neisworth & R. M. Smith (Eds.), *Mental retardation: Issues, assessment and intervention.* New York: McGraw-Hill, 1978. (b)

Ysseldyke, J. E., & Foster, G. G. Bias in teachers' observations of emotionally disturbed and learning disabled children. *Exceptional Children*, 1978, **44**, 613–614.

Ysseldyke, J. E., & Sabatino, D. A. Statistically significant differences between subtest scaled scores and psycholinguistic ages on the ITPA. *Psychology in the Schools*, 1972, **9**, 303–313.

Ysseldyke, J. E., & Salvia, J. A. Diagnostic-prescriptive teaching: Two models. *Exceptional Children*, 1974, **41**, 181–186.

THOMAS OAKLAND • D. L. GOLDWATER

5   Assessment and Interventions for Mildly Retarded and Learning Disabled Children

The school psychologist is an important member of a professional team devoted to advancing students' growth and development. The greatest trials as well
as rewards for many school psychologists come through their work with children
who are mentally retarded (MR) or learning disabled (LD). While working with
these children, school psychologists have opportunities to work cooperatively with
teachers and parents, to assess and evaluate, to advise, to plan, to help, to
encourage—to add an important *psychological* dimension.

There are many issues related to the school psychologist's work with the
mentally retarded and learning disabled that deserve discussion. This chapter
focuses on major historical trends, incidence and prevalence figures, and characteristics of the retarded and the learning disabled. Issues pertinent to diagnosis
and intervention are stressed, since they are central to the roles of school psychologists. The readers also are encouraged to conceptualize how school psychology
may provide new directions leading toward the improvement of psychoeducational
services.

Historical Overview

The fields of mental retardation and learning disabilities have been strongly
affected, perhaps even revolutionized, by recent legislation and litigation concern-

123

SCHOOL PSYCHOLOGY
Perspectives and Issues

ing the rights of handicapped children to educational services. The changes that have occurred are even more dramatic when contrasted with the somewhat bleak history that shows little significant progress until the past few decades—except for the contributions of a few major pioneers.

Ancient Societies

The diagnosis and treatment of the mentally retarded are poorly recorded in ancient history. The discovery of prehistoric human skulls suggest that microcephalus and hydrocephalus were conditions known to primitive people. Early civilizations did not show much advancement in their medical, educational, or psychological approaches to the retarded, preferring to rely on explanations of evil spirits and treatment by magic and incantations. The ancient Egyptians and Babylonians failed to record anything about mental deficiency despite careful records on other phenomena. The few references the Bible provides usually are accompanied by an explanation of demonic possession. The Talmud, however, notes that "from the day of destruction of the Temple, the art of prophesy was taken away (from the learned) and given to the fools." This may have been the basis for the later maxim, "A complete fool is half a prophet [Kanner, 1964]."

In ancient Greece, Hippocrates and Euripides referred to mental illness but not to mental deficiency. Hippocrates did pioneer the attempt to offer an organic etiological basis rather than mystical explanations for the disorder. Plato also looked for an organic basis for mental illness and emphasized the brain as the main factor. Aristotle, on the other hand, emphasized the heart.

In ancient Rome, the physician Celsus recommended corporal punishment for treatment of insanity. The only clear mention of mental defectives was in their use as servants in the homes of wealthy Romans. Similarly, mental defectives later were used as buffoons in the French courts, and as *hofnarren* in Germany. Legends remain about a few persons who reportedly administered to all the needy, including the mental defectives (Kanner, 1964).

The Middle Ages and Renaissance

During the Middle Ages, with the rise of Christianity and less emphasis on medicine, illnesses often were explained and treated through mysticism (e.g., exorcisms, incantations, and astrology). The era also was marked by inconsistencies. While compassion and justice were preached, Luther and Calvin were denouncing the mentally retarded for being possessed by demons. During this era, the distinction between retarded and normal behavior was often difficult to make because the majority of people were uneducated (Nowrey, 1945).

Toward the end of the Renaissance, productive and enduring movements finally began to emerge. Jean Luis Vives [1540][1] lobbied for the education of the poor and hospital treatment for the ill. Agrippa [1535] and one of his pupils, Johann Weyer, advocated similar positions. One reform specifically designed for the mentally defective was the shrine of St. Dyniphia in Gheel, Belgium, where humane treatment of handicapped persons was provided. Paracelsus [1541] wrote what is considered to be the first treatise on the mentally defective in which he asked rhetorically, "Why did God allow fools to be born who cannot understand the sacrifice God made for them?" He concluded that the retarded must be innately pure in spirit since they are not intelligent enough to seek or understand salvation. In 1602 Felix Platter, a Swiss physician, wrote a detailed account of cretinism (i.e., arrested physical and mental development with dystrophy of bones and soft tissues) and of milder forms of retardation. Finally, in 1690 Locke offered one of the first differentiations between the mentally defective and the mentally ill: "Herein seems to lie the difference between idiots and madmen, that madmen put wrong ideas together and reason from them, but idiots make very few or no propositions and reason scarce at all [Doll, 1962, p. 23]."

The Eighteenth and Nineteenth Centuries

The movements continued to focus on differentiating the mentally defective from normals. More impetus for intervention came from the humanitarian reforms that swept across eighteenth-century Europe in fields such as education, social welfare, and medicine. Revolutionary ideas in education came from great thinkers such as Rousseau and Basedar. In this spirit, Jacob Rodrigues Pereire [1780] developed novel approaches for teaching deaf-mutes, many of which are still used today. Pereire's methods included direct observation, attention to case history, development of individual treatment plans, sensory substitution and reinforcement, developmental sequences, education in terms of social needs, and proceeding from the known to the unknown (Doll, 1967). The major ideological contribution of his work was that the handicapped indeed could learn and be taught to communicate. During this period Pinel unshackled the mentally ill in institutions in Bicetre and Salpetriere in France, and Havy opened the first school for the blind in Paris in 1794.

The spirit of educating the handicapped—rather than seeking miraculous "cures" for them—continued. In 1801, the so-called "wild boy of Averon" was brought to Jean Mare Gaspared Itard [1838], a young and enthusiastic physician. Found roaming through the woods, the boy was completely uncivilized. Itard and his wife spent 5 intense years trying to socialize the boy before his premature death due to natural causes. Although his efforts were not totally successful, the

---

[1]Dates in brackets refer to dates of death.

French Academy of Science recognized Itard's work as monumental. Recognition of the mentally retarded grew, and various governments (including King Victor Amedee of Spain and Napoleon Bonaparte) began to seek information and conduct censuses of cretins. At the same time, Franz Joseph Gall, a physician in Vienna, became the first to clearly document disorders of spoken language, now understood as a specific learning disability. Jean Baptiste Bovillard, Pierre Paul Broch, and John Hughlings Jackson later continued to explore the etiological bases of such disorders in the brain.

Continuing with the momentum of education, Edward Seguin in 1866 revised the approaches of his teacher, Itard, and established schools for mental defectives at Salpetriere and Bicetre. Other attempts to establish schools, although unsuccessful, were made by Ferrett in 1828, by Falret in 1831, and by Voisin in 1834. Meanwhile, a young Swiss physician, Johann Guggenbuhl [1863], devoted himself to curing cretinism after having viewed a cretin praying at a cross. He established an innovative instructional program at Aldenberg that won wide acclaim, and later he was instrumental in opening other centers. The goals in these institutions focused on the development of sensory-motor and vocational skills. In Germany, the psychophysiological laboratories of Helmholtz, Wundt, and Fechner encouraged a behavioral approach that was instrumental in inspiring the focus on skill training for the mentally defective (Doll, 1967). Finally, the first public school classes for the mentally defective were established in Dresden, Germany in 1867.

While some favored strong educational approaches, others continued to focus on etiology. Henry Bastian and Carl Wernicke studied the etiology of speech disorders. Francis Galton [1911] pioneered the eugenics movement, which focused on genetic explanations for mental retardation. The eugenics movement was furthered by case studies of "familial" retardation (Dugdale, 1877; Goddard, 1912). The implications of this work dimmed the enthusiasm for educational interventions and instead encouraged the development of custodial care (MacMillan, 1977).

The United States caught onto the European trends, aided by Seguin's arrival in Vineland, New Jersey in 1848. W. E. Fernald focused on training prekindergarten retardates. Dorothea Dix's work to reform institutions for the mentally ill indirectly played a role in the development of state schools for the retarded. Dr. Samuel Howe, a pioneer in social reform for all handicapped persons, successfully fought for the opening of an "experimental school for idiots" in a wing of Boston's Perkins Institute for the Blind in 1848. Under Howe's leadership the school emphasized building self-reliance skills, beginning with basic hygiene and dressing, and moving on to vocational skills. Other institutions in America and Europe developed similar programs. By 1876, 12 schools for defectives existed in eight states. The same year, the Association of Medical Officers of American Institutes for Idiots and Feeble Minded Persons was formed—an organization that later became the American Association on Mental Deficiency (AAMD).

Prior to these new educational movements, all types of mental defectives were grouped under the main category of cretinism. However, as interest in the field grew, more specific delineations evolved. The American Association on Mental Deficiency altered its classification system by adding the category of "morons" to the categories of "idiots" and "imbeciles." In 1866 John Down described a Mongolian type of idiocy that was later confirmed by Fraser and Mitchell in Edinburgh. Down then attempted to delineate other ethnic categories. He soon abandoned this idea, moving instead to divisions according to etiology—congenital, developmental, and accidental types of idiocy. Ten years later, William Ireland in his major work "On Idiocy and Imbecility" suggested 12 categories for cretins. More specific syndromes of retardation subsequently were noted by Bourneville in 1880, Pelizaeus in 1885, Tayin in 1881, and Sachs in 1887.

Precursors to the modern learning disabilities movement, reviewed by Head (1926), explored spoken language disorders as correlates of retardation. Hinshelwood (1917) and Orton (1937) focused on written language disorders, while Goldstein (1939) and Strauss and Werner (1942) stressed perceptual–motor disorders. Contributions from these and others later were to impact the field of learning disabilities.

The Twentieth Century

Classification systems were strongly aided by the development of intelligence tests. Binet and Simon established norms to distinguish the mentally defective from the normal in French public schools. Their tests later were revised in America by Goddard and Terman. The development of the Alpha and Beta tests for screening during World War I provided unequivocal evidence as to the utility of using tests for practical purposes.

Trends begun earlier in this century continue to be relevant today. For example, the need for comprehensive community planning for the mentally retarded was emphasized in 1917 by Wallin. Folling (1934) contributed to building interest among the medical ranks with his discovery of phenylketonuria as a major determinant of retardation. Also, placement according to classification became more popular. Ingram published his major work, "Education of the Slow Learning Child" in 1935, which served to maintain the field of education as a primary arena interested in the mentally retarded. By 1911 there were public school classes for the mentally retarded in 99 American cities (Farber, 1968). That number more than quadrupled by 1948; by 1963 over 400,000 children were being served. The IQ cutoff for defining retardation was raised to 84, increasing the number of persons eligible to be classified as educable mentally retarded (EMR). Increased state and federal funds were also channeled into programs for the trainable mentally retarded (TMR).

Recent Developments

Research in the 1960s showed that special class placement was not necessarily beneficial to children. This provided much of the impetus for the current normalization, or mainstreaming, movement. Parents and educators organized, lobbied, and went to court, inspiring legislation and litigation that induced major revisions in education of the handicapped. The constitutional rights of handicapped persons and their parents to due process and quality educational programs were established firmly in court cases. The field has also moved toward more specific forms of diagnostics. New testing techniques were developed for use by the practitioners working within the major disciplines of medicine, psychology, education, and sociology. Tests were also revised, questioned, and severely challenged in light of new information about minority children and social deprivation (Oakland & Laosa, 1977). The field of education came under attack for its methods and goals; accountability became an important issue.

Major contributions in the area of learning disabilities were made by Osgood (1953), Wepman, Jones, Bock, and Van Pelt (1960), McGinnis (1963), Eisensen (1954), and Kirk and Kirk (1961) during what Wiederholt (1974) describes as the transition phase of the field of learning disabilities. Also during that phase, Kirk (1940), Fernald and Keller (1921), Gillingham and Stillman (1936), and others focused on written language disorders. Perceptual–motor disorders continued to be explored by Kephart (1960), Cruickshank, Bentzner, Ratzeberu, and Tannhausser (1961), and Frostig and Horne (1964). Finally, around 1963, in the "integration phase" of the study of learning disabilities (Wiederholt, 1974), disorders of spoken language, written language, and perceptual–motor processes were merged to form a new field called learning disabilities. The field contributed to a new awareness of the more subtle educational needs of learning disabled children in comparison with the needs of the mentally retarded. The field also brought with it new issues revolving around etiology, definition, and diagnosis.

Mental Retardation and Learning Disabilities:
Concepts in Search of Definitions

Defining mental retardation and learning disabilities has been difficult. The problems occur for a variety of reasons. One is that there are different focal points for the definitions. Some emphasize biological and etiological aspects, whereas others emphasize psychological, social, or academic determinants. Further confusion often occurs within each focal point. For example, within the psychological focus, IQ is a major variable. Psychometrically oriented definitions differ on specific IQ cutoff points for defining mental retardation, or the amount of disparity between verbal and performance IQs in defining learning disability.

Another major problem lies in the differing purposes for formulating a definition. A definition may be written to emphasize diagnostic classifications useful for monitoring incidence and service provision, classification for determining intervention modes, or for research. Finally, definitions have become crucial to legislation, in part because they serve to define the persons and programs eligible for federal and state financial support.

Mental Retardation

The problem of defining mental retardation has been subject to the factors previously discussed as well as to other general problems. For example, some definitions have relied heavily upon psychometric measures, with cutoff points determined from a normal distribution to identify from 1 to 16% of the population as mentally retarded. More socially oriented definitions have proposed that mental retardation should be evaluated on the basis of ability to perform expected roles within the home, school, and community, with peers, and as an earner and consumer (Mercer & Lewis, 1978). Educationally oriented definitions have emphasized ability to learn and profit from instruction. Each definition has important implications for the incidence and prevalence of the disability and the types of social, psychological, and educational services the individuals receive.

The main categories usually include the educable mentally retarded (EMR) with IQs between 50 and 70, trainable mentally retarded (TMR) with IQs between 30 and 50, and the profoundly mentally retarded (PMR) with IQs below 30. The EMRs, under consideration in this chapter, are assumed to have the ability to learn basic educational skills and eventually be able to function independently in society.

While a multitude of definitions have been offered, the most widely accepted and used have come from the American Association on Mental Deficiency (AAMD). The AAMD definitions combine several of the focal points discussed previously. Its original definition, drawn up in 1959, stated that mental retardation "refers to subaverage general intellectual functioning which originates in the developmental period and is associated with impairment in adaptive behavior [Heber, 1961, p. 3]." Such phrases as "subaverage general intellectual functioning" and "impairment in adaptive behavior" were confusing and subject to varying interpretations. As a result a manual was published in 1960 that attempted to interpret and clarify all points. Several distinct characteristics of this definition emerged. The IQ cutoff was placed at one standard deviation below the mean, creating a very high cutoff that allowed for 16% of the population to be classified as mentally retarded. Also, the definition emphasized present functioning, not prognosis or learning capacity. Furthermore, the definition was unconcerned with etiology and did not distinguish between mental retardation as a primary or secondary disorder.

The 1959 AAMD definition was criticized on a number of points. It failed to point out the importance of general adaptive behavior as an important index of retardation. Furthermore, there was a growing awareness of social and environmental factors, such as the effects of labeling a child as mentally retarded and the effects of social deprivation in reducing IQ scores.

Responding to these and other criticisms, the AAMD offered a revised definition in 1973: "Mental Retardation refers to significantly subaverage general intellectual functioning existing concurrently with deficits in adaptive behavior and manifested during the developmental period [Grossman, 1973, p. 5]." The new definition lowered the cutoff point from −1 standard deviation to −2 standard deviations, thereby eliminating the borderline category (IQ 70–84) of mental retardation. It further raised the upper end of the developmental period from age 16 to 18. One possible effect of the changes is to protect persons from being inadvertently mislabeled mentally retarded who are developmentally delayed. Another effect is to exclude borderline children from receiving special services in the public schools under the category of mental retardation. Much legislation has been based on the AAMD definition, including most state laws and policies governing who can receive special services. While we often think of the definitions affecting education, they also have been the basis for other decisions (e.g., determining whether a juvenile should receive services for the mentally retarded or be adjudicated as a delinquent).

Even the revised definition can be criticized for its combination of focal points, the lack of adequate means for determining adaptive behavior, and reliance on testing procedures that some feel are culturally biased.

Learning Disabilities

Attempts to define learning disabilities also have encountered serious problems. The term "learning disabilities" is more heterogeneous than the term "mental retardation." Mental retardation is a fairly homogeneous category that is largely differentiated on the basis of degree of severity (i.e., EMR, TMR, and PMR). Learning disabilities, on the other hand, encompass a variety of subtypes that may or may not have similar problems or symptoms. Thus, classifying learning disabilities becomes a complicated process of determining a specific disability rather than determining the degree of a disability. The most common terms used to describe learning disabilities (LD) include minimal brain injury, minimal brain dysfunction, aphasia or dysphasia, dyslexia, perceptual–motor impairment, specific language disability, neurological impairment, word blindness, hyperactivity, and dyspraxia. There is a growing availability of instruments to differentiate these and other specific disabilities. Also, the search continues for the factors common to all the subtypes of learning disabilities in an effort to form a more precise definition and understanding of learning disabilities.

Another problem in defining learning disabilities is in determining what constitutes an actual learning disability as opposed to a developmental delay or mental retardation. Opinions differ as to the IQ score necessary to rule out the possibility of mental retardation; some propose a cutoff as high as 90 or as low as 70. Also, there is no agreement regarding the symptoms that actually reflect learning disabilities. To a large extent, this reflects a controversy in etiology. Some persons cite neurological factors and thus define the disabilities when they reflect neurological impairment. Others who are unconcerned with etiology focus on present functioning and include within the LD category problems that may be attributed to developmental delays, environmental deprivation, or emotional disturbance.

As with MR, definitions for LD become legitimized through legislation. As defined in recent legislation, a specific learning disability reflects:

> A disorder in one or more of the basic psychological processes involved in understanding or in using language, spoken or written, which may manifest itself in an imperfect ability to listen, think, speak, read, write, spell, or to do mathematical calculations. The term includes such conditions as perceptual handicaps, brain injury, minimal brain dysfunction, dyslexia and developmental aphasia. The term does not include children who have learning problems which are primarily the result of visual, hearing, or motor handicaps, of mental retardation, of emotional disturbance, or of environmental, cultural, or economic disadvantage [*Federal Register,* 1977].

This definition is clearly intended to focus on children manifesting disabilities of a psychoneurological origin. Various problems occur with this definition, two of which are the lack of adequate techniques for ruling out environmental effects on language and school achievement and the lack of consensus on the etiology of learning disabilities. Some argue that etiology is unimportant (Bijou, 1963; Wolfensberger, 1965) and that anyone manifesting a disability should be eligible for services, regardless of causation (Chalfant & Scheffelin, 1969; Kirk, 1972). Others contend that neurological impairment may underlie most learning disabilities and thus should be reflected more strongly in the definition (Strauss & Kephart, 1955; Clements, 1966; Myklebust, 1963). Finally, arguments remain as to whether LD symptoms actually represent a learning disability (i.e., a specific weakness), a learning disorder (i.e., specific neurological impairment), or a syndrome (i.e., a combination of symptoms that manifest an underlying cause).

Thus, defining both mental retardation and learning disabilities has many general problems. Both definitions are arbitrary and can be expected to change. Changes in definitions have important implications for the quality and kinds of services provided to children; implications also are apparent on attempts to determine prevalence estimates for the categories.

Incidence and Prevalence

Before reviewing statistics on the prevalence of mental retardation and learning disabilities, an important distinction must be drawn between incidence and prevalence. Incidence refers to the total number of people at any point in time who *have had* the particular problem under consideration. Prevalence, on the other hand, specifies a time frame so as to determine the number of people at any one point in time who *are presently* manifesting the problem. For example, the incidence of mental retardation in a school district would include the percentage of all children who had ever been classified as MR. The prevalence would refer to the percentage of all children who are now in classes for the retarded. The confusion of the two terms has been partially responsible for the varying estimates of the number of mentally retarded or learning disabled children. Prevalence estimates in themselves are difficult to obtain for several reasons. First of all, the definition of MR itself has an effect on estimating prevalence. For example, when the IQ cutoff for defining mental retardation is change from -1 to -2 standard deviations, prevalence estimates drop from 16 to 2%. Second, special populations such as the mentally retarded have a much higher mortality rate than do normal people, thus affecting estimates. Prevalence estimates are also difficult to specify because of variations across the population, including male versus female, urban versus rural, race, and socioeconomic status. Age can also clearly affect estimates. Graphs of the numbers of mentally retarded and learning disabled show higher prevalence in school-age children and lower prevalence in preschoolers and adults. This may reflect the greater likelihood of detecting mild cases of EMR and LD once a person enters school.

Even with variations in estimates, the most common incidence figure cited for mental retardation is 3% of the population. The President's Committee on Mental Retardation (1962) noted that mental retardation affects 10 times more individuals than diabetes, 20 times more than tuberculosis, 25 times more than muscular dystrophy, and 600 times more than infantile paralysis. It is exceeded only by mental illness, cardiac disease, arthritis, and cancer. The President's Task Force on the Mentally Handicapped (1970) cited 6 million people affected, with an estimated 215,000 institutionalized, and 690,000 receiving special education services. The 3% figure refers to incidence. More recent surveys of Tarjan, Wright, Eyman, and Keeran (1973) and Mercer (1973) suggest a prevalence estimate closer to 1%, with the large majority in the EMR range.

Prevalence and incidence estimates for learning disabilities are even more difficult to obtain than those for mental retardation because of the greater confusion in defining the learning disabled, as well as because they are less likely to be readily identified and are less likely to be receiving special services. The majority of surveys on LD seem to indicate prevalence rather than incidence.

The National Advisory Committee on Handicapped Children (1968) estimated that 1 to 3% of all school-age children were learning disabled. In a later estimate, the United States Office of Education (1972) estimated 1% of the school-age children evidenced learning disabilities. Based on more empirical data from a survey, Myklebust and Boshes (1969) determined that 15% of the public school children screened were learning disabled. However, when the cutoff score was lowered from 90 to 85 on Myklebust's learning quotient, the percentage fell to about 7%. Accurate prevalence and incidence estimates are difficult to make owing to problems that begin in the definitional stage. These estimates remain critical for determining the need for services, training personnel, funding, and legislation.

The Six-Hour Retarded Child: Fact or Fiction

The President's Committee on Retardation and the Bureau of Education for the Handicapped sponsored a conference in the summer of 1969 to discuss the problems of educating children in the inner city. A conference report, entitled "The Six-Hour Retarded Child," has had a strong impact on education in at least three ways. First, the report delineates seven important recommendations to improve the educational opportunities of inner-city students. These recommendations served as strong and important guidelines directed toward improving educational programs within inner-city schools.

Second, the report contains an implicit denunciation of public education. The failure to educate inner-city children was laid largely at the feet of public education. The roles and impact that other factors and institutions exert on the inner-city mentally retarded were largely ignored.

The third impact of the report arises from its title, "The Six-Hour Retarded Child." The publication opens with an anonymous quotation: "We now have what may be called a 6-hour retarded child—retarded from 9 to 3, five days a week, solely on the basis of an IQ score, without regard to his adaptive behavior, which may be exceptionally adaptive to the situation and community in which he lives." The quote unwittingly serves as a definition for the mentally retarded—not for the inner-city or EMR child. The title and quotation have had a widespread impact on the attitudes toward special education despite the fact that this particular publication provides virtually no support for the existence of a 6-hour retarded child. There has been considerable pressure from many quarters to change the term mental retardation to educational retardation, assuming no underlying psychological differences or deficiencies within persons who are mentally retarded.

The report's title (although not the content of the report itself) raises the question as to whether our mentally retarded classrooms are filled with children who are below normal intellectually but normal or above in terms of other qualities and characteristics. The overriding evidence (e.g., Hobbs, 1975) does not support this viewpoint. It is true that many children function at an average level in nonacademic areas that require different abilities and attitudes. Others, however, do evidence problems in perception, conceptual thinking, language, reading, hyperactivity, distractability, perseveration, motor coordination, and other areas not assessed by adaptive behavior measures that limit their nonacademic success as well.

To classify a person "solely on the basis of an IQ score" (as the introduction states) is both unpardonable and extremely rare. The novice may envision school psychologists administering IQ tests to all children and routinely labeling those with subaverage IQs as mentally retarded. This, of course, does not happen. Moreover, to attribute the problems of the inner-city child to IQ scores overly simplifies issues and negates our need to address other factors that more dramatically and forcefully impinge upon children's academic, social, and emotional development. Too much time has been wasted trying to make IQ scores the scapegoat for children's academic failures.

The ultimate goal of education is to develop individuals with functional skills who can participate effectively in various roles. Consistent with Mercer and Lewis' (1978) concept of adaptive behavior, we may characterize a functioning individual as one who functions effectively with peers, family, and community, and can earn a living and be an informed consumer; a functioning individual has the self-help skills that allow independence and has the ability to assume responsibility for the welfare of others. Knowing that a child's out-of-school adaptive behavior is average or above average may help to discover and develop potential strengths undetected through other evaluation techniques.

School psychologists are faced with a dilemma. With one clock we are confident in telling the correct time; with two clocks we are never sure. When mental retardation is defined as subnormal performance on a test of intelligence, we can confidently classify persons. With measures of both intelligence and adaptive behavior, we may be less sure. To confidently classify people, there should be agreement between the two measures. However, we are finding average adaptive behavior scores on many children with subaverage IQs (Oakland, 1977; Gridley & Mastenbrook, 1977). Perhaps as many as 75% of the EMR population would be declassified if we insisted upon below average performance on both IQ and adaptive behavior measures. This would serve to severely decrease the number of children mislabeled, but it might also deny to them special resources available through this classification (Oakland, 1979). The use of this dual standard clearly is in keeping with an attempt to declassify and to avoid labeling as many persons as possible. This is consistent with the notion that it is better not to label a problem if one exists than to risk labeling a problem that does not exist.

One prevalent theme throughout this chapter is that assessment activities do not constitute an end result. Rather, they represent the beginning stage in a process that hopefully provides and augments programs and services that benefit the individual. Placing this within the context of education, assessment activities, to be useful to students, should be fused with appropriate interventions. The fusion of assessment and intervention practices into one process encourages us to more effectively utilize our time and resources during the assessment phase, to seek more direct and relevant information through assessment regarding intervention issues, and to encourage us to clarify and highlight the importance of intervention.

Process of Diagnosis and Intervention

The multistage diagnostic–intervention model put forth by Cromwell, Blashfield, and Strauss (1975) helps conceptualize a realistic and viable approach to acquiring information important to understanding children and to using this information in developing appropriate interventions. Our discussion of this model is limited to its first four components (labeled A, B, C, and D).

The first component (A) is concerned with acquiring *historical information* to assist us in understanding a child. Emphasis is placed on the child's medical, social, psychological, and educational history. This information of a historical nature helps us to identify and understand important antecedent events. The second component (B) seeks information that describes the child's *current characteristics.* Medical, social, psychological, and educational characteristics are also important here. The third component (C) focuses on *interventions,* which can include curricula, instructional arrangements, teaching strategies, grouping practices, social relationships, and other components of the educational process over which the schools have control. Interventions are developed from information gathered from components A or B, or both. The fourth component (D) attempts to estimate the successfulness of the interventions. Given a particular history of behaviors (A), together with a set of current behaviors (B), and employing certain intervention strategies (C), what is likely to occur? That question is addressed through this fourth component (D). Thus, a complete assessment–intervention program would acquire historical (A) and current (B) information on children, would relate this information in order to draw associations between the child's previous and current characteristics (e.g., relationships between A and B), and would use this information pool to specify viable interventions (C). We also should be able to say that, given these prior and current characteristics, this intervention is likely to be more effective than any other in stimulating growth—that in 9 to 12 months we should be able to see a significant improvement in certain areas. Each of the model's two major components—assessment and intervention—are considered in greater detail in the following sections.

Using the Cromwell *et al.* (1975) model, assessment should focus on relevant information from the child's past, relevant information concerning current behavior, and then relate this information to specific and effective interventions. But what information do we need to know? How can we acquire this information efficiently and economically? Do we need to give special attention to differences due to culture, race, or ethnicity? Who collects and interprets the information?

Assessment programs in most schools recognize the importance of acquiring information about children's medical, psychological, social, and educational characteristics. Information from these four areas is often considered by a committee in recommending that a child be placed in a special education class or retained within a regular program. Medical information may be acquired by a school physician or nurse, or it may be supplied by the family's physician. Information regarding social, psychological, and educational characteristics may be acquired by one specialist (e.g., a school psychologist) or through a multidisciplinary team involving school social workers, educational diagnosticians, classroom teachers, and school psychologists.

Each school district ultimately devises its own assessment program so as to be in accord with federal and state guidelines together with local needs and resources. Each district selects the assessment instruments that it prefers because an entire package of assessment techniques has not been available from one company—at least until recently.

The System of Multicultural Pluralistic Assessment

The System of Multicultural Pluralistic Assessment (SOMPA) (Mercer & Lewis, 1978) does provide a comprehensive method of assessing and interpreting various characteristics typically seen as important to school success. While not necessarily advocating its use, we do want to discuss it somewhat fully because of widespread interest in the SOMPA and because it provides measures of most of the dimensions considered most important to a full appraisal. An understanding of the conceptual model underlying the SOMPA hopefully will help in understanding the use of each of the instruments.

Models of Assessment

Children are viewed from three assessent models within the SOMPA: a medical model, a social systems model, and a pluralistic model. The *medical model* defines abnormality in terms of the presence of biological symptoms. Thus, the measurement instruments assess biologically determined symptoms. To interpret data from these measures, one typically does not need to know the children's sociocultural or racial characteristics; the measures used in this model should not yield results that are racially discriminatory. In interpreting data from these measures, one should take the view that to assume no pathology when one exists is worse than to assume that pathology exists when there is none (i.e., it is better to say a person is sick if he is not than to say he is not sick when he is).

The *social systems model* defines normality as behavior that conforms to the expectation of other members of the group and abnormality as behavior that does not meet the expectations of others. Thus, the definition of normal behavior depends upon the particular group in which a person is functioning and the particular role a person plays within the group, because group expectations for social roles vary from group to group and from one role to another in a group. Measures within this model assess social competence in the performance of roles. Social system test scores, according to Mercer and Lewis, are both role specific and system specific and cannot be generalized to other roles or systems.

The *pluralistic model* attempts to make testing procedures more responsive to cultural differences and is less tied to the dominant Anglo-American cultural traditions in American society. The use of this model assumes that differences in learning potential within racial–ethnic and cultural groups exist, but that differences in test scores between cultural groups are due to biased testing procedures. Three approaches are suggested to pluralistic assessment (Mercer & Ysseldyke, 1977). One involves the development of culture-specific tests that enable children to be evaluated on cultural materials with which they are familiar. The Black Intelligence Test for Children (Williams, 1974) is one example of a culture-specific measure designed for a culturally restricted group. The second approach to pluralistic assessment involves estimating children's learning potential by teaching them relevant skills after pretesting and before posttesting, thus permitting a measure of the amount of growth made as a result of this learning opportunity (Budoff, 1972). This technique assesses the ability to profit from experience.

The third approach, and the one advanced by Mercer and Lewis (1978), is to develop many sets of norms for each test and to use those norms that are the most appropriate for a given child. Instead of having only one general norm for a test (usually based on children's ages or grades), separate norms also would be available for different sociocultural, socioeconomic (SES), racial–ethnic, and geographic groups. The performance of any one child could be compared with that of other children who are similar in terms of age, sociocultural, SES, racial–ethnic, and geographic group membership. According to Mercer and Ysseldyke (1977), a slightly different and technically more sophisticated way of developing these multiple norms is

> to use multiple regressions to predict the average score for persons from a variety of sociocultural backgrounds. The sociocultural characteristics of the child's family then are inserted in the multiple regression equation, each characteristic is multiplied by its weight, and the equation is solved to determine the average score on the test which would be predicted for a person from the same background as the child. Then the child's score is compared with this predicted score. Whether he/she is evaluated as normal, subnormal, or superior depends upon the location of his/her score in the distribution of scores predicted for other children from similar sociocultural settings [p. 84].

The three techniques proposed within the pluralistic model attempt to control for cultural and racial–ethnic differences, and thus the results from these techniques should not be discriminatory.

SOMPA Measures

The System of Multicultural Pluralistic Assessment presents a comprehensive battery of measures, some of which are administered directly to children and some of which are completed in a parent interview conducted in the child's home.

THE MEDICAL MODEL MEASURES

The SOMPA provides six medical model measures. The Physical Dexterity Tasks is a newly developed measure of fine and gross motor coordination and balance. The seven subtests include measures of placement, ambulation, involuntary movements, fine motor sequencing, synchronized movements, equilibrium, and finger–tongue dexterity. Combined with other information, these data are helpful in identifying neurologically impaired children. The Bender–Gestalt measure, familiar to most school psychologists, is administered and scored according to Koppitz's procedures (Koppitz, 1964). Its nine figures are presented to the subject one at a time, and the child has to reproduce each figure on a blank piece of paper. The perception and reproduction of the figures are determined by biological principles of sensory–motor action and vary depending upon the child's growth patterns and maturation levels together with any pathological conditions that may be either functionally or organically induced (Koppitz, 1964). The figures can be scored for errors due to distortions, rotations, perseverations, or disintegration. This measure is also used to evaluate perceptual maturity and neurological functioning.

The Health History Inventory is a newly developed instrument used in an interview with the mother to review the child's past and current health conditions and to help identify children who may need a thorough examination by a physician. Five major categories assessed in the Health History Inventory include pre- and postnatal conditions (e.g., complications during pregnancy, premature birth), traumas (e.g., high temperature, serious injuries, or operations), diseases and illnesses, and vision and hearing inventories.

Visual and auditory acuity are also assessed in the medical model. Visual acuity is assessed by the standard Snellen test with norms available from the U.S. Public Health Service. Auditory acuity should be assessed by audiometrists or other qualified personnel using appropriate equipment. These results help to ensure that a child does not have undiagnosed acuity problems hampering his or her growth and development. A height by weight index is the final measure used within the medical model.

The Social Systems Model Measures

Two measures within the SOMPA are used to assess the children's adaptive behavior in various social roles. The Adaptive Behavior Inventory for Children (ABIC) has stimulated the greatest interest of any measure included in the SOMPA. The ABIC contains 242 questions that are asked of the mother in order to determine the child's level of role performance within the family and community, with peers, as an earner and consumer, in nonacademic school situations, and in terms of self-help skills. In addition to a total ABIC score, separate subtest scores are provided for each of these six subtests; the reliability and validity of the scores are aided by scores reflecting how truthful the mother's responses are, how much she knows about the child's behaviors, and the degree of opportunity allowed a child to assume appropriate role behaviors. If the mother's veracity is questioned, for example, the validity of information provided in the interview is suspect.

The Wechsler Intelligence Scale for Children-Revised (WISC-R) is used within the SOMPA to assess the child's functioning within the dominant culture of the school. The WISC-R and school psychologists are often caricatured as being fellow travelers. The test is probably the most frequently used individually administered test of intelligence. Many school psychologists question whether the WISC-R is really a measure of school culture in that they tend to think of it as a measure of broader hereditary and acculturation processes (including nonschool culture). Nevertheless, within the SOMPA, both the ABIC and the WISC-R are used to appraise adaptation in different environments. The WISC-R is used to assess the child's role performance with respect to the school's academic culture, and the ABIC is used to assess a child's role performance with respect to important nonacademic cultural components.

The Pluralistic Model Measures

The sociocultural background of the student is assessed by the Sociocultural Scales. These scales include four subtests that assess the family's urban acculturation, socioeconomic status, structure, and size. This information is used both to characterize an important setting in which the child is being reared and, within the pluralistic model, to adjust scores from other measures in order to estimate the child's learning potential.

The SOMPA also provides an estimated IQ, which is determined by using a child's weighted sociocultural modality scores (i.e., family size and structure, SES, and urban acculturation). This estimated IQ is "the average score predicted for persons having a particular combination of sociocultural characteristics. In other words the estimated (IQ) score can be interpreted as the average score of persons from a particular sociocultural background, the norm for that group [Mercer, 1977]." Thus, the estimated IQ reflects an estimate of a group and is not based upon a child's WISC-R performance.

The concept of pluralistic assessment is also introduced. Pluralistic assessment denotes having many different norms available for a test and using those norms that are most appropriate. The number of norms available for one test equals the number of possible combinations of sociological scores—thus the term "pluralistic." A child's performance is compared only with others from the same sociocultural background. All estimated IQs are transformed into standard scores having a mean of 100 and a standard deviation of 15; these scores are referred to as the estimated learning potential (ELP). The formula for determining the ELP is as follows:

$$\text{ELP} = (\text{actual IQ} - \text{estimated IQ}/SE_{est})\,(15) + 100$$

The use of separate multiple regression equations for Anglos, Blacks, and Mexican-Americans presumably enables us to equalize the children's backgrounds and to make more equitable comparisons.

The SOMPA offers a comprehensive diagnostic battery that attempts to overcome some of the limitations of using separate and at times poorly standardized instruments. Only recently has it become available for use. Thus, the little research presently available (e.g., Oakland, 1979) is not sufficient for judging its utility.

Two Emerging Areas of Assessment: Psychoneurology and Adaptive Behavior

One area to which school psychologists are devoting more time and attention is the assessment of psychoneurological characteristics. During the last 10 years, psychoneurological diagnosis has become more refined and sophisticated, growing alongside advancements made through research in understanding biochemical (Hughes, 1976; Wender, 1976; Conners, 1976) and neurological (Reitan & Davison, 1974; Gazzaniga, 1970) influences on behavior.

Psychoneurological Assessment

Most evaluations of children occur through informal observations. We are interested in detecting prevailing personality and ability traits, changes in these characteristics over time, and changes due to situational circumstances. There are at least six school-related behaviors that tend to be easily recognizable and that may suggest neurological or brain dysfunction: school learning problems, hyperkinesis (particularly among preschool children), impulsivity, low tolerance for frustration, emotional lability, and auditory memory problems. These behaviors, all somewhat easily recognizable by teachers and parents, may be used to screen children in order to identify those most likely to be brain injured or neurologically impaired.

Bender's (1947) delineation of soft signs of neurological damage include children's awkwardness and clumsiness, choreiform movements, speech disorders, the late acquisition of laterality, synkinesia, and reflex asymmetry. Children who demonstrate severe problems in one or more of these areas probably need a more formal assessment of neurological characteristics. Additional symptoms include convulsions, bowel or bladder dysfunction, or muscle weakness or paralysis. The disorders may be congenital or their origins may be more recent—the result of an accident or disease. Thus, the presence of chronic or severe physical, mental, language, or perceptual disorders suggests the need for a complete psychoneurological examination.

The Psychoneurological Examination

A neurological part of the psychoneurological examination is always performed by a physician with advanced training in neurology. The examination is usually conducted in the physician's office with little special equipment needed. It proceeds from an inspection of the person's general appearance and behaviors to an examination of the cranial nerves, motor functions, sensory perception, and reflex responses. Each of the eight areas included in the exam is discussed briefly.

1. An examination of a person's *general appearance* and *behavior* helps to determine whether the person is alert, dull, confused, in a stupor, or in a coma. This information is important in determining whether the examination can continue (e.g., if the person is in a stupor or coma there is no point in continuing).

2. The individual's *mental status* is determined by assessing the following five areas: judgment and insights (awareness of illnesses and conduct is appropriate), orientation (awareness of self, where he/she is, and has an adequate concept of time and date), memory (the ability to recall general long- and short-term information), affect (euphoric, depressed, or dull), and cognition (ability to identify similarities and differences and do simple calculations).

3. Both receptive and expressive *language* are assessed. Particular attention is devoted to detecting whether the person manifests dysarthria (slurred or inarticulate speech), dysphonia (nasal speech), aphasia (disorders in expressing or comprehending language), or mutism (an inability or refusal to speak).

4. The person's *gait* and *posture* are observed, noting particularly any uncoordinated feet and hand movements.

5. The *head* and *cranial nerves* are examined for asymmetry, tenderness, and auscultation of the orbits. The following nerves are examined: olfactory nerve, optic nerve (including visual acuity and the visual field), the nerve associated with eye movements (eyelids, pupils, ocular movements, nystagmus), trigeminal nerve,

facial nerve, vestibulocochlear nerve, glossopharyngeal and vagus nerves, spino-accessory nerve, and the hypoglossal nerve.

6. The *motor system* functions are observed and tested with respect to muscle size, involuntary movements, muscle strength, muscle tone, and muscle coordination.

7. The *sensory system* is evaluated by noting the person's ability to detect a light touch, superficial pain (e.g., pin prick) and deeper pain, heat, cold, and temperature changes, and vibrations from a tuning fork, as well as ability to discriminate sensations on two parts of the body.

8. Three groups of *reflexes* are assessed: the deep tendon reflexes (e.g., biceps and triceps jerks), the superficial reflexes (e.g., the downward curling of the toes), and the abnormal reflexes (e.g., the Babinski sign and forced grasp reflex).

In addition to the examination of these areas, a number of laboratory studies can be ordered that help to support the diagnosis of neurological or brain disorders. The laboratory studies include the electroencephalograph (which examines dysrhythmias in the electrical discharges in the brain), auditory and visual acuity, skull x-rays, urinary screening tests for abnormal metaeolites, and urine chromatography for amino acids.

Various technologies are being developed and used that increase our sophistication in diagnosing neurological dysfunction and brain injury. The computerized axial tomogram (acronymed either CAT or EMI—after the manufacturers of the first instrument) is one new radiological technique that allows for the study of the brain, its ventricles, and the bone structure about the brain and the upper part of the face. The person lies quietly with either the head or complete body inside a large cylinder. A narrow scanning x-ray beam is used to assess the x-ray absorption throughout the skull, brain, and cerebral ventricles. The data are collected by a computer, which then converts the information into two formats. The first is in the form of a printout showing a "picture" of the different absorption areas. The second uses a cathode-ray (TV) display to show the anatomy in axial, frontal, and lateral planes. This technical output provides information that aids in diagnosing diseases and determining prognoses. Improved diagnostic understanding can alter plans for additional diagnostic tests or therapeutic plans. Through more accurate diagnoses and improved therapies, the EMI is expected to significantly improve patient outcomes (Fineberg, Bauman, & Sosman, 1977). Even though in widespread use for less than 4 years, the EMI has been found to be effective in the detecting of cerebral atrophy, dilated lateral ventricles, and porencephalic cysts; it is also helpful in planning surgical approaches and discovering postoperative complications (Becker, McCarthy, Chase, Converse, & Genieser, 1976), thus significantly reducing the need for other diagnostic tests and increasing the accuracy of therapies (Fineberg *et al.,* 1977; Sarwar, 1977).

Another promising but less tried technique is the Quantitative Electrophysiological Battery (QB), a computer analysis of brain waves (Goldman, 1976). Fashioned after the principles that underlie the electroencephalogram (EEG), the QB reportedly monitors 57 different sites within the brain in less than 1 hour. Sensory, perceptual, attentional, language, and other disabilities are diagnosed. The initial results suggest that people who have learning disabilities, brain diseases, certain forms of psychosis, or are mentally retarded or senile, display abnormal diagnostic patterns on the QB. Research is expected soon from E. Roy John and others at New York Medical College's Brain Research Laboratory that will help us evaluate the QB's effectiveness in diagnosing the mentally retarded and learning disabled.

The psychologist has important responsibilities in the psychoneurological assessment process. The psychological phase of the psychoneurological examination augments the evaluation by considering general intellectual abilities, lateralization, right or left hemiphere dysfunction, and localization within the hemispheres.

The Halstead–Reitan battery contains most of the trusted and popular techniques for assessing brain injury by psychologists. Its long history of use and its strong research base (Reitan & Davison, 1974) clearly make it the most preferred instrument to assess psychoneurological characteristics.

There are four principal methods of analyzing psychoneurological data. The psychologist can analyze: (*a*) level of performance; (*b*) presence of pathonomic signs; (*c*) patterns of test results; and (*d*) evidence of laterality. *Levels of performance* are generally considered average or below average. A low level of performance on both the verbal and performance scales of the WISC-R, for example, suggests the presence of more diffuse and general dysfunction. *Pathonomic signs* are serious indications suggesting pathology. Aphasia, for example, is a pathonomic sign of left hemisphere damage, whereas dyslexia suggests problems in the right hemisphere. Finally, many tasks have been developed that specifically assess the abilities *lateralized* within the right or left hemispheres. Occupational therapists and some psychologists have become interested in assessing children's sensory integration and lateralization as a means of screening for brain injury or identifying possible learning disabilities in children with normal IQs but subnormal achievement. Sensory integration is assessed somewhat informally by tasks that often are unstandardized yet related to the person's sensory–neurological intactness. In assessing sensory integration children are asked to perform tasks such as:

1. To extend their arms and then touch their right and left fingers to their nose (first with their eyes opened and then their eyes closed)
2. To walk a chalk line on the floor (with eyes opened and closed)
3. To stand on their right foot and then on their left foot for at least 30 seconds (first with eyes opened, then closed)
4. To squeeze a dynameter to determine right and left hand strength

5. To lie on one's back and hold bent legs off the floor for 30 seconds
6. To lie on one's stomach and hold head and legs off the ground for 30 seconds
7. To manifest ocular control by having each eye follow a penlight's movement
8. To imitate gross physical movements (e.g., angels in the snow)
9. To reproduce visual forms (such as those on the Bender measure) noting their form, placement on the page, accuracy with respect to midline, and the use of both the right and left hands

Adaptive Behavior[2]

The assessment of adaptive behavior is a second area in which school psychologists increasingly devote more time and attention. Consistent with AAMD's definition of mental retardation, adaptive behavior data must be considered together with intelligence test data in judging whether a person is mentally retarded. Also, Public Law 94-142 requires that placement decisions be based on information from a variety of sources including adaptive behavior.

CONCEPTS OF ADAPTIVE BEHAVIOR

The philosophical foundation for the concept of adaptive behavior can be traced to early Grecian and Roman civilizations, which judged persons' mental abilities on the basis of their taking an active and productive role in the activities of their community. The Greek word for idiot, for example, signified a person who was unable to take part in the public affairs of the community. Thus, in a broad sense, a person's mental ability was evaluated in terms of specific behaviors deemed important within the social and cultural system.

Viewed historically, the construct of adaptive behavior in psychology has been strongly intertwined with the concept of intelligence and more specifically with the construct of mental retardation. Itard, Seguin, and Binet emphasized the importance of recognizing that intelligence is reflected by many different kinds of behaviors displayed in various settings. In essence, they suggested a multidimension and multilevel definition of intelligence. This was in opposition to Galton, James, Cattell, and Goddard, who conceptualized intelligence as a more unitary trait that could be assessed primarily through formal psychometric tests. By defining intelligence empirically, we have produced a number of well-developed tests of intelligence, but we may have lost sight of certain historically important notions regarding the nature of intelligence. For example, the notion that intelligent behaviors can be reflected in nonacademic settings may have been lost. We have

---

[2]The authors want to acknowledge the prior contributions by Richard Scheir and Kevin Buckley in preparing this section on adaptive behavior.

retained Binet's psychometric contributions but have largely discarded his definition of intelligence, which also emphasized behaviors that are now regarded as being in the realm of adaptive behavior.

While we continue to define intelligence in a more narrow empirical fashion, its broader notions, including those suggested by the term adaptive behavior, have not been forgotten totally. Self-help skills, self-directed behaviors, vocational and economic pursuits, and being responsible for other persons retain their importance. For some people these represent the true and significant goals of education and mark the well educated. However, these behaviors have been separated from those associated with the concept of intelligence. Thus, we have two concepts, intelligence and social maturity, which are largely distinct within academic psychology.

However, various professionals from education, clinical and school psychology, anthropology, sociology, and law have urged that the two concepts should not be distinct; that we should either return to the older notion of intelligence, which includes adaptive behaviors, or we should use the two simultaneously in order to define intelligence.

We are currently being encouraged to follow the second option—to use the two simultaneously. As previously discussed, the AAMD definition (Grossman, 1973) of mental retardation includes the two dimensions of intelligence and adaptive behavior. Adaptive behavior is defined as the "effectiveness or degree with which the individual meets the standards of personal independence and social responsibility expected of his age and cultural group. Since these expectations vary for different age groups, deficits in adaptive behavior will vary at different ages."

Deficits during infancy and early chidhood might be reflected in sensory–motor skill development, communication skills, self-help skills, and socialization; during childhood and early adolescence deficits may be reflected in the application of basic academic skills, in daily life activities, in appropriate reasoning and judgment, and in the mastery of environment and social skills; during late adolescence and adult life deficits may be reflected in vocational and social responsibilities and performances. Delays in the acquisition of these skills represent potential deficiencies in adaptive behavior and become part of the criteria for diagnosing mental retardation. It is important to note that measures of intelligence and adaptive behavior are used simultaneously to define and measure the construct of mental retardation as well as the broader construct of intelligence.

The meaning and use of the construct of adaptive behavior is far from clear. First, there is no single concept of adaptive behavior—just as there is no single concept of intelligence. Second, to be useful in an applied setting, further work is needed to examine the relevance of adaptive behavior for non-mentally retarded persons. The close tie of adaptive behavior with the concept of mental retardation may be an inappropriate limitation. Third, there is a need to examine the construct of adaptive behavior through accepted empirical techniques. For example, we need to determine its relationships with more established measures of psychological, social, and educational characteristics.

In the meantime, there is a need to be cautious in inferring that adaptive behavior yields a more accurate definition of mental retardation, gives a more equitable and fair assessment of minority group children, or leads to educationally relevant interventions.

MEASUREMENT OF ADAPTIVE BEHAVIOR

Adequate and relatively complete measures of adaptive behavior are not readily available. An evaluation of a measure's suitability often considers information regarding the kinds of behaviors assessed, its age range, who can administer the scale, and the availability of data on reliability and validity. Information on these and other issues is summarized in Figure 5.1.

The Cain–Levine Social Competency Scale is designed for use with TMR children. Although a sound scale, it is not recommended for use beyond an IQ of 59 (Buros, 1965).

The Camelot Behavioral Checklist is intended to provide useful information for placement and programming decisions. In addition, the scale includes sections on job and work-related skills. However, the Camelot is also designed mainly for the TMR population.

In 1959 when the AAMD decided to incorporate the assessment of adaptive behavior into the definition and determination of mental retardation, no instruments met its definition of adaptive behavior. As a compromise, the AAMD recommended the use of the Vineland Scale (Doll, 1953) as a means of measuring adaptive behavior, even though the many limitations of the Vineland for this use were recognized. The Vineland does not assess the three factors of personal independence, social maladaption, and intrapersonal maladaption that constitute adaptive behaviors as defined by the AAMD study. Also, it is primarily developmental in nature, and its subscales do not adequately measure a full range of adaptive behaviors within age levels.

As a consequence, the AAMD sponsored the development of the Adaptive Behavior Scales. This instrument, now called the Clinical Version of the Adaptive Behavior Scales, is designed for use with severely handicapped persons and is normed on an institutional population.

In the early 1970s, the Adaptive Behavior Scale Public School Version was developed to assess adaptive behavior in school settings with less severely handicapped children (Lambert, Windmiller, & Cole, 1974). The instrument is normed on California school children using teachers as the respondents. The scale has two parts. The first section measures one's ability to adapt to the natural demands of the environment, and the second section assesses the ability to cope with social demands. The scale was constructed principally to provide information for remediation and rehabilitation rather than placement per se.

Behaviors Assessed

Measurement scales	Physical development/sensory-motor/locomotion	Self-direction	Language and communication	Vocational and occupational skills	Economic	Social	Self-help/independent functioning/self-maintenance	With peers	In school	In the family	In the community	Age range	Population type: Clinical	Population type: School	Purpose: Screening	Purpose: Placement	Purpose: Programming	Examiner: Teacher	Examiner: Diagnostician	Examiner: Paraprofessional	Respondent: Teacher	Respondent: Parent/family	Respondent: Child	Reliability and validity of data available (Yes/no)	Scores: Grade equivalent/age	Scores: Percentile	Scores: Scaled score	Administration time (minutes)
AAMD Clinical Version (Nihira et al., 1974)	X	X	X	X	X	X	X					3–adult	X			X	X		X	X		X		Yes		X		45–60
AAMD Public School Version (Lambert et al., 1974)	X	X	X	X	X	X	X					7–13		X		X	X	X	X	X	X	X		Yes		X		45–60
Cain–Levine (Cain et al., 1963)		X	X	X	X	X	X					5–13				X		X	X	X	X	X		Yes		X		20
California Preschool (Levine et al., 1969)			X			X						2–5			X			X	X	X	X	X		Yes		X		20
Camelot (Foster, 1974) Behavioral Checklist	X	X	X	X	X	X	X					2–adult		X		X	X	X	X	X[a]	X	X		Yes				60
Adaptive Behavior Inventory for Children (Mercer & Lewis, 1978)				X	X	X	X	X	X	X	X	5–11		X		X		X	X	X[a]	X	X		Yes		X	X	60
Preschool Attainment Record (Doll, 1966)	X	X	X			X	X					birth–7				X		X	X	X	X	X		No	X	X	X	20
Vineland Scale (Doll, 1965)	X	X	X	X	X	X	X					birth–25	X			X		X	X		X	X	[a]	Yes			X	20

[a] With extensive training in interviewing

FIGURE 5.1. *Evaluation of the suitability of a measurement of adaptive behavior.*

As previously discussed, the Adaptive Behavior Inventory for Children Scale (ABIC) developed by Mercer and Lewis (1978) approaches the assessment of adaptive behavior from a social systems model. It is designed to measure the social roles of children in different environments, age 5 through 11 years. While standardizing the ABIC, Mercer found no ethnic differences between the mean raw scores on the six subscales for Anglo, Black, and Mexican-American children. The scale is very comprehensive and provides extensive evaluation of the child's social role performance. The scale does have drawbacks, however. Administration and scoring is time consuming and standardization is incomplete. Also, programming and remediation ideas remain to be developed for the scale. Thus, while adaptive behavior measures exist, care is needed in selecting the measure best suited to the needs of the user.

Intervention:
The Psychologist's Role after Diagnosis

Once a child has undergone appropriate diagnostic procedures, the question becomes one of determining the appropriate intervention. Rarely is only one person responsible for formulating or carrying out interventions. These responsibilities increasingly are shared by members of a team composed of one or more teachers, a counselor, school psychologist, educational diagnostician, speech and language specialist, administrater, school nurse, and social worker.

Conceptualization of service delivery on the systems level has been aided by the Cascade Model (Deno, 1970), which proposes a continuum of special education services ranging from inpatient programs to placement of the handicapped in the regular classroom (see Figure 5.2).

The Cascade Model has been used as the basis for conceptualizing the least restrictive alternative mode so frequently mentioned in legislation. Beyond this conceptual model, however, remain many situational factors that further influence system decisions. Such factors include the context (classrooms available, class sizes), financing, materials, and staffing.

The next level influencing intervention decisions is the curriculum. Curriculum may be defined as all school-oriented experiences for the child. Curriculum-level models are grounded in the assumptions about the underlying intellectual capacities of EMR or LD individuals. The choice of curriculum interacts with broad objectives and the means for achieving those objectives (e.g., texts, films, training of teachers). Each influences the others. Assuming average intelligence, curriculum planning for learning disabled children focuses on correction of deficits while maintaining the usual levels of information input, although alternative learning channels may be utilized.

To a large extent the learning disabled child receives a typical academic curriculum, although offered in a slightly altered fashion. The assumptions un-

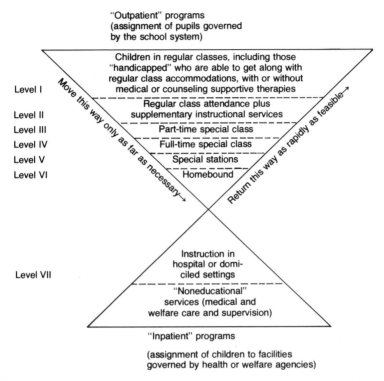

"Outpatient" programs
(assignment of pupils governed
by the school system)

Children in regular classes, including those
"handicapped" who are able to get along with
regular class accommodations, with or without
medical or counseling supportive therapies

Level I

Move this way only as far as necessary→

Return this way as rapidly as feasible→

Level II   Regular class attendance plus
supplementary instructional services

Level III   Part-time special class

Level IV   Full-time special class

Level V   Special stations

Level VI   Homebound

Level VII   Instruction in
hospital or domi-
ciled settings

"Noneducational"
services (medical and
welfare care and supervision)

"Inpatient" programs

(assignment of children to facilities
governed by health or welfare agencies)

FIGURE 5.2.   *Deno's Cascade Model of special education services.* [*Adapted from Deno (1970).*]

derlying curriculum planning for the EMR child are different as indicated in Figure 5.3. The EMR children are categorized as such because they are incapable of average achievement but are capable of learning the basic skills necessary to function independently in society. Thus, the initial emphasis is on basic academic skills (reading, writing, and arithmetic); as the child matures the focus tends to become more functionally oriented toward career education and vocational training.

Finally, intervention plans are determined at the individual level based on the multiplicity of information regarding learning abilities, degrees of disability and retardation, personality, home environment, emotional status, and adaptive behavior. Interventions at the individual level detail specific objectives for the child (as opposed to the broad objectives determined by curriculum choice).

There are also techniques that are designed to advance the academic development of learning disabled brain injured children; many of these techniques are reviewed more completely elsewhere (e.g., Cruickshank *et al.*, 1961; Strauss & Lehtinen, 1947). Some of the more specific techniques include those offered by the Gillingham remedial training method (Gillingham & Stillman, 1936, 1965;

Curricular content areas by organizational levels in EMR programs.

Level	Preprimary	Primary	Intermediate	Advanced
Age (approx.)	Under 6	6 to 11	12 to 18	Over 18

I SELF-HELP, BASIC READINESS, AND INDEPENDENT LIVING SKILLS

- ambulation
- manipulation
- coordination
- visual perceptual training
- physical education
- sense training & stimulation
- health habits
- gymnastics
- grooming
- securing assistance
- simple travel
- toileting
- auditory perceptual training
- intersensory integration
- proper dress
- bathing
- eating
- dressing
- safety training
- individual play

II COMMUNICATION, ORAL LANGUAGE, AND COGNITIVE DEVELOPMENT

- speech development
- attention training
- sign language
- simple number concepts
- simple spatial concepts
- simple time concepts
- simple writing
- concept formation
- general information
- simple reading
- puzzle solving
- creative expression
- simple science concepts
- simple social studies concepts
- simple problem solving

III SOCIALIZATION AND PERSONALITY DEVELOPMENT SKILLS

- group play
- sharing
- greetings
- conversation
- listening to others
- emotional control
- parties and picnics
- group projects
- dramatization
- handling ridicule
- scouting
- dancing
- manners
- social roles

IV VOCATIONAL, RECREATIONAL, AND LEISURE SKILLS

- observing others
- following instructions
- music and rhythmics
- art
- independent work habits
- work training
- arts and crafts
- yardwork
- housekeeping chores
- group work habits
- sheltered workshop

Instructional emphases (per cent): 10 to 100

FIGURE 5.3. Curricular content areas by organizational levels in EMR programs. [From Campbell (1968). Reprinted by permission of the State Department of Education in Sacramento, California.]

Orton, 1966), the Fernald (1943) remedial training program, and the Frostig program for the development of visual perception (Frostig & Horne, 1964). Attention to social and emotional behaviors through behavior management programs, modeling, counseling, and other techniques also may help. Of course, physical and occupational therapists and other specialists often offer professional expertise that is central to the advancement of self-help and social behaviors.

The effectiveness of school psychologists depends largely upon their ability to work cooperatively with teachers. A true collegial relationship depends, in part, upon teachers and school psychologists viewing issues in similar ways and taking similar actions, given the same information. There is some information that suggests that school psychologists and teachers may be far apart on important issues and that mutual understanding and cooperation are, at best, distant goals toward which to work (Wickman, 1928; Shrupp & Gjerde, 1953; Hunter, 1957; Bower, 1960).

Recent research, however, provides evidence that teachers and psychologists may not be very far apart on the information they feel is important in understanding children and the kinds of special education decisions they would make, given the same information (Matuszek & Oakland, 1978). Teachers and psychologists were asked to read 106 case studies of pupils who differed in terms of 16 characteristics. After reading each case study, the teachers and psychologists recommended one of the following: a regular classroom, a regular classroom in which consultants are provided to the teacher, a regular classroom plus a resource room, a part-time special class for at least ½ hour each day, a full-time special class, or a special school setting.

Results suggest that teachers and psychologists generally make decisions on similar kinds of information. Both agree that achievement measured by classroom and standardized tests as well as IQ are important. They also agree that the child's ethnicity, language, values, anxiety, and class behavior, and relationships with peers, classmates, teachers, and other adults are relatively unimportant in making placement decisions. However, psychologists see socioeconomic status as important, whereas teachers do not. Teachers see adaptive behavior and self-concept as being important, but psychologists do not. Thus, teachers and psychologists tend to be consistent in identifying which characteristics in children are or are not important for determining special class placement.

Improving Diagnostic–Intervention Services

A central issue before education seems to be how diverse professional groups can work together more effectively and compatibly, pursuing common goals by providing different services. School boards, parents, and the general public are not particularly interested in the wording on our professional credentials. They are seeking—and demanding—better psychoeducational services. Problems facing education require committed, well-trained persons from diverse fields. The goal to establish strict territorial rights to certain areas may provide a sense of security for the moment but ultimately may forecast the group's demise. The goal to seek ways to improve our services is sounder and helps to ensure our survival.

The origin of school psychology lies in working with children of special needs. Examining the history of research in the field of mental retardation permits us to see the progress made in defining and identifying the mentally retarded, in developing humanistic services directed toward educational, vocational, and personal growth, and in establishing an attitude of "can do," not just "can't do." Similar developments are occurring with the learning disabled. Mainstreaming, least restrictive alternatives, Public Law 94-142, new assessment techniques, and research from the biological and social sciences are but some of the areas that presently give shape to these two fields. Our definitions for the mentally retarded and learning disabled are very arbitrary and continually changing. These changes cause problems throughout the fields and result in significant changes in incidence and prevalence estimates.

The fields are marked by many new developments, two of which are particularly important for school psychology—the new approaches to psychoneurology and adaptive behavior. Assessment programs are also being developed (i.e., SOMPA) that attempt to be particularly sensitive to issues associated with minority groups and that hopefully enable us to diagnose more accurately and to discover abilities masked by sociocultural and racial–ethnic factors.

School psychologists are participating in an important shift away from assessment for the purposes of classification toward diagnostic–intervention strategies that consider information on children's history and current characteristics and utilize this information to develop interventions that have some degree of success. We realize that we have legitimate roles after diagnosis, too.

Our effectiveness often is contingent on our ability to work cooperatively with parents, teachers, and other support personnel. School psychologists and teachers are close together on many important issues. Parents continue to look to school psychology for help and guidance. A central issue before education is how diverse professional groups and parents can work together more effectively and compatibly, pursuing common goals by providing different services. A major theme of this chapter is that school psychology can offer many unique and quality services for the mentally retarded and learning disabled.

References

Bijou, S. W. Theory and research in mental (developmental) retardation. *The Psychological Record,* 1963, **13,** 95–110.
Bower, E. *Early identification of emotionally handicapped children in school.* Springfield, Illinois: Charles C Thomas, 1960.

Becker, M., McCarthy, J., Chase, N., Converse, J., & Genieser, N. Computerized axial tomography of craniofacial malformations. *American Journal of Childhood Diseases*, 1976, **130**, 17–20.

Bender, L. Clinical study of one hundred schizophrenic children. *American Journal of Orthopsychiatry*, 1947, **17**(40).

Budoff, M. Measuring learning potential: An alternative to the traditional intelligence test. In G. R. Gredler (Ed.), *Ethical and legal factors in the practice of school psychology* (Proceedings of the First Annual Conference in School Psychology). Philadelphia: Temple University, 1972.

Buros, O. *The mental measurements yearbook.* Highland Park, New Jersey: Gryphon Press, 1965.

Cain, L., Levine, S., & Elzey, F. *Cain–Levine social competency scale.* Palo Alto, California: Consulting Psychologists Press, 1963.

Chalfant, J., & Scheffelin, M. *Central processing dysfunctions in children: A review of the research* (NINDS Monograph No. 9). Bethesda, Maryland: Department of Health, Education and Welfare, 1969.

Clements, S. D. *Minimal brain dysfunction in children* (Public Health Service Publications, No. 415). Washington, D.C.: U.S. Government Printing Office, 1966.

Conners, C. Drugs and LD—theoretical implications. In R. Knights & D. Bakkor (Eds.), *The neuropsychology of learning disorders.* Baltimore: University Park Press, 1976.

Cromwell, R. L., Blashfield, R. K., & Strauss, J. S. Criteria for classification systems. In N. Hobbs (Ed.), *Issues in the classification of children* (Vol. 1). San Francisco: Jossey-Bass, 1975.

Cruickshank, W. M., Bentzner, F. A., Ratzeberu, F. H., & Tannhausser, M. T. *A teaching method for brain-injured and hyperactive children.* Syracuse: Syracuse University Press, 1961.

Deno, E. Special education as developmental capital. *Exceptional Children*, 1970, **37**, 229–237.

Doll, E. A. *Measurement of social competence.* Circle Pines, Minnesota: American Guidance Service, 1953.

Doll, E. A historical survey of research and management of mental retardation in the United States. In E. P. Trapp & P. Himelstein (Eds.), *Readings on the exceptional child.* New York: Appleton-Century-Crofts, 1962.

Doll, E. *Vineland social maturity scale.* Circle Pines, Minnesota: American Guidance Service, 1965.

Doll, E. *Preschool attainment record.* Circle Pines, Minnesota: American Guidance Services, 1966.

Doll, E. (Ed.). Historical review of mental retardation, 1800–1965: A symposium. *American Journal of Mental Deficiency*, 1967, **72**, 165–189.

Dugdale, R. L. *The Jukes.* New York: Putnam, 1877.

Eisenson, J. *Examining for aphasia.* New York: The Psychological Corporation, 1954.

Farber, B. *Mental retardation: Its social context and social consequences.* Boston: Houghton Mifflin, 1968.

Federal Register, 1977, **42**(250).

Fernald, G. M. *Remedial techniques in basic school subjects.* New York: McGraw-Hill, 1943.

Fernald, G. M., & Keller, H. The effect of kinesthetic factors in the development of word recognition in the case of nonreaders. *Journal of Educational Research*, 1921, **4**, 355–377.

Fineberg, H., Bauman, R., & Sosman, M. Computerized cranial tomography. *Journal of the American Medical Association*, 1977, **238**(3), 224–227.

Folling, I. A. Ausscheidungen von phenylbrenztraubensaüre in den harn als stoffwech selanomalie in verbindung mit imbezillität. *Hoppe-Seyler's Zeitschr:f Für physiologische Chemie*, 1934, **227**, 169–176.

Foster, R. *Camelot behavioral checklist.* Parsons, Kansas: Camelot Behavioral Systems, 1974.

Frostig, M., & Horne, D. *The Frostig program for the development of visual perception.* Chicago: Follett, 1964.

Gazzoniga, M. *The bisected brain.* New York: Appleton-Century-Crofts, 1970.

Gillingham, A., & Stillman, B. W. *Remedial work of reading, spelling, and penmanship.* New York: Sachett & Wilhelms, 1936.

Gillingham, A., & Stillman, B. W. *Remedial training for children with specific disability in reading, spelling, and penmanship.* Cambridge, Massachusetts: Educational Publishing Service, 1965.

Goddard, H. H. *The Kallikak family: A study of the heredity of feeble-mindedness*. New York: MacMillan, 1912.

Goldman, D. A new computer test of the brain. *Psychology Today*, May 1976, 44–48.

Goldstein, K. *The organism*. New York: American Book, 1939.

Gridley, G., & Mastenbrook, J. *Research on the need for local norms for the ABIC*. Paper presented at the meeting of the American Psychological Association, San Francisco, 1977.

Grossman, H. H. (Ed.). *Manual on terminology and classification in mental retardation*. Washington, D.C.: American Association on Mental Deficiency, 1973.

Head, H. *Aphasia and kindred disorders of speech* (Vols. I and II). London: Cambridge University Press, 1926.

Hinshelwood, J. *Congenital word blindness*. London: Lewis, 1917.

Heber, R. F. A manual on terminology and classification in mental retardation. *American Journal of Mental Deficiency Monograph* (Prev. ed., Supp. 64), 1961.

Hobbs, N. *The futures of children*. San Francisco: Jossey-Bass, 1975.

Hughes, J. Biochemical and EEG correlates of LD. In R. Knights & D. Bakker (Eds.), *The neuropsychology of learning disorders*. Baltimore: University Park Press, 1976.

Hunter, E. Changes in teachers' attitudes toward children's behaviors over the last thirty years. *Mental Hygiene*, 1957, **41**, 3–11.

Kanner, L. *A history of the care and study of the mentally retarded*. Springfield, Illinois: Charles C Thomas, 1964.

Kephart, C. *The slow learner in the classroom*. Columbus, Ohio: Charles E. Merrill, 1960.

Kirk, S. A. *Teaching reading to slow children*. New York: Houghton Mifflin, 1940.

Kirk, S. A. *Educating exceptional children*. Boston: Houghton Mifflin, 1972.

Kirk, S. A., & Kirk, W. P. *Psycholinguistic learning disabilities: Diagnosis and remediation*. Urbana: University of Illinois Press, 1961.

Koppitz, E. *The Bender–Gestalt test for young children*. New York: Grune & Stratton, 1964.

Lambert, N., Windmiller, M., & Cole, L. *AAMD adaptive behavior scale* (public school version). Washington, D.C.: American Association on Mental Deficiency, 1974.

Levine, S., Elzey, F., & Lewis, M. *California preschool social competency scale*. Palo Alto, California: Consulting Psychologists Press, 1969.

MacMillan, D. L. *Mental retardation in school and society*. Boston: Little Brown, 1977.

McGinnis, M. A. *Aphasic children*. Washington, D.C.: Volta Bureau, 1963.

Matuszek, P., & Oakland, T. Factors influencing teachers' and psychologists' recommendations regarding special class placement. *Journal of School Psychology*, 1978, **00**, 000–000.

Mercer, J. R. The myth of 3% prevalence. In R. K. Eyman, C. E. Myers, & C. Tarjan (Eds.), *Sociobehavioral studies in mental retardation* (Monographs of the American Association on Mental Deficiency, No. 1). Washington, D. C.: American Association on Mental Deficiency, 1973.

Mercer, J. R. *System of multicultural pluralistic assessment*. Riverside: University of California, Riverside, 1977.

Mercer, J., & Lewis, J. *System of multicultural pluralistic assessment*. New York: The Psychological Corporation, 1978.

Mercer, J., & Ysseldyke, J. Designing diagnostic–intervention programs. In T. Oakland (Ed.), *Psychological and educational assessment of minority children*. New York: Brunner/Mazel, 1977.

Myklebust, H. R. Psychoneurological learning disorders in children. In S. A. Kirk & W. Becker (Eds.), *Conference on children with minimal brain impairment*. Urbana: University of Illinois, 1963.

Myklebust, H. R., & Boshes, B. *Minimal brain damage in children* (Final report, Contract 108-65-142, Neurological and Sensory Disease Control Program). Washington, D.C.: Department of Health, Education and Welfare, 1969.

National Advisory Committee on Handicapped Children. *Special education for handicapped children* (First annual report). Washington, D.C.: Department of Health, Education and Welfare, 1968.

Nihira, K., Foster, R., Shellhaas, M., & Leland, H. *AAMD adaptive behavior scale* (Rev. ed.). Washington, D.C.: American Association on Mental Deficiency, 1974.

Nowrey, J. E. A brief synopsis of mental deficiency. *American Journal of Mental Deficiency*, 1945, **49,** 319–357.

Oakland, T. *Pluralistic norms and estimated learning potential.* Paper presented at the meeting of the American Psychological Association, San Francisco, 1977.

Oakland, T. Research on the SOMPA. *School Psychology Digest*, **8**(2), 1979.

Oakland, T., & Laosa, L. Professional, legislative, and judicial influences on psychoeducational assessment practices in schools. In T. Oakland (Ed.), *Psychological and educational assessment of minority children.* New York: Brunner/Mazel, 1977.

Orton, S. T. *Reading, writing and speech problems in children.* New York: Norton, 1937.

Orton, J. L. The Orton–Gillingham approach. In J. Money (Ed.), *Disabled reader.* Baltimore: Johns Hopkins Press, 1966.

Osgood, C. E. *Method and theory in experimental psychology.* New York: University Press, 1953.

President's Committee on Mental Retardation. *Report to the President: A proposed program for national action to combat mental retardation.* Washington, D.C.: U.S. Government Printing Office, 1962.

President's Task Force on the Mentally Handicapped. *Action against mental disability.* Washington, D.C.: U.S. Government Printing Office, 1970.

Reitan, R., & Davison, L. (Eds.). *Clinical neuropsychology: Current status and applications.* New York: Wiley, 1974.

Sarwar, M. Computed cranial tomography: Experiences at the University of Texas Medical Branch. *Texas Medicine,* September 1977, **73,** 42–61.

Shrupp, M. & Gjerde, C. Teacher growth in attitudes toward behavior problems in children. *Journal of Educational Psychology*, 1953, **44,** 203–214.

Strauss, A., & Kephart, N. C. *Psychopathology and education of the brain injured child.* New York: Grune & Stratton, 1955.

Strauss, A., & Lehtinen, L. *Psychopathology and education of the brain injured child.* New York: Grune & Stratton, 1947.

Strauss, A., & Werner, H. Disorders of conceptual thinking in the brain-injured child. *Journal of Nervous and Mental Diseases*, 1942, **96,** 153–172.

Tarjan, G., Wright, S. W., Eyman, R. K., & Keeran, C. V. Natural history of mental retardation: Some aspects of epidemiology. *American Journal of Mental Deficiency*, 1973, **77,** 369–379.

United States Office of Education. *Estimated number of handicapped children in the United States, 1971–72.* Washington, D.C.: Author, 1972.

Wender, P. Possible biochemical bases for MBD. In R. Knights & D. Bakker (Eds.), *The neuropsychology of learning disorders.* Baltimore: University Park Press, 1976.

Wepman, J. M., Jones, L. V., Bock, R. D., & Van Pelt, P. Studies in aphasia: Background and theoretical formulations. *Journal of Speech and Hearing Disorders*, 1960, **25,** 323–332.

Wickman, E. *Children's behavior and teachers' attitudes.* New York: Commonwealth Fund, 1928.

Wiederholt, J. L. Historical perspectives on the education of the learning disabled. In L. Mann & D. Sabatino (Eds.), *The second review of special education.* Philadelphia: Journal of Special Education Press, 1974.

Williams, R. Scientific racism and I.Q.—the silent mugging of the black community. *Psychology Today*, 1974, **7**(12).

Wolfensberger, W. Diagnosis diagnosed. *Journal of Mental Subnormality*, 1965, **11,** 62–70.

KATHRYN CLARK GERKEN

Assessment of High-Risk Preschoolers and Children and Adolescents with Low-Incident Handicapping Conditions

A national goal set before us in 1975 by Public Law 94-142 (Abeson & Zettel, 1977; Ballard & Zettel, 1977) is to provide appropriate educational programs for all handicapped children by 1980. If the goal is to be attained, continued education of the public and the professionals who are expected to serve the handicapped must take place. Professional personnel from many disciplines must work together in an effort to screen, evaluate, and plan programs for children with handicapping conditions.

In 1977, the Bureau of Education for the Handicapped (BEH) reported that in the United States and its territories, 3.7 million children received special education and related services during the 1976–1977 school year. The high-incident handicapping conditions of speech impairment, mental retardation, and learning disabilities accounted for 82.8% of the total number of handicapped children. Within the area of mental retardation, there is a minority group for whom services within the public schools is a new phenomenon (Sontag, Smith, & Certo, 1977). This group is the severely/profoundly retarded who comprise approximately 3.3% of the retarded population. Thus, relative to the BEH report (1977), 32,067 severely/profoundly mentally retarded children received special educational services during the 1976–1977 school year. The BEH report makes it clear that there are other low-incidence groups within the handicapped population. There were 89,744 children with hearing impairments, 87,302 children

157

SCHOOL PSYCHOLOGY
Perspectives and Issues

with orthopedic impairments, and 38,464 children with visual impairments receiving some type of special service during the same year. In addition to those children who form a minority group because of their low-incident handicapping conditions, there is another minority group of handicapped children that requires special attention because of their age. The BEH report (1977) indicates that 11,800 infant to 2-year-olds and 196,287 3- to 5-year-olds received special services.

One could question the number of children who belong to low-incidence groups within special education because of the variability in reporting prevalence, incidence, and service statistics. Yet it does seem apparent that in the past there have been enough children in these categories to warrant special services, but not enough to guarantee the provision of trained personnel to provide the best possible services. Regardless of prevalence, high-risk preschoolers and children/ adolescents with low-incident handicapping conditions do present problems in assessment because of their age and type of handicap. Often, those who are supposed to provide special services in the schools are ill-equipped to provide such services. Many school psychologists who have not been trained to work with preschool children or children with low-incident handicapping conditions are expected to provide assessment and consultation services for these children. The purpose of this chapter is to provide guidelines for the appropriate assessment of these minority children. Hopefully, the guidelines will aid the school psychologist in the assessment process and the provision of optimal services.

Composition of the Groups

Definitions and classifications can be dangerous, yet they appear to be essential for communication. For the purposes of this chapter, the following adaptations of the definitions in the *Federal Register* (1977) will be used to delineate which children and adolescents are being discussed.

1. *Handicapped preschoolers* are handicapped children ages 3 through 5 (p. 42481).

2. *Hearing impaired,* or *deaf* students, have hearing impairments which are so severe that the child is impaired in processing linguistic information through hearing, with or without amplification, and which adversely affect educational performance. The term *hard of hearing* refers to a hearing impairment, either fluctuating or permanent, that adversely affects educational performance, but children who are hard of hearing would not be considered "deaf" (p. 42478).

3. *Visually impaired* refers to an impairment which, even with correction, adversely affects educational performance. Partially seeing and blind children are included under the definition of the visually handicapped (p. 42479).

4. *Orthopedically impaired* refers to severe orthopedic impairment that adversely affects a child's educational performance and includes impairments caused

by congenital anomalies, disease, and other causes. In this chapter, children with disabling orthopedic and neuromuscular impairment are discussed (p. 42478).

5. *Severely/profoundly mentally retarded.* A definition for the mentally retarded is given in the *Federal Register* (1977, p. 42478), but the severely/profoundly retarded are a minority group within the mentally retarded population who usually function intellectually four or more standard deviations below the mean on a standardized intelligence test (Robinson & Robinson, 1976, p. 24).

It is recognized that there are multihandicapped children and deaf–blind children who have concomitant impairments that make assessment a difficult task. However, assessment guidelines for the multihandicapped will not be presented.

The Ties that Bind the Group

The diversity of these groups of children is obvious, yet there are ties that bind them together. Each group member has an impairment and is in need of special services and/or education. Although special services and programs have been provided for the children with hearing, vision, and orthopedic impairments for some time, there has been a scarcity of skilled and knowledgeable school psychologists to provide services to the children in the schools. High-risk preschoolers and severely/profoundly retarded children are new additions to school populations and few psychologists have adequate knowledge or skills to work with them.

One reason for the psychologists' lack of knowledge and skills has been a neglect or de-emphasis of these areas in many school psychology training programs. Bardon and Wenger's (1976) survey of training programs indicated that "needs of exceptional children" was listed by only 17 of 140 graduate programs as one of the three most important emphases in the program. When school psychologists have had coursework in special education, it has usually been a survey course on exceptional children or introductory courses in mental retardation and/or learning disabilities. Even though school psychologists are usually involved in the assessment of every handicapped child in the schools, they may have very limited knowledge and experience concerning the handicapping condition. This is especially true of the preschool and low-incidence handicapped children discussed in this chapter (Bauman, 1968; Levine, 1974; Mittler, 1970; Seaton, 1975).

One reason for the lack of emphasis in the training programs is the small number of children who fall within these categories. Programs by necessity emphasize the knowledge and skills the psychologist will be using daily. It may not be feasible to train all psychologists to be competent in working with all children. However, it is a necessity that some psychologists be trained in these specific areas. The ethical codes promulgated by the American Psychological Association (APA) in 1977 and the National Association of School Psychologists (NASP) in 1976 have always included principles regarding competency and the provision of services. However, neither APA nor NASP could ensure competency. A series of court rulings, consent agreements, and Public Law 94-142 (1975; Abeson & Zettel, 1977; Ballard & Zettel, 1977) have now mandated that the competencies needed to work with these children be attained. The National Association for Retarded Citizens (1974) issued a statement concerning the competencies of school psychologists who work with mentally retarded individuals. Levine (1976) initiated and spearheaded the first National Conference of Psychological Workers with the Deaf in 1975 where special competencies needed by psychologists were listed. The state of Iowa has delineated the functions and competencies of school psychologists who work with high-risk preschoolers, hearing impaired, emotionally disabled, chronically disruptive, or severely/profoundly retarded children and adolescents.

Another strong tie that binds this diverse group together, as well as the school psychologists who attempt to provide services for them, is the paucity of reliable, valid, and useful assessment instruments. In the areas of hearing, vision, and orthopedic impairment, the market for appropriate instruments is very small, thus testing corporations have not invested large amounts of time and money in test development. Modifications of the "best sellers" are used most often along with ad hoc instruments developed by individuals. Preschool assessment instruments were developed from the mid-1960s on because of the emphasis on compensatory education. However, many of these instruments were developed with little regard to accepted standards of technical adequacy.

Problems caused by communications gaps and the attitudes of others are also common to the diverse groups of children discussed in this chapter. Communication is necessary for valid assessment, yet it may be limited by specific impairments that the children have and/or by the psychologist's inability to understand and use varied means of communication. Both positive and negative attitudes toward the disabled have been attributed to society (Burgemeister, 1962; Chesler, 1965; Comer & Pilavin, 1975; Kleck, Ono, & Hastorf, 1966; Wright, 1960) and both seem to affect the functioning of the disabled.

Common Needs

The concern with appropriate assessment of exceptional children is not new (Weiner, 1967). The goal of assessment should be to acquire relevant information that will contribute to decisions about interventions for cognitive and/or social behaviors. Diagnoses and predictions that end in attaching labels without effective interventions are useless. Assessment must be viewed as a continuous process that leads up to effective interventions for children. The basic assumptions underlying assessment described by Newland (1971) and Ysseldyke (Chapter 4 of this volume) have often been disregarded in services provided to these groups. The need to meet all assumptions and to provide descriptions and specific prescriptions is essential. There is dissatisfaction with the currently available tests and techniques. However, a multifactorial approach to assessment that includes systematic and nonsystematic observational procedures (Anastasi, 1976; Boehm & Weinberg, 1977; Cartwright & Cartwright, 1974; Weiner, 1967) results in precise and useful information. The complete assessment should include the significant others in the child/adolescent's life, historical information, general and specific medical reports, behavioral observations in various settings, multiple assessment instruments, consultation, and intervention–treatment.

The Challenge for School Psychologists

LaVor's (1977) review of federal legislation for exceptional children provides a historical perspective of the programs and funds that have been provided to assist exceptional children. It is apparent that during the nineteenth century federal laws for the handicapped were primarily designed to meet the problems of specific disability groups, such as the "deaf" and "blind." However, these services were usually provided out of the "mainstream" in state-operated or state-supported residential schools. With the enactment of the Elementary and Secondary Education Act (ESEA) in 1965 and the amendment in 1966 to establish the Bureau of Education for the Handicapped (BEH), funds were provided for the expansion of state services to meet the educational and related needs of handicapped children. In 1968, experimental preschool programs for the handicapped were established, the forerunners to later services for preschoolers. The original versions of the Vocational Rehabilitation Act, 93-112, was vetoed as was its successor in 1973. However, a significant revision of the act resulted in a powerful charge to the public and to those who served handicapped individuals (Abeson & Zettel, 1977; Ballard & Zettel, 1977; LaVor, 1977).

Section 504 of the bill outlawed discrimination against handicapped individuals. The first priority for rehabilitation services was to be given to those individuals with the most severe handicaps. The Education Amendments of 1974, Public Law 93-380, increased the authorization level of funding for handicapped children and moved toward guaranteeing rights to the children and parents (Abeson & Zettel, 1977; LaVor, 1977). These laws paved the way for Public Law 94-142 (1975), which requires that appropriate service be provided for all handicapped children (Abeson & Zettel, 1977; Ballard & Zettel, 1977; *Federal Register,* 1977; LaVor, 1977). Certain aspects of this law apply directly to high-risk preschoolers and children and adolescents with low-incident handicapping conditions (see Monroe, Chapter 2 of this volume). Especially relevant is Section 121a.532(c) which states that:

> Tests are selected and administered so as best to ensure that when a test is administered to a child with impaired sensory, manual, or speaking skills, the test results accurately reflect the child's aptitude or achievement level or whatever other factors the test purports to measure, rather than reflecting the child's impaired sensory,

manual, or speaking skills (except where those skills are the factors which the test purports to measure) [*Federal Register,* 1977, p. 42496].

If these guidelines are followed, there should be a resultant decrease in inappropriate labeling and placement. Public Law 94-142 now requires what ethical standards have always proposed. Psychologists and others cannot close their eyes to the challenge, nor should they take refuge in the fact that the passage of a law does not guarantee that the intent or objectives of the law will be met. Classification and grouping of children may be necessary for communication and funding, but they are not sufficient for meeting the minimum standards established by Public Law 94-142 and for providing the best possible services to children. Psychologists working in the schools can no longer expect to be men and women for all seasons, continuing to test all types of exceptional children of all ages without specific training to do so. Inservice training is one aspect of Public Law 94-142 that psychologists and other school personnel should demand be carried out. The courts will no longer allow the schools and school personnel to plead ignorance as an excuse for negligence. The psychologist in the schools has a responsibility beyond testing, and if he/she cannot perform assessment that complies with the standards set forth in the law, arrangements should be made for someone else to do so.

The psychologist who complies with the ethical standards of the profession and the legal mandates in Public Law 94-142, will contribute effectively as a team member in preventive and child-find programs, assessment, intervention, consultation, counseling and program design, and evaluation.

Preschool Handicapped

A growing awareness of the importance of early childhood experiences has resulted in an emphasis on educational programming for the preschool child (Haskins, Finkelstein, & Stedman, 1978; Hodges, Lapides, & Phillips, 1977). BEH included early childhood education as one of its target areas for the 1970s. Its stated objective was "to secure the enrollment by 1978 of 850,000 (85%) preschool aged handicapped children in federal, state, and local educational day care [Soeffing, 1974, p. 437]." The inclusion of programming for handicapped preschool children along with an incentive grant in Public Law 94-142 is further proof that the public has recognized the need for early intervention programs.

As a result of the emphasis placed on programming for preschool children, emphasis is also being placed on the use of assessment procedures with these children. Herein lies a major problem, since uncertainty and controversy abound in relation to the assessment of preschoolers. A perusal of test catalogs and the professional literature reveals that numerous preschool screening instruments such as checklists, inventories, and tests have been developed and used by specialists in different disciplines. The abundance of preschool assessment techniques has been viewed by some professionals as a welcome solution to their lack of knowledge and skill in working with handicapped preschool children. Tests are used to perform the diagnosis and prescription. Even if these tests did meet the basic assumptions of reliability and validity, sole reliance on tests has always been ethically inappropriate and is now illegal.

School psychologists and others who work with preschool children soon find out that it is a long way from infancy to 5 years. It is mandatory that the school psychologist obtain a thorough knowledge of typical and atypical child development and have practicum experiences with typical and atypical preschoolers before beginning assessment of preschool children. Assessment with preschoolers requires demonstrated skill in gathering data within the home, school, and other environments. It is not necessary for the psychologists to gather all data, but they must know what data are needed and how they can be obtained. The following outline is suggested as a sequential guide to data gathering:

1. Conduct interviews with the parent or guardian to gather historical and current data relative to development, health, and environmental factors.
2. Obtain pertinent information from all other agents or agencies who have been in contact with the child.
3. Obtain current medical assessment including vision and hearing testing.
4. Conduct systematic observations of the child in various settings over time.
5. Administer formal and informal tests as indicated by data collected in 1–4.
6. Conduct a staff meeting that includes all participants in the assessment process. Describe the child and provide a useful prescription.

The psychologist should be involved in the entire assessment process, but items 4 and 5 necessitate that the psychologist have knowledge of and be able to select appropriate assessment instruments and techniques.

Early studies of mental development concluded that infant tests were limited as predictors of later intelligence (Bayley, 1949), and more recent reviews still indicate that the test performances of preschoolers are generally quite variable and have limited predictive validity except for children within the lowest ranges of intellectual development (Gallagher & Bradley, 1972; Rutter, 1970; Thomas, 1970; Uzgiris & Hunt, 1975; Werner, Honzik, & Smith, 1968). These data certainly raise questions concerning the reliability and validity of preschool assessment instruments in general. One must attempt to evaluate the plethora of assessment instruments and techniques that are currently available before using them. There are screening, diagnostic, and prescriptive instruments for infants, up to 2 years old, and nursery children 2–5 years old. There are instruments that have been developed specifically for handicapped children, but the majority have not. The content of the instruments for ages up to 2 years is simple, readily observable motor actions, whereas the instruments for ages 3–5 years usually measure communication, motor, cognitive, self-help, and preacademic skills. A thorough assessment should utilize more than one type of instrument, and the end result should be an individualized program for a child. Since evaluations of most of the current instruments are available, there will be no attempt to evaluate specific instruments in this chapter. However, the appendix to this chapter lists the resources for assessment which include information on these instruments.

Hearing Impaired

Information concerning the psychology of deafness and the need for appropriate psychological testing of children, adolescents, and adults who are hearing impaired has been available since 1960 (Levine, 1960, 1974, 1975; Myklebust, 1960; Vernon, 1967; Vernon & Brown, 1964). Yet Levine (1974) and Seaton (1975) conducted surveys that make it all too clear that school psychologists and others who are currently working with hearing impaired clients do not have adequate academic training or practical experience. Many persons are unfamiliar with the needs of the hearing impaired, are often unable to communicate with the client, and generally are incapable of using any assessment instrument other than those developed for the hearing. There is general agreement (Levine, 1975; Reed, 1970) that the psychologist who works with deaf clients must be prepared to deal with a range of abilities and potentials that are often hidden behind a unique communication barrier. "To penetrate the barrier and get to the individual demands unusual skills and exceptional competencies [Levine, 1976, p. 290]." If school psychologists are going to work with children/adolescents with hearing impairments, they can ask no less of themselves than to obtain these competencies.

The greatest single handicap that results from hearing loss during the prelingual years is the barrier to learning language. If language remains unlearned, communication with the rest of the world becomes a problem. Special education services and programs can ameliorate the impact of hearing loss on communication to some extent, but this remains the most serious problem. Schlesinger and Meadow (1972) have used Erickson's developmental model to assess the impact of deafness on the passage through the life cycle. It appears that cognitive and social development are influenced not only by the communication and experiential restrictions imposed by deafness itself, but also by the attitudes and reactions of the individual and significant others.

Reviews of the literature concerning the intellectual ability of children with hearing impairments reveal inconsistencies (Darbyshire & Reeves, 1969; Meyerson, 1963). At one point, being deaf carried with it the connotation of retardation. However, Hess (1969) and Mindel and Vernon (1971) report that deafness per se does not affect IQ scores on performance-type tests. The conclusion regarding the impact of deafness on intellectual ability is dependent on the kind of research, definition of intelligence, and type of test used.

Almost universally, the achievement testing of hearing impaired children indicates below normal functioning with the absolute amount of educational retardation increasing with age (Bonvillian, Charrow, & Nelson, 1973; Meyerson, 1963). The child who is deaf or hard of hearing is unable to progress in the normal sequence of mastery of language, which is comprehending, speaking, reading, and writing; thus, the major academic problems are in reading, writing, and spelling. The hearing impaired child with a mild loss may have a 1- to 3-year academic delay, whereas only 5% of the children in schools for the deaf attain a tenth-grade or above achievement level, and 30% are considered functionally illiterate. The general curriculum objectives for the hearing impaired are *not* different from those for the hearing, but different techniques are used to meet the objectives. Although there is still considerable debate among the educators over educational placement of hearing impaired children and the method of communication (Davis, 1977; Meyerson, 1963; Reed, 1970), there is no debate over the need to begin the educational program as soon as possible.

Research on the relationship between personality and hearing impairment is also contradictory. Early studies indicated many hearing impaired individuals exhibited a greater degree of emotional disability and social maladjustment. Levine and Wagner (1974) found that the deaf subjects with the greatest linguistic handicap were those with the greatest psychological handicap. However, Levine (1975) reports that most of the research was conducted on small undifferentiated groups, the instruments used to assess personality characteristics were designed for and standardized on hearing subjects, and the researchers were unfamiliar with the deaf population and generally unable to communicate with the deaf. Adjustment patterns of deaf individuals are a result of an interaction between environmental factors and hearing loss. Extreme caution should be taken in drawing conclusions about social and emotional adjustment in view of confounding factors present in most studies. The findings on the social–emotional adjustment of hard-of-hearing children resemble the findings on the hearing population (Meyerson, 1963).

The fact that fewer deaf individuals are employed in higher professional, managerial, clerical, and sales areas than the general population may be due to the need for greater verbal communication in these jobs, but it may also be due to attitudes of the individual and the public. The degree to which communication, language, and educational level approach normal is a major consideration in the job market. It may be necessary for psychologists and educators to spend some of their time effecting attitude changes in order to counteract the underemployment problems of the hearing impaired.

To be an effective member of a team that works with hearing impaired individuals, the psychologist not only needs to understand the impact the hearing impairment has on communication, intellectual, academic, and emotional functioning, but must also have knowledge of the medical and audiological implications of the hearing impairment. What is the degree of loss? Is the loss permanent or fluctuating? Is it a conductive or sensori–neural loss? Is there a treatment for the loss? Is amplification desirable; if so, what type? Vernon's (1976) report on multiply handicapped deaf individuals makes it very clear that the etiology of the hearing impairment may be a necessary factor to consider when planning an educational program.

The studies of characteristics of hearing impaired children/adolescents are very difficult to interpret because the studies have usually been conducted with children from special schools or special classes without clear delineation of the population. Thus, although a psychologist should be aware of the literature concerning the psychology of deafness, the heterogeneity of the group requires that the psychologist be sensitive to each hearing impaired person as an individual. The academic and social/emotional needs of the individuals are dependent on many variables other than loss of hearing. One of these variables is the communication skills of the individual and other persons in his/her environment. A well-known but frequently ignored fact is that psychologists who work with the hearing impaired need to be able to communicate with their clients. The results and interpretations of tests given to hearing impaired individuals by a psychologist not experienced in communicating with or assessing hearing impaired individuals are often in error. The skill of communication is of major import and a precursor to actual assessment (Darbyshire & Reeves, 1969; Levine, 1971, 1975, 1976; Mindel & Vernon, 1971; Reed, 1970; Vernon, 1976; Vernon & Brown, 1964). The use of an interpreter who expresses the psychologist's directions in finger spelling and sign language is questionable. Ideally, the interpreter should be knowledgeable about psychological testing, psychology of deafness, and assessment procedures (Levine, 1975, 1976).

Assessment

The following seven considerations are thought to underlie effective psychological evaluation of children/adults with hearing impairment (Vernon, 1967, 1974, 1976; Vernon & Brown, 1964).

1. To be valid, the measure of intelligence must be a nonverbal, performance-type instrument.
2. The scores on preschool and primary school hearing impaired children are unreliable.
3. There is more danger in a low IQ score being wrong than a high one.
4. There is greater error present in tests given by a psychologist not experienced with hearing impaired individuals.
5. One should administer more than one performance scale to determine level of functioning.
6. The results of untimed tests are usually more valid.
7. Group testing should be used only as a gross screening device.

Levine (1971, 1976) suggests that psychologists working with hearing impaired individuals must not only display the usual professional competencies, but also demonstrate specific competencies in communicating with and assessing this population. Yet, these are the two areas that Levine (1974) and Seaton (1975) found to be major problems for the psychologists working with the hearing impaired.

Although the specific assessment procedure to be followed is determined by the individual's needs and the intended purpose of assessment, certain information should be obtained for a complete multidisciplinary, multicriteria assessment of hearing impaired individuals. In addition to the usual areas included in the multifactored assessment, particular attention should be devoted to communication status, vocational factors, social participation, and medical and audiological information. What appears to be of major import is the knowledge the examiner brings to a setting concerning hearing impaired individuals and the ability to use that knowledge to appropriately interpret assessment information. It is this knowledge and the associated communication skills that separate the effective psychologist from the noneffective.

In 1963, Levine (1971) conducted a rigorous search of the United States and various foreign countries for tests that had been specifically standardized on the deaf. The search uncovered 11 tests, 9 of which were intelligence tests. A search in 1978 would reveal few changes. The evaluations of the instruments that are commonly used with the hearing impaired reveal the following:

1. There are no formal language tests that have norms for the hearing impaired.

2. The most appropriate learning ability test would be a nonlanguage performance test that has been standardized on hearing impaired children. The Hiskey–Nebraska Test of Learning Aptitude has been the most appropriate test available in the United States. Recently the WISC-R Performance Scale was also standardized for deaf children (Anderson & Sisco, 1977).

3. The Stanford and Metropolitan achievement tests have norms for hearing impaired and there are other tests that are easily adapted.

4. There are no personality/behavior tests with norms for hearing impaired, but research using the Missouri Children's Picture Series and the Behavior Problem Checklist with hearing impaired subjects has been reported (Reivich & Rothrock, 1972; Vegely, 1971).

5. The use of observation and behavior rating scales seems more appropriate when assessing hearing impaired individuals than the use of projective drawings and tests.

6. Appropriate vocational instruments measuring dexterity, specific aptitudes, and interests are available.

7. There has been little use of social competency/adaptive behavior scales with hearing impaired individuals other than the Vineland Social Maturity Scale, which is outdated.

8. A review of the various modifications suggested for intelligence tests indicates the effects of the modifications are unknown or they result in a lower IQ score than if the subtests were administered using total communication.

The sources for listings and evaluative comments regarding the tests being used with hearing impaired individuals are provided in the appendix at the end of the chapter.

Visually Impaired

The classification of visual impairment encompasses a diverse group of people. There are many types of visual defects, and the school psychologist is not expected to have a thorough understanding of each, but a general knowledge of what the defects mean to the child/adolescent is necessary. Each defect may create different difficulties. Knowledge of the defect will be helpful in understanding the individual's needs and in turn will help establish an individualized educational program. In order to provide appropriate assessment, knowledge concerning functional vision is as important as knowledge of visual acuity. Etiology and age of onset are also important considerations. Lowenfeld (1973) reports that children who lost their sight before 5–7 years of age generally do not retain useful visual imagery nor any idea of color. The sudden onset of blindness versus a gradual onset may also have differential effects.

Blindness may cause limitations in three important areas of cognitive functioning: (a) in the range and variety of experiences; (b) in mobility; and (c) in the interaction with the environment (Lowenfeld, 1971, 1975). Studies of intellectual ability indicate that the percentage of blind children functioning in the average and superior ranges is lower, and a larger percentage are functioning in the defective range. However, the distribution of scores is not significantly different from normal on tasks that use the auditory vocal or haptic motor channels. Favorable opportunities for learning appear to be more important than degree of blindness, intelligence, or socioeconomic status in determining level of functioning (Norris, Spaulding, & Brodie, 1957). Norris et al. (1957) also suggest that under favorable conditions the blind child can develop into an independent, fully functioning child whose use of potential would compare favorably to that of most sighted children. Others have posited a less favorable picture and cite results from the 1940s that indicated that blind children were behind their sighted peers in achievement (Ashcroft, 1963; Hayes, 1941; Lowenfeld, 1945, 1963). Langan's (1970) history of the assessment of visually impaired persons as well as Bauman's reviews of assessment instruments (Bauman, 1968, 1971, 1972a, 1972b, 1973, 1974, 1976) make it clear that there were few appropriate assessment instruments available when most of the early studies on blindness and cognition were conducted. Thus, cautious interpretation should be made of such studies.

Lowenfeld's (1971, 1975) historical review reveals perceptions of blind people as helpless and dependent. There is a plethora of literature describing the personality and social characteristics of the blind, but actual research is limited. It is interesting to note that some of the dependency behavior noted in the blind child (Imamura, 1965) seems to disappear by adolescence or adulthood or can be accounted for by environmental expectations (Lukoff & Whiteman, 1970). Lowenfeld (1971) reports that emotional disturbance and maladjustment may result more frequently from the conditions and social attitudes in the environment than from the visual handicap itself. A significant study (Cowen, Underberg, Verrillo, & Benham, 1961) investigated the relationship of parental behavior to adjustment of blind adolescents and compared the adjustment of blind and sighted adolescents. The three groups of adolescents were blind residential school students, blind public school students, and sighted public school students. For all three groups, a high degree of parental understanding correlated consistently and significantly with good adjustment. However, there was no significant relationship between maternal attitudes and adjustment of adolescents nor any systematic or consistent differences in personality attributes or adjustment among the three groups of adolescents. Jervis (1959) found no significant difference in self-concepts of blind and sighted adolescents. The major difference in the latter two studies and earlier studies was that Jervis (1959) and Cowen *et al.* (1961) developed instruments directly applicable to visually impaired adolescents. Tests of personality assessment of the seeing are of questionable value when used with blind individuals. The relationship between blindness and personality and social factors can best be summarized as follows: There appear to be no essential and consistent differences in blind and sighted adolescents as a group. Also, behavioral studies provide increasing evidence that blindness, if uncomplicated by other disorders of an organic or environmental nature, does not cause developmental disturbances (Lowenfeld, 1971).

Pitner, Eisenson, & Stanton's review of literature concerning partially sighted children in 1941 revealed that little was known about the children and the effects their visual impairment had on development. Lowenfeld (1971) reports that conditions have changed very little. Part of the reason for the lack of research seems to be that for most practical purposes, the children function as seeing children with only slight deviations. Differences in cognition have not been substantiated, and the most significant educational effect appears to be underachievement. It is apparent that differentiation within the heterogeneous group labeled visually impaired is necessary in future research efforts that attempt to connect specific behavior with visual impairment.

Assessment

The goals of assessment with visually impaired children/adolescents are the same as those for sighted individuals. The same factors in the assessment process

TABLE 6.1

Instrument	Age range	Norms for visually impaired	No modification necessary	Easily modified	Difficult to modify	Evaluated by Bauman[a]
Learning ability						
1. Verbal measures						
a. Wechsler Verbal Scales	4–12			WAIS WISC	WPPSI	X
b. Interim Hayes–Binet	7–12	X	X			Dated items X
2. Performance measures						
a. Blind Learning Aptitude Test	7–17	X	X			Limited information X
b. Wechsler Performance Scale	4–adult				X	X
c. Nonlanguage learning test	Preschool–adult	X	X			X
d. Haptic Intelligence	16–adult	X	X			Needs revision X
e. Stanford–Kohs Block Design Test	16–adult	X	X			X
f. Vocational Intelligence Scale for the Adult Blind	16–adult	X	X			X
g. Tactual Reproduction Pegboard	16–adult	X	X			Not commercially available
Aptitude and proficiency tests						
1. Manual dexterity						
a. Minnesota Rate of Manipulation	10–adult	X	X			X
b. Penn Bi-manual Work Samples	10–adult	X	X			X
c. Crawford Small Parts Dexterity Tests	10–adult	X	X			X
d. Form Boards		X	X			X

	Age range				American Printing House for the Blind
2. Others					
a. Roughness Discrimination Test	Preschool–adult	X	X		X
b. Scholastic Aptitude Test	Jr. & sr. high		Adapted		X
c. Tactile Analogue of Boehm Test of Basic Concepts	Kdg.–grade 3		Adapted		X
Achievement tests					
1. Stanford Achievement Tests	Elem. & sec. school		Adapted		X
2. Sequential Tests of Educational Progress	Elem. & sec. school		Adapted		X
Social competency					
1. Maxfield–Buchholz Social Maturity Scale	0–6	X	X		X
2. Overbrook Social Competency Scale	Through young adult	X	X		X
Personality					
1. Questionnaires					
a. Emotional Factors Inventory	Adults	X	X		X
b. Adolescent Emotional Factors Inventory		X	X		X
2. Auditory Projective Test	Adult	X	X		X
3. Sound Test	16–adult	X	X		X
Measures of interest					
1. Kuder Preference	Adolescents–adults			X	X
2. California Occupational Interest Inventory	Adolescents–adults			X	X
3. Strong Vocational Interest Blank	Adolescents–adults			X	X
4. Bauman's PRG Interest Inventory	Adolescents–adults	X	X		X

[a]See 1968, 1972, 1973, 1974, and 1976 references.

must be considered, but with the addition of information on the cause, degree, and onset of the visual impairment and the current condition of the eye.

Langan (1970) reports that there are few administration problems that cannot be remedied when assessing a *partially sighted* child as long as consideration is given to the factors cited previously. Margach and Kern (1969) recommend techniques in administration and interpretation of the WISC for partially sighted children. However, it should be noted that there are varied opinions as to the usefulness of instruments that have been modified (Parker, 1969) and as to whether or not modifications destroy validity.

Bauman (1968) sent questionnaires to every known psychologist working with blind people in the United States and Canada in order to find out what tests were being used and how they were evaluated. The results of her study revealed that most respondents had little training and experience in evaluating visually impaired individuals; half of them saw fewer than 10 blind clients per year. Bauman also found that psychologists generally use the instruments for nonhandicapped when assessing blind individuals. The need to depart from the usual directions, and the fact that the instruments were not standardized on blind populations, may reduce the reliability and validity of the instruments. Observation of a child/adolescent should always be included in the assessment process, and when reliable and valid assessment instruments are not available, observation assumes more importance (Norris *et al.*, 1957).

Tillman's (1973) review of the use of intelligence scales with the blind further supports the importance of observational data. Psychologists should be cautious in making predictions about blind children based on the use of the WISC. Skills in assessment of environments and ability to differentiate between failures of the child and failures of the environment are necessary. A new test of general intelligence, which has been standardized on visually impaired and sighted children is needed as well as predictive validity studies of the Wechsler Verbal Scales with visually impaired.

Bauman (1971, 1972b, 1973, 1974, 1976) offers comprehensive guidelines for psychological and educational assessment of blind students and provides evaluative information concerning the instruments that are available. Bauman suggests that a useful guideline in the testing situation is to tell the blind person all pertinent information that a seeing person would naturally obtain through sight. Available test batteries at the preschool, school, and vocational levels as well as detailed discussions of tests that are unique to the evaluation of the blind are discussed by Bauman (1974). Table 6.1 lists most of the tests that are commonly used with blind individuals. References to Bauman's work as well as references to other resources are provided in the appendix at the end of the chapter.

Orthopedically Impaired

Understanding the medical aspects of orthopedic and/or neuromuscular impairment is a prerequisite to good psychological services. Information on etiology, age at onset, scope of involvement, neurological component (if any), and prognosis are all important to a full understanding of the person.

There are excellent resources that review what is currently known concerning the psychological aspects of orthopedic impairments (McDaniel, 1969; Mittler, 1970; Wright, 1960). However, it is clear that there is little *empirical research* concerning the psychological effects of physical disabilities. Depending on the nature and severity of orthopedic impairment, limitations may result in communication, perception, locomotion, dexterity, body image, self-concept, and intellectual functioning. However, these variables interact with early experiences, attitudes of significant others, and cultural attitudes to produce a wide range of individual differences within this group. Significant factors in overall adjustment are the expectancies and attitudes of the handicapped and others that influence social and vocational activities (Klapper & Birch, 1966).

It appears that negative and inconsistent attitudes of others make the goal of sound mental health difficult to attain. Freedman's (1967) comprehensive review indicates environmental factors are at least as important as the handicap itself in the genesis of emotional disturbances. The physically disabled individual may be more vulnerable to emotional and behavioral problems. However, available research indicates that as a group, the physically disabled to not differ qualitatively from normals in adjustment. Wright (1960) found no substantial evidence that the physically impaired differ from normals in general adjustment. When lower adjustment scores are reported for physically impaired persons, they may be attributable to inappropriate measurement instruments. Furthermore, no clear evidence of an association between type of disability and specific personality characteristics has been established. Wright's major conclusion was that the physically disabled are a heterogeneous group and that it is not the impairment per se that affects personality, but the attitude toward the impairment.

The psychologist who is involved in the assessment of orthopedically impaired children/adolescents must be concerned about what the impaired person will do when he/she completes formal education and must adjust in a world that seldom makes allowances for disabilities. The preparation for the world of work must be part of the orthopedically impaired individual's first individualized educational program, as well as the last. The psychologist who is unaware of the interaction effects of impairment, psychological and social adjustment, educational experiences, vocational opportunities, and internal and external attitudes on total adjustment will not contribute fully to the assessment process. Also, the psychologist must have enough contact and experiences with orthopedically impaired children/adolescents to be aware of his/her own attitudes before becoming involved in the assessment of orthopedically impaired children.

Assessment

Assessment of the orthopedically impaired child should take place as early in the child's life as possible. It should be a continuous process that is multicompo-

TABLE 6.2
Assessment Instruments that Are Used with Orthopedically Impaired Children/Adolescents

Instrument	Age range	Norms for physically handicapped	No modification necessary	Easily modified	Difficult to modify	Evaluation source
Adaptive behavior scales						
1. 18 different scales	0–adult					Coulter & Morrow, 1977
2. 136 checklists	0–adult					Walls, 1977
Intelligence–learning ability						
1. Ammons & Ammons Full Range Picture Vocabulary Test	2–adult			X		Allen & Collins, 1955
2. Cattell Infant Intelligence Scale	3–30 months					Katz, 1955
3. Columbia Mental Maturity Scale	3–6 to 9–11 years		X			Anastasi, 1976; Allen & Collins, 1955; Reynell, 1970; Sattler, 1974
4. French's Pictorial Test of Intelligence	3–8		X			Allen & Collins, 1955; Sattler, 1974
5. Gesell Developmental Schedules	0–8 years				X	
6. Leiter International Performance Scale	2–18			X		Allen & Collins, 1955; Anastasi, 1976; Sattler, 1974; Sattler & Tozier, 1970;

Test	Age range	Adapted			References
7. Peabody Picture Vocabulary Test	2½–18		X		Anastasi, 1976; Conner et al., 1971; Reynell, 1970; Sattler, 1974; Sattler & Anderson, 1973
8. Porteus Mazes	3–12 years, year 14, adult				Allen & Collins, 1955; Anastasi, 1976
9. Raven's Progressive Matrices	6–11	Adapted			Allen & Collins, 1955; Reynell, 1970; Sattler & Tozier, 1970
10. Stanford–Binet	2–6, 2–adult		X		Katz, 1955, 1958; Sattler, 1974; Sattler & Anderson, 1973; Sattler & Tozier, 1970
11. WISC					
a. Verbal scale	5–0 to 15–11		X		Reynell, 1970; Sattler, 1974
b. Performance scale				X	
Visual–motor perception					
1. Marble Board		Adapted			Conner et al., 1971
2. WISC—Block Design Subtest	5–15				Conner et al., 1971; Sattler & Peters, 1964
3. Custom Battery		Adapted			
Achievement					
No specific tests listed					
Behavior/personality					
MMPI	16–adult	Adaptation possible			Taylor, 1970

nent and multidisciplinary. Knowledge of the child/adolescent's ability to respond and evaluation of vision, hearing, speech, sitting balance, arm and hand use are all prerequisites to formal assessment (Sattler, 1974). Very few instruments have been normed on orthopedically impaired individuals, thus, there is little knowledge on the effects of modifications on the obtained results. Most examiners create their own tests rendering the norms useless. The results of the available studies on the effects of modifications have been equivocal (Sattler, 1974; Sattler & Tozier, 1970). However, there is evidence to suggest that the time limits and procedures of unmodified tests underestimate ability in direct proportion to the severity of handicap, reflecting the extensiveness of the handicap rather than level of intellectual or cognitive ability (Sattler & Tozier, 1970). Studies are needed that include both normal and handicapped children when evaluating the effects of modifications. Improved ways of modifying as well as new methods of assessment are also needed. Correlational studies that only indicate the relationship between modified and unmodified instrumentation are not sufficient. There can be high correlations between test results, yet significant differences for individuals. Table 6.2 contains information and resources about assessment instruments that are used with orthopedically impaired individuals and the appendix at the end of the chapter contains a list of resources.

Severely and Profoundly Mentally Retarded

Public school personnel were not prepared to serve severely and profoundly mentally retarded individuals prior to the litigation that brought about public education for this group, and many are still not prepared. The educational, psychological, and health services usually offered in the schools are not sufficient to meet the needs of this new population. The majority of these students have neurological damage that limits intellectual functioning and many adaptive behaviors. The lack of sufficient services should not be viewed as gross negligence on the part of the school personnel. These professionals face questions that were not discussed in most training programs before the 1970s and for which there are no easy answers.

In recent years the American Association for the Education of the Severely/ Profoundly Handicapped was founded and many training programs for school personnel and educational programs for children were established (Haring, 1976; Haring & Brown, 1976; Sontag, Smith, & Certo, 1977). However, there is still a need for trained personnel, and specifically personnel who have been trained in assessment. The results of a survey by Lynch, Shoemaker, and White (1976) revealed that 76% of the respondents desired further training in measurement and evaluation techniques with this group. Most educators and psychologists are aware that appropriate assessment of the severely/profoundly retarded requires a total team approach to assessment, including a medical/health consultant, a physical and/or occupational therapist, a speech/communication clinician, a psychologist/consultant, and an educator. Although the diagnosis of severe or profound retardation occurs at or soon after birth, screening procedures should be the initial stage of the assessment process with appropriate instrumentation leading to intervention; intervention and follow-up are the final stages in the process.

The removal of the barriers to optimal evaluation services can only be accomplished by training programs in which knowledge is acquired and skills are developed. Numerous training programs for educators have been developed at the preservice and inservice levels, and such programs will also have to be developed for psychologists. One attempt to provide such training via continuing education workshops has resulted in better psychological services to severely/profoundly retarded individuals and programs (Gerken & Grimes, 1977). Such training must include practicum experiences. Continued research and development in every aspect of severe and profound retardation is necessary for removing the barriers to optimal services.

Assessment

Shakespeare (1970) lists four major purposes for assessment of severely subnormal children: (a) general diagnosis; (b) determination of degree of handicap; (c) development of a plan for training; and (d) prognosis. Although the general diagnosis is usually not a problem, the severity of the handicap(s) can cause an underestimation of potential. The attempt to determine degree of handicap is a continuous process, and the major component of the process is careful assessment of an individual's functioning in all areas of development in order to formulate a precise educational program.

Two basic approaches to assessment have been used with the severely/profoundly retarded—the developmental approach and the behavioral approach (Haring, 1977; Shakespeare, 1970; Stephen & Robertson, 1965). When using the developmental approach, the severely/profoundly handicapped are assessed with norm-referenced devices such as scales developed for young normal children, scales designed for assessing subnormal children based on normal development, and scales comparing the child with other handicapped children. The behavioral approach to assessment uses criterion-referenced devices that focus on observable behaviors, frequent measures, environmental factors, and the relationship of measures to intervention goals (Haring, 1977).

A three-phase assessment and prescription system consisting of screening, programming, and community entry levels have been suggested by Reavis, Morrey, and Hamel (1976) to reintegrate the severely and profoundly handicapped into the community. From the limited experiences to date in assessment of severely/profoundly retarded individuals, it is apparent that there is no one system or process that by itself is adequate for all individuals in all programs. The choice of which approach or combination of approaches to use is dependent upon many factors. Hopefully, training, research, and evaluation will assist the psychologist and educators in making the best choices in the future. Psychologists who work

TABLE 6.3
Assessment Instruments that Are Used with Severely/Profoundly Mentally Retarded Individuals

Type of instrument	Age range	Norms for severe/profound	Assessment linked to curriculum	Evaluative information
Screening				
1. Apgar	Birth			Haring, 1977
2. Neonatal Behavior Assessment Scale	1–4 weeks			Brazelton, 1973; Haring, 1977; Tronick & Brazelton, 1975
Diagnostic/programming				
1. Standardized instruments for cognition				
a. Bayley Scales	2–30 months			Anastasi, 1976; Haring, 1977; Shakespeare, 1970
b. Cattell Infant Intelligence Scale	3–30 months			Shakespeare, 1970
c. Gesell Developmental Schedules	4 weeks– 6 years			Anastasi, 1976; Shakespeare, 1970
d. Griffith's Mental Developmental Scale	0–2 years			Shakespeare, 1970
2. Standardized instruments for motor skills				
a. Bayley Scales of Mental Development	2–30 months			Anastasi, 1976; Haring, 1977; Shakespeare, 1970
b. Vineland Social Maturity Scale	0–25+ years			Anastasi, 1976; Shakespeare, 1970
3. Standardized instruments for communication				

178

Item	Age			References
a. Vineland Social Maturity Scale	0–25+ years			Anastasi, 1976; Shakespeare, 1970
4. Adaptive behavioral scales	0–adult			
a. Rating of 136 checklists		Some	Some	Walls, 1977
b. Review of 18 scales		Some	Some	Coulter & Morrow, 1977
5. Developmental inventories				
a. Down's Syndrome Performance Inventory			X	Down's Syndrome, 1975; Haring, 1977
b. Individual assessment guide			X	Haring, 1977; Sommerton & Turner, 1975
c. Application of Piaget's theory				Shakespeare, 1970; Woodward, 1959
6. Observation/behavioral checklists				
a. Uniform performance assessment system			X	Bendersky, Edgar, & White, 1976; Haring, 1977
b. Progress assessments chart				Gunzberg, 1963; Shakespeare, 1970
c. Diagnostic checklist			X	Bender, Valletutti, & Bender, 1976
d. A prescriptive behavioral checklist for severely and profoundly retarded			X	Popovitch, 1977
e. Behavior evaluation checklist				Morris, 1976
7. Videotapes				Boehm & Weinberg, 1977; Cartwright & Cartwright, 1974
8. Daily logs				

with severely/profoundly retarded individuals soon find out that they have entered a new arena in which they must provide a variety of services in addition to assessment. Some of these services include support to the families and teachers in the intervention/change process, evaluation of the programs and services, and suggestions for change. Familiarity with the instruments that are being used with the severely/profoundly handicapped (see Table 6.3) and a review of the resources on assessment (see the appendix to this chapter) are necessary components of the psychologists' training.

Beyond Assessment

The psychologist who is actively involved in the assessment process for the children/adolescents discussed in this chapter will also be involved in intervention. One aspect of the intervention program that the psychologist may assume primary responsibility for is counseling which, like assessment, should be a continuous process. The parents or guardians usually need guidance after the initial assessment and at various stages of the child's development, whereas the child's need for guidance seems to occur concurrently with the introduction to school and continues or reappears at certain stages of development.

It is apparent that school psychologists cannot perform adequate assessment nor can they go beyond assessment without specific training to do so. There has been limited training of school psychologists to work with high-risk preschoolers and children/adolescents with low-incident handicapping conditions, and there is a great need for some psychologists to become specialists in these areas. National and state organizations, groups of psychologists, and school psychology training programs are attempting to provide such specific training now via continuing education programs. However, now is also the time to consider a revamping of the initial training of school psychologists by providing the means to specialize to those students who exhibit the competencies required to function effectively as generalists as well as to those who express an interest in specializing in the delivery of services to children with low-incident handicapping conditions. It is not reasonable to expect an individual psychologist to provide adequate services to clients from 0–21 years of age who have diverse handicapping conditions.

Appendix: Resources for Assessment

High-Risk Preschoolers

GENERAL ASSESSMENT INFORMATION

Anastasi, 1976; Frankenburg & North, 1974; Friedlander, 1975; Friedlander, Sterritt, & Kirk, 1975; Gallagher & Bradley, 1972; Haeussermann, 1952, 1958;

Hayden & Edgar, 1977; Hellmuth, 1967, 1971; Karnes & Zehrbach, 1977; Meier, 1973; Mowbray & Salisbury, 1975.

Lists/Bibliographies

Hayden & Edgar, 1977 (Resources, 91–93); Jordan, Hayden, Karnes, & Wood, 1977 (Appendix B, 301–304); Mardell & Goldenberg, 1972.

Evaluation of Assessment Instruments

Brazelton, 1973; Buros, 1972; Cairns & Butterfield, 1975; Cross & Goin, 1977; Gallagher & Bradley, 1972 (Table 2, Sample Measures, 105–107); Guthrie, P. D., 1971; Guthrie, P. E., 1971; Hayden & Edgar, 1977 (85–88); Hoepfner, Stern, & Nunmedal, 1971; Jedrysek, Pope, Klapper, & Wortis, 1972; Meier, 1973 (Appendix A); *Preschool Test Matrix,* 1976; Rosen, 1971; Rosenblith, 1975; Stott & Ball, 1965; Technical Assistance Development System, 1973; Thomas, 1970; Tronick & Brazelton, 1975; Uzgiris & Hunt, 1975 (Chapters 10–17, Ordinal Scales of Psychological Development); Zehrbach, 1975.

Hearing Impaired

General Assessment Information

Anastasi, 1976; Anderson & Sisco, 1977; Cantor & Spragins, 1977; Donoghue, 1968; Donoghue & Bolton, 1971; Gerweck & Ysseldyke, 1975; Hess, 1969; Levine, 1971, 1974, 1975, 1976; Meyerson, 1963; Reed, 1970; Sattler, 1974; Vernon, 1967, 1974, 1976; Vernon & Brown, 1964.

Lists/Bibliographies

Levine, 1971 (Tables 1, 2, & 3); Levine, 1974 (Table 1); Seaton, 1975.

Modifications

Murphy, 1957; Neuhaus, 1967; Reed, 1970; Sattler, 1974; Sullivan, 1977, 1978.

Evaluation of Assessment Instruments

Buros, 1972; Gerweck & Ysseldyke, 1975; Reed, 1970; Smith, 1967; Vernon, 1974 (Tables 6.1 & 6.2); Vernon, 1976 (Table 7, Update of 1964); Vernon & Brown, 1964 (Tables 1 & 2, Suggested Test Batteries for Various Ages).

Visually Impaired

Psychological Factors

Bauman, 1972a; Cowen *et al.,* 1961; Hardy & Cull, 1972; Lowenfeld, 1971, 1973, 1975; Lukoff & Whiteman, 1970; Norris *et al.,* 1957; Pintner, Eisenson, & Stanton, 1941; Raskin, 1962; Wright, 1960.

General Assessment Information

Anastasi, 1976; Bauman, 1968, 1971, 1973, 1974, 1976; Bauman & Hayes, 1951; Blechman, 1970; Clark & Jastrzembska, 1970; Dickman, 1972; Hepfinger, 1962; Langan, 1970; Lowenfeld, 1971; Margach & Kern, 1969; Norris *et al.*, 1957; Parker, 1969.

Lists/Bibliographies

American Foundation for the Blind, 1975; Bauman, 1968, 1971, 1972a, 1973, 1974, 1976; Bauman & Hayes, 1951; Morris & Nolan, n.d.; Sattler, 1974; Scholl & Schnur, 1976.

Evaluation of Assessment Instruments

Bauman, 1968, 1971, 1972b, 1973, 1974, 1976; Bauman & Hayes, 1951; Buros, 1972; Dauterman, Shapiro, & Suinn, 1967; Kenyon, 1959; Langan, 1970; Malikin & Freedman, 1970; Margach & Kern, 1969; Newland, 1969; Parker, 1969; Tillman, 1973.

Orthopedically Impaired

Psychological Factors

Conner, Rusalem, & Cruickshank, 1971; Freedman, 1967; Lamm & Fisch, 1955; McDaniel, 1969; Peters, 1964; Wright, 1960.

General Assessment

Conner, Rusalem, & Cruickshank, 1971; Haeussermann, 1952; Mittler, 1970; Reynell, 1970; Sattler, 1974.

Lists/Bibliographies

Anastasi, 1976; Conner *et al.*, 1971; Reynell, 1970; Sattler & Tozier, 1970.

Modifications

Allen, 1958; Allen & Collins, 1955; Anastasi, 1976; Katz, 1955, 1958; Peters, 1964; Sattler, 1974; Sattler & Anderson, 1973; Sattler & Tozier, 1970.

Evaluation of Assessment Instruments

Allen & Collins, 1955; Allen & Jefferson, 1962; Anastasi, 1976; Buros, 1972; Reynell, 1970; Sattler, 1974.

Severely/Profoundly Handicapped

General Assessment Information

Assessment: Guide 1 to Materials for the Severely Handicapped, 1976; Baumeister, 1965; Cabanski, 1969; Haring, 1977; Haring & Brown, 1976; Reavis *et al.*, 1976;

Shakespeare, 1970; Sontag, Smith & Certo, 1977; Sontag, Smith & Sailor, 1977; Stephen & Robertson, 1965.

ADAPTIVE BEHAVIOR INFORMATION

Bhattacharya, 1973; Congdon, 1973; Coulter & Morrow, 1977; Robinson & Robinson, 1976; Schwartz & Allen, 1975; Walls, 1977.

LISTS/BIBLIOGRAPHIES

Catalog of Materials for the Severely Handicapped, 1970.

EVALUATION OF ASSESSMENT INSTRUMENTS

Buros, 1972; All references listed in Table 6.3

References

Abeson, A., & Zettel, J. The end of the quiet revolution: The Education for All Handicapped Children Act of 1975. *Exceptional Children,* 1977, **44**(2), 114–128.

Allen, R. M. Suggestions for the adaptive administration of intelligence tests for those with cerebral palsy. *Cerebral Palsy Review,* 1958, **19,** 6–7.

Allen, R. M., & Collins, M. G. Suggestions for the adaptive administration of intelligence scales for those with cerebral palsy. *Cerebral Palsy Review,* 1955, **16,** 27–33.

Allen, R. M., & Jefferson, T. W. *Psychological evaluation of the cerebral palsied person.* Springfield, Illinois: Charles Thomas, 1962.

American Foundation for the Blind. *Assessment for the educational readiness of the child with visual impairments: Three workshops.* New York: American Foundation for the Blind, 1975.

American Psychological Association. Revised ethical standards of psychologists. *APA Monitor,* March 1977, 22–23.

Anastasi, A. *Psychological testing* (4th ed.). New York: MacMillan, 1976.

Anderson, R., & Sisco, F. *Standardization of the WISC-R Performance Scale for deaf children* (Series T, Number 1). Washington, D.C.: Gallaudet College, Office of Demographic Studies, 1977.

Ashcroft, S. C. Blind and partially sighted children. In L. M. Dunn (Ed.), *Exceptional children in the schools.* New York: Holt, 1963.

Assessment: Guide 1 to materials for the severely handicapped. Tallahasee: Information Series, Retardation Program Office, Department of Health and Rehabilitation Services, State of Florida, 1976.

Ballard, J., & Zettel, J. Public Law 94-142 and Section 504: What they say about rights and protections. *Exceptional Children,* 1977, **44**(3), 177–184.

Bardon, J. I., & Wenger, R. D. School psychology training trends in the early 1970's. *Professional Psychology,* 1976, **7**(1), 31–37.

Bauman, M. K. *A report and a reprint: Tests used in the psychological evaluation of blind and visually handicapped persons and a manual of norms for tests used in counseling blind persons.* Washington, D.C.: American Association of Workers for the Blind, 1968.

Bauman, M. K. Tests and their interpretation. In G. D. Carnes, C. E. Hansen, & R. M. Parker (Eds.), *Readings in rehabilitation of the blind client.* Austin, Texas, 1971.

Bauman, M. K. Psychological factors associated with blindness. In R. E. Hardy & J. G. Cull (Eds.), *Social and rehabilitation services for the blind.* Springfield, Illinois: Charles C. Thomas, 1972. (a)

Bauman, M. K. Special problems in the psychological evaluation of blind persons. In R. E. Hardy & J. G. Cull (Eds.), *Social and rehabilitation services for the blind.* Springfield, Illinois: Charles C. Thomas, 1972. (b)

Bauman, M. K. Psychological and educational assessment. In B. Lowenfeld (Ed.), *The visually handicapped child in school*. New York: Day, 1973.

Bauman, M. K. Blind and partially sighted. In M. V. Wisland (Ed.), *Psychoeducational diagnosis of exceptional children*. Springfield, Illinois: Charles C. Thomas, 1974.

Bauman, M. K. Psychological evaluation of the blind client. In B. Bolton (Ed.), *Handbook of measurement and evaluation in rehabilitation*. Baltimore: University Park Press, 1976.

Bauman, M. K., & Hayes, S. P. *A manual for the psychological evaluation of the adult blind*. New York: The Psychological Corporation, 1951.

Baumeister, A. A. The usefulness of the IQ with severely retarded individuals: A reply to MacAndrew and Edgerton. *American Journal of Mental Deficiency*, 1965, **69**, 881–882.

Bayley, N. Consistency and variability in the growth of intelligence from birth to 18 years. *Journal of Genetic Psychology*, 1949, **75**, 165–196.

Bender, M., Valletutti, P. J., & Bender, R. *Teaching the moderately and severely handicapped* (Vols. I, II, and III). Baltimore: University Park Press, 1976.

Bendersky, M., Edgar, E., & White, O. *Uniform Performance Assessment System (UAAS)* (Working paper No. 65). Seattle: Experimental Education Unit, Child Development and Mental Retardation Center, University of Washington, 1976.

Bhattacharya, S. Adaptive behavior scale refinement. *Mental Retardation*, 1973, **11**, 27.

Blechman, R. O. *What do you do when you see a blind person?* New York: American Foundation for the Blind, 1970.

Boehm, A., & Weinberg, R. A. *The classroom observer*. New York: Teachers College Press, 1977.

Bonvillian, J. D., Charrow, V. R., & Nelson, K. E. Psycholinguistic and educational implications of deafness. *Human Development*, 1973, **16** 321–345.

Brazelton, T. B. *Neonatal behavioral assessment scale*. Philadelphia: Lippincott, 1973.

Bureau of Education for the Handicapped. *BEH Data Notes*, Sept. 1977, 1–4.

Burgemeister, B. B. *Psychological techniques in neurological diagnosis*. New York: Harper & Row, 1962.

Buros, O. K. (Ed.). *Seventh mental measurements yearbook*. Highland Park, New Jersey: Gryphon Press, 1972.

Cabanski, S. Psychological diagnosis and evaluation of the severely retarded: A programmatic approach. In R. C. Scheerenberger (Ed.), *Mental retardation, selected conferences papers*. Springfield, Illinois: Department of Mental Health, 1969.

Cairns, G. F., & Butterfield, E. C. Assessing infant's auditory functioning. In B. Z. Friedlander, G. M. Sterritt, & G. E. Kirk (Eds.), *Exceptional infant* (Vol. 3). New York: Brunner/Mazel, 1975.

Cantor, D., & Spragins, A. Delivery of psychological services to the hearing impaired child in the elementary school. *American Annals of the Deaf*, 1977, **22**, 330–336.

Cartwright, C. A., & Cartwright, G. P. *Developing observation skills*. New York: McGraw-Hill, 1974.

Catalog of materials for the severely handicapped. Tallahassee, Florida: Department of Health and Rehabilitative Services, State of Florida, 1970.

Chesler, M. Ethnocentrism and attitudes toward the handicapped. *Journal of Personality and Social Psychology*, 1965, **2**, 877–882.

Clark, L. L., & Jastrzembska, Z. Z. *Proceedings of the conference on new approaches to the evaluation of blind persons*. New York: American Foundation for the Blind, 1970.

Comer, R. C., & Pilavin, J. A. As others see us: Attitudes of physically handicapped and normals toward own and other groups. *Rehabilitation Literature*, 1975, **36**, 206–221.

Congdon, D. The adaptive behavior scale modified for profoundly retarded. *Mental Retardation*, 1973, **11**(1), 20–21.

Conner, F. P., Rusalem, H., & Cruickshank, W. M. Psychological considerations with crippled children. In W. M. Cruickshank (Ed.), *Psychology of exceptional children and youth* (3rd ed.). Englewood Cliffs, New Jersey: Prentice-Hall, 1971.

Coulter, A. W., & Morrow, H. W. (Eds.). *The concept and measurement of adaptive behavior within the scope of psychological assessment*. Austin: Texas Regional Resource Center, 1977.

Cowen, E. L., Underberg, R. P., Verrillo, R. T., & Benham, F. G. *Adjustment to visual disabilities in adolescence.* New York: American Foundation for the Blind, 1961.

Cross, L., & Goin, K. *Identifying handicapped children: A first chance series.* New York: Walker, 1977.

Darbyshire, J. O., & Reeves, V. R. The use of adaptations of some of Piaget's tests with groups of children with normal and impaired hearing. *British Journal of Disorders in Communication,* 1969, **4**(2), 197–202.

Dauterman, W. L., Shapiro, B., & Suinn, R. M. Performance tests of intelligence for the blind reviewed. *International Journal for the Education of the Blind,* 1967, **17,** 8–16.

Davis, J. (Ed.). *Our forgotten children: Hard-of-hearing pupils in the schools.* Minneapolis: University of Minnesota Press, 1977.

Dickman, I. R. *Living with blindness.* New York: American Foundation for the Blind, 1972.

Donoghue, R. J. The deaf personality—a study in contrasts. *Journal of Rehabilitation of the Deaf,* 1968, **2,** 37–52.

Donoghue, R., & Bolton, B. Psychological evaluation of deaf rehabilitation clients. *Journal of Rehabilitation of the Deaf,* 1971, **5**(1), 29–38.

Down's Syndrome Performance Inventory, Levels 1–7. Seattle: Experimental Education Unit, Child Development and Mental Retardation Center, University of Washington, 1975.

Federal Register, 1977, **42**(163), 42474–42517.

Frankenburg, W. K., & North, A. F. *A guide to screening for the Early and Periodic Screening, Diagnosis, and Treatment Program (EPSDT) under Medicaid* (Document No. [SRS] 74-24516). Washington, D.C.: Department of Health, Education and Welfare, 1974.

Freedman, R. D. Emotional reactions of handicapped children. *Rehabilitation Literature,* 1967, **19,** 274–282.

Friedlander, B. Z. Notes on language: Screening and assessment of young children. In B. Z. Friedlander, G. M. Sterritt, & G. E. Kirk (Eds.), *Exceptional infant* (Vol. 3). New York: Brunner/Mazel, 1975.

Friedlander, B. Z., Sterritt, G. M., & Kirk, G. E. (Eds.). *Exceptional infant* (Vol. 3). New York: Brunner/Mazel, 1975.

Gallagher, J. J., & Bradley, R. H. Early identification of developmental difficulties. In I. J. Gordon (Ed.), *Early childhood education. The seventy-first yearbook of the National Society for Education.* Chicago: The University of Chicago Press, 1972.

Gerken, K. C., & Grimes, J. *Escape from obsolescence: Implementation and evaluation of continuing education workshops for school psychologists.* Unpublished manuscript, The University of Iowa, 1977.

Gerweck, S., & Ysseldyke, J. Limitations of current psychological practices for the intellectual assessment of the hearing impaired: A response to the Levine study. *Volta Review,* April 1975, **77,** 243–248.

Gunzberg, H. C. *Progress assessment charts.* London: National Association of Mental Health, 1963.

Guthrie, P. D. *Head Start test collection report: School readiness measures (an annotated bibliography).* Princeton: Educational Testing Service, August 1971.

Guthrie, P. E. *Head Start test collection report: Measures of infant development (an annotated bibliography).* Princeton: Educational Testing Service, December 1971.

Haeussermann, E. *Evaluating the developmental level of preschool children handicapped by cerebral palsy.* New York: United Cerebral Palsy Association, 1952.

Haeussermann, E. *Developmental potential of preschool children.* New York: Grune & Stratton, 1958.

Hardy, R. E., & Cull, J. G. (Eds.). *Social and rehabilitation services for the blind.* Springfield, Illinois: Charles C. Thomas, 1972.

Haring, N. (Ed.). *Teaching severely/profoundly handicapped individuals.* New York: Grune & Stratton, 1976.

Haring, N. G. Measurement and evaluation procedures for programming with the severely and profoundly handicapped. In E. Sontag, J. Smith, & N. Certo (Eds.), *Educational programming for the severely and profoundly handicapped.* Reston, Virginia: Division on Mental Retardation, The Council for Exceptional Children, 1977.

Haring, N. G., & Brown, L. (Eds.). *Teaching the severely handicapped: A yearly publication of the American Association for the Education of the Severely/Profoundly Handicapped* (Vol. 1). New York: Grune & Stratton, 1976.

Haskins, R., Finkelstein, N. W., & Stedman, D. J. Infant-stimulation programs and their effects. *Pediatric Annals,* 1978, **7**(2), 99–128.

Hayden, A. H., & Edgar, E. B. Identification, screening and assessment. In J. B. Jordan, A. H. Hayden, M. B. Karnes, & M. M. Wood (Eds.), *Early childhood education for exceptional children.* Reston, Virginia: Council for Exceptional Children, 1977.

Hayes, S. P. *Contributions to a psychology of blindness.* New York: American Foundation for the Blind, 1941.

Hellmuth, J. (Ed.). *Exceptional infant* (Vol. 1). New York: Brunner/Mazel, 1967.

Hellmuth, J. (Ed.). *Exceptional infant* (Vol. 2). New York: Brunner/Mazel, 1971.

Hepfinger, L. M. Psychological evaluation of young blind children. *New Outlook for the Blind,* 1962, **56,** 309–315.

Hess, D. W. Evaluation of the young deaf adult. *Journal of Rehabilitation of the Deaf,* 1969, **3**(2), 6–21.

Hodges, W. L., Lapides, J., & Phillips, B. N. School psychology and early childhood education. *Journal of School Psychology,* 1977, **15**(2), 99–191.

Hoepfner, R., Stern, C., & Nunmedal, S. G. (Eds.). *CSE-ECRC preschool/kindergarten test evaluations.* Los Angeles: University of California, Los Angeles Graduate School of Education, 1971.

Imamura, S. *Mother and blind child.* New York: American Foundation for the Blind, 1965.

Jedrysek, E., Pope, L., Klapper, Z., & Wortis, J. *Psychoeducational evaluation of the preschool child.* New York: Grune & Stratton, 1972.

Jervis, F. M. A comparison of self concepts of blind and sighted children. In C. J. Davis (Ed.), *Guidance programs for blind children. A report of a conference.* Watertown, Massachusetts: Perkins Institute for the Blind, 1959.

Jordan, J. B., Hayden, A. H., Karnes, M. B., & Wood, M. M. (Eds.). *Early childhood education for exceptional children: A handbook of ideas and exemplary practice.* Reston, Virginia: Council for Exceptional Children, 1977.

Karnes, M. B., & Zehrbach, R. R. Early education of the handicapped: Issues and alternatives. In B. Spodek & H. Walberg (Eds.), *Early childhood education.* Berkeley: McCutchan, 1977.

Katz, E. Method of selecting Stanford–Binet Intelligence Scale tasks for evaluating the mental abilities of children severely handicapped by cerebral palsy. *Cerebral Palsy Review,* 1955, **16,** 14–17.

Katz, E. The "pointing modification" of the revised Stanford–Binet Scales, Forms L and M, years II through VI: A report of research in progress. *American Journal of Mental Deficiency,* 1958, **62,** 698–707.

Kenyon, E. L. Diagnostic techniques to be applied with blind children. In C. J. Davis (Ed.), *Guidance programs for blind children: A report of a conference.* Watertown, Massachusetts: Perkins Institute for the Blind, 1959.

Klapper, Z. S., & Birch, H. G. The relation of childhood characteristics to outcome in young adults with cerebral palsy. *Developmental Medicine and Child Neurology,* 1966, **8,** 645–656.

Kleck, R., Ono, H., & Hastorf, A. The effects of physical deviance upon face to face interaction. *Human Relations,* 1966, **19,** 425–436.

Lamm, S. S., & Fisch, M. L. Intellectual development of the cerebral palsied child as a factor in therapeutic progress. *American Journal of Mental Deficiency,* 1955, **59**(3), 452–457.

Langan, W. Visual and perceptual difficulties. In P. Mittler (Ed.), *Psychological assessment of mental and physical handicaps.* London: Methuen, 1970.

LaVor, M. Federal legislation for exceptional children: Implications and a view of the future. In R. D. Kneedler & S. G. Tarver (Eds.), *Changing perspectives in special education.* Columbus: Merrill, 1977.

Levine, E. S. *The psychology of deafness.* New York: Columbia University Press, 1960.

Levine, E. S. Mental assessment of the deaf child. *Volta Review,* 1971, **73,** 80–105.

Levine, E. S. Psychological tests and practices with the deaf: A survey of the state of the art. *Volta Review,* 1974, **76,** 298–319.

Levine, E. S. *Psychological evaluation of the deaf client* (Working paper), 1975.

Levine, E. S. Psychological evaluation of the deaf client. In B. Bolton (Ed.), *Handbook of measurement and evaluation in rehabilitation.* Springfield, Illinois: Charles C. Thomas, 1976.

Levine, E. S., & Wagner, E. E. Personality patterns of deaf persons: An interpretation based on research with the Hand Test. *Perceptual and Motor Skills,* 1974, **39,** 1167–1236 (Monograph Supplement).

Lowenfeld, B. *Braille and talking book reading: A comparative study.* New York: American Foundation for the Blind, 1945.

Lowenfeld, B. The visually handicapped. *Review of Educational Research,* 1963, **33,** 38–41.

Lowenfeld, B. Psychological problems of children with impaired vision. In W. M. Cruickshank (Ed.), *Psychology of exceptional children and youth* (3rd ed.). Englewood Cliffs, New Jersey: Prentice-Hall, 1971.

Lowenfeld, B. *The visually handicapped children in school.* New York: Day, 1973.

Lowenfeld, B. *The changing status of the blind: From separation to integration.* Springfield, Illinois: Charles C. Thomas, 1975.

Lukoff, I. F., & Whiteman, M. *The social source of adjustment to blindness* (Research Series No. 21). New York: American Foundation for the Blind, 1970.

Lynch, V., Shoemaker, S., & White, O. Training needs survey. *American Association for the Education of the Severely/Profoundly Handicapped Review,* 1976, **1**(4), 1–16.

Malikin, D., & Freedman, S. Test construction or adaptation for use with blind adults. In L. L. Clark & Z. Z. Jastrzembska (Eds.), *Proceedings of the conference on new approaches to the evaluation of blind persons.* New York: American Foundation for the Blind, 1970.

Mardell, C. D., & Goldenberg, D. S. *Instruments for screening of pre-kindergarten children.* Chicago: State of Illinois, Department of Public Instruction, Handicapped Children Section, 1972.

Margach, C., & Kern, K. C. Visual impairment, partial sight, and the school psychologist. *Journal of Learning Disabilities,* 1969, **2**(8), 407–414.

McDaniel, J. W. *Physical disability and human behavior.* Elmsford, New York: Pergamon, 1969.

Meier, J. *Screening and assessment of young children at developmental risk* (H.E.W. Publication No. (OS) 73-90). Washington, D.C.: Department of Health, Education and Welfare, 1973.

Meyerson, L. A psychology of impaired hearing. In W. M. Cruickshank (Ed.), *Psychology of exceptional children and youth* (2nd ed.). Englewood Cliffs, New Jersey: Prentice-Hall, 1963.

Mindel, E., & Vernon, M. *They grow in silence.* Silver Spring, Maryland: National Association of the Deaf, 1971.

Mittler, P. (Ed.). *The psychological assessment of mental and physical handicaps.* London: Methuen, 1970.

Morris, J. E., & Nolan, C. Y. *Bibliography of tests for the visually impaired.* Louisville, Kentucky: Educational Research, Development, and Reference Group, American Printing House for the Blind, n.d.

Morris, R. J. *Behavior modification with children.* Cambridge, Massachusetts: Winthrop, 1976.

Mowbray, J. K., & Salisbury, H. H. *Diagnosing individual needs for early childhood education.* Columbus, Ohio: Merrill, 1975.

Murphy, K. P. Tests of abilities and attainments. In A. W. G. Ewing (Ed.), *Educational guidance and the deaf child.* Manchester, England: Manchester University Press, 1957.

Myklebust, H. *The psychology of deafness.* New York: Grune & Stratton, 1960.

National Association for Retarded Citizens. *Competencies of persons responsible for the classification of mentally retarded individuals.* Washington, D.C.: Author, 1974.

National Association of School Psychologists. *Principles for professional ethics.* Washington, D.C.: Author, 1976.

Neuhaus, M. Modifications in the administration of the WISC performance subtests for children with profound hearing loss. *Exceptional Children,* 1967, **33,** 573–574.

Newland, T. E. *The blind learning aptitude test.* Washington, D. C.: Department of Health, Education and Welfare, 1969.

Newland, T. E. Psychological assessment of exceptional children and youth. In W. M. Cruickshank (Ed.), *Psychology of exceptional children and youth* (3rd ed.). Englewood Cliffs, New Jersey: Prentice-Hall, 1971.

Norris, M., Spaulding, P. J., & Brodie, F. H. *Blindness in children.* Chicago: University of Chicago Press, 1957.

Parker, J. Adapting school psychological evaluation to the blind child. *The New Outlook for the Blind,* 1969, **63**(10), 305–311.

Peters, D. M. Developmental conceptual components of the normal child. A comparative study with the C.P. child. *Cerebral Palsy Review,* 1964, **25,** 3–7.

Pintner, R., Eisenson, J., & Stanton, M. *The psychology of the physically handicapped.* New York: Appleton-Century-Crofts, 1941.

Popovitch, D. *A prescriptive behavioral checklist for the severely and profoundly retarded.* Baltimore: University Park Press, 1977.

Preschool test matrix. Lexington: Coordinating Office for Regional Resource Centers, University of Kentucky, March 1976.

Public Law 94-142, *Educational for All Handicapped Children Act,* November 29, 1975.

Raskin, N. J. Visual disability. In J. F. Garrett & E. S. Levine (Eds.), *Psychological practices with the physically disabled.* New York: Columbia University Press, 1962.

Reavis, H., Morrey, J., & Hamel, K. Behavioral assessment procedures for community reintegration. *American Association for the Education of the Severely/Profoundly Handicapped Review,* 1976, **1**(4), 37–46.

Reed, M. Deaf and partially hearing children. In P. Mittler (Ed.), *Psychological assessment of mental and physical handicaps.* London: Methuen, 1970.

Reivich, R., & Rothrock, I. Behavior problems of deaf children and adolescents: A factor-analytic study. *Journal of Speech and Hearing Research,* 1972, **15,** 93–104.

Reynell, J. Children with physical handicaps. In P. Mittler (Ed.), *Psychological assessment of physical and mental handicaps.* London: Methuen, 1970.

Robinson, N. M., & Robinson, H. B. *The mentally retarded child* (2nd ed.). New York: McGraw-Hill, 1976.

Rosen, P. *Head Start test collection report: Language development tests (an annotated bibliography).* Princeton: Educational Testing Services, 1971.

Rosenblith, J. F. Prognostic value of neonatal behavioral tests. In B. Z. Friedlander, G. M. Sterritt, & G. E. Kirk (Eds.), *Exceptional infant* (Vol. 3). New York: Brunner/Mazel, 1975.

Rutter, M. Psychological development—predictions from infancy. *Journal of Child Psychology and Psychiatry,* 1970, **11,** 49–69.

Sattler, J. *Assessment of children's intelligence* (Rev. reprint). Philadelphia: W. B. Saunders, 1974.

Sattler, J. M., & Anderson, N. E. The Peabody Picture Vocabulary Test, Stanford–Binet, and the Modified Stanford–Binet with normal and cerebral palsied children. *The Journal of Special Education,* 1973, **7**(2), 119–122.

Sattler, J., & Tozier, L. L. A review of intelligence test modifications used with cerebral palsied and other handicapped groups. *The Journal of Special Education,* 1970, **4**(4), 391–398.

Schlesinger, H., & Meadow, K. P. *Sound and sign.* Berkeley: California University Press, 1972.

Scholl, G., & Schnur, R. *Measures of psychological, vocational, and educational functioning in the blind and visually handicapped.* New York: American Foundation for the Blind, 1976.

Schwartz, B. J., & Allen, R. M. Measuring adaptive behavior: The dynamics of a longitudinal approach. *American Journal of Mental Deficiency,* 1975, **79,** 424–433.

Seaton, J. Communication disorders: The school psychologist's role. *Language, Speech, and Hearing Services in Schools*, 1975, **6**, 106–112.

Shakespeare, R. Severely subnormal children. In P. Mittler (Ed.), *Psychological assessment of mental and physical handicaps*. London: Methuen, 1970.

Smith, A. J. Psychological testing of the preschool deaf child: A challenge for changing times. In *Proceedings of international conference on oral education of the deaf* (Vol. 1). Washington, D.C.: A. G. Bell Association for the Deaf, 1967.

Soeffing, M. Y. BEH officials identify and discuss significant federal programs for the handicapped. *Exceptional Children*, 1974, **40**, 437–442.

Sommerton, E., & Turner, K. *Pennsylvania training model: Individual assessment guide*. Harrisburg: Pennsylvania Department of Education, 1975.

Sontag, E., Smith, J., & Certo, N. (Eds.). *Educational programming for the severely and profoundly handicapped*. Reston, Virginia: Division on Mental Retardation, The Council for Exceptional Children, 1977.

Sontag, E., Smith, J., & Sailor, W. The severely and profoundly handicapped: Who are they? Where are we? *Journal of Special Education*, 1977, **11**, 1.

Stephen, E., & Robertson, J. Normal child development and handicapped children. In J. G. Howells (Ed.), *Modern perspectives in child psychiatry*. Edinburgh and London: Oliver and Boyd, 1965.

Stott, L. H., & Ball, R. S. *Evaluation of infant and preschool mental tests*. Detroit: Merrill Palmer Institute, 1963. [Also in *Monographs of the Society for Research in Child Development*, 1965, **30**(3), Serial No. 101.]

Sullivan, P. M. *The influence of total communication on the WISC-R performance scale with hearing-impaired children*. Dubuque: Education Specialist Research Project, University of Iowa, 1977.

Sullivan, P. M. *A comparison of administration modifications on the WISC-R performance scale with different categories of deaf children*. Unpublished doctoral dissertation, University of Iowa, 1978.

Taylor, G. P. Moderator-variable effect on personality-test-item endorsements of physically disabled patients. *Journal of Consulting and Clinical Psychology*, 1970, **35**(2), 183–188.

Technical Assistance Development System. *Evaluation bibliography: Tadscript #2*. Chapel Hill: University of North Carolina, 1973.

Thomas, H. Psychological assessment instruments for use with human infants. *Merrill-Palmer Quarterly*, 1970, **16**(2), 179–223.

Tillman, M. H. Intelligence scales for the blind: A review with implications for research. *Journal of School Psychology*, 1973, **11**(1), 80–87.

Tronick, E., & Brazelton, T. B. Clinical uses of the Brazelton Neonatal Behavioral Assessment. In B. Z. Friedlander, G. Sterritt, & G. E. Kirk (Eds.), *Exceptional infant* (Vol. 3). New York: Brunner/Mazel, 1975.

Uzgiris, I. C., & Hunt, J. M. *Assessment in infancy*. Urbana: University of Illinois Press, 1975.

Vegely, A. Performance of hearing impaired children on a non-verbal personality test. *American Annals of the Deaf*, 1971, **116**, 427–433.

Vernon, M. A guide for the psychological evaluation of deaf and severely hard of hearing adults. *The Deaf American*, 1967, **19**(9), 15–18.

Vernon, M. Psychological aspects of the diagnosis of deafness in a child. *EENT Monthly*, 1973, **52**, 60–66.

Vernon, M. Deaf and hard of hearing. In M. Wisland (Ed.), *Psychoeducational diagnosis of exceptional children*. Springfield, Illinois: Charles C. Thomas, 1974.

Vernon, M. Psychologic evaluation of hearing-impaired children. In L. L. Lloyd (Ed.), *Communication assessment and intervention strategies*. Baltimore: University Park Press, 1976.

Vernon, M., & Brown, D. A guide to psychological tests and testing procedures in the evaluation of deaf and hard-of-hearing children. *Journal of Speech and Hearing Disorders*, 1964, **29**(4), 414–423.

Walls, R. T. Behavior checklists. In J. D. Cone & R. P. Hawkins (Eds.), *Behavioral assessment: New directions in clinical psychology*. New York: Brunner/Mazel, 1977.

Weiner, B. B. Assessment: Beyond psychometry. *Exceptional Children,* 1967, **33**(6), 367–370.

Werner, E. E., Honzik, M. P., & Smith, R. S. Prediction of intelligence and achievement at ten years from twenty months pediatric and psychologic examinations. *Child Development,* 1968, **39**(4), 1063–1075.

Woodward, M. The behavior of idiots interpreted by Piaget's theory of sensori–motor development. *British Journal of Educational Psychology,* 1959, **29,** 60–71.

Wright, B. A. *Physical disability: A psychological approach.* New York: Harper & Row, 1960.

Zehrbach, R. R. Determining a preschool handicapped population. *Exceptional Children,* 1975, **42**(2), 76–83.

DONALD J. TREFFINGER • MICHAEL C. PYRYT
M. MADON HAWK • ELWOOD D. HOUSEMAN

7 Education of the Gifted and Talented: Implications for School Psychology

Concern for the gifted and talented has been a part of our cultural heritage since antiquity. In his *Republic,* Plato urged the development of one's talent to the fullest. Presently, there is widespread concern about our limited natural resources; there needs to be greater concern, however, for the development of our greatest natural resource—our gifted and talented youth (Marland, 1971). Failure to meet the needs of these youth may result in a great loss of human potential since, contrary to a popular stereotype, gifted children do not always "make it on their own."

School psychologists have an integral role to play in encouraging the development and education of gifted students. In school systems with well-defined programs for the gifted, school psychologists are often called upon for assistance in the planning and implementation of identification procedures. In school systems that do not have such programs, school psychologists often become "one-person task forces" for the gifted and talented. In addition to assisting in identification procedures, school psychologists are frequently called upon to consult with educators in planning programs for gifted students. As formal requirements such as individual educational programs (IEPs) increase, the role of the school psychologists will take on added significance. The school psychologist may be called upon to make programming suggestions that will help to minimize the variety of problems encountered by gifted students when their unique needs have not been met.

191

SCHOOL PSYCHOLOGY
Perspectives and Issues

School psychologists will also become increasingly involved in direct services to gifted and talented students. For these reasons, it is important that school psychologists have an understanding of the major questions, issues, and concepts now being raised in relation to the education of the gifted. In this chapter, we shall address four basic concerns: (*a*) Who are the gifted? (*b*) How are they identified? (*c*) What special problems do they face? and (*d*) How can we assist them?

Nature and Characteristics of Gifted Children

The first large-scale study of intellectually gifted children was begun at Stanford University by Lewis Terman in 1921. The purpose of the study was to discover the characteristics of intellectually superior children, the kinds of adults they would become, and the factors that would influence their later achievements. The search for subjects was confined chiefly to medium to large urban areas of California. Classroom teachers were asked to indicate the brightest, second brightest, third brightest, and youngest children in their classes. Nominated children were given a standardized intelligence test. For children below high school age, the criterion for selection was a score of 140 or higher on the Stanford–Binet (S–B). Selection of high school students was based on scores on the Terman Group Test, in which students were required to score within the top 1% of the general school population on which the norms had been established. Terman selected 1528 subjects (857 boys and 671 girls) who averaged 11 years of age at the time of testing. In addition to the intelligence scores, data were collected concerning the subjects' developmental history, health and physique, family background, school history, interests and personality, and school achievement. These subjects have been followed up at several points during the past 50 years.

Terman and Oden (1959) reviewed some of the major findings of the initial study. According to Terman, the typical gifted child in his study was the product of superior parentage—superior in cultural and educational background and heredity. He found that due to the interaction of heredity and environment, gifted children were physically superior to their less able age peers. During the elementary school years, the majority of gifted children were 2–3 years above grade level achievement on standardized tests. Gifted children in this sample had a wider range of interests and read more than average children.

Oden (1968) demonstrated that these gifted children tended to become superior adults. They maintained their intellectual ability, as measured by their scores on Terman's Concept Mastery Test. Some 90% of the subjects reported good or very good health. Also, the mortality rate was lower than that found in the general population. The incidence of serious mental illness was no greater than that found in the general population. Studies of their academic and occupational achievements showed that 71% of the men and 67% of the women were college graduates; 68% of the men and 24% of the women held one or more graduate degrees; and 86% of the men were employed in professional or semiprofessional occupations; the achievements of these men are remarkable. In 1968 at the time of writing, Oden found that they had published 2500 articles and papers and more than 200 books in the arts and sciences, and they had obtained 350 patents. Of the women, 42% were employed full-time, with 60% of the employed women doubling as housewives. Employed women tended to be school teachers or secretaries. Those women who did pursue professional careers were highly successful.

One fascinating section of Oden's (1968) report concerns the comparison of the 100 most successful men (Group A) with the 100 least successful men (Group C). Parents of the men in Group A tended to be higher in socioeconomic status (SES) than parents of the men in Group C. Parental divorce was markedly lower among Group A than among Group C. A's reported more often than C's that their parents encouraged initiative and independence and expected school success and college attendance. A's also reported having above-average energy, vocational planning at an earlier age, and greater satisfaction in their work than C's. A's were more accelerated in their grade placement than C's, finishing both eighth grade and high school at younger ages. Twice as many A's as C's graduated from college. A's tended to have greater perseverance, self-confidence, and ambition for excellence in work, recognition for accomplishments, and vocational advancement.

The most recent follow-up of Terman's sample was conducted in 1972. Pauline Sears and Barbee (1977) reported the most recent findings for the women in the sample. They found that 79% of the income workers, as opposed to 62% of the homemakers, reported high satisfaction with their career work patterns. Work satisfaction patterns were not related to family income. Life satisfaction was also studied, with results indicating that satisfaction was positively related to the subjects' level of education, occupation, health, and ambition. It was also positively related to the subjects' ratings of parental encouragement, their admiration for their parents, and their own early feelings of self-confidence and ambition.

R. R. Sears (1977) reported follow-up data for the male subjects. Occupational satisfaction and work persistence at age 62 were best predicted by feelings of satisfaction, ambition, and good health expressed as early as age 30. Despite their many accomplishments, these men placed greater importance on achieving satisfaction in their family life than in their work. These men were successful in realizing satisfaction in their family lives. Family life satisfaction and success in marriage were predicted by good childhood social adjustment, positive attitudes toward their parents, and by the Terman Marital Happiness Test (taken at age 30).

Gowan (1977) has listed several limitations in Terman's *Genetic Studies of Genius* (1925). These included: (*a*) Terman's narrow, unidimensional view of intelligence; (*b*) lack of control for SES; (*c*) neglect of creativity; and (*d*) lack of explicit hypotheses to guide the research. Stanley, Keating, and Fox (1974) noted that Terman's study was not a true experiment, since there was no explicit control group, single- or double-blind procedures were not employed, and the subjects and their parents knew that they were chosen as being extremely bright. The use of the term "genius" rather than simply "gifted" may have had potent effects for a large number of subjects. Keating (1975) also suggested a possible sampling bias in Terman's study. In reference to the normal curve, there were a greater number of subjects with IQ scores 170 or higher and fewer subjects in the 140–150 IQ range than one would expect. Despite the shortcomings, the *Genetic Studies of Genius* comprise our most extensive longitudinal investigation of the gifted; these studies have provided a foundation for many other investigations.

Broadening Conceptions of Giftedness

Terman conceived of intelligence as unidimensional; he believed it to be adequately and comprehensively measured by intelligence tests such as the Stanford–Binet. As a result of his longitudinal study, giftedness has historically been defined solely on the basis of IQ scores. The only variability in the definition among early theorists and researchers was the arbitrary IQ cutoff. Many educators, however (including Thurstone, Witty, Guilford, Torrance, Getzels and Jackson, Taylor, and Gowan), found this view of giftedness and intelligence to be too narrow. The pioneering work of Thurstone (1938) and Guilford's development of the Structure of Intellect model (1959, 1967) stressed the multidimensionality of human intelligence. This multifactor approach led to broadened conceptions of what it means to be gifted.

Since the early 1950s, creativity has become increasingly important in our conceptions of giftedness. Gowan (1977) proposed that *giftedness* should be defined as the potential to become verbally creative and *talent* as the potential to become nonverbally creative. Renzulli (1977) argued that the origins of giftedness may be traced to three factors: above-average (but not necessarily superior) intelligence, creativity, and task commitment. By focusing solely on IQ, one is likely to miss creative and potentially gifted students. Witty (1958) urged that the term gifted be used to describe those who show remarkable performance in any potentially valuable area of human endeavor. Taylor (1968) proposed that if a school system cultivated at least six dimensions of talent, approximately 30% of the school population would be in the top 10% in at least one of those areas.

The call for an expanded conception of giftedness has not gone unheeded. According to the current United States Office of Education definition (Marland, 1971), gifted and talented children are those who are capable of high performance in one or more of six talent areas. These areas are: (*a*) general intellectual ability; (*b*) specific academic aptitude; (*c*) creative or productive thinking; (*d*) leadership ability; (*e*) ability in the visual or performing arts; and (*f*) psychomotor ability.

Characteristics of the Gifted and Talented

Since the IQ definition has dominated the field for about 40 years, characteristics of the gifted as seen in the literature most often describe the intellectually gifted child. Salient characteristics of such gifted children include: an unusually large vocabulary for age or grade, a vast storehouse of information, and quick mastery and recall of information. The intellectually gifted child tries to discover the "how and why" of things, not just the "what." He or she is a keen and alert observer who looks for similarities and differences in people, events, and things. The gifted child likes to read on her/his own and may show preferences for biographies, autobiographies, encyclopedias, and even atlases. Intellectually gifted students are easily bored by routine tasks. They are interested at early ages in many "adult" problems and value issues such as religion, politics, sex, race, and death (Renzulli, Hartman, & Callahan, 1971). Highly creative students are often characterized by wide interests, openness to emotions and feelings, aesthetic sensitivity, self-awareness, lack of self-defensiveness, curiosity, tolerance for ambiguity, independence, and willingness to take risks (Dellas & Gaier, 1970). Gifted students are usually self-confident with peers and adults, have good verbal facility, carry responsibility well, can adapt to new situations, and enjoy being around people who show signs of leadership ability (Renzulli *et al.*, 1971). In the visual and performing arts, giftedness is characterized by technical proficiency in one's medium as well as expressiveness, spontaneity, and originality. Flexibility and bodily coordination are indicators of psychmotor ability.

Of course, any list of characteristics is a statistical synopsis of the results of many research findings and clinical case studies; the list is intended to illustrate a wide range of traits that will often be displayed by gifted students. It should not be construed as a "check list" of characteristics that are *necessarily* present in any individual gifted child or adult.

Contemporary Large-Scale Studies

Expanded conceptions of giftedness have led researchers to initiate studies investigating the various aspects of giftedness in greater detail. Several important longitudinal studies are now in progress.

The Study of Mathematically Precocious Youth (SMPY) at Johns Hopkins University, under the direction of Julian Stanley, is one of the largest current studies of exceptionally gifted children. The purposes of SMPY are threefold: (*a*) to identify mathematically gifted youth; (*b*) to study their characteristics; and (*c*) to facilitate their educational development.

The students are selected to participate in SMPY by means of a mathematical talent search. To be eligible, students must be seventh, eighth, or underage ninth graders who score at the ninety-eight percentile on the mathematical subtest of a standardized achievement test such as the Iowa Test of Basic Skills (ITBS). Students who meet these criteria are given the Scholastic Aptitude Test (SAT). Although the SAT is normally given to high school juniors and seniors, Stanley and his associates have used it to identify more than 3000 mathematically precocious young people. Top scorers on the mathematical section on the SAT are then invited to Johns Hopkins University for further testing, including measures of other specific abilities, such, as mechanical comprehension, career interests, and personality. Results of the testing are used in conjunction with the talent search results in recommending possible educational strategies for each student.

In meeting the needs of the mathematically gifted, SMPY utilizes many different accelerative opportunities. Students are informed of a variety of opportunities, such as subject matter acceleration, advanced placement courses, fast-paced math classes, college courses, and early admission to college. They are encouraged to select among these according to their abilities, needs, and interests. Participation in all phases of SMPY is completely voluntary on the student's part. So far, SMPY has had considerable success in enabling mathematically precocious youth to accelerate their progress (Stanley, Keating, & Fox, 1974; Keating, 1976; Stanley, 1977). During the course of the study, more males than females have been identified as precocious mathematical reasoners, and the girls who have been identified by SMPY have been less likely than boys to utilize the various accelerative strategies. Lynn Fox, Coordinator of the Intellectually Gifted Child Study Group (IGCSG) at Johns Hopkins University, is now studying the effectiveness of various intervention strategies aimed at increasing participation in appropriate activities among these gifted girls (Fox, 1976, 1977a, 1977b).

Longitudinal research has also been conducted in the area of creativity. Torrance (1977) reported data from a 1971 follow-up of students who had taken the Torrance Tests of Creative Thinking (TTCT) while in high school in 1959. Young people who were identified as creative in the high school years tended to become creative achievers as adults. Those who expressed interest in "unusual" occupations in high school were employed in those areas as adults. A larger portion of highly creative subjects included study in a foreign country as part of their career development. Highly creative students more frequently reported withdrawal experiences for periods of renewal or for creating new life styles. Creative achievements in writing, science, medicine, and leadership, however, were more easily predicted by creativity tests administered in high school than were creative achievements in music, the visual arts, business, and industry. Further follow-up studies of these students are being planned.

Parnes and Noller (1972) reported the effects of four semester-long courses in creative studies at Buffalo State University College. Compared with other students, those who participated in the creative studies courses demonstrated greater ability to cope with real-life situation tests and were better able to apply their creative abilities in other courses. These students also performed significantly better than control group students on several measures of cognition, divergent production, and convergent production (Reese, Parnes, Treffinger, & Kaltsounis, 1976). Creative studies participants also reported gains in their own creative behavior and greater productivity in areas of nonacademic achievement (Parnes & Noller, 1972).

Another large-scale study is being conducted by Halbert Robinson and his associates at the University of Washington. The purpose of their project is to identify and study extremely precocious preschool children (Robinson, Jackson, & Roedell, 1977).

These contemporary studies will lead to a better understanding of students who are gifted in many areas of human endeavor. The following section discusses assessment and various methods and procedures for identifying gifted and talented children.

Identification of Gifted and Talented Students

The problem of locating gifted and talented students at times may seem like an Easter egg hunt. Some children will search under bushes and trip over obvious eggs. Others will choose to hunt only for blue eggs, perhaps never realizing that there are no blue eggs! Our hunt for the gifted may begin with wild enthusiasm, but may later be reduced to a stalemate if no one knows what to look for or where to search. In this section, we offer some guidelines for "hunters." These guidelines will follow four important stages: (*a*) assessment of district needs and resources; (*b*) initial nomination and screening of students; (*c*) comprehensive review and evaluation of candidates; and (*d*) decisions concerning selection and placement.

Assessment of District Needs and Resources

Before initiating any identification procedures, it is best to determine the *needs of the school population* and to evaluate the *resources that the district can provide* for meeting those needs. Although we all would like to live in a world in which we could provide for every need, our sense of hope must be tempered by reality. In this case, we are suggesting that one must begin by taking into account the *realities* of the values and resources of the schools. In determining the needs of the students there are several valuable sources of information: school records, counselors' reports, psychological evaluations, and teacher, parent, and student nominations. Whether looking through school records or interviewing individuals, the

TABLE 7.1
Questions Relating to Screening and Identification of the Gifted

1. Does the district have a substantial incidence of students with superior general intellectual ability?
2. Does the district have a greater incidence of students with talents in specific areas?
3. Do these students seem to be properly provided for in the present school situation?
4. In what ways do these students demonstrate their gift/talent?
5. Are there students who demonstrate outstanding abilities in the visual or performing arts? In leadership?
6. Are there students who give evidence of creative potential?
7. Who are these students? Where are they? How many are there?

TABLE 7.2
Questions Relating to Resources for Programs for the Gifted

1. What current personnel have training and capabilities in the various areas of giftedness?
2. What community resources and leaders are available?
3. Where are there facilities available for the gifted program to utilize?
4. What financial resources and contingencies must be considered?
5. How might additional facilities and resource materials be made available to the program?
6. What needs and resources are there for transportation?

questions to be answered relating to screening and identification of the gifted include those presented in Table 7.1.

Once the needs of the gifted have been assessed, the resources of the district must be analyzed. In analyzing school resources, consult with building principals, curriculum directors, personnel managers, business officers, superintendents, and board members. Pertinent resource data relate to such questions as those identified in Table 7.2.

It is most desirable to synthesize this information into a statement of program philosophy and goals. Such a document must be amended, of course, as program development proceeds. However, the initial statement will be useful in guiding efforts during the planning of identification procedures.

Initial Nomination and Screening

The initial nomination and screening of students should involve many interest groups. Any group or individual involved must clearly understand the program goals. Requests for nominations should be prefaced with explanations of the significant characteristics that gifted students will display, with examples of typical behaviors manifested in school or at home, and with examples of accomplishments that might provide documentation. The directions should emphasize that gifted students display these characteristics to a considerably greater degree than would be normally associated with a student of that age. A good source of information on characteristics and screening devices is Ruth A. Martinson's *The Identification of the Gifted and Talented* (1974).

At this stage, we should remember our earlier analogy of the egg hunt. We may look under bushes, but we must also take care not to overlook the obvious. The school records may provide information about test results (ability or achievement), academic history, behavior, parent–teacher conferences, health, and attendance. Interviews with parents, teachers, counselors, and students may provide information about spontaneous expressions of the child's abilities in and out of school; thus all sources should be consulted who have had the opportunity to observe the child's *typical* behavior. Presentations that explain the program goals to parent–teacher organizations might be followed by written communications or personal contacts for nominating students who demonstrate the characteristics at home or at school. Classmates can provide peer nominations by naming the students whom they believe to be very capable in various areas, or who demonstrate various characteristics of the gifted. Principals and counselors can further the nomination process when asked about students who demonstrate consistently superior accomplishments or even who display boredom and frustration with school routines and requirements. By using the media—community newspaper articles, radio or television interviews—it is also possible to solicit nominations from neighbors, scout leaders, and church people who have seen certain behaviors that fit the descriptions. Lastly, do not discredit the person who steps forward saying, "That's me." This person may be quite cognizant of his/her own abilities.

Thus, the initial nomination process should involve input from a broad spectrum of groups and sources. Some students will demonstrate their gifts and talents to everyone who knows them, but there will also be students, equally gifted, who have hidden their abilities except to a few close individuals. This necessitates "looking under bushes." It would all be *easy* if gifted and talented students would consistently behave and perform in the same way; however, they do not. There is no such thing as a single description to fit all gifted and talented students. As surely as one will fit, another will not. Therefore, we must keep an open mind to many sources of information, explain clearly that there are many characteristics associated with childrens' talents, and be aware that no one student will be likely to display *all* of the characteristics, *all* of the time, to every observer.

After receiving a nomination, there should be additional screening to obtain more information about the individual. Martinson (1974) provided numerous examples of instruments that can be used, for example, to learn about the child's early development, hobbies, travel experiences, reading interests. Teachers can describe behaviors observed in the classroom, such as rapid learning, insightful questioning, unusual retention, or leadership ability. Information can also be gathered directly from the students by asking them to describe their own interests, hobbies, career expectations, and concerns. The Scales for Rating Behavioral Characteristics of Superior Students (Renzulli *et al.,* 1971) summarizes characteristics in the areas of learning, motivation, creativity, leadership communication, and the arts, and can be completed by teachers or others who have observed students' performance in these areas. Aside from these informal assessments of the student's abilities, interests, and accomplishments, the screening process can also make use of more formal tools, such as group tests of achievement or ability. Many districts have these data available in the school records. If group testing has not been done, it would be advisable to invest the necessary time and expense to administer an appropriate testing program as part of a district-wide "talent search." Often the initial nomination and screening will provide a very extensive list of students who may require special educational services. To develop a comprehensive individual evaluation for all, including individual testing, may be too time consuming and costly. Group testing in the screening process may help schools to ascertain which students should be referred for further evaluation.

Comprehensive Review and Evaluation

The comprehensive review and evaluation reduces the possibility of wrongly identifying and placing, or wrongly rejecting, any student on the basis of a single test score or nomination. The individual intelligence test will often constitute an important part of the evaluation. However, there should be other information to help document the child's gifts/talents as well.

The information needed for the comprehensive evaluation will vary in relation to the nature of the program to be initiated. In a program for intellectually gifted students, for example, a composite score on an individual intelligence test may be a valid source of information, whereas in a program for creatively talented students, we might gain more vital information from tests of creative thinking. When dealing with a specific talent, achievement tests or tests with content validity for the specific talent area should be considered. A very common flaw is to use many different criteria for identification, but then to place all the students in a single program. It is extremely important that there should be *consistency* among program goals, identification procedures, and program alternatives.

Much of the information gathered in the initial nomination and screening will be useful in the comprehensive review and evaluation. A partial list of representative sources of such information is presented in Table 7.3.

As in the nomination process, a wide variety of people will be able to provide information about the student. It would be a great injustice to dismiss a student on the basis of the report of only one person who sees that student in a dismal manner because of personality or value differences.

How can the great volume of data thus obtained be integrated and evaluated in a workable fashion? An effective comprehensive review and evaluation may take

TABLE 7.3
Representative Sources of Information for Comprehensive Review

Biographical and autobiographical information
Interest surveys
Career aspirations
Developmental information from parents
Academic history from school records
School behavior patterns
Home behavior patterns
Accomplishments
Awards
Peer nomination and evaluations
Systematic teacher nominations over various desired characteristics
Interview information from principals, teachers, parents, counselors, and students
Personality assessments
Learning and perception assessments
Observation of the student in various environments

several forms. A format that involves chronological sequencing is the *case study approach*. This is a method of organizing the information gathered into a biographical profile of the child. From early childhood developmental information supplied by parents, the case study traces the child's school career, interests, successes, behavior, and testing results to the present. In this manner, it becomes possible to view the development of the student and to observe influential patterns of behavior. The case study provides a clear picture of the individual and assists in understanding and analyzing his/her current level of performance. Case study information may not lend itself readily to quantitative selection decisions, however, and must be utilized carefully (especially in explaining decisions to teachers and parents).

Another alternative is to organize all available evidence into a matrix and to develop specific profiles for each student using appropriate quantitative methods. If well-qualified measurement specialists and computer facilities are available, the review may involve quite sophisticated statistical procedures for combining data from many sources. A quantitative assessment of the data may also be accomplished, in a somewhat less complex approach, using procedures such as those proposed by Gowan (1967) or Baldwin and Wooster (1976).

Selection and Placement Decisions

It is important to keep in mind that collecting data about students and assembling test scores in complex arrays is not the same as making actual *decisions* about students for educational programs. Thus, once the data have been gathered in the comprehensive review, we must also examine the action that should follow. Given the goals and objectives of the program and given the data about students' abilities, needs, and interests, which students will be selected? Or, if different program options are available, how can we best assign students to them?

In the case of a single program with specific objectives, the comprehensive review should enable the staff to identify those students most highly qualified. In such programs, typically referred to as programs for "academically talented" or "intellectually gifted" students, it is common to seek to identify the top 3 to 5% of the students. These students will be those whose personal and learning characteristics will be sufficiently unique from those of other students that special educational provisions must be made for them. It is important, of course, that the students and their parents be fully informed of the nature, goals, and procedures of the program, and they must consent to placement in the program. In some schools, program placement involves the same individualized program planning (with IEPs) and due process considerations that are provided for handicapped children under Public Law 94-142. Program placement should always be understood as flexible, and no student who is uncomfortable or unable to function effectively in a particular program should be forced to continue to participate. Selection decisions should not be excessively rigid!

It would be very desirable, of course, for the school to recognize that there are many different ways for giftedness to be expressed and to try to provide a variety of educational programs for students with exceptional talents in many areas. This implies that, given identification procedures that enable us to find outstanding talents, we should provide unique program options for many individuals or groups. Certainly, if our identification criteria help us locate many children with outstanding but different talents, we should not assume that a single program will be satisfactory for all of them. While many talents can readily be defined, such as in the current United States Office of Education definitions, educators have not found it equally possible to provide appropriate programs for gifted children in every area. Practical constraints of time and resources, and the tradition of group instruction by age levels, seem to make this goal difficult to attain. The number of students for whom special programs would be needed under this model would, of course, be considerably greater than 3 to 5% of the population. Even allowing for some "duplication" of students with exceptional potential in several areas, it might be necessary to include 15% or more of the students in special programs. Taylor's "multiple talent teaching" is one approach that emphasizes selection of many students for different programs.

Whether the school decides to identify one major area of giftedness for which it will seek to provide special programming, or whether it decides to identify several talent areas, effective student selection is based upon adequate specification of goals and objectives, and selection decisions must be made from the comprehensive review data that can be justified (to parents, students, and our colleagues) in relation to these goals.

Controversial Issues in Identification

There are several aspects of the identification process that are controversial. These may be of particular concern to the school psychologist, who may frequently be called upon to help parents, teachers, or administrators deal with these issues.

One very important issue, of course, is the *fairness* and *validity* of the tests that are employed in efforts to identify gifted students. This may involve general questions, typically expressed in such forms as:

"Do these tests really give us any valuable information?"
"Are those IQ tests really any good"
"I've heard that tests are just used to put labels on people; shouldn't we avoid that?"

Of course all of us should be concerned with these questions. It is not possible for us to summarize here all of the debate and research about educational testing here; most school psychology training programs provide consideration of such issues. However, specifically in relation to the identification of the gifted, we recommend that:

1. The better one has specified the program's goals and objectives and selected tests accordingly, the better one will be able to answer such questions. One should be able to explain specifically how the tests used in the identification procedure give information relevant to the goals.
2. One should recognize the possible limitations of test data for some students (culturally different or disadvantaged, for example), and seek effective alternative procedures (e.g., Block & Dworkin, 1976; Loehlin, Lindzey, & Spuhler, 1975; Samuda, 1975).
3. One should be able to explain why such concerns lead to the conducting of a comprehensive evaluation that includes many different sources of data so that no child will be denied services on the basis of a single test score.

Another important issue often confronting school psychologists is that of measuring creative abilities. This is a very challenging problem, since test development in this area has not been nearly as extensive as traditional intelligence testing. Many problems continue to challenge us in identifying creative abilities (Treffinger, Renzulli, & Feldhusen, 1971). There are some helpful sources of information, however, that school psychologists should study. The *Journal of Creative Behavior* has frequently published information about the validity, reliability, and availability of tests. Khatena (1978) has offered valuable, practical suggestions for parents and teachers concerned with identifying creative ability. Biondi and Parnes have also edited a two-volume set entitled *Assessing Creative Growth* (1976).

Some individuals will express concern that identification of the gifted and talented singles out certain students for privileges or rewards. Once again, it is important to be able to explain how selection procedures are designed to identify those students who, by virtue of their characteristics and interests, *require* particular education programs in order to be served adequately by the school. We do not identify children for privileges, but to determine how best to meet their needs; this should be the goal of *all* educators.

Special Problems of the Gifted

It is very easy, and all too common, to view the gifted student in one of two stereotyped ways: either as a puny, excessively studious introvert who always walks around with an open encyclopedia in hand, or as an all-around, constantly energetic, healthy and happy "wonder child." Doubtless some gifted children would fit one or the other of these patterns (although, as we noted at the beginning of the chapter, the former stereotype is especially uncharacteristic of gifted students as a group).

It is important, however, to help educators, administrators, and parents understand that it is not really productive for us to deal in such stereotypes. The child who is "labeled," whether with one view or the other, is always at a disadvantage, since real behavior does not respect our stereotyped expectations!

While recognizing the strengths and the talents of gifted students, then, it is also urgent to recognize that they do have problems that require our help and guidance. Some of these may be the same problems that every child confronts at some time in his or her life—for gifted students are *children*. They are not exempt, by virtue of their talents, from childhood stresses and anxieties. But there are also some unique concerns of gifted students to which the school psychologist must be alert and responsive. These include:

1. *Self-acceptance and understanding one's own talent.* It is not uncommon for gifted students to feel that something is "wrong" with them because of their ability. Many students learn that "being average" or being like everyone else is desirable and that to be different in any way is a problem. One must help students to understand the reality of individual differences among all people and to become better able to accept their own strengths and limitations.

2. *Acceptance of others.* Some gifted students can become so involved in their own ideas and so immersed in others' praise and expectations, that they become negative and cynical toward other students. It is important for the adults who work with them to help them recognize and value the strengths of other people and to accept the ideas and contributions that others can make.

3. *Need for adequate social relationships.* The gifted student faces, even more strongly than others, the complex problem of relating effectively to other people in a social setting. The student must learn to deal with others, but not merely to conform blindly to social pressures; at the same time, the student may need to learn to be independent without withdrawing entirely from social interaction.

4. *Need for controlled curiosity.* Gifted students may have a wide range of interests and activities, both in and out of school. They must learn, however, to control their curiosities and channel their energies lest they become ineffective people who are forever beginning projects and never finishing them. There must be balance between creative exploration, on the one hand, and self-disciplined inquiry on the other.

5. *Need for independent learning skills.* Because a student has the potential to be an autonomous learner does *not* mean that the student has already developed the necessary skills. Gifted students need instruction in effective thinking, problem solving, and study methods. They must learn how to set goals, develop and carry out plans, and evaluate and report on their efforts.

6. *Sustaining motivation for learning.* Occasionally the gifted child faces the problem of overcoming boredom with learning; it can be easy to become intellectually "lazy" when, with little effort, a gifted child can do as well as some other students do with much greater effort. The student may need assistance in setting reasonable, challenging goals and providing the effort required to attain a

complete and satisfying product or solution. Continuing boredom in the classroom, of course, may require much more than an adjustment by the student. There must be challenging and appropriate opportunities for learning.

7. *Responding to concerns for values.* Many gifted children are not content to learn facts and information, or even to learn how to be better logical thinkers or creative problem solvers. They also want to deal with value questions, with issues of merit and worth, and with right and wrong. Instruction in value clarification and assessment may therefore be extremely valuable (Treffinger, Borgers, Render, & Hoffman, 1976). It is also beneficial to help gifted children learn about the *people* who have made important contributions to our world.

8. *Coping with pressures from parents and teachers.* Some adults create pressures that can become extremely difficult or threatening for gifted students. Parents may be exceedingly demanding, leaving the child little latitude for growth, experimentation, or play. Teachers may also create excessive pressures by falsely assuming that "gifted students never make errors." Such problems require careful efforts with the adults (to reduce or modify arbitrary pressures and demands) as well as with the students (to help them learn how to deal with such situations without being overwhelmed by anxiety or frustration).

9. *Setting reasonable self-expectations.* Parents and teachers often report that gifted students are sometimes reluctant to share, submit, or display their work unless it is perfect to the last detail. The child's standards may be considerably more severe than those of anyone else. Quality workmanship must be encouraged, of course, without creating the idea that anything less than total perfection is inadequate. The student needs to learn how to establish standards that are reasonable and consistent with the demands of the task and the setting.

10. *Avoiding withdrawal and loneliness.* At times, the gifted student may feel isolated and lonely; he or she may respond by withdrawing into a private shell of thoughts and dreams. It is important to help the child learn constructive ways of dealing with emotions, fears, and problems and to help him or her recognize that many alternatives are available.

11. *Eliminating arbitrary sex role stereotypes.* Many gifted people, especially girls and women, must overcome the formidable problem of arbitrary sex role stereotypes. Many personal and professional alternatives have too long been viewed as suitable only for one sex or the other, rather than suited to people with certain interests and abilities. We must help students recognize that a wide range of possibilities are open to them, and that their efforts need not be thwarted because of their sex.

The school psychologist may be involved in dealing with these problems in a variety of ways, including providing services directly to children; consulting with teachers, counselors, and administrators; working with parents individually or in groups; or working with policymakers (school boards, legislators, etc.) to provide

for effective responses to important problems (Broedel, Ohlsen, Proff, & Southard, 1960; Drews, 1965; Gross & Sabbatino, 1965; Jordan & Keith, 1965; Tisdall
& Birch, 1965; Torrance, 1967; Wyne & Skjei, 1970; Fine, 1977).

How Can We Assist Gifted Children?

Of course, it would be impossible to provide within a single chapter a comprehensive summary of the wide variety of program models or prototypes that have
been proposed for educating gifted students. Many such prototypes have been
described by Gallagher (1975) and Kaplan (1974). In this section, then, we shall
summarize briefly some of the major issues and directions in program development, with particular focus upon challenges for school psychologists.

Enrichment

Although school personnel often think of enrichment as a type of program or
activity, following Kaplan (1974), we prefer to use this term in relation to a *goal*
for gifted education. The goal may be attained using any number of different
program models or "prototypes." According to Kaplan, "Enrichment is experiences

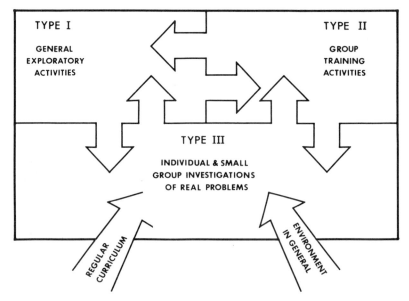

FIGURE 7.1.   *The Enrichment Triad model.* (From Renzulli [1977]. Reproduced with permission of
the publisher.)

which replace, supplement, or extend learnings. . . . Enrichment is the reason for the development or adaptation of any program prototype [1974, p. 46]."

Complex Cognitive and Affective Processes

In striving to accomplish "enrichment" for gifted students, many educators and psychologists have stressed the importance of complex cognitive and affective outcomes. Drawing from the widely known work of Bloom (1956), Krathwohl, Bloom, and Masia (1964), and Guilford (1967), many writers have admonished educators that adequate instruction for the gifted and talented must not rest solely upon increases in the rate and/or amount of basic information that is memorized and repeated upon demand (e.g., Feldhusen, Treffinger, & Elias, 1969; Williams, 1971; Torrance, 1965; Gallagher, 1975). Beyond the acquisition and retrieval of facts and basic concepts, gifted students must have opportunities for application, analysis, synthesis, creative problem solving, inquiry, and evaluation. In addition, they must have opportunities to deal with feelings, values, and attitudes, as well as knowledge and information. These concerns will not be elaborated here, inasmuch as they are widely discussed throughout the educational literature in behalf of *all* children (not only the gifted).

Renzulli (1977) has significantly advanced our understanding of ways in which learning can be enriched for gifted students. His model, called the Enrichment Triad, is illustrated in Figure 7.1.

Type I enrichment, "General Exploratory Activities," involves the freedom to explore areas of interest. This can be partially accomplished by developing categorical interest centers in the classroom. Activities in these centers should give information such as: Why study this topic? What does this subject do for humanity? Where does this information come from? What are some major issues and problems related to this topic? What are some great discoveries in this area? Field trips and special speakers may also be used as Type I activities.

Type II enrichment, "Group Training Activities," involves programs for the development of thinking skills. These include: critical thinking, problem solving, reflective thinking, inquiry, divergent thinking, self-concepts, and awareness development. Mental processes and operations are emphasized at complex levels of Bloom's taxonomy (1956) or Guilford's model (1967).

Type III enrichment, "Individual and Small-Group Investigations of Real Problems," occurs when the student becomes an investigator of real problems. It stresses the active use of appropriate methods of inquiry. By putting together unorganized bits of information, conclusions of others, and investigative techniques to add new knowledge, problems are solved. The student becomes a producer of knowledge, not merely a consumer of other peoples' ideas.

Type I and Type II enrichment activities are appropriate for all children, not only gifted students. Type III activities are seen as especially appropriate for gifted students.

Acceleration

Acceleration is a complex topic, little understood in many schools, and even less practiced. Despite extensive research on the topic, which has generally been very positive, we are often restrained by the anxieties and reservations of teachers, administrators, counselors, and parents (Pyryt, 1977; Tobin, 1977).

Research on acceleration has been recently reviewed by Daurio (in press). He divided acceleration research into studies of early entrance to college and studies involving acceleration prior to college. In both, acceleration seems to have benefited gifted students academically without hindering them socially.

One of the most extensive programs of research on acceleration has been conducted at Johns Hopkins University; it was briefly described earlier in this chapter (see pp. 195–196). Such programs as SMPY, under the direction of Professor Julian Stanley, as well as the Intellectually Gifted Child Study Group, under the direction of Dr. Lynn Fox, have provided many insights into the potential benefits of systematic acceleration, especially for students with outstanding aptitude in specific areas. Stanley (1977) has listed some of the benefits of the SMPY model. These include: increased zest for learning, enhanced feelings of self-worth, more realistic understanding of students' ability, and better preparation educationally, especially in mathematics. SMPY students tend to enter selective colleges. By getting into college, graduate school, and a profession earlier, they have more time and energy for creative pursuits. The accelerates have increased opportunities to explore more specialities and hobbies and more time to explore various careers before marriage. In addition, accelerative practices save money for students and their parents.

Are Acceleration and Enrichment Incompatible?

Proponents of acceleration have been sharply critical of some educational "enrichment" efforts. Stanley (1976) has argued that most enrichment activities either consist primarily of busy work, are irrelevant to gifted students' individual needs, or are appropriate for all students.

Certainly, it is apparent that these criticisms are too often well founded; they should help us to be alert to some of the ways in which enrichment efforts can be unsatisfactorily implemented with gifted students in some school settings.

On the other hand, proponents of more systematic approaches to enrichment have also expressed concern for acceleration efforts. They point to the concern that intensive content acceleration may channel or direct a student's efforts too narrowly, too soon, before the student has had significant opportunities to explore many possible fields of interest and aptitude. In addition, content acceleration may lead to an overemphasis on acquisition of facts and "lesson learning," and inhibit creative thinking, problem solving, and active inquiry (Renzullli, 1977). Acceleration is too often viewed, say its critics, as simply moving a child arbitrarily from one grade level to another.

These views are not necessarily mutually exlusive or inherently contradictory. It is certainly plausible, in our view, that an adequate individual educational plan for a gifted student should involve *both* systematic provisions for exploration, curiosity, creative thinking, problem solving, or inquiry into real problems (enrichment) *and* continuous involvement with content instruction as rapidly as the student's progress or mastery makes possible (acceleration).

Self-Directed Learning

Gifted students are frequently described as independent in thought and judgment (e.g., Torrance, 1965). We now realize, however, that a child may have the *potential* for independence, but not possess the *skills* necessary for effective, independent action. Thus, some recent efforts have emphasized procedures for helping teachers to create an environment in which students can *develop* the ability to be self-directed, independent learners (Treffinger, 1975, 1978). Students can learn to participate in the development of the goals and objectives of learning, to assess their own strengths and weaknesses, to plan and conduct appropriate learning activities, and to evaluate their own work.

Settings for Educational Intervention

Is it necessary to separate gifted and talented students from their age peers in order to provide adequate educational programs? This question has led to many heated discussions among educators. Although, as Daurio's (in press) review pointed out, grouping students by age in our schools does not have as long a tradition as some believe, alternative arrangements are frequently discomforting for educators; we are often reluctant to implement programs that will "take children away from their peers." But who is the peer of the gifted child? It is very likely that, for many activities, the child's peers are other people who share his or her interests and skills, regardless of their chronological age. Of course, it is also true that for some *other* activities that occur in the course of the school day, a different peer group would be more appropriate. Thus, it does not seem likely that any single grouping plan, whether on the basis of age, IQ, or any other variable considered in isolation, will always be optimal for the gifted student. The most desirable plan would be one in which students are grouped for instruction (and other school activities) or regrouped as appropriate on the basis of their abilities and skills in those particular activities. In such an arrangement, students would participate in some activities with their age peers, others with their social peers, and yet others with their intellectual peers.

Such an arrangement, of course, may be very difficult to establish in the rather fixed methods of operation of some schools. It is hoped that one of the functions of an effective school psychologist, as a psychoeducational consultant in the schools, will be to assist schools in developing new patterns of organization that will facilitate such instructional programs. This will be a more productive effort than merely "taking sides" in favor of, or against, a particular plan for gifted education.

Once the commitment has been made to the goal of providing instruction that is tailored as closely as possible to the individual talents, characteristics, and needs of students, many program options are available. The majority of these do *not* assume that gifted children will be separated entirely from other children. The most complete current description of program alternatives has been provided by Kaplan (1974). She has described more than 40 different program prototypes; these are summarized in Table 7.4.

The major concern in any setting in which programs are implemented is to provide instruction that is *qualitatively* different, that is, to take into account the most unique needs of the gifted learner.

Role of the School Psychologist

We believe that, in many schools, there will be an increasingly important role for the school psychologist to play in the education of the gifted. This role will extend beyond participation in the identification process and assisting in working with problems encountered by some children (although both of these roles will also be present). Some other important contributions may include:

1. Helping teachers in the interpretation of test data and the utilization of appropriate data in planning individual educational programs for gifted students. Teachers will not only require assistance in working with students with deficiencies and disabilities, but they will also need assistance in recognizing students with exceptional talents and building upon their talents.

2. Assisting teachers in learning how to observe students, interpret their behavior accurately, and develop appropriate responses to the needs they identify among their students. The school psychologist cannot be a curriculum or materials specialist, of course, but may provide valuable assistance to teachers by helping them learn how to study their students' characteristics and needs and plan accordingly.

3. Assisting teachers in working effectively with parents and community resources (such as aides or mentors) and in developing community support for gifted programs.

4. Participating in the planning and implementation of program evaluations.

5. Providing support and encouragement for teachers' efforts to develop new, more flexible instructional programs for many students with special educational needs.

Programs for gifted and talented students are still in "an infant stage of development" in many schools. Knowledgeable, concerned school psychologists can provide significant leadership in their successful development, implement, and evaluation in the 1980s.

TABLE 7.4
Enrichment Program Prototypes

Grouping	Acceleration	Guidance
Provisions that facilitate the student's access to learning opportunities	Activities that promote learning beyond regularly prescribed curriculum	Experiences that promote understanding of the self and others and explore opportunities for careers
Cluster grouping within the regular class	Early entrance or preschool classes	Individual conferences
Special regular classes	Double-grade promotion	Group meetings
Part-time groups before, during, after school, or on	Advanced placement classes	Career and vocational counseling
Saturday seminars	Ungraded classes	Educational counseling
	Multi-age classes	Community programs and sponsorship
Minicourses	Tutoring	
		Scholarship societies
Team teaching	Correspondence courses	
		Study groups
Alternative schools	Extra classes for extra credit	
		Special education classes
Resource room or demonstration classroom	Credit by examination	Tutoring
Itinerant or resource teacher	Independent study	
	Continuous progress curriculum	
Field trip and cultural events		
	Year-round school	
Special summer classes	Flexible scheduling	
	Block or back-to-back classes	

Source: Kaplan (1974).

References

Baldwin, A., & Wooster, J. *The baldwin identification matrix.* Buffalo: DOK, 1976.

Biondi, A., & Parnes, S. J. *Assessing creative growth* (Vols. 1 & 2). Great Neck, New York: Creative Synergetic Association, 1976.

Block, N. J., & Dworkin, G. (Eds.). *The IQ controversy.* New York: Pantheon, 1976.

Bloom, B. S. *Taxonomy of educational objectives: Cognitive domain.* New York: David McKay, 1956.

Broedel, J., Ohlsen, N., Proff, F., & Southard, C. Effects of group counseling on gifted underachieving adolescents. *Journal of Consulting Psychology,* 1960, **24,** 103–170.

Daurio, S. P. Educational enrichment vs acceleration: A review of the literature. In W. C. George, S. J. Cohn, & J. C. Stanley (Eds.), *Acceleration and enrichment: Strategies for educating the gifted,* in press.

Dellas, M., & Gaier, E. L. Identification of creativity: The individual. *Psychological Bulletin,* 1970, **73**(1), 55–73.

Drews, E. M. Counseling for self-actualization in gifted girls and young women. *Journal of Counseling Psychology,* 1965, **12,** 167–175.

Feldhusen, J. F., Treffinger, D. J., & Elias, R. M. The right kind of program instruction for the gifted. *NSPI Journal,* 1969, 8–11.

Fine, M. J. Facilitating parent-child relationships for creativity. *Gifted Child Quarterly,* 1977, **22,** 487–500.

Fox, L. H. Sex differences in mathematical precocity: Bridging the gap. In D. P. Keating (Ed.), *Intellectual talent research and development.* Baltimore: The Johns Hopkins University Press, 1976.

Fox, L. H. Sex differences: Implications for program planning for the intellectually talented. In J. C. Stanley, W. C. George, & C. H. Solano (Eds.), *The gifted and the creative: A fifty-year perspective.* Baltimore: The Johns Hopkins University Press, 1977. (a)

Fox, L. H. *The effects of sex role socialization on mathematics participation and achievement.* Paper prepared for Education and Work Group, Career Awareness Division, National Institute of Education, U.S. Department of Health, Education, and Welfare, Contract Number FN17 400-76-0114. Washington, D.C.: U.S.Government Printing Office, 1977. (b)

Gallagher, J. J. *Teaching the gifted child.* Boston: Allyn and Bacon, 1975.

Gowan, J. C. Identification-responsibility of both principal and teacher. *Accent on Talent,* 1967, **2,** 1.

Gowan, J. C. Background and history of the gifted-child movement. In J. C. Stanley, W. C. George, & C. H. Solano (Eds.), *The gifted and the creative: A fifty-year perspective.* Baltimore: The Johns Hopkins University Press, 1977.

Gross, F. P., & Sabatino, D. A. Role of the school psychologist in evaluating an experimental program for gifted students. *Journal of School Psychology,* 1965, **3,** 56–61.

Guilford, J. P. The three faces of intellect. *American Psychologist,* 1959, **14,** 469–479.

Guilford, J. P. *The nature of human intelligence.* New York: McGraw-Hill, 1967.

Jordan, J. E., & Keith, J. P. The counselor's role in working with gifted students. *Gifted Child Quarterly,* 1965, **9,** 136–140.

Kaplan, S. N. *Providing programs for the gifted and talented: A handbook.* Ventura, California: Ventura County Schools, 1974.

Keating, D. P. Possible sampling bias in genetic studies of genius. *Educational and Psychological Measurements,* 1975, **35,** 657–662.

Keating, D. P. (Ed.). *Intellectual talent: Research and development.* Baltimore: The Johns Hopkins University Press, 1976.

Khatena, J. *The creativity gifted child: Suggestions for parents and teachers.* New York: Vantage Press, 1978.

Krathwohl, D. R., Bloom, B. S., & Masia, B. B. *Taxomony of educational objectives: The affective domain.* New York: David McKay, 1964.

Loehlin, J. C., Lindzey, G., & Spuhler, J. N. *Race differences in intelligence.* San Francisco: W. H. Freeman, 1975.

Marland, S. P. *Education of the gifted and talented* (2 Vols). Washington, D.C.: U.S. Government Printing Office, 1971.

Martinson, R. A. *The identification of the gifted and talented.* Ventura, California: Ventura County Public Schools, 1974.

Oden, M. H. The fulfillment of promise: 40-year follow up of the Terman gifted group. *Genetic Psychology Monographs,* 1968, **77,** 3–93.

Parnes, S. J., & Noller, R. B. Applied creativity: The creative studies project II. The results of the two-year program. *Journal of Creative Behavior,* 1972, **6,** 164–186.

Pyryt, M. C. *Survey of teachers' attitudes towards gifted students.* Paper presented at the 24th annual meeting of the National Association for Gifted Children, San Diego, California, October 1977.

Renzulli, J. S. *The enrichment triad model.* Weathersfield, Connecticut: Creative Learning Press, 1977.

Renzulli, J. S., Hartman, R. K., & Callahan, C. M. Scale for rating the behavioral characteristics of superior students. *Exceptional Children,* 1971, **38,** 211–214; 243–248.

Reese, H. W., Parnes, S. J., Treffinger, D. J., & Kaltsounis, A. Effects of a creative studies program on structure of intellect factors. *Journal of Educational Psychology,* 1976, **64,** 401–412.

Robinson, H. B., Jackson, N. E., & Roedell, W. C. *Early identification of advanced children.* Paper presented at the annual convention of the National Association for Gifted Children, San Diego, California, October 1977.

Samuda, R. J. *Psychological testing of american minorities: Issues and consequences.* New York: Dodd, Mead, 1975.

Sears, P. S., & Barbee, A. H. Career and life satisfactions among Terman's gifted women. In J. C. Stanley, W. C. George, & C. H. Solano (Eds.), *The gifted and the creative: A fifty-year perspective.* Baltimore: The Johns Hopkins University Press, 1977.

Sears, R. R. Sources of life satisfaction of the Terman gifted men. *American Psychologist,* 1977, **32,** 119–128.

Stanley, J. C. Identifying and nurturing the gifted child. *Phi Delta Kappan,* 1976, **58,** 234–237.

Stanley, J. C. Rationale of the study of mathematically precocious youth (SMPY) during its first five years of promoting educational acceleration. In J. C. Stanley, W. C. George, & C. H. Solano (Eds.), *The gifted and the creative: A fifty-year perspective.* Baltimore: The Johns Hopkins University Press, 1977.

Stanley, J. C., Keating, D. P., & Fox, L. H. *Mathematical talent: Discovery description and development.* Baltimore: The Johns Hopkins University Press, 1974.

Taylor, C. W. Cultivation new talents: A way to reach the educationally deprived. *Journal of Creative Behavior,* 1968, **2,** 83–90.

Terman, L. M. Mental and physical traits of a thousand gifted children. *Genetic studies of genius* (Vol. I). Stanford, California: Stanford University Press, 1925.

Terman, L. M., & Oden, M. H. The gifted group at mid-life. *Genetic studies of genius* (Vol. 5). Stanford, California: Stanford University Press, 1959.

Thurstone, L. L. Primary mental abilities. *Psychometric Monographs,* 1938, No. 1.

Tisdall, W. J., & Birch, J. W. The school psychologist in a program of early admission for mentally advanced children. *Journal of School Psychology,* 1965, **3,** 48–55.

Tobin, D. *Counselor stereotypes of gifted youth.* Paper presented at the 24th annual meeting of the National Association for Gifted Children, San Diego, California, October 1977.

Torrance, E. P. *Rewarding creative behavior.* Englewood Cliffs, New Jersey: Prentice-Hall, 1965.

Torrance, E. P. Helping gifted children through mental health information and concepts. *Gifted Child Quarterly,* 1967, **11,** 3–7.

Torrance, E. P. Creatively gifted and disadvantaged students. In J. C. Stanley, W. C. George, & C.

H. Solano (Eds.), *The gifted and the creative: A fifty-year perspective*. Baltimore: The Johns Hopkins University Press, 1977.

Treffinger, D. J. Teaching for self-directed learning: A priority for gifted education. *Gifted Child Quarterly*, 1975, **19**, 46–59.

Treffinger, D. J. Guidelines for encouraging independence and self-direction among gifted students. *Journal of Creative Behavior*, 1978, **12**, 14–20.

Treffinger, D. J., Borgers, S. B., Render, G. F., & Hoffman, R. M. Encouraging affective development. *Gifted Child Quarterly*, 1976, **20**, 47–65.

Treffinger, D. J., Renzulli, J. S., & Feldhusen, J. F. Problems in the assessment of creative thinking. *Journal of Creative Behavior*, 1971, **5**, 104–112.

Williams, F. E. *Classroom ideas for encouraging thinking and feeling*. Buffalo: DOK, 1971.

Witty, P. Who are the gifted? In N. D. Henry (Ed.), *Education for the gifted. Yearbook of the national society for the study of education*, 1958, **57** (Part II), 41–63.

Wyne, M. D., & Skjei, P. The counselor and exceptional pupils: A critical review. *Personnel and Guidance Journal*, 1970, **48**, 828–835.

DANIEL J. RESCHLY

Nonbiased Assessment

When in danger, when in doubt,
Run in circles,
Yell and shout.

The issues of bias in tests and in assessment have provoked high-frequency behaviors of the type suggested in the anonymous saying quoted here. Much heat has been generated through the yelling and shouting, but relatively little light. Illumination of improved practices in psychology and education, especially procedures that would expand opportunities and improve competencies for children, have been conspicuously absent in most of the discussions.

Perhaps the main difficulty stems from a focus on the wrong problems and the wrong questions in the discussion of nonbiased assessment. The major concern has been with the assessment of minorities, particularly questions related to whether specific tests are biased or unfair when used with black, Latino, or Native American children. The issues related to the use of tests with children from minority backgrounds are legitimate and important to raise. However, a more significant issue to address is whether we can ensure educational experiences that maximize competencies and opportunities.

Several of the wide assortment of definitions and criteria for determining bias in tests or assessment are discussed and evaluated in this chapter. Although each of these conceptions has merit, a more comprehensive view of bias in assessment is proposed. Bias in tests, or bias in assessment generally, should be evaluated according to the criterion of outcomes for individuals. If assessment activities result in needed services, effective interventions, or expanded opportunities for

215

SCHOOL PSYCHOLOGY
Perspectives and Issues

individuals, then assessment is useful, and by the definition proposed here, unbiased. If the assessment activities do not lead to appropriate services and are not related to effective interventions, then the assessment activities must be regarded as useless for the individual, and biased or unfair if members of minority groups are differentially exposed to inappropriate services or ineffective interventions as a result of assessment activities. The major problem then in nonbiased assessment is ensuring usefulness and fairness of assessment and interventions for all persons. The focus on usefulness and fairness of both assessment and interventions provides a broader perspective on the problem of nonbiased assessment and directs our attention beyond the typical, narrow questions of whether this item or that item, this test or that test is biased and unfair. Consideration of outcomes of assessment can improve the assessment practices used with all children as well as reduce the alleged bias in current assessment practices used with minority children.

Nonbiased assessment is not simply a debate within academic settings. Legislation has been enacted, judicial inquiry has occurred and continues, and various directives from federal and state agencies have resulted. The issues that led to these events are discussed, and implicit assumptions are clarified in this chapter. Most important, specific recommendations are made that reflect an attempt to provide a guide to school psychologists for our efforts to ensure quality in assessment for all children, including nonbiased assessment with minority persons.

Concerns about bias in assessment did not originate in school psychology and can perhaps be understood best within the context of the historical process of removing race, class, and ethnic discrimination. Similar issues of bias in assessment that will be discussed within the context of school psychology are present in the broader contexts of public education, employment settings, and professional school selection. Indeed, recent events such as the introduction of resolutions suggesting the outright elimination of all standardized tests (Houts, 1977) and the *Bakke* court case (1978) demonstrate the widespread contemporary concerns over bias and usefulness. Furthermore, concerns over bias in tests are not a recent phenomenon. Issues similar to those debated today were the topic of heated discussions in the 1920s. These discussions, like those today, appeared in both the professional and popular literature (Block & Dworkin, 1976).

Perhaps the most critical issue, often ignored in current and previous debates on bias in tests, is the net effect of standardized tests in the process of eliminating discrimination and expanding opportunities. There was a close parallel in the 1920s to the current discussions of the hereditary potential for intellectual development of specific racial or ethnic groups. Only in the 1920s, the primary concern was over the "innate abilities" of southern and eastern Europeans and persons of Jewish ancestry (Kamin, 1974). Tests were also used to document the hereditary inferiority of these groups. However, it is highly likely that the same kinds of tests, used earlier as proof of inferiority, served later as instruments of social mobility for many individuals of Jewish and eastern or southern European ancestry. The net effect of standardized tests on eliminating discrimination against various groups has probably been positive for many groups, and more importantly, suggests a different set of criteria for us to consider in current discussions of test bias. The most significant criteria in judging the effects of standardized tests are usefulness and fairness, especially in terms of outcomes for individuals. The debate over alleged bias in this test or that test probably cannot be resolved. Furthermore, whether or not cultural bias exists in a test may be largely irrelevant to the issue of ensuring more effective educational outcomes and expanded opportunities for children.

Although the concerns about bias in tests are not new, and did not arise only within school psychology, school psychology and intelligence tests have been among the most targeted areas for expressions of concern. Perhaps the most dramatic expressions of concern have occurred in the form of litigation over the past 10 years. The litigation bearing upon bias in tests was concerned with special education placement, principally the placement of minority-group students in classes for the mildly retarded. The court decisions have had a significant impact on recent legislation and the practice of school psychology.

Special Education Litigation

All of the provisions of recent federal legislation regarding the handicapped (see Monroe, Chapter 2 of this volume) appeared earlier in one or more of the court cases (Turnbull, 1978). Two types of court cases have been extremely influential. One type of case was initiated by parents of handicapped children, usually moderately or severely retarded, against public schools. Parents contended that constitutional guarantees existed to protect children from discrimination solely because of handicapping conditions. The fact that many school districts did not admit children with more severe handicaps was discriminatory according to the parents. In a landmark decision (PARC, 1971) a Pennsylvania federal district court upheld the contentions of parents and ordered the state to provide free and appropriate educational services for handicapped children.

The second type of case was concerned with the overrepresentation of minority students in special education programs for the mildly retarded. A number of cases have been before the courts on the placement issue. The net effect of these cases has been to raise serious questions about traditional assessment practices, to institute a variety of protections for parents and students, and to establish guidelines for assessment of minority students. The effects and implications of these cases are sufficiently far-reaching to warrant closer examination.

Hobson v. Hansen

The *Hobson* v. *Hansen* case (1967), although not directly related to special education placement, considered issues and established a precedent that appeared in subsequent cases. *Hobson* was the first case in which the courts considered technical issues related directly to psychological testing. The basic issue was the constitutionality of the tracking system used in Washington, D.C. public schools. Although a test was not the only source of information used to assign students to an ability level, it was apparently the most identifiable component, at least in the deliberations of the court. The group ability test per se was not ruled unconstitutional, but rather the *use* of the test, on the basis of evidence that black students were overrepresented in lower tracks and underrepresented at higher (gifted) levels. The court reasoned that since the outcome of the test was discriminatory, the test itself was biased or unfair to black students.

In retrospect, it is obvious that the reasoning of the court in the *Hobson* v. *Hansen* case was clearly relevant to issues in special education classification where poor and minority students were also overrepresented. The overrepresentation of minorities in classes for the mildly retarded was certainly well known in the 1960s, but it was regarded widely in the literature and in university classes as the "natural" outcome of "cultural–familial" factors. School psychologists, the author included, should probably have recognized the obvious parallels of this case to special education practices and either undertaken appropriate corrective action or collected data to defend overrepresentation. In point of fact most of us expressed curiosity over the decision and ignored the implications.

Diana v. State of California

The *Diana* case (1970) was the first court action related directly to overrepresentation of minorities in special education. *Diana* was a class action suit filed on behalf of bilingual children in Monterey County, California who were placed in special education classes for the mildly retarded. The plaintiffs contended that inappropriate intelligence tests were used to place minority students in the programs. The tests were regarded as inappropriate due to emphases on verbal facility and middle-class values and symbols. Furthermore, the tests were administered in English, although the children enrolled in the classes were from homes in which Spanish was the primary language (and possibly the primary language of the children). The plaintiffs also contended that through the *use* of the tests the children were denied their Fourteenth Amendment rights to equal protection of the laws, specifically the right to equal educational opportunities. Implicit in this contention was the assumption of ineffectiveness of the special education program and the deleterious effects of the label "educable mentally retarded." The crucial, and apparently most persuasive, evidence was the percentage of Spanish surnamed children in the district in comparison to the percentage of Spanish surnamed children enrolled in special education classes for the mildly retarded. In Monterey County, Spanish surnamed students constituted 18.5% of the total school enrollment, but 33.3% of the enrollment in classes for the mildly retarded was Spanish surnamed. The suit was settled out of court through negotiations between the plaintiffs and representatives of the school district and the California State Department of Education. A consent decree was then issued by the court that had far-reaching effects upon assessment procedures in California and implications for assessment elsewhere.

The consent decree in *Diana* required the following:

1. Assessment of primary language competence prior to administration of other assessment procedures. If the child's primary language competence was determined to be Spanish, subsequent assessment procedures had to be administered in Spanish.
2. Unfair portions of current tests such as knowledge of English word meanings were to be deleted, and greater emphasis was to be placed on the results of nonverbal or performance measures.
3. All bilingual children enrolled currently in special classes for the mildly retarded were to be reevaluated within a short time period using procedures consistent with points 1 and 2 above.
4. School districts and the State Department of Education were required to develop services to assist those children who were returned from special education to regular classes as a result of the reevaluations.
5. The California State Department of Education was required to develop and standardize a more appropriate test for Latino youth. (Author's note: Apparently this project was never initiated.)
6. Finally, the consent decree included a rather strongly worded warning to districts that disproportionate numbers of any ethnic or racial group placed in special education programs must be explained and justified.

Two direct and immediate outcomes of the *Diana* case can be identified. First, the court decision resulted in the immediate return of several thousand minority children to regular classrooms. The social and academic adjustment of these "decertified" students was better than expected, though still well below average, despite the haphazard nature of the court-mandated transition services (Yoshida, MacMillan, & Meyers, 1976). The fact that many students, previously classified as educably mentally retarded, were "successful" in regular classroom programs illustrates the need for periodic and thorough review of placement decisions, and perhaps, demonstrates the wisdom of routinely returning special class students to regular classrooms on a trial basis (Hewett & Forness, 1974).

The second direct outcome of the *Diana* case was the issuing of an Office for Civil Rights (OCR) memorandum in 1972 (Oakland, 1977a) that specified certain procedures to guide the assessment of minority students. This memorandum was particularly concerned with the possible relationship of overrepresentation of minority students in special education to the broader issue of segregation in the public schools.

Guadalupe v. Tempe Elementary District

The *Guadalupe* case (1972) was nearly identical to the *Diana* case in terms of issues (overrepresentation) and method of resolution (consent decree). *Guadalupe* is important to this discussion in that the consent decree went even further in specifying assessment procedures. In addition to the same requirements concerning assessment included in *Diana, Guadalupe* required the following:

1. No child shall be placed in programs for the mildly retarded unless the intelligence test score is two or more standard deviations below the mean. (Note: The Arizona educational definition of mental retardation at that time was IQ of less than 75 and the AAMD criterion prior to 1973 was one standard deviation or more below the mean.)
2. Intelligence test results shall not be the exclusive or the primary basis for classifying children as mentally retarded. (Note: This same statement has appeared frequently in legislation and rules and regulations over the past 5 years.)
3. If the child's primary language competence was determined to be in some language other than English, classification decisions were to be based upon nonverbal or performance-type measures.
4. Assessment of adaptive behavior must be done through, but not limited to, an interview with the parents or guardian in the child's home.

The *Guadalupe* case also required several other procedures that were later incorporated in federal legislation, such as informed consent for evaluation and placement, due process, integration of programs for handicapped and normal students, and accountability of school districts in terms of data on "prior effectiveness of special education programs [*Guadalupe* v. *Tempe,* p. 6]."

Larry P. v. Riles

The *Larry P.* case (1972, 1974, and pending) is also a class action suit related to the basic issue of overrepresentation of minority students in programs for the mildly retarded. *Larry P.* was filed on behalf of black children placed in programs for the mildly retarded. The case was filed originally in November 1971; an injunction was issued by the Federal District Court for Northern California in June 1972; an expanded injunction was issued in 1974, and a final decision in the case is expected some time in 1978.

The preliminary injunction in *Larry P.* restrained the San Francisco School District from

> placing Black students in classes for the educable mentally retarded on the basis of criteria which place primary reliance on the results of IQ tests as they are currently administered, *if* the consequence of use of such criteria is racial imbalance in the composition of such classes [*Larry P.* v. *Riles* Court Injunction, 1972; emphasis added].

In 1974 the plaintiffs requested and obtained an expansion of the original injunction to include all school districts in the state of California. This resulted in California State Board of Education action forbidding the use of individual intelligence tests for *all* students in California schools *if* the outcome of such tests was a classification decision of mental retardation (California State Board of Education, 1975). Intelligence tests were not banned generally by the courts in California as is commonly believed, and use of intelligence tests in California was permissable as long as a decision of mental retardation was not under consideration.

The *Larry P.* case is potentially much more far-reaching than any of the previous court suits. The case was filed on the basis of constitutional law in a federal district court, and the case will be decided by judicial opinion rather than a consent decree negotiated out of court. Finally, both sides in the case are reportedly committed to appeal the decision, possibly to the Supreme Court. Massive amounts of evidence in the form of documents and expert testimony were presented in the *Larry P.* court hearings that began in October 1977 and extended through March 1978. A judicial opinion is expected during the latter half of 1978. Although the *Larry P.* case may seem remote and irrelevant to school psychologists outside of California, the *Larry P.* decision may have a decisive influence on the nature of assessment throughout the country.

The basic issues in *Larry P.* include the same concerns addressed in *Guadalupe* and *Diana* with certain crucial additions. In both *Diana* and *Guadalupe* the plaintiffs requested *revision* and *reform* of current assessment practices. In *Larry P.* the plaintiffs originally requested *elimination* of all standardized tests including, of course, individual intelligence tests. The plaintiffs argued that the resolution of previous cases such as *Diana* did not go far enough. To substantiate this assertion the plaintiffs cited data from 1974 that indicated large overrepresentation of ethnic or racial minorities in special education programs in California despite the *Diana* decision. In both 1972 and 1974 when injunctions were issued by the court, the plaintiffs argued that black children were overrepresented in programs because of inherent biases in the tests. Further, the plaintiffs contended the programs were ineffective, the labels attached to children were stigmatizing and humiliating, and the overrepresentation constituted an abridgment of the Fourteenth Amendment guarantee of equal protection. Although a number of issues *in addition* to cultural bias in tests were implicit in the contentions of the plaintiffs, the court focused on the issue of test bias in both of the preliminary injunctions.

Summary on Litigation

The litigation in special education has clearly been a crucial influence on state and federal legislation and on professional practices in school psychology. Although other factors were certainly important in influencing this legislation, litigation must be recognized as one of the most important influences.

It is also essential to understand the judicial mechanism as a means of resolving professional or scientific issues. The fundamental purposes of the courts are somewhat different from the aims of science or professions. The legal system is primarily concerned with justice whereas science is concerned primarily with truth. The issues addressed by the courts in the special education placement litigation are at best ambiguous. These issues, for example, labeling effects, bias in tests, and effectiveness of special education programs, are all sources of intense debate within the scientific and professional communities. None of these issues can be resolved "beyond a shadow of doubt" with the currently available *empirical* evidence. All of the issues mentioned previously, however, are related to rights and opportunities that are, of course, legitimate areas of judicial inquiry. The problem is that the courts, usually reluctantly, must ultimately resolve the issues on the basis of very ambiguous, sometimes technical evidence. The courts by their nature resolve the disputes in "absolute" language such as "shall" or "must" when, in fact, the evidence is at best at the level of "might" or "should."

Another notable feature of the litigation to date is the question of burden of proof. In the *Larry P.* case injunctions, the court shifted the burden of proof from the plaintiffs to the defendants on the basis of the evidence on overrepresentation. The court viewed the fact of overrepresentation as "inherently suspicious" within the broader context of the legality of segregation. The burden of proof is crucial in that it is probably impossible to prove or disprove unequivocally whether or not standardized tests are biased on the basis of the available evidence. The fact that the defendants have been responsible for proving their case has been a distinct disadvantage. However, many other issues are implicit in the special education litigation on placement. These issues are probably more important in terms of the rights and opportunities of children than the narrow issue of test bias.

Analysis of Court Decisions

A number of unresolved issues and implicit assumptions are apparent from close examination of the previous and current litigation over special education placement. These issues involve fundamental questions about the nature of intelligence, the direct and indirect effects of classification and educational services for the mildly retarded, and the outcomes of intelligence tests for culturally different persons. The court decisions have appeared to ignore many of these issues. Understanding these issues is crucial to the development of fairer and more effective assessment procedures and educational interventions.

Nature versus Nurture

The nature versus nurture debate over intellectual differences is an old controversy that even precedes the development of IQ tests (Galton, 1892). The issue is far from new, the general outline of the debate has not changed, and the issue is no closer to resolution now than it was in the 1800s. However, the debate has been intensified since the late 1960s for a variety of reasons. Reactions to Jensen's (1969) highly controversial evaluation of and explanation for the disappointing effects of the Head Start program are a crucial component of the current attacks on intelligence tests. Jensen has published widely on the alleged genetic inferiority of blacks. Although Jensen's conclusions are usually stated in the tentative and conditional style favored and required by the scholarly community, the conclusions of several other "scholars" have been nothing short of inflammatory. For example, the following statement by Schockley (1971), which appeared a few years ago in a highly regarded academic journal, was based largely on Jensen's conclusions: "Nature has *color coded* groups of individuals so that statistically reliable predictions of their adaptability to intellectually rewarding and effective lives can *easily* be made and *profitably* be used by the pragmatic man in the street [p. 377, emphasis added]."

The statement is, of course, absurd. The fact that such statements are made, and even appear occasionally in academic journals, provides a basis for understanding the sense of outrage expressed by many black Americans regarding the use (misuse) of IQ tests. However, in the judgment of the present author, elimination of current tests would accomplish little in reducing racism and might in fact be counterproductive to that effort.

A complete review of all of the data on the nature–nurture issue is far beyond the scope of this chapter (see Brody & Brody, 1976; Loehlin, Lindzey, & Spuhler, 1975; Samuda, 1975). Two points must be emphasized. First, elimination of standardized tests would not settle the nature–nurture controversy, and would, in all likelihood, reduce the chances of overcoming existing barriers to the full participation of all persons in the economic and social order. Second, the professional personnel responsible for using the tests have an ethical and moral obligation to ensure that test results are interpreted accurately and test use leads to expanded, not diminished, opportunities and competencies for children.

Meaning of IQ Test Results

Perhaps the most immediate challenge for professional personnel who use standardized tests is to once again attempt to clarify the meaning of IQ test results. Alfred Binet was the first to warn of the misuse and misunderstanding of the meaning of IQ test results. Others have issued similar warnings over the past 70 years. The myths that IQ scores are fixed, unitary, and predetermined by heredity are all too prevalent among consumers for us to ignore. Much testimony in the court cases including *Larry P.* (*APA Monitor,* 1977) was directed at disproving these myths. This testimony has a "straw man" quality. It is not hard to substantiate charges that confirm the obvious. Unfortunately, we have not done enough to eliminate the misconceptions about IQ. One step we might take is to develop a kind of "surgeon general's warning" about IQ that could be printed on every test protocol, every test report, and placed in every file where IQ test results are included. The following is one example of a warning statement that we have used recently in school psychology practica settings:

> IQ tests measure only a portion of the competencies involved with human intelligence. The IQ results are best seen as predicting performance in school, and reflecting the degree to which children have mastered middle class cultural symbols and values. This is useful information, but it is also limited. Further cautions—IQ tests do not measure innate-genetic capacity and the scores are not fixed. Some persons do exhibit significant increases or decreases in their measured IQ.

Unfortunately, one of the issues in the litigation has been whether or not measured intelligence is unitary, fixed, and predetermined. The testimony that once again proves these assertions to be myths may be important to the resolution of the *Larry P.* case.

Labeling Effects: Meaning of Mild Mental Retardation

A closely related set of implicit assumptions in the court cases involves the meaning of mild mental retardation, labeling effects, and the efficacy of special classes for the mildly retarded. The courts have apparently been convinced that the label "educable mentally retarded" is humiliating, stigmatizing, and solely responsible for a negative self-fulfilling prophecy. Further, the courts have examined the term "mental retardation," and apparently have understood it to imply permanent, global incompetence with a biological etiology (*APA Monitor,* 1977). The available factual evidence related to these assumptions reveals a quite different state of affairs.

The alleged effects of labels have dominated much of the discussion of the outcomes of special education programs over the past 10 years. Four basic questions seem to be especially important in this discussion.

1. Do labels create expectancies? The evidence generally confirms this assertion; however, the outcomes of these studies may be an artifact of the methodology used. In studies where subjects (college students or teachers) are given only the label and/or no or only brief exposure to the child bearing the label, a rather large expectancy effect is typically reported (e.g., Ysseldyke & Foster, 1978). The studies essentially involve telling the subject that Johnny is retarded, then asking the subjects to rate Johnny's likely or briefly observed performance on an academic task. In other studies using the same basic methodology, but providing lengthy exposure to the "labeled child," the expectancy effect is not observed or diminishes over time (Yoshida & Meyers, 1975; Reschly & Lamprecht, in press). The evidence from experimental studies on the relationship of labels to expectancies is unclear, and few studies have been conducted in natural situations.

2. There is even less support for the question raised as to whether there is a

relationship between expectancies and the self-fulfilling prophecy phenomena described by Rosenthal and Jacobson (1968). The basic idea of the self-fulfilling prophecy is widely cited as fact, and apparently is consistent with certain philosophical or political orientations. However, the data simply do not support the assertion (MacMillan, Jones, & Aloia, 1974; Humphreys & Stubbs, 1977).

3. A related, and usually unexamined, issue in the litigation is the kind of informal label used in the public schools and the "prelabeling" experiences of children classified as mildly retarded in the schools. From reading the testimony in the placement cases, one is perhaps led to believe that no one ever saw the students as academic or behavioral problems prior to their being labeled by a psychologist. The erroneous impression that school psychologists and IQ tests were the first and most important step in classifying school children as mildly retarded has been refuted (Meyers, Sundstrom, & Yoshida, 1974), but this misconception is prominent in the litigation. In fact, teacher referral is the most important step in the process whereby children are classified as mildly retarded. Many children referred as suspected cases of mild retardation are not diagnosed as such by psychologists (Ashurst & Meyers, 1973), and many children who would fail the IQ criterion are never referred (Mercer, 1973). These data suggest the possibility that IQ tests have protected children, especially minority students, from being misclassified as mildly retarded. Surprisingly, very few studies of the numbers of majority and minority children referred versus the number placed in programs have appeared in the literature. The minimal data available presently (e.g., Zucker & Prieto, 1977) suggest that elimination of IQ tests would likely result in greater rather than less overrepresentation of minorities in special education programs.

4. Evidence on the final question of the meaning of the diagnosis of mild mental retardation and the reactions of persons so labeled is much clearer. Most persons misinterpret the meaning of mild retardation (see Oakland and Goldwater, Chapter 5 of this volume). The diagnostic construct of mild or educable mental retardation does not imply permanence, comprehensive impairment, or biological origin; this is contrary to the apparent understanding of the courts. Mildly retarded persons are deficient only in a fairly narrow range of skills and most become self-supporting, independent functioning adults (Baller, Charles, & Miller, 1967). The widespread misconceptions about the meaning of mild mental retardation suggest the need for a revision in the classification system. The most frequent source of misunderstanding is confusion of mild mental retardation with more severe levels of mental retardation, which are generally permanent, relatively global, and related to biological origin. Clearer separation of types or levels of mental retardation or use of completely different terminology is obviously needed. Until such changes are made, diagnostic personnel must devote more effort toward communicating the meaning and implications of different levels of mental retardation to the public, parents, educators, and students.

The evidence on the final question related to labeling, that is, the reactions of persons who bear the label, provides reason for sober reflection on the part of all diagnostic personnel. Persons who bear the common labels find them highly aversive (MacMillan *et al.,* 1974; Jones, 1972; Edgerton, 1967). Classification activities do involve risks to the individual. The risks clearly supported by the data are misunderstanding of the common labels by others and negative reactions of the individual bearing the label. Elimination of classification activities is probably impossible and potentially damaging to the provision of needed services (Hobbs, 1975). Therefore, the only course of action available to diagnostic personnel is to attempt to minimize the risks and maximize the potential benefits associated with classification. Movement toward a classification system that uses more precise, behavioral, descriptive terminology could reduce some of the risks. Provision of effective interventions as a result of classification (and assessment) is crucial to maximizing the benefits.

Effectiveness of Special Education Interventions

Perhaps the most important allegation by plaintiffs, implicitly accepted by the courts, was the presumed ineffectiveness of special classes for the mildly retarded. The effectiveness of these programs has been questioned (Dunn, 1968) and debated (Kolstoe, 1976). The defendants in the cases (states and local districts) have generally not attempted to defend the efficacy of the educational programs in benefiting the children classified as mildly retarded (Meyers, MacMillan, & Yoshida, 1978). Testimony from parents and others focused on the ineffectiveness of the programs. Since the defendants did not attempt to rebut this testimony, the courts assumed the programs were inferior to regular classrooms. Although the court decisions focused on IQ tests and the overrepresentation of minority children, the ineffectiveness of special classes was a crucial assumption in the decisions. However, if the educational programs were as ineffective as alleged, then the programs as such were a denial of the constitutional rights of any child, regardless of racial or ethnic status!

The litigation may reflect "worst case" situations (MacMillan, 1977). Special education programs for the mildly retarded generally (and the psychological services associated with these programs) may not have been represented accurately by the situations brought to litigation. MacMillan has pointed to a wide variety of inappropriate services involved with the *Diana* case that may not have been typical of special education programs or psychological services in other settings. In addition to the alleged inferiority of the academic programs and the negative effects of labels, the courts were concerned with the degree of segregation involved in the self-contained classes. The recent concept of least restrictive alternative along with efforts to improve academic services through individualized educational programs with annual review are important to meeting the concerns of the courts and to ensuring the benefits of classification and assessment for individuals.

Disproportionate Numbers Equated with Bias

Evidence on the overrepresentation of minority students in classes for the mildly retarded has been a major component in all of the court decisions cited earlier and still represents the major emphasis of the Federal Office for Civil Rights. Overrepresentation of minorities has been regarded as inherently suspicious by the courts. Two facets of the overrepresentation data bear closer analysis. First, the overrepresentation data are sometimes misinterpreted and/or exaggerated in attacks on the uses of intelligence tests with minorities. The percentages can be very misleading if not understood properly. For example, in the *Larry P.* case, black students constituted 28.5% of the total district enrollment, but nearly 66% of the enrollment in special education classes for the mildly retarded. These data have sometimes been understood to mean that two-thirds of all black students were diagnosed as mentally retarded through the use of intelligence tests. In fact, as Table 8.1 illustrates, a much smaller percentage of black students were actually diagnosed as mildly retarded.

The only assumption made in the example in Table 8.1 is that 2% of the total student population is classified as mildly retarded. The assumption of 2% is an estimate based upon actual special education enrollment data from a variety of sources. The actual enrollment for a specific district may be slightly higher or lower. The main point is that even with the unusually large degree of overrepresentation involved in the *Larry P.* case, only a relatively small percentage of minority students were actually classified as mildly retarded. These data certainly do not support the assertion that the primary function of IQ tests is to label minority students as "uneducable and retarded."

Curiously, persons with other equally obvious demographic characteristics are also overrepresented in special education programs. For example, the ratio of

TABLE 8.1
Application of Overrepresentation Data to a Hypothetical Population of Students

Data	Percentage of student enrollment	Student enrollment (N)
Larry P. case		
Minority student enrollment	28.5	
Minority enrollment in programs for the mildly retarded	66	
Total student population in programs for the mildly retarded	2	
Apply these data to a hypothetical population of 40,000 students		
Minority student enrollment	28.5	11,400
Total enrollment in programs for mildly retarded	2	800
Minority enrollment in programs for the mildly retarded	66	528
Minority students classified as mildly retarded	4.6	

males to females in programs for children with mild retardation or learning disabilities is at least 3:1, and probably much higher. More important to our present discussion is the overrepresentation of children from economically poor homes in programs for the mildly retarded. If we divided a student population into two groups simply on the basis of median family income, and then analyzed the income characteristics of students in programs for the mildly retarded, it is likely that even greater disproportionality would result. The fact is that very few children from middle- and upper-class homes obtain intelligence test scores within the mildly retarded range, which of course is one of the criteria for the diagnosis of mild mental retardation (Zigler, 1967). This relationship, that is, the association of poverty with mild mental retardation along with the income characteristics of certain minority populations, raises an intriguing question. Are minorities overrepresented in programs for the mildly retarded because of minority status or because of socioeconomic status?

The purpose in raising these questions is not simply to defend the overrepresentation of minorities in special education. As mentioned earlier, if the programs for the mildly retarded were (are?) as bad as alleged, then placement in such programs is inappropriate for any child, regardless of racial or ethnic status. However, these questions may direct our attention to more relevant issues, for example, the usefulness and fairness of assessment procedures generally, rather than the narrow preoccupation with test bias that unfortunately has been the focus of the litigation.

Legislation Requiring Nonbiased Assessment

Two recent federal laws provide nearly identical guidelines for the assessment and placement of handicapped children. Section 504 of the Rehabilitation Act of 1973 (*Federal Register,* May 4, 1977) and Public Law 94-142, the Education for all All Handicapped Children Act of 1975 (*Federal Register,* August 23, 1977), reflect the clear influence of the special education placement litigation. Most pertinent to this chapter is the following requirement from Public Law 94-142: "Testing and evaluation materials and procedures used for the purposes of evaluation and placement of handicapped children must be selected and administered so as not to be racially or culturally discriminatory [p. 42496]."

This requirement, commonly referred to as nonbiased assessment, is one of the most important features of the legislation, but potentially, one of the weakest, since no clear definition and only limited discussion of the meaning of bias in assessment appeared in the rules and regulations. In view of the differing interpretations and contradictory evidence on bias in tests or assessment, the practical effects of the requirement are unpredictable.

Perhaps in response to the potential confusion, the Bureau of Education for the Handicapped (BEH) awarded a large contract to the Coordinating Office for

Regional Resource Centers (CORRC) to explore the meaning of bias in assessment. The CORRC project has issued three reports on bias in assessment. Volume II of this series entitled *With Bias Toward None* (CORRC, 1976; also available as Oakland, 1977a) is the most substantive and pertinent of the reports. The CORRC projects have not resulted in clearly stated definitions of bias or specific guidelines for eliminating bias in assessment. Both the CORRC reports and the federal rules and regulations have apparently concluded that although bias cannot be defined unequivocally, evaluation procedures are likely to be less biased if procedural safeguards are followed and a broad variety of information is gathered and considered. The most important features of the Public Law 94-142 rules and regulations regarding assessment are:

1. Procedural safeguards which provide for informed consent and due process are required.
2. The assessment must be conducted in child's native language if at all possible.
3. Tests and other evaluation devices are validated for the specific purpose for which they are used, and administered by trained personnel.
4. Classification and placement decisions are *not* based on a single source of information (such as IQ) and areas of specific educational need are identified in the evaluation process.
5. Inferences about aptitude or achievement are not made from evaluation procedures which reflect the child's impaired sensory, manual, or speaking skills.
6. Assessment must be conducted in broad variety of areas and placement procedures shall draw upon information from aptitude and achievement tests, teacher recommendations, physical conditions, social or cultural background, and adaptive behavior. Further, information from the above sources must be documented and carefully considered.
7. Decisions are made by a multidisciplinary team with participation of parents.
8. Placement options are selected according to the principle of least restrictive alternative and an individualized educational program is developed.
9. The educational program is reviewed annually and a comprehensive reevaluation which meets the requirements stated above is conducted at least every 3 years.

It might be noted that the nonbiased assessment requirements appear to be concerned primarily with two populations of children. First, there is the obvious concern about the kind of assessment conducted with culturally different students, which has been the focus of this chapter. Second, there is concern (see No. 5 in the preceding list) about the assessment of children with sensory, manual, or speaking impairments, which is discussed by Gerken in Chapter 6 of this volume. These legislative guidelines are nearly identical to consent decrees issued by the courts in the early 1970s. The guidelines are stated in general terms with few precise or specific suggestions for practitioners. For example, consider the question of sociocultural background which, according to the legislation, must be considered, and the consideration must be documented in making placement decisions. There is no specification of how sociocultural background is to be assessed or how it might be taken into account by the multidisciplinary team. These issues, which are considered in a later section, will undoubtedly be the subject of much discussion and research in the future.

Bias in Tests:
Differing Conceptions and Empirical Results

There have been many efforts to define bias in tests and assessment (e.g., Novick & Petersen, 1976; Oakland & Matuszek, 1977; Hunter & Schmidt, 1976), but consensus on theoretical or research criteria and agreement on practical implications has not been achieved. Analyses of bias in specific tests have ranged from speculative judgments about specific items to sophisticated statistical examinations of test results and prediction systems. The conclusions of these efforts are largely contradictory. Analyses using subjective judgments of bias usually lead to identification of many examples or sources of bias in current tests. Analyses of data from various groups usually result in conclusions of little or no bias in current tests. Throughout the discussions of test bias, conclusions are confounded by confusion about, or differing interpretations of, the meaning of IQ test results.

Some agreement concerning the categories of bias that may exist in tests or assessment procedures appears to be emerging from this very complex literature. The major elements of possible bias can be organized around the concepts of content bias, atmosphere bias, and bias in use. Information on each of these kinds of bias has appeared in the literature, including some research evidence.

Content Bias

Allegations of cultural bias in the items used on conventional tests have been and continue to be the most popular of the criticisms of standardized tests. In fact examination of *an* item from a current standardized test to support the allegation of bias in *all* of the items appears to be an increasingly popular indoor sport. Examples of subjective judgments of item bias are numerous (e.g., *APA Monitor,* 1977; Dent, 1976; Williams, 1971). The implicit assumption is that all items on the test are biased if one or a few of the items are apparently biased. If the test is presumed to be biased on the basis of inappropriate items, then the test results are presumed to be "inaccurate" and unfair. If the items are biased, usually meaning that opportunity to learn the content of the item is not common to all environments, then the test results certainly do not reflect, and cannot be interpreted as evidence of, "innate" intelligence. However, as discussed previously, the IQ test results are *not* direct measures of innate ability for any group.

The distinction between cultural bias and cultural loading is important to this discussion. The degree of cultural loading of an item, that is, the likelihood of success on the item for persons with different backgrounds and experiences, varies on a continuum. At one end of the continuum are items that could only be answered correctly by persons with highly specific backgrounds and experiences. An example might be an item that asks "Name three presidents of Iowa State University over the past century" (the present author can name only two). The item is similar to those used on many intelligence tests in terms of the type of thinking required. However, only a very limited sample of persons would have an opportunity to be exposed to this information and thereby answer the item correctly. The item reflects a very high degree of cultural loading and would be regarded by most as culturally biased (as well as trivial). Some items on current standardized tests require similar kinds of thought patterns and also vary in degree of cultural loading. The degree of cultural loading of an item, however, depends upon the characteristics of the persons taking the test, not the item per se.

The "person-specific" nature of item bias has been illustrated well in the development of "counterbalanced" or culturally specific intelligence tests (e.g., Dove, undated; Williams, 1975). These tests require highly specific information that is usually possessed only by persons with particular backgrounds or experiences. Knowledge of "What is a short dog?" or "In C. C. Rider, what does 'C. C.' stand for?" or "What was a zoot-suiter?" is common only to persons with very specific experiences.

In addition to subjective judgments, critics of current tests also point to the differences among various groups as evidence of item bias. The differences in average performance among various groups are attributed to item bias and/or atmosphere bias. The fact that certain groups of white Anglo-Saxon Protestants (e.g., low socioeconomic status Appalachian whites) also obtain lower scores on conventional tests is usually not mentioned by the critics and suggests the differences are not simply due to the factors of race or ethnicity.

A solution attempted earlier, and mentioned only occasionally in recent years, was the development of culture-free or culture-fair tests. Generally, nonverbal or performance tests have been regarded as less culturally loaded, although not all minority groups perform better on nonverbal or performance tests. Nonverbal or performance tests are now generally recognized as falling short of the goal of freedom from cultural influences, and attempts to develop culture-fair verbal tests (e.g., Davis & Eells, 1951) are recognized as failures. Current thinking suggests that the original concept of culture free or culture fair was probably faulty (Anastasi, 1976) in view of the usual purposes of tests, that is, to predict or evaluate performance within a cultural context.

Relatively little empirical research or critical examination of the allegations of item bias has appeared in the literature. Subjective judgments of item bias, however, are not necessarily consistent with empirical data. The following item, "What is the thing to do if a boy (girl) much smaller than yourself starts to fight with you?" which appears on the WISC-R comprehension subtest, has been criticized as biased against the experiences of urban black children where it is presumably more acceptable to respond physically (incorrect answer) than verbally (correct answer). Empirical data on this item, however, suggests that it may be *relatively* easier for blacks than whites (Jensen, 1976). Empirical examinations of item bias for different groups have been relatively rare, but the minimal data that exist suggest caution in conclusions based only on subjective judgment. Furthermore, some of the allegations of item bias (as well as some of the items from culturally specific tests) reflect negative racial or ethnic stereotypes. The criticism of the item from the WISC-R subtest cited earlier implies that urban black children are taught by parents and peers that it is acceptable to beat up smaller and younger children. I doubt very much that such attitudes or behaviors are any more typical or acceptable among blacks than among whites. Another example is the item from the BITCH Test (Williams, 1975), "What is Mother's Day?" (correct answer is, "The day the welfare checks arrive"), which suggests the incorrect stereotype that all black children are from families supported by welfare, and is of course, unfair to the millions of black children from intact families where the sole source of support is income from jobs held by parents.

The evidence on item bias is simply inconclusive. Test items do vary in amount of cultural loading. Items on current tests are culturally loaded to varying degrees, as they must be if tests are to predict or evaluate important behaviors that occur only within a cultural context. Subjective judgments of item bias are not necessarily accurate, and revision of current tests either in the direction of greater or lesser cultural loading might have the effects of simultaneously increasing or maintaining group differences and reducing validity.

Atmosphere Bias

In addition to bias in content, a frequent criticism of standardized tests is that the *atmosphere* of the testing situation is unfair to minority children. Two general aspects of the testing environment are mentioned most frequently as possible sources of unfairness: (*a*) the kinds of responses and nature of the effort required on the test may be unfamiliar; or (*b*) the nature of the interaction with the examiner may be inconsistent with the child's background or experiences.

It is essential to recognize the basic assumption of maximum effort on achievement, ability, and aptitude tests. If the child cannot or does not perform as well as possible owing to unique features of the testing environment, the results of the test are inaccurate reflections of the child's thinking competencies or academic skills. In such cases comparisons of the child's performance to that of the normative sample are inappropriate.

A great amount of research has been conducted on atmosphere bias, and this research is well reviewed by Sattler (1970, 1973, 1974). The interested reader is encouraged to pursue further information in the sources cited. The major conclusions from this research are the following:

1. Much of the research was poorly designed.
2. Some of the studies used experimental manipulations that are atypical and inconsistent with good testing practices. For example, token reinforcers provided for correct answers.
3. The results of reasonably well-controlled studies in which the variables manipulated were within the range of good testing practices are contradictory. For example, the degree of warmth, amount of encouragement, time devoted to establishing rapport prior to testing, and sex or race of examiner or examinee, have been studied with mixed results. Inconsistency is the rule rather than the exception in studies of examiner effects (Samuel, 1977).
4. Examiner expectancies for performance may influence scoring of responses on items where there is some subjectivity in evaluating responses, for example, vocabulary subtest of the Wechsler scales.
5. When differences due to atmosphere effects are reported, the size of the differences is usually fairly small.

The results of this research do not necessarily generalize to all natural settings or to the performance of all individuals. Professional personnel who administer tests to culturally different persons must be sensitive to individual variations in values, motivation, language, and cognitive style, all of which could influence the results of the test. One of the most important roles of the examiner in individual evaluations is to establish the kind of climate that will elicit the child's maximum effort and performance. The test results are invalid to the degree that maximum performance is not elicited.

Bias in Use

The third concept of bias in tests is concerned with how tests are used. Two different approaches to analyzing bias in use have emerged from the recent literature. One approach, favored generally by leaders in test theory and psychometric research, emphasizes the relationships of tests to other criteria for different groups. The second approach emphasizes the implications and outcomes of test use for individuals and groups of persons. The two approaches to bias in use will be discussed separately since they use different criteria and result in different conclusions.

BIAS IN USE: PREDICTIVE VALIDITY

Academic psychologists and test publishers have generally emphasized the technical adequacy of tests in predicting various criteria for different groups. Several definitions of test bias have been proposed to guide examinations of the degree to which tests function in the same way for persons regardless of group membership. The Cleary definition (1968) characterized test use as biased if the predictions or decisions based upon the test were different as a function of group membership. Stated simply, Cleary and most leaders in psychometric theory see test use as unbiased if the same predictions are made for persons with the identical test scores regardless of group membership (Cleary, Humphreys, Kendrick, & Wesman, 1975). A number of variations of the Cleary definition have been proposed, most notable of which are those that stress the social utility of test use (Darlington, 1971; Novick & Petersen, 1976).

Although some of the definitions of bias in test use become very complex (Petersen & Novick, 1976), certain basic features are prerequisite to fairness in test use. Tests cannot be regarded as fair unless they predict with equal accuracy for all groups. Most pertinent to our concerns in school psychology is the question: Do IQ tests predict academic achievement equally well for different groups?

The data from a variety of studies conducted with prospective employees, prospective graduate and undergraduate students, and school-age children suggest that conventional standardized tests predict the usual criteria equally well for all groups. For example, the correlations between the WISC-R and either teacher ratings of achievement or a standardized test of achievement are virtually identical for Anglo, black, and Latino groups (Reschly & Reschly, in press). Furthermore, the regression equations and factor sturctures for different groups, although not identical, are highly similar (Reschly, 1978a; Reschly & Sabers, 1978; Silverstein, 1973). When differences in regression systems were found in these and other studies, the effects were overprediction for non-Anglo groups and underprediction for Anglos. The available evidence supports the conclusion that current tests predict equally well for the different groups studied thus far, and from one perspective on bias in use, conventional tests can be regarded as fair to all groups.

Bias in Use: Social Consequences

The definitions of test bias previously cited, although important, are inadequate in terms of the overall influence of tests upon the lives of persons. Testing does have social consequences. Tests, even those that predict accurately, have been misused to justify race, social class, and ethnic discrimination. Test results have led to reduction of opportunities for persons and have qualified persons for apparently ineffective interventions that may have been stigmatizing and humiliating. To defend tests simply on the basis of predictive accuracy is to miss entirely the points raised by recent critics of tests.

For example, Williams (1974) charged that IQ tests predict achievement as well for blacks because of the intervening variable of bias. In his view, both the predictor (IQ test) and the criterion (school achievement) are contaminated by racial bias, hence the correlation is significant and positive, but meaningless.

Jackson's (1975) response to Cleary et al.'s (1975) report of the American Psychological Association (APA) Committee on Educational Uses of Tests is even more to the point. Jackson saw the report as largely irrelevant to the concerns expressed by minorities. The report defended the technical adequacy of the tests when in fact the major concerns of black and Chicano psychologists (Bernal, 1975) are with how tests affect the lives of persons. The fact that tests have been used to justify racist ideology and otherwise have been misused or misinterpreted in inferences about the potential of individuals are facts acknowledged even by the authors of the APA report. Thus, to defend tests on the basis of evidence of common regression systems or to attempt to separate the issues of technical adequacy from those of social consequences is insufficient.

The ultimate criteria that should guide our evaluations of test bias are the implications and outcomes of test use for individuals. Succinctly stated, test use is fair if the results are more effective interventions leading to improved competencies and expanded opportunities for individuals. Test use is unfair if opportunities are diminished or if individuals are exposed to ineffective interventions as a result of tests.

Implementation of Nonbiased Assessment Procedures

Prerequisities to Nonbiased Assessment

A number of conditions are best seen as prerequisites to nonbiased assessment. If these conditions are not present, nonbiased assessment, or more generally, fair and useful assessment is usually impossible. The discussion of these prerequisites is brief since most are considered in other chapters in this volume.

PROCEDURAL SAFEGUARDS

Both informed consent and due process have been ignored frequently by special educators and school psychologists in the past. These issues were considered by the courts in the special education placement litigation where in several instances parents testified that they were not even informed of the decision to place their child in a special education program. Although informed consent and due process were established as legal requirements only recently, professional ethics and standards for best practices have always emphasized the importance of good communication with and involvement of parents. Both concepts are best understood as processes whereby lines of communication are established and facilitated and rights and interests protected (Abeson, Bolick, & Hass, 1975). A good guideline for most professionals to use in evaluating their performance in carrying out the spirit of informed consent and due process is, "Would you be satisfied that your rights and interests were respected and considered by the communications used if the child under consideration were your own?"

MULTIDISCIPLINARY CONTRIBUTIONS

Past standards for best professional practices and current guidelines require the involvement of a multidisciplinary team in assessment and placement of children. In particular, the guidelines require that no single source of information be used as the sole basis for placement and that a broad variety of information be gathered and considered. The source of these guidelines in the legislation may be the erroneous assumption that school psychologists and IQ tests were solely responsible for the overrepresentation of minorities in special education programs for the mildly retarded. Regardless of the source of the guideline, the intent is crucial to effective assessment and intervention. Special education placement decisions are significant events in the lives of children. Since instruments (and persons) are fallible, no single person or single measure should be the basis for a special education placement decision. A variety of information collected by different persons should result in better decisions and more effective interventions.

The sometimes difficult task in practical situations is to ensure that different disciplines are involved not just as participants in the final staffing, but also as independent data collectors, observers, and interpreters of assessment information. The intent of a multidisciplinary team is to ensure that a variety of disciplines and perspectives will be involved in the solution of a problem. Multidisciplinary teams that involve collection of data by only one or two of the team members fail to achieve the potential benefits of the multidisciplinary approach.

PLACEMENT OPTIONS AND EFFECTIVE PROGRAMS

If bias in assessment is conceptualized in terms of outcomes, then the availability of effective educational programs and alternative placement options are absolute prerequisites to implementing nonbiased assessment procedures. In the situations that resulted in the special education placement litigation, the educational programs were apparently ineffective and the range of options limited. Many school psychologists can recall vividly cases where we knew the child was not "really" retarded, but in view of very low achievement accompanied by increasingly negative attitudes toward school and self, the self-contained, segregated class appeared to be the best option.

This situation has changed, or is in the process of change. A wide range of options are increasingly available, the principle of resorting to the least restrictive alternative is the law of the land, and greater emphasis is placed on effectiveness of interventions through individualized educational programs with annual review. These changes provide the opportunity for assessment activities in a broader variety of areas (see Ysseldyke's discussion in Chapter 4 of this volume of the purposes of assessment). In addition to classification decisions, assessment should be directed toward decisions concerning choice of least restrictive alternative and toward the content of interventions, especially identifying specific areas of "educational" need in terms of social, emotional, and academic development. Assessment should also yield information concerning the approach to intervention, specifically, changes in antecedent, situational, and consequent environments that can be used to carry out interventions. Finally, we need to gather information that is relevant to and/or can assist others in evaluating the effectiveness of interventions (see Phye, Chapter 9 of this volume).

The kind of information collected by school psychologists and other members of the staffing team is crucial to minimizing the risks and maximizing the benefits of classification. Obviously, classification, even if conducted with great skill, is not sufficient. Intellectual assessment, while important to classification, provides only limited information about the kind and nature of interventions necessary. If effective interventions result from the classification decisions that school psychologists have always and will likely continue to participate in, then the special education bargain described by Gallagher (1972) is worthwhile for children, regardless of ethnic or racial status. The kind of assessment conducted will be a crucial part of the effort to deliver effective interventions and to achieve fair treatment of minority students.

Changes in Assessment

The recent litigation and legislation require changes in two general areas of assessment. The *procedural* changes such as due process, multidisciplinary teams, and informed consent have been discussed previously in this and other chapters. The required changes in the *content* of assessment are that a comprehensive or multifactored evaluation be conducted that includes information on language dominance, adaptive behavior, and sociocultural background. The measurement and use of these types of information in classification decisions are likely to be sources of controversy in the near future.

MULTIFACTORED ASSESSMENT

The concept of multifactored assessment has been the apparent solution to the dilemma of defining and describing the requirement of nonbiased assessment. The requirement of multifactored assessment is suggested in Public Law 94-142 rules and regulations and is even more prominent in the reports from the CORRC project on nonbiased assessment. The underlying assumption is that assessment is likely to be less biased if a broad variety of information is collected and considered systematically in making classification decisions.

Tucker (1977) described the categories of information that should be developed in a comprehensive assessment of children "for possible mildly handicapping conditions." For the most part, the categories of information are fairly standard and consistent with traditional descriptions of comprehensive psychoeducational evaluations. The arrangement of the categories of information, especially the *sequence* suggested for collecting the information, is somewhat unique (see Table 8.2). Especially noteworthy is the placement of "psychological assessment" (personality and intelligence) at the end of the sequence of assessment procedures.

TABLE 8.2
Sequential Outline of Multifactored Assessment[a]

Type of data	Purpose	Data source
1. Observational	Determine degree of deviance from expectations	Natural setting; teachers and others who have direct contact with child
2. Other data available	Disconfirm or corroborate the nature and extent of problem; consider other factors such as medical or temporary, situational conditions	Cummulative records, previous evaluations of child, records and/or test scores from previous years
3. Language dominance	Determine child's primary language, assess whether the school-related problem is due to language differences, and decide appropriate language for administration of other instruments	Tests of primary language and interviews with parents
4. Educational	Determine level, pattern, and strengths and weaknesses in academic areas; confirm or disconfirm discrepancies established in previous steps	Formal and informal achievement measures administered by trained diagnosticians
5. Sensory–motor (optional)	Determine whether deficits in process areas are possible explanations for the learning problem	Usually formal tests administered by trained diagnosticians
6. Adaptive behavior	Determine social competence outside of school in relation to age and cultural expectations	Usually structured interview with parents by trained diagnosticians
7. Medical and/or developmental	Determine if medical, sensory, or health factors are related to the onset or treatment of the learning problem	Developmental history, medical records, and if indicated, physical examination
8. Personality assessment, including self-report	Determine degree of emotional involvement (if any) and obtain student's perception of problem	Interviews and formal or informal devices administered and interpreted by appropriately trained persons
9. Intellectual	Predict level of achievement, and with other data, classify if appropriate	Formal tests measuring verbal and nonverbal abilities administered by trained specialists

[a] Adapted from Tucker (1977).

Implicit in Tucker's description of multifactored assessment is the concern about misuses of IQ test information. The placement of intellectual assessment data at the *end* of the sequence appears to be a conscious effort to emphasize the importance of other data. The other data were seen as important both for the interpretation of IQ test results and for decisions about special education placement. Interestingly, the area of sociocultural background was not mentioned as a separate category in Tucker's description of comprehensive (multifactored) assessment. However, concerns about sociocultural background are implicit in the descriptions of language dominance and adaptive behavior. Sociocultural background is mentioned as a separate area of assessment in the Public Law 94-142 rules and regulations and should be recognized as an important area in the multifactored assessment.

Multifactored Assessment: Primary Language

The assessment of primary language competence is a logical, common sense procedure as well as a requirement of recent legislation. Non-English-speaking children have apparently been placed in programs for the mildly retarded on the basis of tests administered in English (see *Diana* or *Guadalupe* cases). These classification and programming decisions were inappropriate, although an even larger problem in those situations was the apparent absence of alternative programs for non-English-speaking youth.

Assessment of primary language competence is more difficult than it might appear. Many instruments have been developed recently (Oakland, 1977a), but little systematic work has been conducted on their reliability and validity. Nevertheless, a systematic effort to assess primary language competence is needed. The decision about primary language competence must be based on data. The presence of a Latino surname, for example, is certainly not sufficient to conclude that the child or family uses Spanish as the dominant language.

The information on primary language is important in collecting and interpreting other assessment data and in making decisions about appropriate interventions. If the child is monolingual, non-English speaking, perhaps the wisest course of action is to simply avoid the use of norm-referenced standardized tests of achievement and ability. The use of an interpreter was suggested in court cases. However, due to the many problems that arise when attempts are made to translate tests into other languages, for example, items do not have the same meaning and difficulties of items change, the results of translated tests are of questionable value. *If* inferences must be made about ability, use of nonverbal or performance tests is probably the best course of action (Gerken, 1978). Educational programs for monolingual non-English-speaking students must be provided in the students' native language if at all feasible (*Lau* v. *Nichols* 1974). If only a few monolingual children attend schools in a particular district, then other alternatives should be pursued (see Oakland, 1977a).

Bilingual children may exhibit widely varying competencies in English and another language. The range will extend from limited to high degrees of competence in either or both languages. The language dominance measure that is used to determine primary language should be supplemented by other measures that yield information on competence in both languages. Subsequent assessment activities should be conducted within the dominant language of the child. An important principle to remember is the assumption of maximum performance. Any inference about ability or academic aptitude made in subsequent assessment activities should include consideration of the effects of *differences* in language. Bilingual youth may, though certainly not always, obtain lower scores on verbal measures administered in English due to limited exposure to English. Special education services may not be the appropriate intervention for bilingual children who, on the basis of other data, meet state guidelines for special education classification. Bilingual/bicultural programs may be more appropriate, and children's rights to such services have been established through the *Lau* decision.

Multifactored Assessment: Adaptive Behavior

A subtle but important change in emphasis has occurred since 1963 concerning the criteria for judging adaptive behavior competence among school-age children. The 1961 American Association on Mental Deficiency (AAMD) definition of mental retardation suggested that learning and school achievement were the principal criteria for assessing adaptive behavior for school-age children (Heber, 1961). These criteria have been expanded through litigation, legislation, federal memoranda (e.g., Office for Civil Rights, 1972), and now recently, in revisions in the AAMD *Classification and Terminology Manual* (Grossman, 1973, 1977). Adaptive behavior for school-age children now encompasses activities outside of the school, including the settings of home, neighborhood, and community. Clearly, the criteria have changed, and it is no longer appropriate to judge adaptive behavior on the basis of school performance alone.

Conceptions of and methods for measuring adaptive behavior have been fairly limited until quite recently (see Oakland and Goldwater, Chapter 5 of this volume). Concepts of adaptive behavior have usually been restricted to fairly simple self-help or social behaviors such as dressing, eating, etc. These behaviors are usually mastered by normal and mildly retarded children prior to or soon after school entrance. Most of the instruments available currently reflect these limited conceptions and are not particularly useful for most normal or mildly retarded children.

Perhaps the best example of this type of instrument is the AAMD Adaptive Behavior Scales, which were developed from careful studies of deficit behaviors among samples of persons in institutions for the mentally retarded and later normed on samples selected from institutions for the mentally retarded. A public school version of the AAMD Adaptive Behavior Scales was developed recently (Lambert, Windmiller, & Cole, 1974). The usefulness of the public school version is questionable, since all of the items were selected from the original AAMD version with norms developed on school-age children. The respondent in the AAMD public school version is the classroom teacher, and the content validity of the items is questionable. Similar criticisms apply to most other adaptive behavior scales, nearly all of which were developed through studies of persons exhibiting retardation at the moderate to severe levels.

A major advance provided by the System of Multicultural Pluralistic Assessment (SOMPA) (Mercer & Lewis, 1978) is the development of the Adaptive Behavior Inventory for Children (ABIC), which is designed for normal children and is appropriate for the mildly retarded (see Oakland and Goldwater, Chapter 5 of this volume). The accuracy of the ABIC norms, which are based on California data, for children in other geographic regions has not yet been determined.

Even though much research with adaptive behavior instruments such as the ABIC needs to be conducted, cautious use of the information in three types of decisions seems appropriate. First, classification decisions in mild mental retardation should be refined by the adaptive behavior information. Mercer (1973) suggested that there be a distinction made between the "comprehensively retarded," who obtain low scores on both IQ and adaptive behavior, and the "quasi-retarded," who fail the IQ criterion only. In making classification decisions we might consider two general categories of adaptive behaviors: those associated with academic role performance in the school and those associated with broader social roles in the school, home, and neighborhood. Diagnostic terminology should be refined to reflect different combinations of low performance over the adaptive behaviors and intellectual dimensions. For example, poor academic performance and low IQ in combination with normal social role performance outside of school implies that the difficulties are associated primarily with school-related tasks and might be classified more appropriately as "educational" rather than "mental" retardation.

A second area in which adaptive behavior data will be useful is in the selection of program or service options. Deno's Cascade Model (see Oakland and Goldwater, Chapter 5 of this volume) provides a model for conceptualizing the range of special education services. Children who are eligible for special education services according to IQ and academic criteria, but not according to information on social role performance outside school, would likely be served best in less restrictive programs. The curriculum in *special classes* for the educable mentally retarded has traditionally reflected emphases on social competence and functional academic skills (Kirk, 1972). The emphasis on social competence is justifiable in view of the longitudinal data on the adult adjustment of persons who are mildly retarded. The problems of mildly retarded persons in vocational settings are more likely to arise from deficits in social competence than from limited academic or intellectual skills. However, the ABIC data or data from other sources may confirm that the child has relatively high social competence in the home, neighborhood, and community. If social competence is relatively normal, the traditional special class is probably not the best service option. An educational program that is more specific to the child's academic needs, such as the resource option, is probably more appropriate. The "quasi-retarded," that is, children with low IQs and normal adaptive behavior outside of school, should be served in resource programs in most, perhaps nearly all, cases.

In addition to selection of service option, another important use for adaptive behavior data is educational programming. Deficits in social competence should be viewed as potential goals for interventions. The kinds of data that are provided by the ABIC are probably not sufficient for precise specification of goals for interventions in social competence. The ABIC or other data should be useful for determining whether there are problems with social competence and the general nature of these problems, if any. These data should be supplemented by more precise observation from which interventions could be designed and evaluated.

A number of conceptual and practical issues concerning the assessment of adaptive behavior are discussed by Coulter and Morrow (1978). The discrepancy between what is needed or required in this area and present technology is rather large. Considerable progress in instrument development is needed. In addition to the problems related to currently available instruments, a number of conceptual issues must be resolved. Is adaptive behavior data useful for classification decisions in educational settings? Is adaptive behavior data useful in program planning for other mildly handicapping conditions such as learning disabilities? What is the nature of adaptive behavior in older age groups? The reader is encouraged to consult Coulter and Morrow's (1978) discussion of these and other issues.

Multifactored Assessment: Sociocultural Background

The measurement and use of sociocultural background information in classification and placement decisions presents even more problems than the area of adaptive behavior.

Measures of SES used in research have varied from single-factor occupational scales to more complex measures using occupation, income level, educational level, type of residence, etc. Occupational scales have been used most frequently, since the information needed is usually obtained easily and the results closely approximate the more complex measures. The adequacy of traditional SES measures for equating groups in studies of intelligence or achievement has been questioned recently. Trotman (1977) compared the relationship of a conventional SES measure and a "home intellectuality" scale to measured intelligence. The home intellectuality measure was considerably better than SES as a predictor of achievement and intelligence, and groups of black and white students matched on SES differed substantially on home intellectuality, achievement, and intelligence scores. These results suggest caution in interpreting conclusions from studies where different groups are matched on SES only (e.g., Jensen, 1969) and caution in using simple measures of SES as measures of sociocultural background.

The sociocultural measures (SCM) of the SOMPA provide a relatively complex measure of sociocultural background. The SCM scales were built around variables that have been correlated with IQ results in published studies. Factor analysis results were used to organize the 24 SCM items into nine factors and then into four sociocultural measures. Multiple regression analyses of the SCM and WISC-R scores are used in SOMPA to develop pluralistic norms (see Oakland and Goldwater, Chapter 5 of this volume). Two normative frameworks are used in SOMPA to interpret IQ scores. The WISC-R IQ scores based on the conventional norms are called school functioning level (SFL). The WISC-R IQ scores based on the pluralistic norms are called estimated learning potential (ELP). The latter score, the ELP, will be the topic of considerable debate over the next few years (*School Psychology Digest,* 1979). At the present time, the SOMPA provides the only systematic method for using sociocultural background information in the interpretation of assessment data. Unfortunately, the litigation and legislation requiring consideration of sociocultural background do not provide guidelines for definition, measurement, or use of these data.

The concept of sociocultural background includes the overlapping factors of social class and race or ethnicity. Mercer (1978) uses the concept of *eth-class,* which is a term from sociology that refers to the combined effects of ethnicity and socioeconomic status (SES). The concept of eth-class, or the more commonly used term, sociocultural background, is needed to accurately describe the relationship between sociocultural factors and achievement or intelligence. As is well known, social status and racial or ethnic background are *not* independent in the population of the United States. The concept of SES would be sufficient for our discussions if all racial or ethnic groups of the same social status performed in the same way on measures of achievement and intelligence. This, however, is not the case. In addition to and independent of SES, racial or ethnic factors influence performance on achievement and intelligence tests (e.g., Lesser, Fifer, & Clark, 1965). The results of these and other studies indicate that although SES influences the *level* of performance for all groups, ethnicity or race influences the *pattern* of performance. Thus, social status or ethnicity or race alone are insufficient to account for their combined effects on achievement or intelligence.

The relationship of SES to measures of achievement or intelligence is far from perfect: The correlations are typically in the range of .3 to .4; the range of performance within each SES level is fairly large; and considerable overlap of distributions is typical. The relationship of SES to *average* levels of performance appears to be more impressive. For example, Kaufman and Doppelt (1976) reported mean differences of 9 to 17 points for both blacks and whites between the highest and lowest SES groups in the WISC-R standardization sample.

Several features of the SOMPA, SCM, and ELP scores are apparent from the standardization data (Mercer & Lewis, 1978) and the limited research conducted thus far (Oakland, 1977b; Reschly, 1978b). By the nature of the statistical analysis used to compute the ELP scores, differences in mean IQ scores were eliminated in the SOMPA standardization sample. Differences in mean scores for other ethnic groups and for children in other geographic areas will in all likelihood be reduced but not necessarily eliminated (Reschly, 1978b). Again, there is the problem of the SOMPA norms being based on data from California rather than on a representative national sample. The laborious process of developing local norms suggested by the SOMPA authors will be necessary in cases where local populations differ substantially from the California normative sample in terms of the variables that are used to compute the ELP scores. The frequency of such deviations will, of course, be unknown pending further research.

The SOMPA SCM are more highly related to intelligence test performance than traditional measures of SES. The multiple correlations between the SCM and WISC-R full-scale IQ reported in the SOMPA manual were in the range of .37 to .52. Independent studies of the same ethnic–racial groups in Texas and Arizona (Oakland, 1977b; Reschly, 1978b) yielded multiple correlations that were only slightly lower. Initial results do suggest that the SCM are more valid than the previously used measures of SES.

Validity data on the SOMPA ELP are largely unavailable. A number of studies investigating the relationship of ELP to conventional measures of achievement will undoubtedly appear in the near future, despite Mercer's contention that conventional achievement measures are inappropriate criteria for examining the validity of ELP. In the previously cited studies by Oakland and Reschly, the ELP score was significantly related to achievement, but at a lower level than the conventional score. According to Mercer, a more appropriate criterion in terms of the construct of ELP would be scores from measures of rate of acquiring new information or skills (Budoff, 1975). Unfortunately, we are not likely to see much of this kind of research being done because of difficulties with time, complexity, and selection of appropriate subjects and materials.

The appropriate use of sociocultural background information in classification and placement decisions is far from clear. Some speculations may be in order. The comparison of the ELP and SFL (i.e., conventional) WISC-R scores provides a practical means to recognize the effects of SES and cultural background on measured intelligence. This comparison should be a significant aid in alleviating the common misconception that IQ scores represent innate or hereditarily determined abilities. Renaming the conventional score as "school functioning level" is consistent with the validity evidence for IQ scores. IQ tests do predict, although imperfectly, the likelihood of success in school. However, the relationships of IQ test results to general learning aptitudes and adjustment in other settings is considerably lower. The information provided through intelligence testing is important, but limited. The ELP and SFL concepts in SOMPA should bolster efforts to recognize these limitations and to clarify the meaning of IQ scores.

Systematic use of the SCM and ELP scores in classification and placement decisions may be of dubious benefit to individuals. Depending on how these data are used, they may result in a large reduction in the number of low SES and/or minority children considered eligible for special education services. Would this change be beneficial to children? The answer to this question depends upon consideration of the needs of these children, the effects of special education services, and the possible negative consequences of labels. Few would deny that the students represented in the court decisions regarding classification and placement exhibited significant problems in the classroom. These students typically were achieving well below grade level and/or were not successful in meeting the academic demands in the classroom. These deficits in performance preceded referral and individual evaluation. The individual evaluations in many cases yielded results indicating low IQ (SFL) and confirmed eligibility for special education services according to the criteria in effect at the time. Use of the ELP score would result in adjusted, that is, higher scores for most of these persons. Which scores should be used in classification and placement, the SFL or the higher ELP score? If the ELP score is used, the child will be protected from the negative consequences of labeling but denied special education services. If the SFL score is used, services will be provided but the child will be labeled, and the cumulative effect in individual cases will be the overrepresentation that led originally to the litigation. There is no easy solution to this dilemma, which illustrates the difficult *value* judgment required presently regarding the risks and benefits of classification and placement. In the future, one can hope for substantially more evidence of a positive nature regarding the effectiveness of special education services. Such evidence would provide clearer guidance in resolving this dilemma.

Innovative uses of the sociocultural information and the ELP concept are also possible. For example, this information may be useful in selecting students from disadvantaged backgrounds for programs for the gifted (Mercer, 1976). The concept of giftedness has been broadened in recent years (see Treffinger *et al.*, Chapter 7 of this volume) to include factors other than intellectual ability. Comparisons of persons within the framework of pluralistic norms may be a valuable addition to current practices. The ELP score might also be used in the future as the basis for the comparison of achievement and potential in learning disabilities diagnoses. Although recent federal guidelines for learning disabilities (*Federal Register,* December 1977) continue to mention "environmental, cultural, or economic disadvantage" as an exclusion factor, one might argue that the ELP is a more accurate representation of the child's intellectual abilities. Greater numbers of minority and/or low SES children would have the "severe discrepancy" required in the federal "Procedures for Evaluating Specific Learning Disabilities" if the ELP was used rather than a conventional IQ score.

Nonbiased Assessment:
Some Tentative Conclusions

Nonbiased assessment is obviously an extremely complex issue. Concerns with the meaning and usefulness of IQ test results have dominated much of the discussion of nonbiased assessment. The issues surrounding the meaning of IQ have been debated for at least 60 years and are not likely to be resolved in the near future. However, many other issues, such as the meaning and etiology of mild mental retardation, the rights of parents and students, the effectiveness of special education interventions, and the definition of bias in tests, are clearly involved with our efforts to reduce bias in assessment. These issues have been discussed in this chapter, though certainly not resolved.

There are two possible negative reactions among a range of possible reactions by school psychologists to the pressures for nonbiased assessment that could be damaging to children. One such reaction would be to conclude that the issue is so complex and ill-defined that there is nothing we can do, hence, we should stubbornly defend and simply continue our current practices. This reaction will be maladaptive. There are important changes that we can make that will enhance the fairness and usefulness of assessment for all children. In the interests of children, we need to make these changes. A second maladaptive reaction would be to reject most, if not all, of our current instruments and practices. For example, some have rejected the use of conventional IQ tests with culturally different children. Others have severely limited the numbers of culturally different children in special education programs simply on the basis of their proportions in the population. Such reactions are not in the best interests of children.

Positive reactions to the concerns about nonbiased assessment must first be based on a recognition of the ambiguity of the current situation. There are no easy solutions—and there may never be any.

Recognition of the underlying assumptions in the special education placement litigation provides an orientation to the most important issues in nonbiased assessment. One can only wonder if these cases would have appeared *if* the interventions were effective; *if* due process safeguards had been observed; *if* the interventions had been consistent with the principle of least restrictive alternative, that is, if they had not been provided in segregated, self-contained special classes; *if* the assessment had been multifactored and programs based on specific educational need; and so on. In fact, the assessment by school psychologists and programs in special education did *not* meet these criteria in at least some, and perhaps many instances. The litigation and legislation are attempts to correct these abuses. From the perspective of school psychologists, the current demands for nonbiased assessment, along with the other requirements from the courts and legislation, are the best things that have happened for our profession (and for children).

Three general themes should form the basis for efforts to achieve nonbiased assessment. First, and most important, we must continue and expand our efforts to ensure that assessment procedures result in positive benefits for individuals. This goal is certainly not new. The underlying assumption of positive benefit to individuals has always been the goal in all types of assessment. Realization of this goal requires more concern about the relationship of our assessment activities to interventions and more concern about the effectiveness of these interventions.

TABLE 8.3
Guidelines for Special Education Assessment[a]

I. Programming and Intervention in the Regular Classroom
   A. *Basic principle.* Prior to referral to special education diagnostic services, solutions to classroom learning and adjustment problems should be attempted in the regular classroom.
   B. *Basic principle.* Various resource personnel, for example, remedial reading specialists, curriculum consultants, counselors, psychologists, speech clinicians, and social workers, should be available to assist teachers in developing educational procedures for meeting the child's needs in the regular classroom.
   Considerations
   1. Are specially trained personnel available to assist classroom teachers, and do these personnel provide assistance to teachers in developing alternative procedures in the regular classroom?
   2. What changes are made in the regular classroom programs in order to serve children with diverse backgrounds and diverse characteristics?
   3. What alternative materials and approaches, independent of special education, exist and have been attempted for children with learning and adjustment problems?
   4. In cases referred to special education services, what evidence exists to confirm that attempts were made to solve the problem within the regular classroom? Were special personnel involved? Was an organized plan developed? Was the plan implemented? Was the plan given sufficient time to be successful?
   5. Were efforts made to inform parents of the problem and attempted solutions, and were parents given an opportunity to contribute to solutions attempted in the regular classroom?

II. Screening and Referral Phase
   A. *Basic principle.* Prior to formal diagnostic procedures, adequate information should be obtained that establishes the nature and extent of deviation from reasonable expectations.
   Considerations
   1. Is the concern related to classroom learning or adjustment stated or restated specifically in behavioral terms rather than in terms of a special education category?
   2. Is the concern related to current classroom learning or adjustment supported and illustrated by descriptive samples of behaviors?
   3. Is consideration given to and evidence provided concerning the child's strengths within school and in other situations?
   4. Are other sources of information considered systematically? Is this information consistent or inconsistent with the referral? Other sources of information should include the educational history (evaluations by previous teachers, previous educational methods and materials used, previous grades), achievement test scores, previous evaluations by support personnel, previous and current social and emotional patterns of behavior, etc.
   5. Do the above sources of information confirm the need for consideration of special education alternatives, or does the information suggest that solutions should be attempted within the regular classroom?
   B. *Basic principle.* Parental involvement shall be obtained in all phases of referal, evaluation, and placement. Informed consent and due process procedures should be initiated early and followed throughout.
   Considerations
   1. Are parents informed of the reasons for the referral in precise, meaningful language?
   2. Have all communications been in the primary language of the home?
   3. Does the school use a variety of means to solicit active parental participation in all phases of evaluation and staffing? Are parents informed of their rights to examine all relevant records?
   4. Are parents provided with information concerning the activities and kinds of decisions antici-

Continued

TABLE 8.3
Guidelines for Special Education Assessment[a]

pated in evaluation and staffing along with estimates of time required and specification of personnel responsible?

III. Evaluation
   A. *Basic principle.* The evaluation of children referred for special education services should be conducted by a multidisciplinary team.
      Considerations
      1. Is someone assigned the responsibility of coordinating the work of the team members including; (*a*) evaluating the referral; (*b*) determining the kind of information needed; (*c*) assigning appropriately trained personnel to collect the data; (*d*) facilitating communication among the team members?
      2. Are interim procedures established for assisting the child and classroom teacher while the evaluation and staffing are conducted?
   B. *Basic principle: Multifactored assessment.* Children should be assessed in all areas related to the suspected handicap, including where appropriate, health, vision, hearing, adaptive behavior, sociocultural background, emotional status, academic performance, aptitude (intelligence), language, and psychomotor functioning. No single procedure, such as IQ test results, is used as the primary sosrce of information, and the assessment procedures are used to identify areas of specific educational need. Testing and evaluation materials and procedures used for the purposes of evaluation and placement of handicapped children must be selected and administered so as not to be racially or culturally discriminatory.
      Considerations
      1. *Situational assessment.* Is an assessment of the school or classroom environment conducted that includes a behavioral definition of the referral problem(s)? Are data collected on the frequency and magnitude of the problem(s) and a study made of the antecedent, situational, and consequent conditions related to the problem?
      2. *Health history.* Are data collected on physical/health conditions that may be related to the learning problem? This information would include factors such as developmental history, disease and injury data, sensory status, medication(s) used, and nutrition.
      3. *Personal and social adjustment.* Is personal and social adjustment (adaptive behaviors) in the home, neighborhood, and broader community evaluated using formal and informal data collection procedures?
      4. *Personal and social adjustment.* Is personal and social adjustment (adaptive behaviors) in the school setting evaluated with formal and informal data collection procedures?
      5. *Primary language.* Is the child's primary language dominance determined, and are the assessment procedures administered and interpreted in a manner consistent with the primary language data?
      6. *Social and cultural background.* Is the sociocultural background of the child assessed systematically, and are the results of other assessment procedures interpreted in light of the sociocultural data?
      7. *Educational achievement: Norm referenced.* Is educational achievement assessed with norm-referenced instruments that yield valid information concerning the child's current performance in relation to grade level expectancies?
      8. *Educational achievement: Criterion referenced.* Is educational achievement assessed with criterion-referenced instruments or devices that provide valid information concerning specific skills and deficit areas?
      9. *Aptitude.* Is academic aptitude (that is, general intelligence) assessed with appropriate instruments available, consideration given to variations in performance over different factors of academic aptitude, and results interpreted in view of strengths and limitations of such measures?

Continued

TABLE 8.3
Guidelines for Special Education Assessment[a]

10. *Psychoeducational process.* Are psychoeducational processes and motor skills related to learning assessed, and are the influence of these factors on the learning or adjustment problem considered (e.g., attention, eye–hand coordination, language, visual–motor, visual perception, auditory discrimination, etc.)?
11. *Other information.* Where appropriate, is information from other areas potentially important to placement and educational programming considered (e.g., career and vocational interests and aptitudes)?

IV. Staffing
A. *Basic principles.* Placement decisions should be based upon information from a variety of sources (see previous section). Consideration of the information from the multifactored assessment should be documented in the staffing report. Placement decisions should be made by a group of persons including appropriate professional personnel and parents. The least restrictive alternative principle shall guide the selection of option for serving children.
Considerations
1. What evidence exists to document the consideration of a broad variety of information, including both strengths and deficits, in determining educational needs and selection of placement options?
2. Does the determination of educational needs and selection of placement option include the contributions of relevant professional personnel and parents?
3. Are current educational status and educational needs stated precisely and supported by data?
4. Are alternative options considered for meeting these needs, including regular education with or without support services?
5. Are special education eligibility recommendations made in conformance with the criteria for primary handicapping condition as defined in the Department of Public Instruction Special Education Rules and Regulations?
6. In making the special education eligibility recommendations, did the multidisciplinary team consider a broad variety of information, including adaptive behavior and sociocultural background? How did this information influence the recommendations concerning goals for intervention and placement options?
7. Are a variety of program options considered in view of the information from the multifactored assessment? For example, was information on adaptive behavior outside of school used to choose between special classes and resource options for mild mental retardation?
8. What evidence supports the choice of program option as an appropriate alternative for meeting the child's needs?
9. Is an interim plan developed and implemented to assist the child in the regular classroom until the placement recommendations are carried out?
10. Do the special education personnel inform parents of the primary handicapping condition (if any) and explain the full range of available alternatives for meeting the child's needs?
11. Do parents contribute to decisions concerning the objectives of special education services and to choices concerning type of special education service selected?
12. Are there provisions for members of the multidisciplinary staffing team to express opinions that disagree with the decision of the majority? Are the dissenting opinions in written form expressing the reasons for disagreement?

[a]The *Guidelines* were developed by a committee appointed by George Garcia, Director, Urban Education Section of the Iowa Department of Public Instruction. Committee members included Daniel Reschly (Consultant), George Garcia, Jeff Grimes, Wilbur House, Merry Maitre, Pat O'Rourke, and Wayne Mooers. The *Guidelines* have *not* been approved officially by any division of the Iowa Department of Public Instruction.

Second, there is a need to implement the idea of multifactored assessment. Again, this is not a new idea. However, the degree to which comprehensive assessment has been conducted, documented, and used in planning interventions has varied considerably. The proper role of IQ tests in the multifactored assessment must be recognized. Areas often ignored in the past, for example, adaptive behavior outside of school, primary language competence, and sociocultural background, should be a part of the assessment process. These newer areas of assessment, along with the conventional areas, are important to better understanding of children. Fuller understanding can lead to more refined classification decisions and more effective interventions.

Finally, our understanding of nonbiased assessment and our ability to implement these procedures will be enhanced if we view nonbiased assessment as a *process* rather than as a set of instruments (Iowa DPI, 1978; NRRC, 1977). The process is oriented toward ensuring fairness and effectiveness of assessment and interventions for all children. This process is appropriate in all settings, regardless of the ethnic or racial composition of the student population.

A recent draft of the Iowa DPI *Guidelines for Special Education Assessment* is reprinted in Table 8.3. The *Guidelines* represent an attempt to describe appropriate procedures in sequential order for the assessment–placement process. The *Guidelines* cover appropriate steps and activities *up to* the development of the individualized educational program (IEP). The procedures associated with the IEP and evaluation of short-term objectives and annual goals are covered elsewhere in this volume. (See Phye, Chapter 9 of this volume.)

References

APA Monitor. Exhibit A: IQ Trial. Plaintiffs Take the Stand. December, 1977, p. 4.

Anastasi, A. *Psychological testing* (4th ed.). New York: Macmillan, 1976.

Ashurst, D., & Meyers, E. Social system and clinical model in school identification of the educable retarded. In R. Eyman, E. Meyers, & G. Tarjan, (Eds.), *Sociobehavioral studies in mental retardation*. Washington, D.C.: American Association on Mental Deficiency, 1973.

Abeson, A., Bolick, N., & Hass, J. *A primer on due process*. Reston, Virginia: Council for Exceptional Children, 1975.

Bakke v. *Regents of the University of California*. U.S. Supreme Court, 1978.

Baller, W., Charles, D., & Miller, E. Mid-life attainment of the mentally retarded. *Genetic Psychology Monographs*, 1967, **75**, 235–329.

Bernal, E. A response to "Educational uses of tests with disadvantaged subjects". *American Psychologist*, 1975, **30**, 93–95.

Block, N., & Dworkin, G. *The IQ controversy*. New York: Pantheon/Random House, 1976.

Brody, E., & Brody, N. *Intelligence: Nature, determinants, and consequences*. New York: Academic Press, 1976.

Budoff, M. Measuring learning potential: An alternative to the traditional intelligence test. In G. Gredler (Ed.), *Ethical and legal factors in the practice of school psychology*. Harrisburg: Pennsylvania Department of Education, 1975. (Also, see Budoff *et al.* article in the *American Journal of Mental Deficiency*, 1971, **76**, 159–169.)

CORRC (Coordinating Office on Regional Resource Centers). *With bias toward none.* Lexington: University of Kentucky, 1976.

California State Board of Education. *News release.* January 15, 1975.

Cleary, T. A. Test bias: Prediction of grades of Negro and white students in integrated colleges. *Journal of Educational Measurement,* 1968, **5,** 115–124.

Cleary, T. A., Humphreys, L., Kendrick, A., & Wesman, A. Educational uses of tests with disadvantaged students. *American Psychologist,* 1975, **30,** 15–41.

Coulter, A., & Morrow, H. *The concept and measurement of adaptive behavior.* New York: Grune & Stratton, 1978.

Darlington, R. Another look at "cultural fairness." *Journal of Educational Measurement,* 1971, **8,** 71–82.

Davis, A., & Eells, D. *Davis–Eells tests of general intelligence or problem solving ability.* New York: Harcourt, 1951.

Dent, H. Assessing black children for mainstream placement. In R. Jones, (Ed.), *Mainstreaming and the minority child.* Reston, Virginia: Council for Exceptional Children, 1976.

Diana v. *State Board of Education.* C-70 37 RFP, District Court for Northern California. February 1970.

Dove, A. *Dove Counterbalanced Intelligence Test.* Mimeo, n.d.

Dunn, L. Special education for the mildly retarded: Is much of it justifiable? *Exceptional Children,* 1968, **35,** 5–22.

Edgerton, R. *The cloak of competence: Stigma in the lives of the mentally retarded.* Berkeley: University of California Press, 1967.

Federal Register. Nondiscrimination on Basis of Handicap. Regulations implementing Section 504 of the Rehabilitation Act of 1973. May 4, 1977. Pp. 22676–22702.

Federal Register. Education of Handicapped Children. Regulations implementing Education for All Handicapped Children Act of 1975. August 23, 1977. Pp. 42474–42518.

Federal Register. Procedures for Evaluating Specific Learning Disabilities. December 29, 1977. Pp. 65082–65085.

Gallagher, J. The special education contract for mildly handicapped children. *Exceptional Children,* 1972, **38,** 527–535.

Galton, F. *Hereditary genius* (2nd ed.). London: Macmillan, 1892.

Gerken, K. Performance of Mexican-American children on intelligence tests. *Exceptional Children,* 1978, **44,** 438–443.

Grossman, H. (Ed.). *Manual on terminology and classification in mental retardation* (rev. ed.). Washington, D.C.: American Association on Mental Deficiency, 1977.

Guadalupe v. *Tempe Elementary School District.* District Court for Arizona, 71-435, January 1972.

Heber, R. A manual on terminology and classification in mental retardation (2nd ed.). *American Journal of Mental Dericiency,* 1961, Monograph Supplement 64.

Hewett, F., & Forness, S. *Education of exceptional learners.* Boston: Allyn and Bacon, 1974.

Hobbs, N. *The futures of children.* San Francisco: Jossey-Bass, 1975.

Hobson v. *Hansen.* 269 F. Supp. 401 (1967).

Houts, P. (Ed.). *The myth of measurability.* New York: Hart, 1977.

Humphreys, L., & Stubbs, J. A longitudinal analysis of teacher expectation, student expectation, and student achievement. *Journal of Educational Measurement,* 1977, **14,** 261–270.

Hunter, J., & Schmidt, F. Critical analysis of the statistical and ethical implications of various definitions of test bias. *Psychological Bulletin,* 1976, **83,** 1053–1071.

Iowa DPI. *Guidelines for Special Education Assessment Procedures.* Report of the DPI Committee on Nonbiased Assessment. Des Moines: Department of Public Instruction, Special Education Division, 1978.

Jackson, G. On the report of the ad hoc committee on educational uses of tests with disadvantaged students. *American Psychologist,* 1975, **30,** 88–92.

Jensen, A. How much can we boost IQ and scholastic achievement? *Harvard Education Review*, 1969, **39**, 1–123.

Jensen, A. Test bias and construct validity. *Kappan*, 1976, **58**, 340–346.

Jones, R. Labels and stigma in special education. *Exceptional Children*, 1972, **38**, 553–564.

Kamin, L. *The science and politics of IQ*. Potomac, Maryland: Erlbaum Associates, 1974.

Kaufman, A., & Doppelt, J. Analysis of WISC-R standardization data in terms of stratification variables. *Child Development*, 1976, **47**, 165–171.

Kirk, S. *Educating exceptional children*. Boston: Houghton-Mifflin, 1972.

Kolstoe, O. *Teaching educable mentally retarded children* (2nd ed.). New York: Holt, 1976.

Lambert, N., Windmiller, M., & Cole, L. *Manual: AAMD adaptive behavior scale, public school version (rev. ed.)*. Washington, D.C.: American Association on Mental Deficiency, 1974.

Larry P. et al. v. *Wilson Riles et al.* United States District Court, Northern District of California, Case No. C-71-2270 RFP, 1972, 1974, now in trial.

Lau v. *Nichols*. 414 U.S. Pp. 563–572, 1974. (also see Oakland, 1977a.)

Lesser, G., Fifer, G., & Clark, D. Mental abilities of children from different social-class and cultural group. *Monographs of the Society for Research in Child Development*, 1965, **30**(4), 1–115.

Loehlin, J., Lindzey, G., & Spuhler, J. *Race differences in intelligence*. San Francisco: Freeman, 1975.

MacMillan, D. *Mental retardation in school and society*. Boston: Little, Brown, 1977.

MacMillan, D., Jones, R., & Aloia, G. The mentally retarded label: A theoretical analysis and review of research. *American Journal of Mental Deficiency*, 1974, **79**, 241–261.

Mercer, J. *Labeling the mentally retarded*. Berkeley: University of California Press, 1973.

Mercer, J. *Identifying the gifted Chicano child*. Paper presented at the first symposium on Chicano Psychology, University of California, Irvine, May 1976.

Mercer, J. Theoretical constructs of adaptive behavior: Movement from a medical to a social-ecological perspective. In A. Coulter & H. Morrow, (Eds.), *The concept and measurement of adaptive behavior*. New York: Grune & Stratton, 1978.

Mercer, J., & Lewis, J. *Technical manual: SOMPA: System of multicultural assessment*. New York: The Psychological Corporation, 1978.

Meyers, C., MacMillan, D., & Yoshida, R. Validity of psychologists' identification of EMR students in the perspective of the California decertification experience. *Journal of School Psychology*, 1978, **16**, 3–15.

Meyers, C., Sundstrom, P., & Yoshida, R. The school psychologist and assessment in special education: A report of the Ad Hoc Committee of APA Division 16. *Monographs of Division 16 of the American Psychological Association*, 1974, **2**(1), 3–57.

Novick, M., & Petersen, N. Towards equalizing educational and employment opportunity. *Journal of Educational Measurement*, 1976, **13**, 77–88.

NRRC. Guide for nonbiased assessment. In *Position statement on nonbiased assessment of culturally different children*. Hightstown: Northeast Regional Resource Center, New Jersey, State Department 1977.

Oakland, T. (Ed.). *Psychological and educational assessment of minority children*. New York: Brunner-Mazel, 1977. (a)

Oakland, T. *Pluralistic norms and estimated learning potential*. Paper presented at the annual convention of the American Psychological Association, August 1977. (b)

Oakland, T., & Matuszek, P. Using tests in nondiscriminatory assessment. In T. Oakland (Ed.), *Psychological and educational assessment of minority children*. New York: Brunner-Mazel, 1977.

Office for Civil Rights. *Memorandum to state and local education agencies*. November 18, 1972. (Also in Oakland, 1977a.)

PARC. *Pennsylvania Association for Retarded Children* v. *Commonwealth of Pennsylvania*. 334 F. Supp. 1257 (E.D. Pa. 1971).

Petersen, N., & Novick, M. An evaluation of some models for culture fair selection. *Journal of Educational Measurement*, 1976, **13**, 3–29.

Reschly, D. WISC-R factor structures among Anglos, Blacks, Chicanos, and Native American Papagos. *Journal of Consulting and Clinical Psychology,* 1978, **46,** 417–422. (a)

Reschly, D. *Comparisons of bias in assessment with conventional and pluralistic measures.* Paper presented at the Council for Exceptional Children Annual Convention, May 1978. (b)

Reschly, D., & Lamprecht, M. Expectancy effects of labels: Fact or artifact? *Exceptional Children,* in press.

Reschly, D., & Reschly, J. Predictive utility of WISC-R factor scores for four groups. *Journal of School Psychology,* in press.

Reschly, D., & Sabers, D. *An examination of test bias for Black, Chicano, and Native American Papago children.* Unpublished manuscript, Iowa State University, 1978.

Rosenthal, R., & Jacobsen, L. *Pygmalion in the classroom: Teacher expectations and pupils' intellectual development.* New York: Holt, 1968.

Samuda, R. *Psychological testing of American minorities: Issues and consequences.* New York: Dodd, Mead, 1975.

Samuel, W. Observed IQ as a function of test atmosphere, tester expectation, and race of tester: A replication for female subjects. *Journal of Educational Psychology,* 1977, **69,** 593–604.

Sattler, J. Racial "experimenter effects" in experimentation, testing, interviewing, and psychotherapy. *Psychological Bulletin,* 1970, **73,** 137–160.

Sattler, J. Intelligence testing of ethnic minority-group and culturally disadvantaged children. In L. Mann & D. Sabatino (Eds.), *The first review of special education* (Vol. 2). Philadelphia: The JSE Press, 1973.

Sattler, J. *Assessment of children's intelligence.* Philadelphia: W. B. Saunders, 1974.

School Psychology Digest, 1979, **8**(1). (Entire issue devoted to theme of SOMPA: A symposium.)

Shockley, W. Models, mathematics, and the moral obligation to diagnose the origin of Negroe IQ deficits. *Review of Educational Research,* 1971, **41,** 368–377.

Silverstein, A. Factor structure of the Wechsler Intelligence Scale for Children for three ethnic groups. *Journal of Educational Psychology,* 1973, **65,** 408–410.

Trotman, F. Race, IQ, and the middle class. *Journal of Educational Psychology,* 1977, **69,** 266–273.

Tucker, J. Operationalizing the diagnostic-intervention process. In T. Oakland (Ed.), *Psychological and educational assessment of minority children.* New York: Brunner/Mazel, 1977.

Turnbull, H. The past and future impact of court decisions in special education. *Kappan,* 1978, **60,** 523–527.

Williams, R. Abuses and misuses in testing black children. *The Counseling Psychologist,* 1971, **2,** 62–73.

Williams, R. The problem of the match and mismatch in testing black children. In L. Miller (Ed.), *The testing of black students: A symposium.* Englewood Cliffs, New Jersey: Prentice-Hall, 1974.

Williams, R. The BITCH-100: A culture-specific test. *Journal of Afro-American Issues,* 1975, **3,** 103–116.

Yoshida, R., MacMillan, D., & Meyers, E. The decertification of minority group EMR students in California: Student achievement and adjustment. In R. Jones (Ed.), *Mainstreaming and the minority child.* Reston, Virginia: Council for Exceptional Children, 1976.

Yoshida, R., & Meyers, E. Effects of labeling as Educable Mentally Retarded on teachers' expectancies for change in students' performance. *Journal of Educational Psychology,* 1975, **67,** 521–527.

Ysseldyke, J., & Foster, G. Bias in teachers' observations of emotionally disturbed and learning disabled children. *Exceptional Children,* 1978, **44,** 613–615.

Zigler, E. Familial mental retardation: A continuing dilemma. *Science,* 1967, **155**(20 January), 292–298.

Zucker, S., & Prieto, A. Ethnicity and teacher bias in educational decisions. *Instructional Psychology,* 1977, **4,** 2–5.

INDIRECT SERVICES OF SCHOOL PSYCHOLOGISTS

⎵⎵⎵⎵

A broad variety of indirect services have been emphasized in school psychology role descriptions over the past 50 years. Thus, the kinds of indirect services described in the three chapters in this section are not new. However, in recent years there has been a shift in how these indirect services are viewed in relation to the other more direct services, such as psychoeducational assessment. Traditionally, indirect services were seen as a minor or subsidiary role of school psychologists. This is not to say that the services were seen as unimportant or ineffective. Rather, school psychologists had so many other more pressing demands for direct services that the indirect services had to be regarded as a minor role or even as a luxury. In recent articles there have been many position statements advocating that indirect services, such as consultation, be seen as the primary role of school psychologists. Other roles, particularly the traditional testing or refer–test– report activities, would be less important.

The rationale for increased emphasis on indirect services is complex. One component of this rationale is based on dissatisfaction with the traditional testing role. At this point we should perhaps again remind ourselves of the differences between the traditional testing role and the psychoeducational assessment role. These differences were discussed in Chapter 2, in the introduction to Part II, and in Chapter 4. The traditional testing role has been criticized as time consuming, inefficient, and frequently irrelevant to interventions. A second component of the rationale is the assertion that indirect services, particularly consultation, would reach many more children, could exert positive influences on the system, would be more related to interventions since the psychologists would work with those persons (parents and teachers) who had continuing contact with the child in the natural setting, and so on. These assertions are possibly more belief than fact at the present, but research on consultation is beginning to appear consistently in the journals. The third component of the rationale for greater emphasis on consultation is preliminary research suggesting that consultation is more effective than the traditional roles. Although these results are exciting and have potentially large ramifications for the future of school psychology, our enthusiasm must be tempered by the fact that most studies have used weak designs and/or were not conducted in natural settings.

The psychologist in the schools today often becomes alienated toward articles in journals that exhort him/her to consult rather than test; to do research rather than write test reports; and to prevent rather than diagnose mental health problems. We are sympathetic to these reactions. We, too, are well aware of the pressing demands that preclude full-time commitment to indirect services. However, we are convinced that all school psychologists have at least some opportunity to provide indirect services. The largest barrier for many is how to start these services and how to develop the necessary skills. The opportunity is there and much anecdotal evidence suggests that indirect services, once initiated, can be expanded. The largest barrier to more indirect services, then, may be school psychologists' perceptions of their roles. To quote Pogo, "We have met the enemy and he(she) is us."

The chapters in this section are designed to provide a sample of the indirect services that might be provided by school psychologists. In Chapter 9, Gary D. Phye discusses basic research on learning that can be applied by school psychologists. One of the most useful services that school psychologists can provide is to apply basic research knowledge from learning, development, personality, etc., to practical educational and/or psychological problems of children. In the first half of Chapter 9, Phye explains the application of recent cognitive research to learning problems in the schools. In the second half of Chapter 9, Phye discusses procedures for evaluating individualized educational programs and special projects. The different purposes of these two types of evaluation are explained with implications drawn for the kinds of decisions that are needed.

In Chapter 10, Martin Tombari and Ronald A. Davis discuss one of the consultation models that has been prominent in school psychology. Behavioral consultation is discussed from the perspective of consultation models, verbal interaction, and steps in consultation. We have found this particular consultation model to be highly useful in the school setting. In the final section of Chapter 10, recent advances in behavioral interventions are discussed.

In Chapter 11, Harvey F. Clarizio discusses the mental health needs of children and the possible roles of schools and school psychologists in improving mental health. The conventional concepts of primary, secondary, and tertiary prevention are used to organize the discussion. However, Clarizio goes far beyond the typical presentation of these concepts with extensive discussion and evaluation of different ways to carry out each of the types of prevention. The information presented by Clarizio provides crucial background information for school psychologists' efforts to promote positive mental health through school programs.

GARY D. PHYE

 School Psychologists as Consultants in the Evaluation of Learning and Intervention Outcomes

Although there is a great deal of emphasis on the assessment (identification) of persons who are in need of psychological and educational interventions (Public Law 94-142), the current legislation also requires evaluation of the effectiveness of special programs. Once identified, handicapped children and youth have a right to a free and appropriate education at public expense. If placement procedures determine that the child is in need of educational programming other than that provided in the regular classroom, an individualized educational program (IEP) is developed. The IEP specifies, among other things, instructional objectives and the evaluation of progress in achieving the objective.

Evaluation of special education service at the levels of both individual outcomes and agency effectiveness appears consistent with recent legislation. In the former instance, the handicapped individual's development as a result of individualized educational programming is assessed. At the program level, an agency, such as the school or a preschool project that is responsible for developing IEPs, must demonstrate the effectiveness or impact of their educational curricula designed to provide services for the handicapped. In both cases, the issue is one of accountability through the evaluation of learning and/or development.

For many years emphasis has been placed on research, and more recently on evaluation, as appropriate services and roles for school psychologists (see Tindall and Monroe, Chapters 1 and 2 of this volume). Gray's (1963) description of the

SCHOOL PSYCHOLOGY
Perspectives and Issues

"data-oriented problem solver" is consistent with the kinds of services and roles that are foreseen for school psychologists in this chapter. The current emphasis on IEPs provides the opportunity for nearly all school psychologists to become more involved with questions regarding learning and assessment of outcomes of interventions. Many school psychologists are part of the process whereby the IEP is formulated. Knowledge of cognitive processes, learning styles, and instructional psychology are potentially valuable contributions of the school psychologist to IEP formulation. Annual review of the IEP and reevaluation of placement decisions at least every 3 years also provide opportunities to apply the skills of the "data-oriented problem solver." Evaluation of programs, agencies, or curricula within agencies are potential activities for at least some school psychologists. The measurement and research skills that are apparently an increasingly important component of school psychology training at the sixth-year and doctoral levels (see Brown, Chapter 3 of this volume) can be extremely useful in improving the outcomes of services to exceptional children.

In this chapter, the two general topics of learning and evaluation are discussed with emphasis on applications to the IEP. Prior to a consideration of evaluation designs to be used for the evaluation of either short-term instructional objectives or program effectiveness, the implications of cognitive learning theory and the use of cognitive instructional objectives will be discussed. The focus on cognitive instructional objectives is not intended as an argument against the use of behavioral objectives. Rather, the use of both behavioral and cognitive instructional objectives is to be encouraged in the development of IEPs. The consideration of cognitive instructional objectives and the assessment of change are considered prerequisites for a discussion of formative evaluation that has as its primary focus the promotion of growth and development in a handicapped individual.

Learning

Cognitive Considerations

The last decade has seen a marked increase in the emphasis on an understanding of cognitive processing in education (Farnham-Diggory, 1972). The emphasis on process variables is of primary importance in any cognitive theory. By "cognitive theory" is meant a theory that would consider such covert thinking and problem-solving activities as attention, expectancies, memory storage and retrieval, plans, conscious control, and complex information processing.

The process orientation is an important commonality among cognitive psychologists in their attention to processing details. No longer can the psychologist or educator present stimuli, measure responses, and ignore what happens in the interval between the two. As educationalists (those who teach teachers or train school psychologists), we must help persons working directly with the handicapped determine how cognitive psychology is relevant and how to apply it.

A concern for the identification of process variables in cognitive ability is not new to special education. In certain respects, for example, the Illinois Test of Psycholinguistic Abilities (ITPA) (Kirk, McCarthy, & Kirk, 1968), was a forerunner in the assessment of process variables. While the theory behind the ITPA was more stimulus–response (S–R) than cognitive (Farnham-Diggory, 1977), it does provide an example of cognitive methodology. However, the practical utility of the ITPA for diagnosis and prescriptive teaching has recently come under criticism.

The present emphasis on cognitive theory should not be construed as a rejection of behavioral theories and/or methodology. As has been pointed out by Farnham-Diggory (1972), behaviorism must be considered as method as well as theory (pp. 77–78). In fact, behavioral methodology as a method of objectivity in the experimental sense is common to many psychological theories, including cognitive theories. Methodological objectivity in the experimental sense is necessary for the assessment of IEPs and/or the assessment of intervention program impact. The present position suggests that a consideration of cognitive theory and the nature of cognitive objectives in combination with behavioral methodology increases the instructional and assessment repertoire of school psychologists who will often have the opportunity to be involved with the development of IEPs.

The ubiquity of the cognitive perspective can be seen in the recent work of Donald Meichenbaum (1977). Meichenbaum has provided the foundation for a rapprochement of cognitive and behavioral theory within the context of behavior therapy. This rapprochement is best seen in the proposal that behavioral change in therapy occurs "through a sequence of mediating processes involving the interaction of inner speech, cognitive structures and behavior, and their resultant outcomes [Meichenbaum, 1977, p. 218]." Further, in order for an individual to change his/her pattern of responding, Meichenbaum posits the introduction of an intentional mediational process. For example, Meichenbaum has used cognitive processes successfully in the treatment of a variety of problem behaviors including hyperactivity and impulsivity.

Recent cognitive research suggests that careful attention must be paid to the manner in which information is presented to the learner (Phye, Gugliemella, & Sola, 1976). Prior information available to the learner must be considered in terms of individual background differences. In addition to variables such as mode of instruction and entering behavior, the assumption is made that the learner actively processes information in a manner influenced by background and task variables. This view of the learner as one who actively processes information evokes the assumption of "volition or intent" on the part of the learner. Thus, background variables in combination with intention must be considered to interact to produce individual differences. Both factors will, of course, determine the mode or manner of information presentation in an instructional sequence.

To better understand the relevance and application of cognitive methodology, some theoretical assumptions that are central to any cognitive theory must be examined. No attempt will be made to be exhaustive in the delineation of assumptions. Only those theoretical assumptions that pertain to instructional practice will be considered.

Cognitive Instructional Objectives

A cognitive perspective does not preclude a consideration of educational objectives. As has been demonstrated by Greeno (1976), the compatibility of cognitive theory and behavioral methodology is best demonstrated by the use of cognitive objectives. Greeno's view of cognitive objectives has much in common with the views of those educationalists who recommend that instructional goals be formulated as behavioral objectives. Greeno's view goes further, however, and specifies that "cognitive objectives are developed by analyzing the psychological processes and structures that are sufficient to produce the needed behavior [p. 123]." Needed behavior in this case is defined as behavior required by the learner as a result of the test used to assess learning outcomes.

The specification of cognitive objectives would require a task analysis. In this case, however, the learning task would be analyzed in terms of the cognitive processes and structures required to demonstrate learning. The concept of cognitive structures would introduce into the task analysis a consideration of the level of cognitive development or a consideration of individual differences in the entering behavior of any learner.

The nature of cognitive objectives would vary greatly in terms of complexity. At one end of the continuum, a cognitive objective to be included in an IEP for a young exceptional individual (e.g., low-incidence handicapped) might be a simple algorithm for learning to add or subtract two-digit numbers. For example, the teaching of an algorithm as a cognitive objective would require the analysis of the thinking processes involved. Examples from mathematics would include such formal plans as "invert and multiply" or a logical thinking process such as "the relationship between multiplication and division." At the opposite end of the continuum, a consideration of cognitive objectives for an academically talented and/or intellectually gifted youth would be a more complex matter. An IEP for this individual might include as a cognitive objective the development of a sophisticated algorithm such as the ability to describe possible outcomes of a significant two-way interaction in a statistical design.

Having considered in general terms cognitive instructional objectives, the nature of the dependent variable to be used for assessment purposes must also be addressed. It is undeniable that the educator has a profound interest in correct responses, answers, etc., on the part of the learner. However, this interest may, at times, obscure the pedagogical fact that an analysis of learner errors can also enhance the understanding of the processes involved in cognitive change. The suggestion has been offered elsewhere (Phye, 1977, 1979), that an analysis of both correct responses and errors is required for an accurate understanding of cognitive processing. For example, a correct response may be less informative in terms of the processing involved than an error because it is more ambiguous. Inasmuch as this is the case, the nature of the processing used by the learner is difficult to infer unless we take the time to ask questions of the learner concerning the processing involved. While this approach may be feasible with mature learners, there are many instances where very young or handicapped learners cannot adequately verbalize the cognitive processes they use to arrive at a solution to a problem.

In a discussion of the use of error analysis, Clinchy and Rosenthal (1971) suggest that as teachers we must understand the messages contained in children's errors. The following are examples of problems related to the interpretation of processing involved when a correct answer is given. Consider an instance where the teacher asks the question, "Which planet is closer to the sun, Mercury or Mars?" One learner responds "Mars," the other "Mercury." We know that the child who responded "Mars" needs help in correcting misinformation. But what about the other child? Did he/she know the correct answer or was the reply the result of a lucky guess? At the level of factual information, this potential confounding factor is always present. This factor leads to the ambiguity associated with correct responding. The only way of ascertaining the nature of the process involved (i.e., guessing or application of correct information) would require reassessment.

A germane example at the problem-solving level would be a problem in a mathematics lesson. A child may be asked, "What is 2×2?" In the case of a correct answer, it is tempting to infer that the learner understands the principle or processing involved. For didactic purposes, assume that our math student responded "4" to our query. On the basis of this correct response, we might infer that he/she knows how to multiply by two's. However, if the child goes on to say that $1 \times 2 = 3$, $3 \times 2 = 5$, and $4 \times 2 = 6$, it is clear that the child is using the incorrect process. On the basis of the initial correct response, we might have inferred that the child could use rules pertaining to the multiplication process, when, in fact, the child was using addition rules. Note however, that this insight into the nature of the processing involved is obtained only through the analysis of errors.

The main objective of this discussion of the role of error analysis is to emphasize the utility of its use in combination with an analysis of correct responses in order to better assess and understand behavioral change as a result of intervention. As suggested by Clinchy and Rosenthal (1971), error analysis reveals not only what a child fails to do, but also what he/she does do in the process of thinking. Consequently, errors as well as correct responses can be used as a guide for the development of an effective educational program for the handicapped child. As was pointed out in the earlier consideration of the use of a cognitive task analysis in the development of an IEP, the analysis of errors is the primary means of identifying the level of cognitive development of the learner. In this case, systematic errors occur when the task requirements exceed the level of development of the child and a production or mediation deficiency is observed.

In summary, when considering the nature of the dependent variable, one must pay attention to measurement issues involved with the assessment of change as well as consider the total behavior defined in terms of both correct responses and errors. As a result of the analysis of both correct responses and errors, the developer of an IEP better understands the child's ability to process information. This understanding can serve as a general guide for the preparation of IEP materials, the identification of entering behavior (level of development), and the development of an IEP most appropriate to remediate the specific deficits responsible for a child's handicap. This is really nothing more than a consideration of individual differences in the background and/or abilities of a learner for whom an IEP is written. This emphasis on a learner's uniqueness suggests a consideration of the implications of individual differences for developers of individual educational programs.

Individual Differences

Due to a lack of space and the fact that our focus is on the development of IEPs, primary consideration will be given to intraindividual differences. Intraindividual differences refer to differences within an individual. Intraindividual differences may take the form of differences in the nature or level of development of cognitive abilities. The awareness of this aspect of intraindividual differences is probably best exemplified by the use of differential diagnosis techniques. In addition, however, intraindividual differences may also take the form of differences within an individual on a particular cognitive skill from one occasion to the next.

This variation across time in a particular cognitive ability may be the result of a production deficiency. A production deficiency (Flavell, Beach, & Chinsky, 1966; Phye & Zimmerman, 1978) is said to exist when it has been demonstrated that the necessary cognitive ability or skill is part of a learner's repertoire but is not spontaneously used when its use would aid problem solving. A production deficiency may be the result of an inappropriate strategy or cognitive style. Additional sources of production deficiencies would be a lack of attention or simply a misunderstanding of the requirements of the task. Regardless of source, production deficiencies result in inconsistencies in performance for an individual across abilities that give rise to intraindividual differences. This type of inconsistency in cognitive performance is most frequent when a child is in transition from one stage of cognitive development to the next. This simply reflects the fact that transition from one stage to the next is not an abrupt transition that occurs across all aspects of cognitive ability at the same time.

The development of an IEP is prescriptive in nature and is essentially concerned with the construction of methods or materials that capitalize on entering behavior in order to maximize development. The type of intervention approach taken can vary widely. A factor influencing the type of IEP developed would be one's philosophy of intervention. For example, does one develop an IEP directed at teaching the same material at a level different from that taught in the regular instructional program, or does one develop IEPs that teach different materials to different students (Levin, 1977)? While this issue will not be addressed here, it appears to be an issue best resolved on an individual basis. This conclusion follows from a consideration of the vast interindividual differences in abilities among individuals diagnosed as handicapped (Public Law 94-142).

Regardless of educational philosophy, intraindividual differences must be dealt with in the development of an IEP. Two commonly used techniques developed to serve this purpose have been labeled by Cronbach and Snow (1976) as compensatory and capitalization techniques. These techniques are readily identified by special educational personnel as teaching that is directed toward either the strengths or weaknesses of the learner. For example, compensatory techniques are geared to the identification of learner deficiencies and the prescription of instructional methods that either compensate for or remove those deficiencies. Capitalization techniques identify learner strengths and gear instructional methods to those strengths. As pointed out by Levin (1977, p. 85), compensatory techniques have been around for some time in the form of remedial programs of instruction. Capitalization techniques in education are of more recent vintage and are based on the premise that "different" need not imply anything about "better" or "worse."

Capitalization Techniques

A number of psychologists and educators are beginning to advocate the use of capitalization techniques. This interest is probably best documented by the increasing attention being given to the "aptitude by treatment" interaction (ATI) movement. Capitalization techniques begin with the assumption that individual instructional treatment is called for when teaching learners with differing entering behaviors. Ideally, developers of IEPs would match entering behaviors with known instructional treatment to produce maximal learning and development.

The ATI movement is only one approach to dealing with intraindividual differences. While much of the published research dealing with ATIs have taken a psychometric approach to the identification of aptitudes (Cronbach & Snow, 1976) with group instruction as the treatment, Ysseldyke (1973, 1977) has questioned the feasibility of such an approach with handicapped or very young learners. A case in point would be the identification of the entering behaviors of a preschool handicapped learner. A psychometric approach to the identification of aptitudes would be extremely difficult to carry out owing to the dearth of standardized assessment instruments other than IQ tests available for this population.

An alternative to the psychometric approach to ATI methodology that would be idiographic in nature may have greater utility when developing IEPs for preschool or handicapped individuals. For instance, the first step in the development of an IEP would be to do a task analysis of the cognitive processes (Greeno, 1976) that are required to successfully complete the learning task under consideration. Then having determined the cognitive processing involved, the nature or level of development required of the learner in order to engage in the processing must also be specified. Thus, a determination of the processing involved defines the instructional objective, and the determination of cognitive structures necessary for comprehension identifies the necessary cognitive abilities.

The feasibility of such an idiographic approach to ATIs and its utility in the development of IEPs would depend upon the abilities of IEP developers to perform a cognitive task analysis of instructional objectives. Further information concerning the use of cognitive task analysis as it applies to the teaching of size concepts to preschoolers (Phye & Zimmerman, 1976), fractions to fourth graders, introductory geometry to high school students, and auditory psychophysics to college freshmen (Greeno, 1976) is available in the research literature.

An example of a cognitive task analysis (see Figure 9.1) is borrowed from Phye and Zimmerman (1976), who were concerned with the identification of the cognitive processes involved in the development of size concepts in preschool children. Figure 9.1 provides a flowchart of the cognitive processing involved in a Piagetian conservation of length task. Following the identification of conservers and nonconservers of length, a size judgment task was administered in order to determine whether or not the process of length conservation was a prerequisite for correct size judgments. The following is a brief account of the procedure used.

> The conservation of length task used to identify consistent conserving and nonconserving children involved the manipulation of two six-inch sticks. In order to determine the consistency of responding, a procedure comparable to that used by Rothenberg (6) was employed. A flowchart of the testing procedure is given in Figure 1.
>   Consistent nonconservers were those who went through the 6, 7, 5 sequence. Consistent conservers followed the 1, 2, 3 sequence. Inconsistent nonconservers followed the 6, 8, 9, 10 sequence, while inconsistent conservers followed the 1, 4, 5 sequence. This procedure was carried out twice with the original position of the

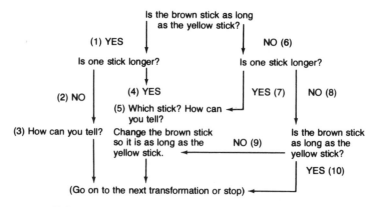

FIGURE 9.1. *Task analysis of conservation of length task.*

sticks in both a vertical and a horizontal position. The position in which the sticks appeared initially was counterbalanced across Ss. In order for children to be included in Experiment I, consistent nonconserving or conserving responses had to be given on both testings. Following the identification of nonconservers and conservers, the judgement of bigger task was administered [p. 69].

While the nature of cognitive task analyses would vary, the example cited is given in order to provide a general frame of reference as to what is meant by a cognitive task analysis.

Assessment of Change

When confronted with the task of specifying instructional objectives for an IEP, attention is almost automatically directed toward some aspect of learning. This is particularly the case with the school-aged child, where many of the instructional objectives will be directed toward the acquisition of academic skills. However, one must not ignore the preschooler or the severely and profoundly handicapped individual of school age. In both of these cases, the goals of an IEP may be the teaching of motor and/or social development rather than the acquisition of academic skills. In all cases, the IEP represents a blueprint for change in important areas of development. The measurement of such change and the cognitive processes involved will be challenging tasks for diagnostic and remediation specialists.

METHODOLOGICAL CONSIDERATIONS

In order to assess behavioral change, a minimum of two measurements at different points in time are required. The standard intervention paradigm of pretest–intervention–posttest is the simplest case in which change can be measured. In our case, pretest would amount to the determination of the entering behavior of a learner and posttest would be the assessment of IEP effectiveness. While this basic paradigm does not exhaust all possibilities, as will be demonstrated later, it is applicable for the assessment of behavioral change for both groups and individuals.

Further, the assessment of behavioral change can occur at several levels. The assessment of a complex educational goal may follow the pretest–intervention–posttest format and the interval between pretest and posttest could be days, weeks, or months. In addition, one must recognize that the assessment of instructional objectives is being dealt with on a continuing basis at all levels of the instructional task. Consequently, either a formal or informal assessment procedure following a pretest–posttest format, or a single-subject time-series format would be necessary whenever a change in instruction was contemplated. This type of procedure would be required in order to effectively monitor the process of behavioral change.

The assessment of behavioral change can be approached from two different frames of reference. On the one hand, developers of IEPs are concerned with the *nature of change.* Did any reliable change in behavior occur? Was the change a positive one, etc.? These types of questions are answered through *formative* evaluation efforts. When this type of evaluation effort is undertaken, the goal is usually the improvement or modification of an IEP or special program. Formative evaluation efforts focus on the needs of the individual and the primary objective is the improvement of services for the handicapped child. On the other hand, evaluation efforts can be directed toward the assessment of overall program effectiveness through the *evaluation of intervention impact.* In this case, the type of evaluation effort is referred to as *summative program* evaluation, and efforts are directed toward determining whether or not observed change was caused by the intervention treatment. Thus, the focus is on the intervention program. In summative evaluation, the program to be evaluated may be an IEP or a special curriculum that provides intervention services for several similar handicapped children or youth.

Within the present context of special education programming for handicapped learners, the following distinction will be maintained. Formative evaluation has as its primary focus the *individual,* while summative evaluation efforts focus on the *program.*

IEP Evaluation

Popham (1975), a leader in the advancement of educational evaluation theory, has made the point that semantic problems abound in the arena of educational evaluation. A case in point, educational research is frequently mistaken for educational evaluation. While both make use of measurement devices and analyze data systematically, the focus of inquiry differs. According to Popham, educational research is concerned with the drawing of conclusions, whereas educational evaluation is concerned with the *decision-making process.*

Formative Evaluation

As previously mentioned, formative evaluation is concerned with the evaluation of the process and products of a program being developed (Perloff, Perloff, & Sussna, 1976). As such, emphasis is placed on the use of evaluation results to facilitate decision making. In the case of IEPs, primary emphasis is on decision making relative to the question, Is the intervention working with a particular child? If not, what changes or modifications need be undertaken? Hence, the basic issue is one of maximizing potential. Phrased differently, the question is, Did change occur that demonstrated growth and development for the handicapped child or youth (see Tombari & Davis, Chapter 10 of this volume)?

Formative evaluation efforts are of great relevance to school psychologists because a primary goal of the evaluative effort is the promotion and optimization of change. Information obtained through the continuous monitoring of cognitive instructional objectives, the use of an error analysis as well as an analysis of correct responses, and an awareness of intraindividual differences are the focus of formative evaluation. At the formative evaluation level, the fact that observed change could be due to any number of causes, among them the effect of intervention, is immaterial.

The point to be stressed is that the formative evaluation of intervention processes through the systematic collection of data is needed in order to improve services to handicapped children. The case study method and the one-group pretest–posttest design to be considered in this section are useful for formative evaluation efforts. While these tools may not be adequate for summative evaluation efforts, they are quite appropriate for the present conceptualization of formative evaluation. Hence, their use is encouraged.

Case Study Methodology

The case study has been included in our discussion of formative evaluation because it is so popular. Its popularity can be traced to such factors as ease of implementation and administration, economy in terms of time and effort, and its familiarity due to its extensive use as a traditional method of assessing psychotherapeutic effectiveness. However, without the establishment of a baseline or pretest, there is no standard of comparison from which change can be inferred.

While the case study design is insufficient for the assessment of change, the case study methodology has a place in the formative assessment of IEPs. The method that involves the formal, continuous observation of behavior is an appropriate modus operandi for evaluation efforts. Consequently, the case study methodology used in combination with an evaluation design that assesses behavioral change would constitute an appropriate formative evaluation format. A case in point would be the use of case study methodology in combination with a single-group pretest–posttest design.

One-Group Pretest–Posttest Design

The one-group pretest–posttest design meets the minimal requirements for the assessment of change. Within the context of formative evaluation, greater interest is expressed for whether or not change occurs than for the cause of the observed change. From this perspective, the one-group pretest–posttest design is adequate for formative evaluation efforts.

Although the pretest–intervention–posttest format is useful in making decisions about IEP processes, since there is no control group for comparison purposes, special emphasis must be placed on reliable measurement. The reliability of measurement is a concern whether the instrument is criterion referenced or norm referenced. In fact, as pointed out by Tallmadge and Horst (1976), norm- and criterion-referenced test characteristics are not mutually exclusive. "On the contrary, the 'norm' and 'criterion' descriptors refer to completely independent test characteristics both of which should probably be included in the description of any test [p. 55]." The dominant characteristic associated with instruments labeled criterion referenced is that their content is clearly defined in behavioral terms. The criterion being referenced is a behavior that is specified in behavioral terms, not a level of proficiency as is frequently, albeit mistakenly, assumed. The mastery issue, which relates to level of proficiency, is an altogether different matter and is encountered with either a criterion- or norm-referenced instrument. The level of proficiency issue is pertinent only when interest is expressed in the amount of change to expect as a result of intervention practices.

The aforementioned requirement of reliable measurement can be dealt with in two ways. When the instructional objective pertains to a behavior that cannot readily be measured with a standardized test, special efforts must be taken to ensure reliable observation of behavior. Training in observational techniques is one way to ensure reliability. A further refinement is possible if personnel permits; this would involve multiple observers and the determination of interobserver reliability indexes. If the behavior evaluated can be measured with a test, the instrument must be standardized with appropriate norm group characteristics and established reliability estimates.

Also, we must start to think in terms of the possibility that a formative evaluation effort for a single child may extend over several years. This is due to the fact that special education efforts may continue for several years with some handicapped children and youth. Hence, a formative evaluation effort under these circumstances would require some type of continuous formative evaluation.

Summative Evaluation

Two factors that have contributed to the impetus for summative evaluation are dissatisfaction with public education in general and shrinking financial support. Not only are federal agencies requiring program evaluation components (e.g., Title I and Title III), but local communities are also more reluctant to indiscriminately provide school-support money (school bonds). In sum, the era of educational accountability is upon us and the need for a formal system of accountability in special education programming demands that attention be given to the evaluation of change at the program level. Also, since the questions asked of summative program evaluation are different from those asked of formative evaluation, attention must be given to methods of determining the impact of special education intervention.

The determination of overall program effectiveness through the evaluation of intervention impact is the goal of summative evaluation efforts. Thus, emphasis is placed on the determination of the cause for observed behavioral change. While it is natural to assume that the observed behavioral change is the result of intervention, that may not be the case. There may be alternative explanations for the observed change. Consequently, summative evaluation is an attempt to build a strong case for the effectiveness of the intervention program in causing the observed change by ruling out alternative explanations.

Summative evaluation efforts appear to be similar to those of educational research. In fact, emphasis on design characteristics is shared by both. This is due to the fact that both are conscious of internal validity factors associated with design methodology that would permit the determination of the cause for observed behavioral change.

For example, a program that provides intervention programming for a preschool handicapped population might have as its focus the provision of educational intervention within the context of the home (Fuqua & Phye, 1978). For each child provided service, an IEP would be developed. An educational specialist would then train the parents to implement the IEP. These sessions would be carried out on a weekly basis. A legitimate question to ask is, Does the home-based intervention work? As indicated in earlier discussions, we are asking the question, What effect did intervention have on observed change?

Note that the question is being asked at the program level. Evaluation at the program level is a requirement of federally funded projects and may eventually become a common requirement of all projects providing educational intervention programming for handicapped persons. Hence, the consideration of frequently used designs for program evaluation.

THE IDEAL DESIGN

In a hypothetical situation, the ideal design for summative evaluation purposes would probably be the pretest–posttest control group design. This design is one of three true experimental designs discussed by Campbell and Stanley (1966). In this hypothetical case, two groups of comparable subjects are randomly assigned to either the treatment or a no-treatment control group. The treatment group would undergo a pretest–intervention (IEP)–posttest sequence. The control group would receive only the pretest and posttest. A comparison of posttest performance would indicate whether or not behavioral change had resulted from the program. Also, with this ideal design, any observed change could be attributed to program intervention because most alternative explanations would be ruled out by design features.

Unfortunately, in the real world of educational program evaluation, the use of a pretest–posttest control group design is almost never possible. This is particularly true in the case of the evaluation of intervention programs for the handicapped. One obvious reason is that many intervention projects have too few individuals in any given program to make possible the use of a group evaluation design.

INTERNAL AND EXTERNAL VALIDITY

In the ideal design, observed behavioral change was attributed to the intervention program. This was possible because the design had high internal validity. Internal validity is the basic minimum without which observed behavioral change cannot unequivocally be attributed to intervention. Phrased differently, internal validity relates to the degree of confidence one has that results were caused by treatment. External validity asks the question of generalizability of findings. Unfortunately, internal and external validity are not independent phenomena. The relationship is a dependent one. This presents the program evaluator with the task of trying to construct an evaluation design reasonably high in both internal and external validity features while knowing that there must be a trade-off. Also, subject characteristics can further complicate matters. As a result of the subject characteristics of the population under consideration (handicapped individuals), design features that are typically employed to enhance both internal and external validity are precluded. In addition, ethical considerations, such as the use of a no-treatment control group, would influence decisions about the evaluation design. Consequently, the confidence in the generalizability of results is a constant issue in any program evaluation of intervention services for the handicapped.

Also, a group falling at one extreme of the ability continuum (handicapped persons) poses unique measurement problems. For example, an obvious threat to internal validity would be statistical regression. This phenomenon is also called regression toward the mean. In this instance, improvement at posttest would occur in extremely low-performing groups even in the absence of intervention treatment. In addition, low-performing persons receiving intervention treatment would appear to gain more from a special program than they actually did. "Regression effects are those inevitable accompaniments of imperfect test–retest correlation for groups selected for their extremity [Campbell & Stanley, 1966, p. 11]." Regression effects would be a factor in either single-subject or group designs, since it is error of measurement that accounts for the imperfect test–retest correlation. Phrased differently, pretest or baseline measures will contain error of measurement, as will any measurement device. Consequently, the selection factor interacts with the regression effect to make this source of invalidity a concern regardless of design (i.e., group or single subject). For example, the use of a single-subject design in combination with a criterion-referenced test when assessing the effectiveness of intervention programs for a handicapped learner will not guarantee that regression effects are not present. Mitigation of regression effects is possible through either design or statistical procedures. However, the procedures are not simple, since regression effects are probably the primary source of invalidity when attempting to evaluate intervention programs for handicapped learners.

To further complicate matters, ethical considerations influence our attempts to mitigate regression effects. For instance, the opportunity to randomly assign handicapped learners to either a treatment or a no-treatment control group would be one means of estimating and controlling for a regression effect. However, the use of a no-treatment control would be an impossibility both legally (Public Law 94-142) and ethically.

Alternative Evaluation Designs

Since the nature of the population under consideration precludes the possibility of using a pretest–posttest control group design or any other "true experimental design," alternative designs must be considered. The following discussion of a single-subject and a group evaluation design is offered in the knowledge that they are viable alternatives. Inasmuch as the designs to be discussed are quasi-experimental designs, they have shortcomings in terms of internal validity. Consequently, the assumption cannot be unequivocally made that the intervention program caused the observed behavioral change. However, an attempt is made to recognize the respective internal validity shortcomings so that efforts may be directed toward minimizing their influence. Also, the following discussion provides the basis for a rapprochement between single-subject and group summative evaluation efforts.

In both instances, the evaluation effort is one of determining the cause of behavioral change. Consequently, some form of time-series design would be required in order to ascertain intervention impact. At a special agency with a large enrollment, some variant of the pretest–posttest group design would be used. At the other end of the spectrum, a single-subject design of the ABAB variety (see the following section) might be employed. In either case, the determination of change as the result of program intervention is the evaluation goal.

The present rapprochement effort takes the form of a continuum approach. As such, the single-subject and pretest–posttest group designs are viewed as opposite ends of the design continuum. Consequently, efforts will not be made to "sell" one approach or the other, but to indicate design considerations with both approaches when the learners to be assessed are handicapped. The decision to include both frequently used types of designs was based on the legislated responsibility of local education agencies. Public Law 94-142 requires the evaluation of IEPs on at least an annual basis. Hopefully, the evaluation of short-term objectives will occur more frequently (Lilly, 1977). The evaluation of intervention programs relative to short-term instructional objectives or annual goals can be conducted using either single-subject or group designs.

SINGLE-SUBJECT DESIGN

The following is a review of one single-subject design. Neither space nor focus permits the comprehensive coverage of all single-subject designs. The present effort is limited to a discussion of the basic time-series design that serves as the basis for a variety of single-subject time-series designs. Persons interested in pursuing the topic further should consult two recent major works in the field, Hersen and Barlow (1976) and Kratochwill (1978). Both sources deal exclusively with single-subject design and research and provide excellent coverage.

THE ABAB DESIGN

This design has been referred to by Kratochwill (1978) as the operant time-series design and is most frequently employed in $N = 1$ behavior modification research. As is indicated by the notational system, the design sequence is as follows: baseline (A)—intervention (B)—baseline (A)—baseline (B). Two common variations of the design involve differing procedures during the third phase.

In a "withdrawal" design, the intervention technique is removed and behavior is observed in order to determine if it returns to the baseline (phase 1) level. In the "reversal" design, instead of the removal of treatment in phase 3, the intervention technique is applied to a behavior deemed "incompatible" (Hersen & Barlow, 1976). If the intervention technique was responsible for the observed change in phase 2, the same treatment applied to an incompatible behavior in phase 3 should produce an opposite behavior pattern.

In passing, it must be noted that when a reversal ABAB design is used, historical and maturational effects are diminished only to the extent that the compatible and incompatible behaviors share 100% of their variance in common. Also, the order in which the behaviors (compatible or incompatible) are treated may influence the effect of intervention. As such, the reversal procedure appears to introduce an additional threat to internal validity through the successive treatment of different behaviors (order effects).

That being the case, the withdrawal ABAB design appears to offer fewer threats to internal validity when evaluating IEPs developed for handicapped learners. However, the logic of the withdrawal design is based on an assumption that is difficult to reconcile with developmental theory. For example, the assumption is made that the intervention effects of phase 2 will disappear when intervention is withdrawn in phase 3. This assumption introduces the issue of the reversibility or nonreversibility of behavior. Can behavior that has been modified as a result of intervention be returned to the initial state observed during baseline (phase 1)? A secondary aspect of the issue relates to the conceptualization of behavioral change. A developmental perspective would conceptualize change as involving both quantitative and qualitative dimensions. Clearly, the logic of the ABAB withdrawal design applies to only the quantitative dimension of behavioral change. In other words, the design permits only the determination of whether or not behavior that was modified in phase 2 can be returned to baseline level, not baseline state or condition, which are aspects of the qualitative dimension.

The question of the nature of behavioral change aside, there are instances where the withdrawal design simply would not be employed. For example, neither a "reversal" nor a "withdrawal" ABAB design would be employed to study behavioral change when intervention techniques had produced irreversible or positive changes such as learned cognitive, social, or motoric skills. In these instances, it would not be educationally feasible to have the child engage in "unlearning" or the learning of "incompatible" behaviors in order to demonstrate a return to baseline conditions. Hence, the single-subject ABAB withdrawal design would appear to be most useful for evaluation programs where the intervention is geared toward the reduction or elimination of undesirable behavior.

Two major sources of internal invalidity in a single-subject design would be the effects of history and maturation. History effects are those events occurring between the pretest and posttest in addition to the intervention treatment. Maturation effects refer to processes within the organism operating as a function of time and not specific to individual events. These processes include growing hungry, tired, older, etc. (Campbell & Stanley, 1966). The obvious control for both effects would be the random assignment of comparable individuals to either the treatment or no-treatment control condition. However, as previously discussed, this is not usually possible.

There is concern over maturation and history effects because they can be plausible alternative explanations for observed change following intervention. History effects become a plausible alternative explanation for change as a result of two factors: the length of the evaluation interval and the nature of the intervention setting. An evaluation effort that attempts to mitigate history effects must attempt to control for such factors as distractions in the intervention setting, educational television, and significant social events that occur during the course of the evaluation effort. As would logically follow, the longer the evaluation interval, the more difficult it is to control for history effects as plausible alternative explanations for observed change.

Maturation effects refer to systematic biological and psychological changes in the individual as a result of the passage of time. These changes would take the form of children growing hungrier, more fatigued, or in a long-term evaluation, older. Maturation is a particular nemesis in the evaluation of IEPs developed for handicapped children, since a case of "spontaneous remission" may be mistaken for the effect of intervention (Campbell & Stanley, 1966). As specified by Campbell and Stanley, change is not spontaneous in a causal sense, but rather it is the cumulative effect of everyday nonintervention experiences that would be operating even if intervention had not been implemented.

Hence, if a no-treatment control condition is not available, two methodological steps should be taken: (a) keep the evaluation interval at a minimum; and (b) make efforts to provide a setting for intervention that reduces, as much as possible, extraneous sources of influence. These safeguards are almost the only alternatives available when attempting to ensure the internal validity of an ABAB single-subject design's use for program evaluation.

Concluding remarks on the ABAB Design

This review of shortcomings associated with the use of an ABAB single-subject design was not undertaken in an effort to militate against its use in program evaluation. To the contrary, single-subject designs will be frequently used because there are few, if any, viable alternatives. Inasmuch as individualized educational programs must be evaluated, the use of single-subject designs will continue. However, the interpretation of change in behavior as a result of intervention must be qualified in terms of alternative explanations (potential sources of invalidity) that are the result of design features. The position taken here is that an awareness of design shortcomings will provide the basis for a more conscientious evaluation effort. An awareness of threats to internal validity is necessary in order to safeguard against them. While there will never be an instance where the degree of confidence is 100% that the intervention program caused the observed change, attempts must be made to maintain as high a level of confidence as possible.

GROUP DESIGNS

Group designs can be used for summative evaluation purposes when a project has sufficient enrollment to warrant a common intervention curriculum. The "ideal group design" discussed earlier is an excellent design for evaluation purposes. However, as noted, it is not possible to use a "true experimental design" with our handicapped population. Consequently, an alternative group design that can be used to evaluate the intervention impact of programs designed for handicapped persons will be discussed.

NONEQUIVALENT CONTROL GROUP DESIGN

One of the more widespread designs used in special education research is the design involving the use of a treatment and a control group where subjects have not been randomly assigned. In this case, random assignment to either the treatment or control group is not possible. These are instances where persons eligible for a program must be served. Thus, the treatment group is always defined as those eligible for the intervention program. The no-treatment control group must, then, consist of noneligible persons similar to the treatment group on all characteristics except those being treated (Campbell & Stanley, 1966).

In terms of our aforementioned preschool program, control group subjects would be nonhandicapped children of a similar age from comparable socioeconomic, ethnic, and geographical backgrounds. The nonequivalent control group design controls for all sources of internal invalidity except potential regression effects and the interactions of selection and history, selection and maturation, and selection and testing.

The interaction of selection and history is a distinct possibility when the evaluation interval is from 9 to 12 months. In this case, the use of a nonequivalent control group would mitigate the effects of large-scale historical influences (i.e., major social or cultural events). However, the history effects unique to the intervention program would still be operating and having a differential effect, since only the treatment group would be exposed. Again, confidence that the observed behavioral change resulted from intervention practices is attenuated by this potential source of internal invalidity.

Due to the nature of the population being evaluated, the possibility of a selection by instrumentation interaction exists when a nonequivalent control group is employed. For example, if the control group is markedly different from the treatment group on the characteristic being evaluated, it may be difficult to find a single assessment instrument that accurately measures pretest and posttest performance. This possibility arises when an instrument's range is restricted and its use with two widely different populations results in either a floor effect or a ceiling effect.

A floor effect would exist if at pretest the instrument selected for assessment purposes was too difficult because it was selected with the control group in mind. This would produce a floor effect in the performance of the treatment group defined as an artificially high index of behavior. This would result from the instrument's inability to accurately measure the low level of behavior being displayed. A ceiling effect would more likely occur at posttest if the instrument selected for assessment was selected with the treatment group in mind. In this case, the development of the control group during the intervention interval is underestimated because of the instrument's inability to measure at posttest the entire range of behavior being displayed. The possibility of either effect attests to the care with which the assessment instrument used for program evaluation purposes must be selected.

The selection by maturation interaction may, in fact, underestimate program intervention effects. This interaction effect is tenable when one group has a higher rate of maturation or autonomous change than another. By definition, our treatment group (handicapped learners) exhibits a slower rate of development than nonhandicapped children of a comparable chronological age who serve as the nonequivalent control group. Consequently, there would be an underestimation of intervention effect for the treatment group due to the differing rates of development exhibited by the two groups.

In other words, for a treatment to be judged effective, the difference between the control and treatment group at posttest must be large enough to compensate for the slower rate of development of the treatment group. In terms of conclusions drawn about the effectiveness of program intervention, there is a greater likelihood of a Type 2 error being made—a Type 2 error in this case being the conclusion that there was no significant effect of intervention practices when, in fact, the program had produced significant growth and development in the handicapped children serviced by the program. Hence, while the selection by maturation interaction is a source of invalidity, its nature is such that treatment effects are underestimated. This statement is accurate only when applied to a treatment group consisting of handicapped children and a nonequivalent control group of nonhandicapped children.

Regression effects provide the only other major source of internal invalidity. Again, since the regression effect cannot be controlled by random assignment to either the treatment or nonequivalent control group, the effects must be controlled statistically. Two commonly employed statistical techniques are covariance analysis and special regression techniques.

CONCLUDING REMARKS ON GROUP DESIGNS

As was the case with single-subject designs, there are no simple solutions. Again, the design problems stem primarily from the inability to employ a no-treatment control group with random assignment from our handicapped population into either the treatment or no-treatment control groups. Were this possible, one would have a "true experimental design" (Campbell & Stanley, 1966). In such a design, all plausible alternative explanations (sources of internal invalidity) for observed behavioral change are eliminated and we would have absolute confidence in our evaluation results. However, this type of design is impossible to employ. Hence, we must know enough design logic to develop quasi-experimental evaluation designs that permit as much confidence as possible in obtained results. Although this review has dwelt on evaluation design shortcomings, the intent is not to discourage summative evaluation attempts to determine program or curriculum impact. On the contrary, an awareness of problems associated with commonly used evaluation designs should improve the quality of summative evaluation in special education projects designed to provide educational intervention for our handicapped children and youth.

Summative Evaluation Pitfalls

Regardless of the group design selected for program evaluation, there are two common data treatments that should be avoided. These pitfalls are common to educational evaluation efforts in general and have special relevance for the evaluation of educational programs for exceptional learners. These pitfalls occur when pretest differences are observed between treatment and control groups and attempts are made to "adjust for" observed differences. Specifically, attention will be given to the use of gain scores and covariance analysis.

Gain Scores

Since the evaluation of intervention is concerned with change over time as a result of treatment, it is tempting to assume that the basic data would be gain scores. However, consensus suggests that the use of gain scores or residual gain scores should be scrupulously avoided (Tallmadge, 1977). As is widely known, the main problem with gain scores is that they are ridden with a regression effect. As previously observed, the greater the measurement error associated with pretest–posttest assessment, the more likely a statistical regression effect. Residual gain scores have been advocated as a means of reducing the statistical regression effects associated with the use of raw gain scores. However, there is considerable difference of opinion concerning the use of residual gain scores (Cronbach & Furby, 1970). Consequently, if possible, it is wise to avoid the use of gain scores in the evaluation of special education programs. Besides, gain scores are difficult for some people to understand and are open to misinterpretation (Nunnally, 1973).

Covariance Analysis

The analysis of covariance is a statistical technique frequently opted for when the researcher is confronted with pretest differences between treatment and control group. However, the covariance analysis should not be used indiscriminately. Caution must be exercised in the use of covariance analysis when the covariate is not perfectly reliable (Campbell & Stanley, 1966). Also, the analysis assumes random assignment to treatment and control group with the control group being similar to the treatment group (Horst, Tallmadge, & Wood, 1975). Consequently, the use of covariance analysis would be difficult to justify in the analysis of data collected from educational intervention programs for handicapped learners. An alternative would be the use of regression procedures that provide an estimation of treatment effects from the performance of noncomparable control groups (Tallmadge & Horst, 1976).

Educational Significance of the Intervention

Assuming that the summative evaluation design (either single-subject or group) was adequate, evaluation pitfalls were avoided, and differences favoring the treatment condition were found, the question remains, Was the effect of the program educationally significant? Unlike the issue of statistical significance, educational significance is a matter of judgment. "In judging the educational significance of an intervention impact, two factors must be considered: the size of the effect, and the area in which it happened [Tallmadge, 1977, p. 31]." For example, an intervention may have a statistically significant impact and still be judged to be educationally insignificant. This type of judgment would be based on the inappropriateness or narrowness of scope of the intervention. By the same token, a small, though statistically significant, impact may be viewed as educationally significant if the impact is broadly defined and considered to have particular educational significance. Attempts at defining educational significance have taken several forms.

When a standardized achievement test is used to evaluate intervention impact, a statistical rule of thumb has been derived that can be used in a definition of educational significance. The rule states that the intervention effect must equal or exceed one-third or one-fourth of a standard deviation associated with the standardized test used to evaluate impact (Tallmadge, 1977).

However, other means can also be used in determining the significance of intervention impact. For example, relevant literature may be researched and summarized to indicate that the intervention is indeed important and that obtained results are in keeping with results from comparable programs. Further, expert testimony may be obtained to support or buttress evaluation data. In this case, an attempt is made to provide the reader of an evaluation report with a frame of reference. For example, the effectiveness of an intervention program may vary considerably as a result of the population served. Consequently, such differential expectations should be related to theory and provided as a context for the judgment of educational significance.

It is apparent, then, that the judgment of educational significance is not a straightforward decision. Hence, it behooves anyone reporting the results of summative program intervention to marshal as much evidence as possible that addresses the question of the educational significance of impact. Thus, the presentation of evaluation efforts should begin with statistical or numerical evidence but should not terminate at that point.

Summary

Having begun this chapter with a consideration of theoretical issues related to learning, and having then dealt with practical advice such as how to present a case for the judgment of educational significance, a great deal of ground has been covered. In order to conclude, a recapitulation of major issues as they relate to the development and evaluation of individualized educational programs is necessary.

The development of IEPs can take several forms. Short-term instructional objectives as well as annual goals can be expressed in either behavioral or cognitive terms. While it is assumed that behavioral objectives will be used in the development of IEPs, a case is made for the inclusion of cognitive instructional objectives when developing educational programs. Whether instructional objectives are approached from a behavioral or cognitive perspective, intraindividual differences are a key to the development of optimal educational interventions.

Following the adoption of a cognitive frame of reference as a guide for the development of instructional objectives, the nature of behavioral change and its assessment are the next factors to be considered. The assessment of behavioral change within a cognitive frame of reference that would include a consideration of error as well as correct responses is an important process in formative evaluation. The use of systematic observation via case study methodology in combination with a single-group pretest–posttest design is encouraged in order to promote formative evaluation of special education programs. The formative evaluation approach, which places special emphasis on the individual, is encouraged as a means of improving services to handicapped children and youth.

Summative evaluation is also encouraged. It is of particular importance for federally funded projects or agencies that provide special education services (educational intervention) for handicapped children and youth. Shortcomings associated with single-subject and group designs frequently used in program evaluation were reviewed. However, the emphasis was placed on the awareness of design shortcomings so that they could be reduced. Adequate summative program evaluation efforts help to answer questions about the effectiveness of a particular curriculum or program used to provide educational services.

Having evaluated an educational program and its worth, only one step remains. This last step is to determine the educational significance of the program. Since there are no unequivocal guidelines in making a judgment of educational significance, it is suggested that an approach be taken comparable to that which a lawyer might take when developing a case for the defense. This would involve marshaling the evidence (i.e., statistical data, corroborative research, expert testimony, etc.) and presenting it in a logical, convincing manner.

References

Campbell, D. T., & Stanley, J. C. *Experimental and quasi-experimental designs for research.* Chicago: Rand McNally, 1966.

Clinchy, B., & Rosenthal, K. Analysis of children's errors. In G. S. Lesser (Ed.), *Psychology and educational practice.* Glenview, Illinois: Scott Foresman, 1971.

Cronbach, L. J., & Furby, L. How should we measure "change"—or should we? *Psychological Bulletin,* 1970, **74,** 68–80.

Cronbach, L. J., & Snow, R. E. *Aptitude and instructional methods: A handbook for research on interactions.* New York: Irvington/Naiburg, 1976.

Farnham-Diggory, S. *Cognitive processes in education: A psychological preparation for teaching and curriculum development.* New York: Harper & Row, 1972.

Farnham-Diggory, S. The cognitive point of view. In D. J. Treffinger, J. K. Davis, & R. E. Ripple (Eds.), *Handbook on teaching educational psychology.* New York: Academic Press, 1977.

Flavell, J. H., Beach, D. H., & Chinsky, J. M. Spontaneous verbal rehearsal in a memory task as a function of age. *Child Development,* 1966, **3,** 283–289.

Fuqua, R., & Phye, G. *The use of a behavioral developmental profile in the evaluation of a rural, home intervention program for handicapped preschoolers.* Paper presented at the meeting of the American Educational Research Association, Toronto, March 1978.

Gray, S. W. *The psychologist in the schools.* New York: Holt, 1963.

Greeno, J. G. Cognitive objections of instruction: Theory of knowledge for solving problems and answering questions. In D. Klahr (Ed.), *Cognition and instruction.* New York: Lawrence Erlbaum Associates, 1976.

Hersen, M., & Barlow, D. H. *Single-case experimental designs: Strategies for studying behavioral change.* New York: Pergamon Press, 1976.

Horst, D. P., Tallmadge, G. K., & Wood, C. T. *A practical guide to measuring project impact on student achievement* (Stock number 017-080-01516-1). Washington, D.C.: U.S. Government Printing Office, 1975.

Kirk, S. A., McCarthy, J. J., & Kirk, W. D. *Examiners manual: Illinois test of psycholinguistic abilities* (Rev. ed.). Urbana: University of Illinois Press, 1968.

Kratochwill, T. R. Foundations of time-series research. In T. R. Kratochwill (Ed.), *Single subject research.* New York: Academic Press, 1978.

Levin, J. L. *Learner differences: Diagnosis and prescription.* New York: Holt, 1977.

Lilly, M. S. Evaluating individualized education programs. In S. Torres (Ed.), *A primer on individualized education programs for handicapped children.* Reston, Virginia: The Foundation for Exceptional Children, 1977.

Meichenbaum, D. *Cognitive-behavior modification.* New York: Plenum, 1977.

Nunnally, J. C. Research strategies and measurement methods for investigating human development. In J. R. Nesselroade & H. W. Reese (Eds.), *Life-span developmental psychology: Methodological issues.* New York: Academic Press, 1973.

Perloff, R., Perloff, E., & Sussna, E. Program evaluation. *Annual Review of Psychology,* 1976, **27,** 569–594.

Phye, G. D. *The role of informative feedback in productive learning.* Paper presented at the meeting of the American Educational Research Association, New York, April 1977.

Phye, G. D. The processing of informative feedback about multiple-choice test performance. Manuscript submitted for publication, 1979.

Phye, G. D., Gugliemella, J., & Sola, J. Effects of delayed retention on multiple-choice test performance. *Contemporary Educational Psychology*, 1976, **1**, 26–36.

Phye, G. D., & Zimmerman, B. Conservation of length and the development of a size concept. *The Journal of Genetic Psychology*, 1976, **128**, 67–76.

Phye, G. D., & Zimmerman, B. *Testing for mediation and/or production deficiencies in lower SES children: A methodological note.* Manuscript submitted for publication, 1979.

Popham, W. J. *Educational evaluation.* Englewood Cliffs, New Jersey: Prentice-Hall, 1975.

Public Law 94-142. Education for all handicapped children act. November 29, 1975.

Tallmadge, G. K. *The joint dissemination review panel ideabook.* Washington, D.C.: U.S. Government Printing Office, 1977.

Tallmadge, G. K., & Horst, D. P. *A procedural guide for validating achievement gains in educational projects.* (Stock number 017-080-01516-1) Washington, D.C.: U.S. Government Printing Office, 1976.

Ysseldyke, J. E. Diagnostic-prescriptive teaching: The search for aptitude–treatment interactions. In A. Sabatino & L. Mann (Eds.), *The first review of special education.* Philadelphia: Journal of Special Education Press, 1973.

Ysseldyke, J. E. Aptitude-treatment interaction research with first grade children. *Contemporary Educational Psychology*, 1977, **2**, 1–9.

MARTIN TOMBARI • RONALD A. DAVIS

10 Behavioral Consultation

The psychological services provided in elementary and secondary schools can be classified into two basic approaches: direct services from a psychologist to children with learning and adjustment problems; and indirect services via a teacher or parent consulting with a psychological specialist (see Monroe, Chapter 2 of this volume). The latter approach, termed psychological consultation, is less prevalent in schools than direct services. However, it has aroused the greater amount of interest and debate within the last decade (Reschly, 1976).

Despite its long-standing tradition in school psychology, the direct services approach has been found wanting primarily in two respects. First, it is time consuming. The large proportion of school referrals—approaching 10% of school enrollment—cannot be handled adequately by a psychologist offering direct services that involve extensive testing, case work-ups, written recommendations, and staffings (Cowen, 1967).

Second, many educators and psychologists question whether, in working with children in a diagnostic role, psychologists contribute anything to teachers' understanding of those children, to the improvement of their teaching skills, or even to the prevention of classroom problems (Kennedy, 1971; Reger, 1967). Some critics believe the testing aspect of direct services should be dropped entirely (Bardon, 1972).

281

SCHOOL PSYCHOLOGY
Perspectives and Issues

Dissatisfaction with the direct services role has spurred a search for more effective forms of service. Moreover, educators have realized that many of the principles of behavior used by psychologists can be taught to teachers or parents. They, in turn, can use these principles to help solve children's problems without the direct intervention of the psychologist. Such reasoning has led to an interest in psychologists acting as consultants.

Thus we can trace two major lines of influence on consultation: one coming from dissatisfaction with traditional forms of services; and the other coming from a desire to have psychologists transmit their knowledge and skill to persons in direct contact with children.

Although consultation is becoming the preferred mode of service for many psychologists, there has never been a satisfactory definition of consultation. Some define it as indirect service where a caretaker (teacher or parent) interacts with a psychologically trained specialist (consultant) to help a child (client) who is experiencing certain problems (Meyers, Martin, & Hyman, 1977). The extent of the "interaction," however, has never been detailed. Under this definition almost anything can be described as consultation just as long as, at some time, a consultant and a consultee sit down to talk about a client.

There is also confusion about the goals of consultation. Are they directed primarily to changing teacher perceptions of problems or teacher behavior? Should the goal of consultation be to change the child's behavior or to change organizational functioning? Depending on the direction of the goal, different models of consultation have emerged: a mental health approach (Caplan, 1970), an organization development approach (Schmuch, Runkel, Saturen, Martell, & Derr, 1972), and a behavioral approach (Bergan, 1977).

This chapter concerns itself with the behavioral approach to consultation. In describing this approach we will attempt to distinguish it from other forms of psychological service, but we do this without claiming to have evolved the complete definition of consultation. We will specify the key influences on the theory and practice of behavioral consultation and describe the problem-solving process used by those who call themselves behavioral consultants. We will review some of the many successful applications of behavioral consultation, discuss problems related to influencing consultees to change their behavior, and deal with some of the myths that have arisen around this approach to psychological services. Finally, the last section of this chapter will be devoted to a review of some of the issues involved in school implementation of behavioral programs with a consideration of alternatives to traditional types of behavioral interventions.

Behavioral Consultation: Critical Attributes

Crises of one sort or another confront us all at various times in our lives. What prevents us from dealing with many of these crises is a natural tendency to perceive problems as more insurmountable than they actually are. The problems are so immediate to our lives that we fail to see some relatively simple steps that can be taken to solve them. At these times, as we all know, it helps to talk with a friend, someone we trust, to help us look at things more objectively.

There is no need to belabor the point that teachers and parents experience many crises in working with children. Many of these crises relate to a child's disruptive behavior or inability to learn. There are means to deal with these problems, but often the parent or teacher fails to see them. They may lack information necessary to handle these problems, but, just as likely, they may perceive the problem as beyond their control. At this point they need someone to help them examine the problem objectively and guide them through a systematic process that leads to problem solution. Behavioral consultation is a problem-solving process for assisting parents and teachers in coping with children's problems.

Behavioral consultation has certain attributes that distinguish it from all other forms of psychological services, whether direct or indirect. These characteristics relate to goals, assumptions, approach to problem solving, and criteria for success.

Behavioral consultation goals concentrate on change in the behavior of clients. Behavioral consultants involve themselves with a broad scope of behavior changes. These problems may be of a social–emotional or academic nature involving attitudes, self-concepts, assertion, obedience, reading comprehension, penmanship, math computation, or creative writing. The only limitations on goals imposed by behavioral consultants is that they be beneficial to the client and capable of behavioral definition.

Underlying behavioral consultation is the assumption that the root of the child's problem lies in the setting in which it takes place. Thus, any plans to change children's behavior must involve manipulations of immediate environmental events. School problems are dealt with by making changes in school conditions, not the home environment. Conversely, parent–child conflict is seen as a function of the home setting, not caused by events in school.

Behavioral consultation is primarily collaborative in nature, with the teacher or parent acting as the primary agent of change. This is often interpreted as prohibiting the consultant from any direct contact with the client. However, the concept of indirect, collaborative services does not preclude consultants from working with children as long as this involvement is in the nature of fact finding that will lead to interventions implemented by the teacher (Severson, 1973).

Behavioral consultants use a systematic problem-solving process to guide parents and teachers to problem solution. First, they work collaboratively to identify problems and set precise objectives. Not only do they decide on objectives, but they also develop strategies to accomplish these objectives. In addition, there must be a joint evaluation to judge success. If these procedures are not followed, then behavioral consultation has not occurred. Merely sitting down with a teacher and discussing problems is not behavioral consultation unless this discussion leads to setting objectives and establishing an intervention. Likewise, if no evaluation takes place, the behavioral consultation process has not been carried out.

Evaluation of behavioral consultation can only be in terms of the change in client behavior for which both consultee and consultant are accountable. Although consultees may be satisfied with consultation and feel more capable of handling similar problems in the future, such testimony is insufficient to assess effectiveness. The only acceptable proof of success is objective evidence that the client met the objective specified at the start of consultation. Thus, the fundamental components of behavioral consultation are behavioral definitions of problems, interventions, data collection, and evaluation all carried out in an indirect, collaborative manner.

Influences on Behavioral Consultation

There have been a number of theoretical influences on the theory and practice of behavioral consultation. While the predominant influence has been from the behavioral psychology of Skinner and his followers, behavioral consultation also borrows concepts from systems theory, instructional psychology, and counseling theory. If we separate behavioral consultation into a process and a knowledge base we can better understand these influences.

The consultation process refers both to the stages through which consultation proceeds and to the style of verbal interaction that the consultant employs. Systems theory has largely influenced the former, while the latter, surprisingly, draws upon nondirective approaches to the counselor–client relationship.

Largely through the influence of systems theory, the process of behavioral consultation is conceived as a total structure with various parts or stages that affect one another (Kaufman, 1971). Within this structure certain activities must take place for the system to work. These events form an invariant sequence of steps, each having objectives that must be accomplished for the succeeding steps to function. In behavioral consultation these steps involve problem identification, problem analysis, plan implementation, and problem evaluation (Bergan, 1977; Dorr, 1973; Goodwin & Coates, 1976). The final step provides feedback to the total structure that helps those involved in the system assess whether it has functioned effectively. If the evaluation suggests that the system has not worked in a particular case, then certain guidelines are provided for trouble shooting, modification, and the development of new plans. Such systems concepts guide the consultant in problem-solving efforts with consultees.

The verbal interaction that takes place in the consultation process is conceived as largely under the control of the consultant. Consultants direct the course of consultation by the sequence of questions that they ask and by the directions that they give. While controlling the interaction during the stages of the consultation, consultants do so in a manner that makes them appear collaborative and nondirective. They accomplish this by eliciting goals and priorities and offering choices, rather than by simply telling the consultee what to do. The theoretical basis for this style of verbal interaction stems from the literature in psychiatry and counseling that stresses the nondirective nature of helping relationships (Rogers, 1961; Sullivan, 1954).

The knowledge base that behavioral consultants draw upon to analyze and solve problems comes largely from research conducted in the behavioral science tradition. More specifically, controlled research into socialization conducted under behavioral and social learning theory is used extensively (Bandura, 1969). Such research has provided principles that are likely to solve clients' problems in home, school, and institutional settings. Furthermore, the behavioral science tradition has developed a technology for evaluating the effectiveness of plans that apply behavioral principles.

Although the behavioral sciences provide the primary knowledge base, behavioral consultants make use of research outside this tradition to expedite problem solution. Thus, the developmental work of Piaget, the writings of persons such as Berlyne on motivation, as well as research into group dynamics and psycholinguistics all provide useful principles that the behavioral consultant can implement in applied settings. A second knowledge base that is used by behavioral consultants comes from instructional psychology, in particular Gagné's research on intellectual skills and the writings of Mager and Popham on instructional objectives and evaluation (Gagné, 1976; Mager, 1962, Popham, 1976). Such research is used primarily in handling academic cases where the behavioral consultant assumes that the problem can best be understood in terms of prerequisite skills rather than hypothetical processes or abilities. Thus Mager and Popham's suggestions for defining precise instructional objectives as the first step in instructional planning and Gagné's research on task analysis and the hierarchical arrangement of intellectual skills are concepts that the behavioral consultant uses to deal with academic problems.

Consultation Methods

Verbal Behavior during Consultation

Problem solving during behavioral consultation takes place during an interview. Since consultation consists almost entirely of verbal interchange, behavioral consultants are trained to focus almost exclusively on the verbal aspects of the interview. The basis for this exclusive emphasis on verbal behavior relates to the specificity with which verbal skills can be defined and measured—not to research tying specific behaviors to the outcomes of consultation. Such process–product research remains more a dream than a reality.

There is much research on verbal behavior during therapeutic or counseling interviews. Such research makes extensive use of content analysis procedures. Content analysis denotes a research technique for the systematic ordering of the content of the communication process. Typically it involves procedures for dividing verbal content into coding units that are then assigned to categories for summarization and statistical manipulation. Inferences are then made about the significance of these categories in the communication process.

Some of the research using content analysis methods to examine the social influence process during the dyadic interview impinges on consultation. Verbal conditioning studies, for example, have demonstrated that verbal behavior can be brought under the control of environmental stimuli and is highly susceptible to change through contingent reinforcement (Kanfer, 1968). The only reported experimental study of verbal influence during consultation was conducted by Tombari and Bergan (1978). They examined the effect of ambiguous statements ("Tell me anything you can about this child") and specific statements ("Tell me about this child's behavior in your class") on consultee descriptions of children's problems, their expectations for problem solution, and their conceptualizations of children's problems. The results suggest that the consultant's statements can control not only how consultees describe children's problems, but also the manner in which they conceptualize problems (behavioral versus medical model) and their expectations for being able to solve them.

Thus, there is some research on the nature of verbal behavior during the interview that has implications for consultation. However, most of the suggestions for conducting the consultation process have no empirical base and are more on the order of do's and don'ts. A summary of these critical verbal skills follows.

Verbal Skills in Behavioral Consultation

During the consultation interviews the consultant attempts to guide the consultee toward problem solution through the skillful use of verbal elicitors and emitters. Elicitors are the questions and requests made by the consultant to gain information from the consultee, whereas emitters are statements that generally specify information or summarize information transmitted between the two interview participants. Skillful selection of elicitors and emitters by the consultant ensures that the discussion will not stray from the major issue of concern—the child's behavior and what to do about it—while at the same time preserving the consultee's role in defining the problem and giving the consultee an important role in problem solution.

In behavioral consultation, the critical verbal skills involve the consultant's ability either to elicit statements that call for the consultee to specify, summarize, validate, or evaluate certain information, or emit statements that do the same. The information that is elicited or emitted deals with the child's behavior, conditions surrounding the behavior, observations of behavior, or plans to solve the problem. Thus, the behavioral consultant is trained to emit statements that focus the interview on topics relevant to problem solution, to elicit relevant information from the consultee, and to summarize and validate periodically the information transmitted in the interview (Bergan, 1977).

Each stage of behavioral consultation has specific objectives, and it is the consultants' knowledge of which objectives need to be attained that guide their selection of verbal statements. For example, once the behavior and behavior conditions have been identified in the problem identification interview, behavioral consultants must develop a procedure to collect baseline data on the problem. Consequently, they use statements that elicit procedures from the consultee for keeping a record on the behavior or they emit suggestions for doing so. The most comprehensive categorization of these verbal skills and their sequence in the various stages of behavioral consultation can be found in Bergan (1977) and Goodwin, Garvey, and Barclay (1971).

A largely unanswered question, related to verbal behavior during consultation, is whether consultants should be directive or nondirective during the interview. The directive role can be operationalized in terms of the percentage of emitters (statements) versus elicitors (questions) that consultants use, by the percentage of interview time they are speaking, and by the use of the personal pronoun "I" as opposed to "we." Most writers on consultation strongly recommend the nondirective approach.

Implicit in the assumption that consultant's should take a nondirective role is the belief that if they do not, consultees will not follow through on procedures to achieve problem solution. Caplan (1970) and Fine and Taylor (1971) conclude that experts (who give direction) lower the self-esteem and sense of adequacy of the teacher, whereas the nondirective consultative relationship leaves the consultee feeling more capable and competent. Lippitt (1967) supports this viewpoint, asserting that the consultant role is to listen, making it easier for the consultee to talk.

Berlin (1967) and Fine and Taylor (1971) report that the role of the consultant is to provide alternatives and never to suggest a specific recommendation, because the teacher is less likely to follow through with a directive. More recently, others (Bergan, 1977; Meyers, 1975; Meyers *et al.*, 1977) have reaffirmed this belief, although no data are reported in the consultation literature to support it.

There are some studies that call into question this long-standing assumption. Derby (1977) predicted that teachers interacting with a consultant who was low in dominance would perceive him/her as more helpful. The prediction was not supported; Derby concluded that the assumption that teachers prefer interacting with a consultant low in dominance may be invalid. Kuehnel (1975), in a study investigating organizational climate in schools and teacher reactions to consultants, found that some teachers did prefer a directive consultation style, but this depended on previous experience in interacting with principals who were task oriented and kept them at a distance. Suinn (1974) reported that while the training staff in their study rated nondirective consultants as more effective, consumers preferred the directive consultant.

There has been only one experimental study examining this issue (Clark, 1978). Clark randomly assigned 20 teachers to two treatment groups: one involving expert behavioral consultation, the other collaborative. Although teachers perceived the consultants' roles as defined (i.e., the experts were perceived as experts, collaborators as collaborators) there were no differences between the groups in extent of plan implementation, goal achievement, or attitudes about the consultants' openness, warmth, or general effectiveness.

In sum, no definitive evidence supports the preference for either a directive or nondirective style. Certainly the effectiveness of the style will interact with other variables such as problem type, work experience of consultant or consultee, prior contact with consultants, the consultant's own personal preference or comfort in a nondirective or directive role, as well as perceptions of the problem as crisis or noncrisis.

Stages in Behavioral Consultation

Almost all models of behavioral consultation conceptualize the process in four stages: (*a*) a problem identification interview (PII); (*b*) a problem analysis interview (PAI); (*c*) a plan implementation (PI); and (*d*) a problem evaluation interview (PEI) (Bergan, 1977; Dornbach, 1972; Dorr, 1973; Goodwin & Coates, 1976). Each stage or interview has specific objectives that must be accomplished before the participants in consultation can proceed to the next stage.

Problem Identification

Problem identification sets the consultant process in motion. Successful completion of this initial stage requires that the following objectives be met: (*a*) there must be precise behavioral definitions of the client's problem; (*b*) goals must be stated in performance terms; and (*c*) there must be a strategy to collect baseline data. Failure to accomplish these objectives reduces sharply the likelihood that continued problem solving will take place (Bergan & Tombari, 1976). Furthermore, the best predictor of plan implementation is successful completion of problem identification.

Problem identification plays this pivotal role because it very likely sets the stage for either a behavioral or a medical model perspective on the child's problem. The behavioral perspective emphasizes the role of immediate environmental events on the problem. The teacher or parent generally can control influences of this type. By contrast, the medical model stresses remote environmental events and internal characteristics as determinants of behavior. Consultees cannot control these variables. The behavioral perspective on the problem is more likely to result in collection of baseline data and a commitment to pursue consultation through subsequent phases. The medical model perspective, on the other hand, provides little direction for collection of precise data related to the problem and is less likely to result in specific classroom or home interventions. Thus, the subsequent phases of consultation are less likely to be pursued.

Failure, then, on the part of the behavioral consultant to elicit a behavioral definition of the problem during the PII will in all probability end the consultative relationship.

PROBLEM ANALYSIS

Problem analysis takes place after adequate baseline data have been collected on the problem identified in the PII. The consultant's task during the PAI is to determine the factors influencing problem solution, to develop a plan with the consultee to solve the problem, and to establish procedures to assess and monitor performance of the child during plan implementation.

During the PAI, the consultant must determine whether the root of the problem lies in the conditions surrounding the behavior or in a lack of skills on the part of the clients that prevent them from behaving as desired (Bergan, 1977). The former is usually the case with adjustment problems, whereas the latter typifies many academic referrals. Variability in performance is an important clue to whether the problem is primarily related to lack of skills or poor performance. Behavior that is highly variable in performance suggests that conditions are a factor in goal attainment. Consequently, the behavioral consultant must conduct a conditions analysis with the consultee. A uniformly low level of performance of the desired behavior, coupled with the observation that conditions are supportive of goal attainment suggests that a skills analysis by the consultant may be necessary. In both cases decisions are based largely on baseline data collected by the consultee.

In a conditions analysis, consultants attempt to elicit from consultees the antecedent and consequent conditions underlying the problem behavior: the proverbial ABC's of behavior. Through this analysis, behavioral consultants learn which conditions in the environment are likely to prevent goal attainment and must be removed, as well as those conditions absent from the environment that can facilitate goal attainment and must be introduced. A variety of such analysis procedures have been developed that detail the steps a consultant must take to assess the ABC's of the client problem (Goodwin & Coates, 1976; Svinicki & Muller, 1974; Vargas, 1975).

During a skills analysis the consultant proceeds with the assumption that the failure of clients to perform a certain skill or behavior is due to their lack of prerequisite sets of behavioral capabilities referred to as intellectual skills (Bergan & Dunn, 1976; Gagné, 1977).

Gagné's hierarchical arrangement of intellectual skills provides the most suitable model for carrying out a skills analysis. Both conditions and skills analysis end with the development of a plan to be implemented in the classroom to help the client.

PLAN IMPLEMENTATION

Although implementation of the details of the plan is the responsibility of the consultee, the consultant's role during implementation cannot be simply to "wait and see." At this time consultants must take care that the plan is implementated as desired and is functioning as anticipated. They must also be ready to make changes in the plan if necessary (Bergan, 1977).

Bergan believes that consultants must assume responsibility not only for assessing the consultees' skills necessary to implement plans, but also to make provisions for skill training and evaluation of that training if they do not possess such skills. Bergan goes further than any other writer on behavioral consultation in detailing this educational aspect of the consultant's role. However others, such as Caplan (1970), see a danger to the consultative relationship when the consultant assumes training responsibilities.

Certainly, although training may be an important factor in determining plan implementation (we will review training studies in the following section), it is unlikely that the consultant will have much time to devote to this responsibility. Thus it is imperative that consultants design their plans with the strengths and weaknesses of consultees in mind avoiding, if at all possible, requiring them to implement plans for which they lack the requisite knowledge or skills.

PROBLEM EVALUATION

Behavioral consultation, more than other models of consultation, stresses evaluation of services strictly in terms of objective data on client performance. Thus, the problem evaluation interview (PEI) phase of behavioral consultation centers on examining records of client behavior. The essential question is, "Did the child achieve the goal specified during problem identification?" If not, the possible reasons for this are discussed with the consultee. This discussion will usually lead to some revision in the plan or to the development and implementation of a new plan. If the goal has been attained, the participants plan for continued behavior monitoring. Thus, the objectives of the PEI involve validation of goal attainment, the development of new plans or revised plans if the goal has not been met, or the provision of procedures for continued monitoring of progress with the likelihood of plan phase-out at some future time.

While the primary focus of the consultant and consultee is on goal attainment, they may also be concerned with determining whether the plan or some fortuitous event brought about behavior change. Although the child may have reached the desired goal, it is impossible to conclude with certainty that it was the plan that led to this, unless the necessary controls were built into the evaluation design (Campbell & Stanley, 1963). While this issue may appear academic, it is important if behavioral consultants are to build up a knowledge base of principles that are validated as effective in helping children to reach behavioral goals. A technology for single-subject research has evolved over the past decade to answer important questions about the effectiveness of plans in behavioral consultation. Such designs are reviewed by Bergan (1977), Herson (1977), and Kratochwill (1977).

Case Studies in Behavioral Consultation

There are many cases reported in journals that establish the effectiveness of behavioral consultation. Following is a brief review of some of these studies using either teachers or parents as change agents to help children achieve both academic and behavior adjustment goals.

Most of the studies in the behavioral consultation literature involve the successful treatment of children's adjustment problems in schools. These cases have involved both individual children or groups of children as clients. Teachers have been successful in improving the attention being paid by boys sitting at adjacent desks (Broden, Bruce, Mitchell, Carter, & Hall, 1970); they have also succeeded in reducing latenesses to the room after morning, noon, and afternoon recess (Hall, Cristler, Cranston, & Tucker, 1970), as well as reducing out-of-seat behavior (Ramp, Ulrich, & Dulaney, 1971), general disruptive behavior of the target child and classmates (Drabman & Lahey, 1974), the use of obscene words and phrases (Lahey, Lahey, & McNees, 1973), stealing (Azrin & Wesolowski, 1974; Switzer, Deal, & Bailey, 1977), and chronic absences (Barber & Kagey, 1977).

Group disruption has been handled by teachers using negative attention (Jones & Miller, 1974), group contingencies such as good behavior games (Alexander, Corbet, & Smigel, 1976; Barrish, Saunders, & Wolf, 1969; Long & Williams, 1973; Medland & Stachnik, 1972; Schmidt & Ulrich, 1969), token economies (Main & Munro, 1977; McLaughlin & Malaby, 1972), and point economies (Ayllon & Roberts, 1974).

Parents have successfully modified the behavior of their children at home in cases involving weight control (Aragon, Cassaday, & Drabman, 1975), thumbsucking (Knight & McKenzie, 1974), refusal to follow requests or commands (Budd, Green, & Baker, 1976; Wahler, 1969a, 1969b), and general inappropriate behavior including tantrums, cursing, and spitting (Green, Budd, Johnson, Lang, Pinkston, & Rudd, 1976).

Behavioral consultation for academic goals has been carried out successfully with teachers to improve study behavior (Bushell, Wrobel, & Michaelis, 1968; Hall, Panyan, Rabon, & Broden, 1968), mathematics response rate (Kirby & Shields, 1972; Lovitt & Curtiss, 1968), digit reversals (Hasazi & Hasazi, 1972), compositional response rate (Van Houten, Morrison, Jarvis, & McDonald, 1974), social studies and math homework assignments (Harris & Sherman, 1974), reading comprehension (Knapczyk & Livingston, 1973; Rosenbaum & Breiling, 1976), printing and writing (Hopkins, Schutte, & Garton, 1971; Rapport & Bostow, 1976), creative writing (Maloney & Hopkins, 1973), and spelling accuracy (Lovitt & Curtiss, 1969).

Group contingency techniques have been used by teachers to raise achievement (McCarty, Griffin, Apolloni, & Shores, 1977). Parents have been used as change agents in the improvement of plural morphemes (Garcia & Batista-Wallace, 1977) and children's question asking (Henderson & Garcia, 1973).

Finally, behavioral consultants have been effective in involving parents and teachers together to reduce general disruptive school behavior such as out-of-seat behavior, disturbing others, and looking out the window, as well as to improve study behavior and participation in group discussions (Bailey, Wolf, & Phillips, 1970; Colman, 1973; Karraker, 1972; Todd, Scott, Bostow, & Alexander, 1976). The school principal can also be an effective consultee in modifying attendance rates, word recognition, and math achievement for an entire class (Copeland, Brown, & Hall, 1974).

Changing the Change Agents' Behavior

Certainly one of the major challenges the behavioral consultant faces in helping clients is that of influencing the consultee to follow through on the procedures developed during the various stages of consultation. It is one thing to agree to do something during an interview and another to carry out the suggestion in the class or in the home. Most writers on consultation, whether behavioral or mental health, make the assumption that the primary variable influencing consultee change is consultant behavior during the interview. They view the interview in terms of a one-to-one learning episode in which consultants motivate consultees to change, provide guidance as to the direction and extent of change, allow sufficient time to "teach" consultees (whether subtly or more overtly) certain principles of learning and development, and finally ensure recall and application of these principles in the problem setting (Bergan, 1977).

While there is some research supporting the assumption that consultants, through their verbal behavior, can influence consultee verbal behavior and attitudes during consultation (Heller, Davis, & Meyers, 1966; Kanfer, 1968; Tombari & Bergan, 1978) no evidence supports the assumption that consultant verbal behavior has a direct effect on consultee problem-solving behavior outside of the interview. There is much anecdotal evidence to suggest that once outside the consultant's immediate influence, consultee's may or may not follow through on the plans evolving from consultation (Tombari & Yelich, 1978).

There are several reasons for this lack of follow through by consultees—only one of which may be due to the ineffectiveness of the consultant during the interview (Bergan & Tombari, 1976). Lack of skill and motivation on the part of the consultee are other possible explanations. For both of these factors, techniques such as training, cuing, feedback, and modeling in the natural setting, contingency contracting, as well as making children change agents for teachers have been applied.

Training

As reviewed previously, parents and teachers have employed behavioral principles successfully to change children's behavior in the natural environment. So the question is no longer whether parents or teachers can modify behavior, but how to guarantee that they will. A variety of training programs for both parents and teachers have been developed to give potential consultees skills in behavior management.

While these programs differ in the format of training, the concepts used, and some of the specific principles that form the basis of the curriculum, they all possess certain common features. They reflect a general acceptance of the assumptions from behavioral learning theory on how behavior is learned and modified; there is also an emphasis on behavioral over attitudinal change, a preference for experimentally validated principles to constitute the content of the programs, and the use of systematic procedures to evaluate the learning of training objectives (Marsh, Handy, & Hamerlynck, 1976).

The targets of such training have been both individuals and groups of parents or teachers (Green *et al.*, 1976; Tams & Eyberg, 1976; Jones & Eimers, 1975). Training has been conducted both inside and outside the natural setting (Brockway & Williams, 1976). The content of such programs has emphasized both the process of behavioral analysis and specific interventions (Brockway & Williams, 1976; Hall *et al.*, 1968; Martin & Twentyman, 1976). The strategies of training have involved modeling, role playing, and instructions (Henderson & Garcia, 1973; Jones & Eimers, 1975; Ringer, 1973). Evaluations of such training programs have been carried out on the basis of direct observation, self-reports of behavior, and subjective reports (Clark, Greene, Macrae, McNees, Davis, & Risley, 1977; Kovitz, 1976).

Feedback and Modeling

Although training has proven effective in helping parents and teachers to acquire behavioral management skills, it is no guarantee that the procedures will be used in the natural setting after training has ceased. As with the interview during the consultation process, consultees may change their verbal behavior during training but fail to act in accordance with the verbal commitments.

The use of feedback in the natural setting has been attempted to help parents and teachers change their behavior. For example, complimenting teachers for their rates of praise to students has been effective in changing rates of praise. Thomas (1971) modified teacher praise rates by having them record their praise rates from daily videotapes. Herbert and Baer (1972) found similar results with self-recording by parents in changing their rates of attention to appropriate behavior in children. Prompting in the natural setting has shown remarkable power in changing teacher praise rates. This has involved either holding up a colored flag or some other cue whenever verbal praise was to be administered (Hall *et al.*, 1968) or using audio cues in the form of "beeps" emitted from a PA system on a regular interval basis (Van Houten & Sullivan, 1975).

Finally, modeling is another promising method for effecting consultee change. Modeling has many advantages as a change technique in that it can add credibility to the consultant's suggestions if the consultee sees the person giving the advice practicing what he or she preaches. Similar suggestions for the training of teacher aides were made by Tharp and Wetzel (1969). There have been few systematic studies of the effects of modeling by consultants on consultee behavior. One reported study has shown that modeling can effect positive interaction by teachers with students (Brown, Reschly, & Wasserman, 1974).

Contingency Contracting

Another strategy for increasing the likelihood of consultee change in the natural setting is contingency contracting, although very few studies of this nature have been reported. Such studies involve establishing performance criteria for teachers to meet and making certain rewards contingent on meeting these criterion levels. One study of this nature has been carried out that successfully changed teacher use of special reading materials with bonus payments as the reward (Harris, Bushell, Sherman, & Kane, 1975). Rewards such as extra preparation time or less lunchroom duty could be made contingent on such changes as higher rates of open-ended versus closed-ended questions, decreased lateness of returning exams and papers, or increased constructive comments on assignments.

Children as Change Agents

Additional techniques for changing teacher behavior come from the notion that not only do teachers affect children's behavior, but also children's behavior has a reciprocal effect on teachers' behavior. Tharp and Wetzel (1969) in describing the social system of the classroom explain that teachers are just as likely to be influenced by reinforcers coming from children as are children influenced by reinforcers coming from teachers. These reinforcers from the children can be in the form of paying attention or behaving well. There is evidence to show that training children in certain behaviors can modify teachers' attention to appropriate behavior. For example, training students to emit more appropriate behaviors has been shown to influence teachers to make more appropriate comments to children (Breyer & Allen, 1975; Sherman & Cormier, 1974).

Behavioral Consultation Mythology

There are as many myths or misconceptions about behavioral consultation as there are about behavior modification. Some of the more outstanding myths are that behavioral consultants ignore the development of the whole child in favor of short-term superficial decreases in behavior problems, that behavioral consultation is a strictly expert model of service delivery, and that behavioral consultants adhere to only the narrowest of principles in helping teachers or parents change behavior. We feel it is necessary to deal with each of these not only because they are false, but also because, in upsetting these myths, we can tie together much of what has been said so far about behavioral consultation.

Winett and Winkler (1972) were among the first to charge that behavior modification has been used primarily to support the status quo in the classroom. Although the specific points of their article have been debated in numerous re-joinders (e.g., see O'Leary, 1972), the notion still persists that behavioral consultants who implement behavioral techniques in the classroom are concerned only with decreases in superficial problem behavior using trivial techniques (Meyers *et al.*, 1977).

While these criticisms certainly apply to many cases reported in the behavioral consultation literature, there is nothing about behavioral consultation that precludes concern for the development of positive changes on the part of children both in the short and long term. Goodwin and Coates (1976), for example, emphasize that it is incumbent upon the behavioral consultant not only to help teachers and parents reduce problem behaviors, but also to help children acquire positive replacement behaviors that will substitute for the inappropriate behaviors. Svinicki and Muller (1974) make a similar point.

Bergan (1977) goes further than any other behavioral consultation theorist by advocating both a problem-centered and a developmental approach to behavioral consultation. The former is used when problems of a critical nature, such as fighting, require immediate solutions. The latter is the preferred style of consultation in noncrisis situations. In such cases the consultant uses the problem identification interview to elicit categories of broad-range goals from the teacher, to set goal priorities, to establish general and subordinate objectives for each goal, to establish a hierarchy for these objectives, and then to initiate data collection and problem analysis on the objective of immediate concern to the teacher or parent. Once an objective has been achieved by the child, an additional objective becomes the focus of problem solving. This reiterative approach to consultation continues, until all the goals and objectives specified during the initial interview are attained. Thus, the developmental approach to behavioral consultation provides for the establishment of a long-term relationship between consultant and consultee and focuses on the development of the child in a number of goal areas important to socialization.

Behavioral consultation has been mistakingly labeled as an expert model of psychological service delivery. In fact almost all writers on behavioral consultation emphasize the collaborative nature of the role and warn against the dangers of assuming the role of expert (Bergan, 1977; Dorr, 1973). A theme woven through all these writings is the educational nature of the consultant's role—an aspect that can best be achieved via a collaborative relationship between consultant and consultee. Goodwin, in particular, views the consultant as an agent of change not only for the client, but also for the consultee. He views consultation as a total learning process that is "a technology for helping consultees develop programs to achieve their objectives but also stands prepared to assist those consultees to develop whatever skills they may need in implementing those programs." According to Goodwin, only by functioning as a collaborator can the behavioral consultant achieve these ends.

It is perhaps unfortunate that behavioral consultation is so named. The term "behavioral" immediately associates it exclusively with behavior modification principles and techniques. Although, as has been described earlier in this chapter, behavioral consultation leans heavily on operant research and theory, it goes far beyond simple reinforcement, extinction, and punishment in developing plans to help consultees change children's behavior. Behavioral consultation, as has been stated many times, is a process of problem solving. Viewed in this sense *any* principle that has been shown to be useful in helping children learn and develop is at the disposal of behavioral consultants. Behavior modification is only one area where such principles have been generated. Additional areas that can be drawn upon come from the study of learning, motivation, perception, memory, cognition, psycholinguistics, and experimental social psychology, to name a few. Bergan (1977) provides a schema for articulating principles generated from this literature to the objectives identified during consultation. Thus, behavioral consultants who limit themselves to the exclusive use of operant conditioning techniques are depriving consultees and clients of the knowledge of other principles that can be effective in achieving positive goals.

Behavioral Consultation in Retrospect

Behavioral consultation has long since been established as a legitimate form of psychological service. There is ample evidence to support its effectiveness in helping parents and teachers solve problems in homes and classrooms. However, despite this success there is a great deal of research that remains to be done both in applied and experimental settings. Particularly important are studies that assess the critical consultation process variables that predict client outcomes. At this point, consultation training is based more on folklore than science. Even Bergan's thorough volume on behavioral consultation suffers from a lack of empirical support for the suggestions he offers in conducting the various problem-solving interviews.

The technology for doing adequate experimental research in consultation is at hand. Content analysis procedures have been developed that allow operational definitions of both independent and dependent variables (Bergan & Tombari, 1976). Likewise, the programmed interview provides a powerful experimental paradigm for investigating the effects of consultation processes on changes in consultee and client behavior (Heller, 1971; Tombari & Bergan, 1976). It is now time, as Meyers *et al.* (1977) state, "to contribute to an increase in the sophistication and quality of consultation research in the future. [p. 12]."

Issues in the Use of Behavioral Interventions

As stated earlier, a fundamental attribute of behavioral consultation is the development of classroom or home-based interventions directed at changing a client's behavior. While specific techniques for doing this are beyond the scope of this chapter, this section will highlight several issues related to designing such plans. We will conclude with a brief synopsis of some alternatives to traditional behavior modification practice.

The Selection of Target Behaviors

From a social psychological perspective, the level of involvement of individuals in a program can be enhanced by incorporating them into the decision-making process (Backman & Secord, 1968). For behavioral consultants this suggests that they not only consult teachers about which behaviors need to be learned, but also consult the client. The notion that people can be conditioned automatically is largely a myth (Bandura, 1975). People can learn through conditioning but only if they recognize what is being conditioned. Client involvement in the goal section process facilitates this change.

Since young children have limited experience and ability in determining their own goals, parents or guardians often are consulted about behavior change. However, Blackman and Silberman (1975) recommend caution here. They point out that behavior that is distressing to parents or teachers is not necessarily maladaptive. The problem may not be with the child but with the person who is upset by the child. Accordingly, Blackman and Silberman suggest that the decision to change a child's behavior include three criteria: (*a*) the behavior presumed to be maladaptive must occur with sufficient frequency; for example, an occasional fight may be considered typical behavior for most children, but if fights occur daily, the behavior may be maladaptive; (*b*) the behavior, if continued, will ultimately be harmful to the child; and (*c*) the behavior impedes subsequent adaption and healthy development. Excessively dependent or infantile behavior, for example, poses serious problems at later ages.

Another promising approach for determining the "seriousness" of problem behavior may involve the use of normative behavioral observational data as suggested by Walker and Hops (1976).

Developing Intervention Techniques

Although behavior analysis involves examining both the antecedent and consequent conditions surrounding behavior, most behavior modification programs manipulate only the latter. While consequent events are necessary ingredients of such programs, equal emphasis should be given to antecedent events. This involves engineering the child's environment to increase the likelihood that the desired behavior will occur. Goodwin and Coates (1976) advocate that sufficient time during consultation be devoted to discussing what can be done to almost "guarantee" that the desired behavior will be elicited.

Behavioral consultants often fall into the habit of using tangible reinforcers to the exclusion of other types (Forness, 1973). One can forcibly argue that tangibles should be the alternative of last resort when other types of reinforcers have been ruled out.

Baker, Burkholder, and Davis (1975) have developed the concept of a reinforcement hierarchy that merits consideration by behavioral consultants. They devised a hierarchy patterned after Maslow's hierarchy of needs that is illustrated in Figure 10.1. Baker *et al.*, postulate that at birth the infant is limited to the lower level of the hierarchy, but it expands the reinforcement repertoire to include the higher levels as development proceeds through interaction with the environment. Many classroom teachers expect children to behave for the enjoyment of learning when the children may not have developed to that level. When developing

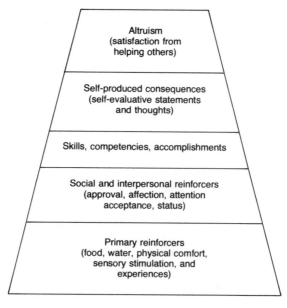

FIGURE 10.1. *Developmental reinforcement hierarchy.* [*From Baker, Burkholder, & Davis (1975). Reprinted by permission.*]

a behavior-change plan, Baker *et al.*, suggest that the change agent determine the highest reinforcement level at which a child can learn effectively. Placement of the child on the hierarchy may be determined by observation of the child, a child interview, or setting up a standardized teaching task using different reinforcement conditions to determine how these conditions affect performance (Severson, 1973).

While consideration of reinforcement hierarchies protects against "reinforcer overkill," a device called the reinforcement menu can help determine truly reinforcing events for an individual child (Addison & Home, 1966). Such menus are developed with the child and specify reinforcing activities or events. The child selects a reinforcer from the menu that will be earned contingent upon the prescribed behavior. This procedure both individualizes the reinforcers and provides for the selection of different reinforcers, thus lessening the likelihood of satiation.

The Use of Aversive Control

Behavior modification has been frequently criticized for the use of aversive procedures in controlling behavior. This has come primarily from the misuse and misunderstanding of the principles of learning by a few rather than a penchant by behavioral consultants to use punitive methods of control. In fact, behavioral psychologists emphasize that punishment is a very poor teacher. At best it teaches what not to do rather than what is appropriate.

The negative effects of punishment have been well documented and the behavioral consultant should use other methods to promote learning and development. When aversive consequences are called for, they should involve the withdrawal of reinforcement rather than the application of an aversive stimulus.

"Time out" is a variant of this procedure that has been demonstrated to be an effective, nonpunitive, behavior control technique (MacDonough & Forehand, 1973). However, there is no standard time out procedure. As Solnick, Rincover, and Peterson (1977) have shown, time out can have both reinforcing and punishing effects, depending on events following *and* preceding the behavior. Thus, in designing time out programs, the behavioral consultant must manipulate conditions related to the succeeding environment, or time out, and the preceding environment, or time in. The relative enrichment of the latter markedly determines the effectiveness of time out.

For those concerned about the "legality" of time out procedures (since they involve exclusion from the class setting) a nonexclusionary time out procedure has been used effectively to reduce problem behavior (Fox & Shapiro, 1978).

Recent Advances in Behavior Change Techniques

Numerous excellent books describe in detail procedures for bringing about behavior change based on learning theory (Bandura, 1969; Blackkan & Silberman,

1975; Martin & Pear, 1978; Sultzer & Mayer, 1972). These texts assume that a change agent such as a teacher or parent will manage the intervention plan. This may not always be a desirable method. This section will review some recent developments in behavior modification that make clients their own change agents.

Self-Control

In reading the school consultation literature, one is struck by the scarcity of studies pertaining to junior or senior high school students. The large majority of studies involve elementary school children or retardates. This may imply that with adolescents and individuals functioning at higher cognitive levels (e.g., formal operations, à la Piaget) self-management plans may be more appropriate.

Self-management plans involve the same components as parent- or teacher-controlled programs, except that the client is the primary change agent. Such programs assume that clients are aware of their problems and have a need to deal with them. The behavioral consultant's role, then, becomes one of helping clients set goals, collect data, intervene in their own behalf, and evaluate the outcome of the intervention. (Strictly speaking, such direct services can no longer be described as consultation.)

Several examples of self-control procedures are described in the following paragraphs. A detailed discussion of these techniques can be found in Thoresen and Mahoney (1974).

STIMULUS CONTROL

Consultants can help clients bring about stimulus control of behavior by assisting them to plan their environment so that a given behavior has an optimal chance of occurring and interfering behaviors are minimized. If study habits are the object of change, the strategy becomes one of planning an environment conducive to studying.

SELF-OBSERVATION (SELF-MONITORING)

Clients are responsible for systematically recording their own behavior. Self-monitored data have high reliability and validity (Broden, Hall, & Mitts, 1971). As an assessment device this method is cost effective, since it does not involve outside observers or any teacher time. Self-monitoring minimizes observer bias. Furthermore, it can produce a variety of data in the form of diaries, check lists, or simple frequency counts. Finally, it is a convenient way of gaining access to private thoughts (McFall, 1977).

SELF-PRESENTED CONSEQUENCES

In self-control plans, individuals take responsibility for rewarding themselves if they have exhibited the desired behavior. Likewise they punish themselves after the performance of a specified negative response (Thoreson & Mahoney, 1974). The latter event may involve removal of a freely available reinforcer or the administration of an easily avoidable aversive stimulus.

COVERT CONDITIONING

Behavioral consultants may help clients manipulate private, internalized events. The term covert conditioning refers to "a set of imagery based procedures which alter response frequency by the manipulation of consequences [Cautela & Baron, 1977]." Here a client is asked to imagine a response to be modified and a consequence to that response.

COGNITIVE SELF-INSTRUCTION

According to Michenbaum and Goodman (1971), "private speech," talk to one's self, has a self-regulatory function that develops through a child's interaction with the social environment. This inner speech can be altered to provide a client with more efficient problem-solving abilities or coping behaviors. Michenbaum and Goodman, using a five-step procedure, successfully altered the behavior of impulsive children. Since that time the technique has been demonstrated to be effective across many different problem areas (Michenbaum, 1977). An interesting offshoot of Michenbaum's procedure has been reported by Bornstein and Quevillon (1976) in the treatment of hyperactive children.

Modeling

While not of as recent vintage as self-control techniques, modeling is an effective, although less widely used, alternative to traditional behavioral methods. Several advantages adhere to the use of modeling. Modeling is used so frequently in the natural environment that its familiarity and acceptance can overcome many objections to behavior modification. It is highly efficient for certain behaviors involving chains of discrete actions. As an alternative to shaping, modeling can often result in the shunting of several steps to get to the terminal behavior.

Modeling can be carried out in the classroom using the teacher or peers as models. The most effective live-modeling procedure may be that of participant modeling (Bandura, 1975). In this procedure the desired behaviors are repeatedly modeled to demonstrate how they can be performed successfully. Next the target child jointly performs the behavior with the change agent guiding successful performance. Though Bandura's work with participant modeling has involved overcoming inhibitions, the procedure would seem to lend itself well to other problem behaviors.

The availability of videotape equipment has opened up the area of modeling as never before. No longer does a live model or a motion picture sequence have to be used. Behaviors can be videotaped and played back immediately. They can also be tailored to the target behaviors of concern with a particular individual.

One innovation of videotape technology is the use of the client as a model for himself or herself (Davis, 1975). In this technique, termed self-modeling, a behavior is first targeted. Then a script is developed delineating the desired behavior. The subject then role plays the desired behavior and is videotaped. As a treatment, the subject repeatedly views himself or herself performing the desired behavior. Positive changes were reported for such behaviors as assertiveness, bed-making, thumbsucking, and verbal interactions (Creer & Miklich, 1970), as well as fighting, attentiveness, and inappropriate verbal responses to teacher imposition of control (Davis, 1975).

Summary

Behavioral consultation is likely to become an increasingly important component of school psychologists' services with children and young adults. Basic and applied research supports behavioral consultation as a systematic and effective approach to solving a wide variety of problems. We anticipate further expansion of the types of interventions and types of problems considered within behavioral consultation. Continued research on the process of consultation and on the application of principles of learning and development to problem behaviors will result in further refinements in the application of behavioral consultation procedures.

References

Addison, R. M., & Homme, L. E. The reinforcing event (RE) menu. *National Society for Programmed Instruction Journal,* 1966, **5,** 8–9.

Alexander, R. N., Corbett, T. F., & Smigel, J. The effects of individual and group contingencies on school attendance and curfew violations with predelinquent adolescents. *Journal of Applied Behavior Analysis,* 1976, **9,** 221–226.

Aragona, J., Cassady, J., & Drabman, R. W. Treating overweight children through parental training and contingency contracting. *Journal of Applied Behavior Analysis,* 1975, **8,** 269–278.

Ayllon, T., & Roberts, M. D. Eliminating discipline problems by strengthening academic performance. *Journal of Applied Behavior Analysis,* 1974, **7,** 71–76.

Azrin, N. H., & Wesolowski, M. D. Theft reversal: An overcorrection procedure for eliminating stealing by retarded persons. *Journal of Applied Behavior Analysis,* 1974, **4,** 577–582.

Backman, C. W., & Secord, P. F. *A social psychological view of education.* New York: Harcourt, 1968.

Bailey, J. S., Wolf, M. M., & Phillips, E. L. Home based reinforcement and the modification of pre-delinquents' classroom behavior. *Journal of Applied Behavior Analysis,* 1970, **3,** 223.

Baker, J. M., Burkholder, R., & Davis, R. A. *A behavioral look at learning disorders.* Paper presented at the Annual Convention of the National Association of School Psychologists, Atlanta, 1975.

Bandura, A. *Principles of behavior modification.* New York: Holt, 1969.

Bandura, A. The ethics and social purposes of behavior modification. In C. M. Franks & G. T. Wilson (Eds.), *Annual review of behavior therapy: Theory and practice* (Vol. III). New York: Brunner/Mazel, 1975.

Bardon, J. I. Overview of issue implications for future trends in school psychology. *Journal of School Psychology,* 1972, **10,** 207–211.

Barrish, H. H., Saunders, M., & Wolf, M. M. Good behavior game: Effects of individual contingencies for group consequences on disruptive behavior in a classroom. *Journal of Applied Behavior Analysis*, 1969, **2**, 119–124.

Bergan, J. R. *Behavioral consultation*. Columbus, Ohio: Charles E. Merrill, 1977.

Bergan, J. R., & Dunn, J. A. *Psychology and education: A science for instruction*. New York: Wiley, 1976.

Bergan, J. R., & Tombari, M. L. Consultant skill and efficiency and the implementations and outcomes of consultation. *Journal of School Psychology*, 1976, **14**, 3–14.

Berlin, I. N. Preventive aspects of mental health consultation to schools. *Mental Hygiene*, 1967, **51**, 34–40.

Blackman, G. J., & Silberman, A. *The modification of child and adolescent behavior* (2nd ed.). Belmont, California: Wadsworth, 1975.

Bornstein, P. H., & Quevillon, R. P. The effects of a self instructional package on overactive preschool boys. *Journal of Applied Behavior Analysis*, 1976, **9**, 179–188.

Breyer, N. L., & Allen, G. J. Effects of implementing a token economy on teacher attending behavior. *Journal of Applied Behavior Analysis*, 1975, **8**, 373–380.

Brockway, B. S., & Williams, W. W. Training in child management: A prevention-oriented model. In E. J. Mash, L. C. Hand, & L. A. Hamerlynck (Eds.), *Behavior modification approaches to parenting*. New York: Brunner/Mazel, 1976.

Broden, M., Bruce, C., Mitchell, M. A., Carter, V., & Hall, R. V. Effects of teacher attention on attending behavior of two boys at adjacent desks. *Journal of Applied Behavior Analysis*, 1970, **3**, 199–203.

Broden, M., Hall, R. V., & Mitts, B. The effects of self-recording on the classroom behavior of two eighth-grade students. *Journal of Applied Behavior Analysis*, 1971, **4**(1), 191–200.

Brown, D., Reschly, D., & Wasserman, H. Effects of surreptitious modeling upon teacher classroom behaviors. *Psychology in the Schools*, 1974, **11**, 366–369.

Budd, K. S., Green, D. R., & Baer, D. M. An analysis of multiple misplaced parental social contingencies. *Journal of Applied Behavior Analysis*, 1976, **9**, 459–470.

Bushell, D., Wrobel, P. A., & Michaelis, M. L. Applying group contingencies to the classroom behavior of preschool children. *Journal of Applied Behavior Analysis*, 1968, **1**, 55–62.

Campbell, D. T., & Stanley, J. C. Experimental and quasi-experimental designs for research on teaching. In N. L. Gage (Ed.), *Handbook of research on teaching*. Chicago: Rand McNally, 1963.

Caplan, C. *The theory and practice of mental health consultation*. New York: Basic Books, 1970.

Cautela, J. R., & Baron, M. G. Covert conditioning, a theoretical analysis. *Behavior Modification*, 1977, **1**, 351–367.

Clark, H. B., Greene, B. F., Macrae, J. W., McNees, M. P., Davis, J. L., & Risley, T. R. A parent advice package for family shopping trips: Development and evaluation. *Journal of Applied Behavior Analysis*, 1977, **10**, 605–624.

Clark, R. D. *The effects of expert and collaborative consultation on plan implementation, goal achievement and attitude toward consultant*. Unpublished doctoral dissertation, University of Texas at Austin, 1978.

Colman, R. G. A procedure for fading from experimenter-school-based to parent-home-based control of classroom behavior. *Journal of School Psychology*, 1973, **11**, 71–79.

Copeland, R. E., Brown, R. E., & Hall, R. V. The effects of principal implemented techniques on the behavior of pupils. *Journal of Applied Behavior Analysis*, 1974, **1**, 77–86.

Cowen, E. L. Emergent approaches to mental health consultation: An overview with directions for future work. In F. L. Cowen, E. A. Gardner, & M. Zax (Eds.), *Emergent approaches to mental health consultation*. New York: Appleton-Century-Crofts, 1967.

Creer, T. L., & Miklich, D. R. The application of self-modeling procedure to modify inappropriate behavior: A preliminary report. *Behavior Research and Therapy*, 1970, **8**, 91–92.

Davis, R. A. *The effect of self-modeling on problem behaviors of school-age children*. Unpublished dissertation, University of Arizona, 1975.

Derby, N. J. F. *The relationship of consultant equalitarianism and teacher-consultant attitude similarity to teacher ratings of consultant helpfulness.* Unpublished doctoral dissertation, University of Texas at Austin, 1977. Dornback, F. *Guidelines for behavioral assessment.* Geneva, Illinois: Learning Disabilities Center, 1972.

Dorr, D. Training for consultation with teachers in behavior modification: Principles and problems. In C. H. Swenson (Chair), *Evaluation of training in consultation.* Symposium presented at the meeting of the American Psychological Association, Montreal, 1973.

Drabman, R. S., & Lahey, B. B. Feedback in classroom behavior modification effects on the target and her classmates. *Journal of Applied Behavior Analysis,* 1974, **7,** 591–598.

Fine, M. J., & Tyler, M. M. Concerns and directions in teacher consultation. *Journal of School Psychology,* 1971, **9,** 436–444.

Forness, S. R. The reinforcement hierarchy. *Psychology in the Schools,* 1973, **10,** 168–177.

Fox, R. M., & Shapiro, S. T. The timeout ribbon: a nonexclusionary timeout procedure. *Journal of Applied Behavior Analysis,* 1978, **11,** 125–136.

Gagné, R. M. *The conditions of learning.* New York: Holt, 1976.

Garcia, E. E., & Batista-Wallace, M. Parental training of the plural morpheme in normal toddlers. *Journal of Applied Behavior Analysis,* 1977, **10,** 505.

Goodwin, D., & Coates, T. *Helping students help themselves.* Englewood Cliffs, New Jersey: Prentice-Hall, 1976.

Goodwin, D. R., Garvey, W. P., & Barclay, J. R. Microconsultation and behavior analysis: A method of training school psychologists as behavioral consultants. *Journal of Consulting and Clinical Psychology,* 1971, **37,** 355–363.

Green, D. R., Budd, K., Johnson, M., Lang, S., Pinkston, E., & Rudd, S. Training parents to modify problem child behaviors. In E. J. Mash, L. C. Handy, & L. A. Hamerlynck (Eds.), *Behavior modification approaches to parenting.* New York: Brunner/Mazel, 1976.

Hall, R. V., Cristler, C., Cranston, S. S., & Tucker, B. Teachers and parents as researchers using multiple baseline designs. *Journal of Applied Behavior Analysis,* 1970, **3,** 247–255.

Hall, R. V., Panyan, M., Rabon, D., & Broden, M. Instructing beginning teachers in reinforcement procedures which improve classroom control. *Journal of Applied Behavior Analysis,* 1968, **4,** 315–322.

Harris, V. W., Bushell, D., Sherman, J. A., & Kane, J. F. Instructions, feedback, praise, bonus payments, and teacher behavior. *Journal of Applied Behavior Analysis,* 1975, **8,** 462.

Harris, V. W., & Sherman, J. A. Effects of peer tutoring and consequences on the math performance of elementary classroom students. *Journal of Applied Behavior Analysis,* 1974, **6,** 587–598.

Hasazi, J. E., & Hasazi, S. E. Effects of teacher attention on digit-reversal behavior in an elementary school child. *Journal of Applied Behavior Analysis,* 1972, **5,** 157–162.

Heller, K., Davis, J. D., & Meyers, R. A. The effects of interviewer style in a standardized interview. *Journal of Consulting Psychology,* 1966, **27,** 117–122.

Henderson, R. W., & Garcia, A. B. The effects of a parent training program on the question asking behavior of Mexican-American children. *American Educational Research Journal,* 1973, **10,** 193–201.

Herbert, F. W., & Baer, D. M. Training parents as behavior modifiers: Self-recording of contingent attention. *Journal of Applied Behavior Analysis,* 1972, **2,** 139–150.

Hopkins, B. L., Schutte, R. C., & Garton, K. L. The effects of access to a playroom on the rate and quality of printing and writing of first-and second-grade students. *Journal of Applied Behavior Analysis,* 1971, **4,** 77–88.

Jones, F. H., & Eimers, R. Role playing to train elementary teachers to use a classroom management skill package. *Journal of Applied Behavior Analysis,* 1975, **8,** 421–434.

Jones, F. H., & Miller, W. H. The effective use of negative attention for reducing group disruption in special elementary school classrooms. *The Psychological Record,* 1974, **24,** 435–448.

Kanfer, F. H. Verbal conditioning: A review of its current status. In T. R. Dixon & D. L. Horton (Eds.), *Verbal behavior and general behavior theory.* New York: Prentice-Hall, 1968.

Karraker, R. J. Increasing academic performance through home managed contingency programs. *Journal of School Psychology,* 1972, **10**, 173–179.

Kaufman, R. A. A possible integrative model for the systematic and measurable improvement of education. *American Psychologist,* 1971, **26**, 250–256.

Kennedy, D. A. A practical approach to school psychology. *Journal of School Psychology,* 1971, **9**, 484–489.

Kirby, F. D., & Shields, F. Modification of arithmetic response rate and attending behavior in a seventh grade student. *Journal of Applied Behavior Analysis,* 1972, **5**, 79–84.

Knapczyk, D. R., & Livingston, G. Self-recording and student teacher supervision: Variables within a token economy structure. *Journal of Applied Behavior Analysis,* 1973, **6**, 481–486.

Knight, M. F., & McKenzie, H. S. Elimination of bedtime thumbsucking in home settings through contingent reading. *Journal of Applied Behavior Analysis,* 1974, **7**, 33–38.

Kovitz, K. E. Comparing group and individual methods for training parents in child management techniques. In E. J. Mash, L. C. Handy, & L. A. Hamerlynck (Eds.), *Behavioral modification approaches to parenting.* New York: Brunner/Mazel, 1976.

Kuehnel, J. M. *Faculty, school and organizational characteristics, and schools openness to mental health resources.* Unpublished doctoral dissertation, University of Texas at Austin, May 1975.

Kratochwill, T. R. N = 1: A research strategy for school psychologists. *Journal of School Psychology,* 1977, **15**, 239–249.

Lahey, B. B., McNees, M. P., & McNees, M. C. Control of an abscene "verbal tic" through time-out in an elementary school classroom. *Journal of Applied Behavior Analysis,* 1973, **6**, 101–104.

Lippitt, G. The consultive process. *The School Psychologist,* 1967, **21**, 72–74.

Long, J. D., & Williams, R. L. The comparative effectiveness of group and individual contingent free time with inner-city junior high school students. *Journal of Applied Behavior Analysis,* 1973, **6**, 465–474.

Lovitt, T. C., & Curtiss, K. A. Academic response rate as a function of teacher and self-imposed contingencies. *Journal of Applied Behavior Analysis,* 1969, **2**, 49–54.

Lovitt, T. C., & Curtiss, K. A. Effects of manipulating an antecendent event on mathematics response rate. *Journal of Applied Behavior Analysis,* 1968, **1**, 329–334.

MacDonough, T. S., & Forehand, R. Response contingent time-out: Important parameters in behavior modification with children. *Journal of Behavior Therapy and Experimental Psychiatry,* 1973, **4**, 231–236.

Mager, R. F. *Preparing objectives for instruction.* Belmont, California: Fearon, 1962.

Main, G. C., & Munro, B. C. A token reinforcement program in a public junior high school. *Journal of Applied Behavior Analysis,* 1977, **10**, 93–94.

Maloney, K. B., & Hopkins, B. L. The modification of sentence structure and its relationship to subjective judgments of creativity in writing. *Journal of Applied Behavior Analysis,* 1973, **6**, 425–434.

Marsh, E. J., Handy, L. C., & Hamerlynck, L. A. *Behavior modification approaches to parenting.* New York: Brunner/Mazel, 1976.

Martin, B., & Twentyman, C. Teaching conflict resolution skills to parents and children. In E. J. Mash, L. C. Handy, & L. A. Hamerlynck (Eds.), *Behavior modification approaches to parenting.* New York: Brunner/Mazel, 1976.

Martin, G., & Pear, J. *Behavior modification—what it is and how to do it.* Englewood Cliffs, New Jersey: Prentice-Hall, 1978.

McCarty, T., Griffin, S., Apolloni, T., & Shores, R. E. Increased peer-teaching with group oriented contingencies for arithmetic performance in behavior-disordered adolescents. *Journal of Applied Behavior Analysis,* 1977, **10**, 313.

McFall, R. M. Parameters of self-monitoring. In R. B. Stuart (Ed.), *Behavioral self-management—strategies, techniques and outcome.* New York: Brunner/Mazel, 1977.

McLaughlin, T. F., & Malaby, J. Intrinsic reinforcers in a classroom token economy. *Journal of Applied Behavior Analysis,* 1972, **5,** 263–270.

Medland, M. B., & Stachnik, T. J. Good behavior game, a replication and systematic analysis. *Journal of Applied Behavior Analysis,* 1972, **1,** 45–52.

Meyers, J., Martin, R., & Hyman, I. *School Consultation.* Springfield, Illinois: C. C. Thomas, 1977.

Michenbaum, D. H. *Cognitive behavior modification.* New York: Plenum, 1977.

Michenbaum, D. H., & Goodman, J. Training impulsive children to talk to themselves: A means of developing self-control. *Journal of Abnormal Psychology,* 1971, **77,** 115–126.

O'Leary, K. D. Behavior modification in the classroom: A rejoinder to Winett and Winkler. *Journal of Applied Behavior Analysis,* 1972, **5,** 505–510.

Popham, W. J. *Educational Evaluation.* Englewood Cliffs, New Jersey: Prentice-Hall, 1975.

Ramp, E., Ulrich, R., & Dulaney, S. Delayed time-out as a procedure for reducing disruptive classroom behavior: A case study. *Journal of Applied Behavior Analysis,* 1971, **4,** 235–239.

Rapport, M. D., & Bostow, D. E. The effects of access to special activities on the performance in four categories of academic tasks with third grade students. *Journal of Applied Behavior Analysis,* 1976, **9,** 372.

Reger, R. The technology of social psychology. *Journal of School Psychology,* 1967, **5,** 148–155.

Reschly, D. School psychology consultation: "Frenzied, faddish, fundamental?" *Journal of School Psychology,* 1976, **14,** 105–113.

Ringer, V. M. J. The use of a "token helper" in the management of classroom behavior problems and in teacher training. *Journal of Applied Behavior Analysis,* 1973, **6,** 671–678.

Rogers, C. R. The characteristics of a helping relationship. In M. J. Stein (Ed.), *Contemporary psychotherapies.* New York: Free Press, 1961.

Rosenbaum, M. S., & Breiling, J. The development and functional control of reading-comprehension behavior. *Journal of Applied Behavior Analysis,* 1976, **9,** 323–334.

Schmidt, G. W., & Ulrich, R. E. Effects of group contingent events upon classroom noise. *Journal of Applied Behavior Analysis,* 1969, **2,** 171–180.

Schmuch, R. A., Runkel, P. J., Saturen, S. L., Martell, R. T., & Derr, C. B. *Handbook of organizational development in schools.* Eugene, Oregon: National Press Books, 1972.

Severson, R. A. Behavior therapy with learning disabled children. In M. B. Rosenberg (Ed.), *Educational Therapy,* 1973, **3,** 29–55.

Sherman, T. M., & Cormier, W. H. An investigation of the influence of student behavior on teacher behavior. *Journal of Applied Behavior Analysis,* 1974, **7,** 11–22.

Solnick, J. V., Rincover, A., & Peterson, C. Some determinants of the reinforcing and punishing effects of time-out. *Journal of Applied Behavior Analysis,* 1977, **10,** 415–424.

Suinn, R. M. Traits for selection of paraprofessionals for behavior modification consultation training. *Community Mental Health Journal,* 1974, **10,** 441–450.

Sullivan, H. S. *The psychiatric interview.* New York: Pergamon, 1954.

Sultzer, B., & Mayer, G. R. *Behavior modification for school personnel.* Hinsdale, Illinois: Dryden Press, 1972.

Svinicki, J. G., & Muller, G. E. *Teaching classroom management in the natural environment.* (Technical report No. 2) Austin: Behavior Analysis Laboratory, University of Texas at Austin, 1974.

Switzer, E. B., Deal, T. E., & Bailey, J. S. The reduction of stealing in second graders using a group contingency. *Journal of Applied Behavior Analysis,* 1977, **10,** 267–272.

Tams, V. & Eyberg, S. A group treatment program for parents. In E. J. Mash, L. C. Handy, & L. A. Hamerlynck (Eds.), *Behavior modification approaches to parenting.* New York: Brunner/Mazel, 1976.

Tharp, R. G., & Wetzel, R. J. *Behavior modification in the natural environment.* New York: Academic Press, 1969.

Thomas, D. R. Preliminary finding on self-monitoring for modifying teacher behavior. In E. A. Ramp & B. L. Hopkins (Eds.), *A new direction for education: Behavior analysis.* Lawrence, Kansas: Support and Development Center for Follow Through, Department of Human Development, University of Kansas, 1971.

Thoresen, C. E., & Mahoney, J. M. *Behavioral self-control.* New York: Holt, 1974.

Todd, D. D., Scott, R. B., Bostow, D. E., & Alexander, S. B. Modification of the excessive inappropriate classroom behavior of two elementary school students using home based consequences and daily report card procedures. *Journal of Applied Behavior Analysis,* 1976, **1,** 106.

Tombari, M. L., & Bergan, J. R. Consultant cues, teacher problem definitions, judgments and expectancies for children's adjustment problems. *Journal of School Psychology,* 1978.

Tombari, M. L. & Yelich, C. *Implementing behavioral consultation programs: An evaluation report.* (Technical report No. 1) Austin: University of Texas at Austin, 1978.

Van Houten, R., Morrison, E., Jarvis, R., & McDonald, M. The effects of explicit timing and feedback on compositional response rate in elementary school children. *Journal of Applied Behavioral Analysis,* 1974, **7,** 547–556.

Van Houten, R., & Sullivan, K. Effects of audio cueing system on the rate of teacher praise. *Journal of Applied Behavior Analysis,* 1975, **2,** 197–202.

Vargas, J. S. *Behavioral psychology for teachers.* New York: Harper & Row, 1977.

Wahler, R. G. Oppositional children: A quest for parental reinforcement control. *Journal of Applied Behavior Analysis,* 1969, **2,** 159–170. (a)

Wahler, R. G. Setting generality: Some specific and general effects of child behavior therapy. *Journal of Applied Behavior Analysis,* 1969, **2,** 239–246. (b)

Walker, H. M., & Hops, H. Use of normative peer data as a standard for evaluating classroom treatment effects. *Journal of Applied Behavior Analysis,* 1976, **9,** 149–168.

HARVEY F. CLARIZIO

11   School Psychologists and the Mental Health Needs of Students

Since the 1960s, there has been a movement in the mental health field away from traditional intervention approaches and toward the development of a variety of innovative service approaches. Much of this reconceptualization of the delivery of psychological services has occurred in conjunction with the community psychology movement. Mental health professionals no longer restrict their services to those confined to state hospitals but are becoming increasingly involved in the life situations of people in the community at key points where adjustment is shaped. Moreover, services are no longer confined to treatment of individuals with existing difficulties. Rather, the focus of psychological intervention has been expanded to include the strengthening of personality development in unafflicted populations. In short, there is now a concern about the mental health of all persons, not just those in need of repair. In this chapter we will examine what mental health means, the school's role in the community mental health movement, the need for prevention, and three varieties of prevention efforts.

Criteria of Mental Health

Defining mental health is no easy matter. The question, "What constitutes mental health?" is best understood not as a question of fact but rather as a

309

SCHOOL PSYCHOLOGY
Perspectives and Issues

question of conventional definition (Scott, 1968). Whereas mental health was defined during the Freudian era as freedom from excessive anxiety and harmony among the three "structures" of personality (id, ego, and superego), it has come to be defined more recently by the community mental health movement in terms of competencies needed for effective adjustment. The notion of competencies is quite complex, of course, as is reflected in the identification of 29 separate factors (e.g., concept of self, fine motor dexterity) by a distinguished panel of experts commissioned by the Office of Child Development (Anderson & Messick, 1974). Bearing in mind that charting the pivotal competencies (those most directly related to adjustment) is a difficult issue, we will offer a picture following the lead of Bower (1970) of what the mentally healthy child might look like in the school setting.

1. *Managing symbols.* A mentally healthy child is one who is able to deal with and manage the symbols of our society. Such symbols include language symbols, mathematical symbols, sound symbols as in music, and art symbols. Without such symbolic skill the child is virtually unable to function in school and later on in the adult society.

2. *Coping with authority.* A mentally healthy child must be able to deal with rules, manage rapid and sometimes arbitrary changes in rules, and be able to accept penalties for breaking rules. It is highly significant that no society of adults or children can go on without goals, rules by which one reaches goals, and penalties for those who do not play by the rules. In the case of children, those who do not play by the rules are often not permitted to play. In adult society those who continually break the rules are sent to institutions that prevent them from functioning in our society. A child has little alternative but to learn how to deal with authority.

3. *Living with peer groups.* As part of the skill of dealing with rules, one must learn how to be an individual and yet function in his/her peer group. The mentally healthy child has learned how to deal with the "give and take" nature of daily associations with classmates and friends.

4. *Regulating emotions.* The mentally healthy child is able to control and manage emotions. This does not mean that a child must give up his/her feelings or inner life in order to become a mentally healthy person. The ability to control one's feelings and desires must also include the ability to loosen controls when such freedom is appropriate and desirable. It suggests freedom to be imaginative, to be spontaneous, or to be emotional when such behavior is enhancing and productive for the individual. Inhibited behavior can be just as irrational in some contexts as impulsive behavior often seems to be. A mentally healthy child needs to have access to his/her affective life and to be able to utilize each success appropriately. One can say that the mentally healthy individual has achieved an integrative balance between emotional and rational capabilities.

Bower's delineation of basic competencies is helpful in specifying the skills that underlie sound adjustment in school children. Yet there are problems in interpreting cause–effect relations. For example, are children made vulnerable to stress by poor peer experiences, or alternatively, do behaviors associated with vulnerability to pathology "turn off" other children and lead to strained peer relations (Hartup, 1978)? Does the inability to manage symbols increase one's vulnerability to mental illness, or does maladjusted behavior lead to academic failure? Definite answers to these questions elude us.

The School's Role in Mental Health

Opinions differ as to the extent to which schools should be concerned with the emotional well-being of students. While viewpoints run the gamut from those who see school as strictly a place for teaching the 3 R's to those who view it as a mental health clinic, probably all would agree upon the minimal objective that a student should be no worse off psychologically as a result of school experience. In my mind, we still have a way to go before we even accomplish this minimal objective. The above statement is not meant to imply that schools should merely attempt to maintain, rather than enhance, student mental health.

Regardless of whether one views dealing with the mental health of students as a *means* to achieve traditional academic outcomes (e.g., reducing excessive anxiety in a student so that he/she can learn to read more effectively) or as an *end* per se (e.g., teaching social problem-solving skills to build psychological strength), there is ample reason to believe that schools can promote the psychological well-being of students. Though no single institution appears adequate to all of the tasks of development and socialization, the school does have some advantages over other institutions, such as religious and recreational agencies. The school has access to large numbers of youth over prolonged periods of time during the formative years. In addition, it has a culturally sanctioned right to "interfere" in the lives of students, at least to the extent that the meddling pertains to the child's educability. Schools also provide a readily available helping resource of persons in the form of concerned and approachable teachers (Allen, Chinsky, Larcen, Lochman, & Selinger, 1976). Finally, the schools are in a position to provide service in a natural setting thereby minimizing the likelihood of separating problem children from their peers and reducing the stigmatizing effects inherent in current mental health practices. This latter advantage is particularly significant in light of Public Law 94-142, which requires that a handicapped student be placed in the least restrictive environment possible.

If school psychologists are to function effectively in schools, they must be aware of the differences in orientation and conflicts in professional paradigms that often exist between mental health professionals and educators.

The values advocated by educators and those favoring a psychiatric model often clash, and the clash has led to a role conflict on the part of teachers. Whereas the mental health movement has championed such attributes as warmth of feeling, spontaneity, insight, a high interest in peers, the ability to communicate feelings, warm teachers, and democratic classrooms, it has been opposed to compulsiveness, competitive striving, intellectualism, achievement orientation, emotional unresponsiveness, as well as the expression of anger or passion, being a loner, not confiding in others, teachers who are curriculum oriented, the regimentation of school life, group tests, red tape, and vice-principles in charge of discipline (White, 1965). Many of these latter attributes are precisely the values espoused by educators committed to the "cognitive" cause.

Because mental hygiene specialists have not fully understood the teacher's role, they have made little available to teachers by way of specific and concrete practical suggestions pertaining to the management of the child's daily behavior. Indeed, mental health concepts advanced by psychodynamically oriented clinicians have proved of little value to teachers on the front lines. Teachers have asked for practical and concrete suggestions, says Morse (1961), only to be given general platitudes. Teachers have, therefore, been forced to rely on their own common sense and ingenuity. Admonitions to be accepting, nonthreatening, and understanding of the child's needs have not helped teachers very much in coping with aberrant behavior. In giving advice to educators, mental health professionals seem to forget about the following aspects of the teacher's role, which make it difficult to heed the advice given:

1. The teacher is a group worker and cannot usually work with just one child.
2. The teacher's primary goal is not to increase the child's personal insights but to achieve certain academic objectives.
3. The teacher must reflect cultural values and therefore cannot be permissively accepting or value-free in his/her approach.
4. The teacher deals primarily with conscious or preconscious processes and is not prepared to handle unconscious processes and materials.
5. The teacher must focus on the reality problems as they exist in the situational present.

In sum, the value differences between mental health professionals and educators commonly lead to differences regarding the best way to deal with the mental health needs of children.

The Need for Multifaceted Intervention Programs

To ensure a comprehensive mental health program, a three-level model of intervention is needed. The first stage is called *primary prevention*. This term means different things to different people, but there is basic agreement that it refers to lowering the rate of emotional disorders in a population and building psychological health and resources in people. Primary prevention as an "in" concept, yet few school psychologists spend much of their time in primary prevention activities. Under the impact of the Education for All Handicapped Children Act (Public Law 94-142), school psychologists may be requested to spend even more of their time as testers. Psychologists and educators might well resist efforts along preventive lines because of the sense of urgency associated with the identification and treatment of students having academic and/or interpersonal difficulties. Moreover, as Fairweather (1972) contends, "An intervention is acceptable to a society in direct proportion to the degree that the innovation does not require a change in the roles or social organization of that society [p. 77]." Despite the difficulties associated with primary prevention, mental health professionals are beginning to implement programs of this nature rather than simply singing its praises from afar.

Whereas primary intervention programs target healthy people, *secondary preventions* target high-risk children. Thus, secondary preventions' efforts focus on the early identification of and intervention with youngsters who already have problems. The basic objective is to remedy problems before they become socially incapacitating. *Tertiary prevention* services concentrate on children and youth who have significant learning and/or personal–social problems. Consistent with its casualty orientation, the fundamental goal of tertiary prevention is to repair psychologically damaged children so that, hopefully, they will be able to function productively in their natural environments.

The reader should be aware that most programs do not fall clearly into one or another of the three intervention categories and that there is some divergence of opinion as to the precise boundaries between these categories (Lemle, 1976). With this caution in mind, we will now examine some of the better known examples of these three levels of preventions.

Primary Prevention

Primary prevention is an appealing but diffuse, abstract term that holds the mysterious, exciting promise of a breakthrough. While this nebulous concept has not yet realized its promise, some concrete, operational "baby-steps" have been taken (Cowen, 1977). The need for primary prevention is best indicated by a consideration of the expense and inadequacy of treatment approaches. As is true of the cost of most services in life, the costs associated with treatment are soaring. In 1972, maintenance of a single child in a special education classroom cost $3500 annually (Dorr, 1972). Incarceration in a juvenile detention facility costs $12,000 per child per year (Report to the Congress, 1977). Internment of a child in a psychiatric hospital can cost as much as $23,000 per year (Commission to Study the Consolidation of Children's Services, 1975). These costs do not include the loss of wasted human resources.

Studies on psychotherapy with children in outpatient clinics (Norman, Rosen, & Bahn, 1962) and in residential facilities (Reid & Hagen, 1952), special class placement for disturbed youngsters (Morse, Cutter, & Fink, 1964), spontaneous remissions in untreated, neurotic children (Shepherd, Oppenheim, & Mitchell, 1966), and studies on the use of stimulant drugs (U.S. Department of Health, Education and Welfare, 1971) all report that two-thirds to three-fourths of children are well or significantly improved 1 to 2 years after having been identified as having behavior problems. Professional rejoicing is tempered by the fact that the base rates for improvement without therapy are the same as those with treatment (Levitt, 1963). In other words, there is no convincing evidence at this time to indicate the superiority of play therapy over dancing lessons in the treatment of shyness nor its superiority over boxing lessons in the case of aggressiveness (Ginott, 1961). Recidivism rates among juvenile offenders in the 60 to 85% range also do little to bolster our faith in correctional schools. Outcome studies of educationally oriented intervention programs with the learning disabled (Koppitz, 1971; Meyers & Hammill, 1976) have not been highly encouraging either. Lastly, studies question the effectiveness of special class placement for the mentally subnormal (Goldstein, Jordan, & Moss, 1962).

Medical science has accomplished much along the lines of mass prevention. Vaccines for polio, measles, and mumps are currently available. Yet the behavioral sciences seem quite content to provide treatment on a one-to-one basis for psychological disturbances. The futility of this approach was well illustrated by Bower (1964), who related an old Cornish custom for determining a man's sanity. According to this method, the suspect was given a scoop and asked to empty the water from a bucket placed under an open tap. If the man turned off the faucet, he was deemed rational and sane. If, on the other hand, he continued to scoop while letting the water run, he was deemed insane. Reasoning analogously, it would appear that most mental health workers might also be deemed irrational. It takes a psychiatrist approximately 12 years to become a fully trained bucket scooper, a Ph.D. psychologist about 8 years, and a social worker about 6 years. As Bower queries, "Is it not time to offer at least a 4-year curriculum in tap turning [p. 9]?"

The Scope of the Problem

The scope of the problem has been estimated by Bower (1970), who indicated that 10% of the children in public schools have mental health problems. Using this figure, Bower estimated that there are now 5.5 million youth, from kindergarten through college, with moderate to severe mental health problems. More recently, it has been estimated that almost 1.5 million youth under age 18 need immediate help and that less than 30% of them are receiving it (Cowen, 1973).

In addition to studying the figures on children with mental health problems, it is important to examine the need for preventive programs with normal children. The fact that the majority of disturbed adults were once normal children clearly highlights the need for preventive actions with this population. Despite the finding that a higher *percentage* of disturbed children (about 30% versus 8%) eventually wind up in the population of disturbed adults, the population of normal children contributes more actual bodies to the population of disturbed adults than does the population of disturbed children. To illustrate this point, 3.6 million (about 8%) of 45 million normal youth will become disturbed as adults in contrast to 1.5 million (30%) of 5 million troubled youth.[1] Thus, based on a ratio of 3.6:1.5, we see that about 70% of disturbed adults come from the population of normal children (Clarizio & McCoy, 1976).

The shortage of trained personnel is a persistent problem. Both Albee (1967) and Sarason (1976) have argued convincingly that there will never be enough trained mental health professionals to handle more than a small fraction of people experiencing adjustment difficulties. The number of trained clinicians has increased dramatically in recent years. Laws at the state and federal levels mandating special education have contributed significantly to the increase in numbers of school psychologists. Yet even conservative estimates of the population that will be in need of service by 1985 indicate a disparity between supply and demand (Report of the Joint Commission, 1973). Even today, it seems to be a rare school district that believes it has sufficient psychological services.

Specific Curriculum Approaches

Some workers believe that one of the most effective ways to promote the mental health of students entails the incorporation of psychological concepts into the curriculum. Such inclusion would not only ensure a definite place for mental health instructors, but it would also accomplish this instruction in a systematic manner. While the present discussion will concentrate on planned curriculum approaches, bear in mind that mental health instruction can also capitalize on teachable moments where in *incidental instruction* is used to deal with real and immediate problems. For example, the teacher and the class might discuss the chronic illness of a hospitalized classmate.

---

[1] These figures are based on studies showing a persistence rate of 30% for troubled children, a 90% rate of normality and 10% abnormality rate among both children and adults, and a solving for the unknown (the rate at which the normal child eventually contributes to the population of disturbed adults). The mathematical calculations are as follows:

$$x90 + \left(\frac{3}{10}\right)10 = 10$$
$$90x + 3 = 10$$
$$90x = 10 - 3$$
$$x = \frac{7}{90}$$
$$x = 7.7\% \text{ or about } 8\%$$

OJEMANN'S CAUSAL APPROACH

Since 1941, Ojemann and his associates have developed and evaluated a curriculum approach to mental health that emphasizes a *causal orientation* to the social environment. By incorporating behavioral science concepts into a curriculum that focuses on the causes or motivations of human behavior, as opposed to the surface or behavioral aspects, Ojemann hopes that the students will be better prepared to solve problems confronting them now and in the future. The basic rationale is that persons who become more fully aware and appreciative of the dynamics of human behavior in general and of their own in particular are better able to cope with personal and social crises.

Ojemann (1967) contends that a sensible arrangement would be to lay a foundation in the causal or motivational approach to behavior in children starting in kindergarten. Then, as children pass into adulthood, they can add to this foundation and apply such a base to the study of marriage and family relationships, employer–employee interactions, and so forth. This approach not only enables the child to surmount current crises, but also establishes a foundation for the solution of crises in later development.

How does Ojemann hope to establish a causal approach? For one thing, he stresses the need to educate the teacher "to live a causal approach in the classroom." As a modeling procedure, daily associations with a teacher who handles situations in an understanding way can go far in developing a causal approach to life.

One teaching strategy used during the primary grades consists of presenting to students narratives in which the surface and causal approaches are contrasted. In kindergarten and first grade, the teacher reads the narratives. In the later grades, the child reads them by him/herself. Each narrative depicts a situation in which a character in the story responds in a surface way initially, but in a causal way after he/she has thought through the situation again. Realistic stories are used. To promote a more generalized approach, stories involve children both older and younger than those in the class, as well as children from different environments. Discussion focusing on the meaning and causes of the behavior in question follows each narrative.

At the elementary and secondary levels, the social sciences and English literature offer numerous opportunities to study the forces influencing the behavior of people. Even in areas such as math and science, the teacher can serve as a model for this type of approach.

Evaluations of Ojemann's approach to date have been promising. The results of more than a dozen research studies indicate that an "appreciation of the dynamics of behavior is accompanied by significant changes in such dimensions as manifest anxiety, tendency to immediate arbitrary punitiveness, antidemocratic tendencies, conception of the teacher and tolerance of ambiguity [Ojemann, 1967, p. 203]." There is some evidence, then, that education in the behavioral sciences can produce youngsters who are less anxiety ridden, less arbitrary, and less authoritarian in handling personal problems. It must be noted that questions pertaining to design and statistical methodology have been raised (Lemle, 1976). Despite these objections, Ojemann's approach is perhaps the best example of a genuine preventive program (Allen *et al.*, 1976).

ROEN'S BEHAVIORAL SCIENCE CURRICULUM

A behavioral science curriculum was developed by Roen (1965, 1967). Roen reports that it was not difficult to recast basic concepts into terms that fourth-grade students could comprehend. A seminar entitled "Teaching the Behavioral Sciences to Children" was used to assist teachers. The course content for fourth graders included such topics as the influences of heredity and environment on development, Erikson's psychosocial stages of development, the self-concept, various learning theory concepts, the concept of intelligence, institutional influences on development, and sociological analysis of the classroom. At the end of the course, each student was asked to write an autobiography discussing his/her uniqueness as a person and the particular forces producing that uniqueness. It is still too early to determine the effectiveness of this behavioral science teaching program. Preliminary evaluation indicates, however, that these elementary school students mastered the course content satisfactorily. Further, the children who were studied responded enthusiastically to the course, and there were no complaints from adults in the community. Evidence on the benefits to mental health, however, is minimal.

COGNITIVE PROBLEM-SOLVING APPROACH

A cognitive problem-solving approach has been described in a recent series of studies by Spivak and Shure (1974, 1976, 1977). The authors reasoned that acquiring interpersonal cognitive problem-solving skills (ICPS) for real-life problems would enhance subsequent social adjustment. Instead of focusing directly on modification of behavior itself, children are taught skills that enable them to think through and solve problems for themselves. After teaching pre-problem-solving thinking skills (e.g., basic word concepts such as *same* and *different*), the training program focuses on the development of the four ICPS components: sensitivity to interpersonal problems, the ability to generate alternative solutions, the ability to understand means–end relationships, and the awareness of the consequences of one's social acts on others. Various versions of the ICPS curricula have been used successfully in class settings with preschoolers, kindergartners, adolescents, and adults (Platt, Spivak, & Swift, 1974; Platt & Spivak, 1976), emotionally disturbed and mentally retarded children (Spivak, Platt, & Shure, 1976), and most recently with inner-city mothers who were trained to teach ICPS skills to their own children (Shure, 1977). In the case of younger children, ICPS are taught through the use of interesting games during daily 5- to 20-minute periods over a 3-month period.

On balance, their studies showed that children in the program improved significantly on such dimensions as concern for others, the ability to take the initiative, and autonomy. The most aberrant children gained the most. Furthermore, gains in social problem-solving skills correlated directly with decreases in maladjustment ratings by teachers on such behaviors as persistence, physical aggression, and proneness to emotional upset.

Special strengths of the program include its sensitivity to developmental principles in social cognition, the specificity with which program operations are identified, the balance between theory and data in development of the ICPS model, the number and variety of replication studies, the use of an "attention" control group, the use of a double-blind methodology that ruled out expectancy effects on the part of parents and teachers, and control for the effect of IQ on outcome measures (Getsen, Apodaca, Rains, Weissberg, & Cowen, 1978; Lemle, 1976).

Spivak and Shure's work shows that behavioral adjustment can be modified. It is not altogether clear, however, that behavior changed because of the child's improvement in ICPS skills, such as their ability to identify alternative modes of acting. In fact, Spivak and Shure recognize that ICPS skills are not the only mediators of behavior. Factors such as emotion and role-taking skills can also play a part. Another factor that might well limit the acceptance of ICPS programs in schools is the fact that students are reinforced for thinking *different* ideas and for thinking about what might happen next, and not for stating the "right" answer. Since a teacher's role does not permit value-free judgments and actions, they may not respond favorably to a curriculum that stresses the "how" to think over the "what" to think. As is true in other intervention programs (Allen *et al.*, 1976), this program seems to be more beneficial for withdrawn youngsters than for impulsive, aggressive ones. It might well be that the base rate for improvement is higher among shy children than it is for aggressive children and that shy youngsters are more apt to improve their adjustment with or without planned intervention (Clarizio & McCoy, 1976). Lastly, one wonders why the most maladjusted children benefited the most from the program. Certainly the most troubled students would seem to have the worst prognosis. Finding the greatest gains among the most disturbed is generally at odds with clinical experience.

THE HUMAN DEVELOPMENT PROGRAM

The theoretical rationale of the human development program derives from several personality theorists. Horney's notion that everyone has a strong drive to achieve competence and to secure approval, together with Sullivan's notion of the delusion of uniqueness, provide much of the ideational scaffolding for this program, which was developed by Bessell and Palomares (1970). Modeled after a structured encounter group format, the program seeks to help children understand and deal with their attitudes, values, and emotions. For preschoolers and kindergarten youngsters, the emphasis is on developing self-control, building self-confidence, increasing understanding of social interactions, increasing tolerance for individual differences, and facilitating skill in verbal expression and listening. Teachers attempt to enhance these skills through the use of daily group sessions. The teacher's task is to facilitate, review, and summarize what the group discussed. Teachers' manuals are available up through the fourth grade.

Despite Bessell's (1973) claim that more than 30,000 professionals and paraprofessionals have been trained in the use of the human development program, research has been disappointingly scarce (Lemle, 1976; Medway & Smith, 1978). What research is available comes from reports disseminated mainly through informal exchange networks. While the preliminary reports are encouraging, they come from satisfied users (Elardo & Elardo, 1976). Like many such programs, they suffer from the fact that they are peripheral to the rest of the school day. Their approach is akin to teaching creativity 20 minutes a day and then returning to the use of convergent thinking for the remainder of the school day. Many psychologists will have reservations about statements made in the theory manuals. Many of these are dogmatically presented as fact when in reality they are speculations or, at best, hypotheses about human behavior. The cost of training teaching staffs in this approach will also limit its use.

DUSO

Developing Understanding of Self and Others (DUSO) centers around eight developmental tasks appropriate for children in kindergarten and the primary grades. The program seeks to accomplish three specific objectives (DUSO, 1970): to label one's feelings; to learn that feelings, goals, and behavior are dynamically interrelated; and to learn to speak freely about feelings, goals, and behavior.

The DUSO materials are appealing because of their clever stories and attractive packaging. Moreover, no special teacher training is said to be necessary. The materials have been field tested in more than 166 classrooms of varying economic, racial, and ethnic make-up (Elardo & Elardo, 1976). Empirical research, however, has been very limited although some studies (Koval & Hales, 1972; Eldridge, Barcikowski, & Witmer, 1973) suggest some limited positive results as a function of the DUSO program.

School-Wide Programs

Competence building is a very appealing pathway toward primary prevention (White, 1975). Another broad area relevant to primary prevention is the analysis and modification of high-impact environments such as families, schools, and churches (Cowen, 1977). The pioneering efforts of Moos (1974) in the Social Ecology Laboratory at Stanford University are noteworthy. He and his co-workers have developed various methodologies for conceptualizing environmental properties and relating these properties to behavior. They discovered that three social climate clusters—relational, personal development, and system-maintenance qualities—characterize obstensibly diverse environments including schools. Relational factors describe the nature of interpersonal relations, such as the support individuals provide for each other. Personal development factors deal with such factors as autonomy, competition, and task orientation. System-maintenance factors assess the extent to which environments are orderly, controlling, change oriented, and so on. Some of the consequences of these clusters have relevance to primary prevention. For example, it has been demonstrated that social environments like schools, which score high in the relational qualities of involvement and support, have occupants who are less irritable and depressed, more satisfied and comfortable, and have higher self-esteem (Moos, 1974a, 1974b). Classrooms that rate high on personal development, such as high student involvement and closer teacher–student relations, generally lead to greater student satisfaction. By contrast, certain system-maintenance dimensions, such as high control, appear to have negative effects. There remain many complexities yet to be unraveled, but a beginning has been made to chart the pathways between the characteristics of high-impact institutions and mental health.

Research involving the entire school environment as it relates to healthy behavior was conducted at the Bank Street School of Education (Minuchin, Biber, Shapiro, & Zimilies, 1969) by a research team that attempted to assess the ramifications of "progressive" versus "traditional" education. These investigators studied the effects of two progressive and two traditional public schools on the cognitive and social functioning and the self-views of fourth graders attending the schools. The traditional schools saw their basic task as fostering the students' mastery of an established body of knowledge and skills. Accordingly, "teaching was directed to a body of knowledge, as organized in textbooks and curriculum syllabi, to be mastered at a level that would make it available to recall and replication on its original form and meanings [pp. 36–37]." The progressive schools viewed their task as that of promoting the children's curiosity, exploration, spontaneity, and self-direction and had in common a preference for instructional methods involving discovery, discussion, experimentation, and activity. The basic findings were as follows:

1. There is little evidence that modern or progressive, schools make for superior or even for systematically different cognitive functioning in comparison with traditional schools. The students of the two types of schools were much alike with regard to problem-solving processes and expressions of degree of imaginativeness in non-problem-solving settings. Qualitative reports suggested that the modern school pupils were more unified and effective in a group problem-solving task, in comparison with traditional school students. This finding may be due to the smaller class sizes in the modern schools, however.

2. With respect to social attitudes, it was found that children from modern schools tended to be more clearly identified with their schools than children from the traditional schools. That is, peer group affiliation is fostered somewhat more

strongly at the modern than at the traditional schools. There were few consistent differences, however, between the two types of schooling in terms of students' ideas of right and wrong and in terms of whether students perceived adults as accepting–benevolent or as controlling–disapproving.

3. The third area of investigation entailed the child's self-views. Specifically, it was hypothesized that children from modern schools would have great self-knowledge. Only one of the six measures supported this hypothesis. In two other aspects of self-views, it was predicted that: (*a*) children from modern schools would show less sex-role stereotyping and therefore less allegiance to their own sex role; and (*b*) there would be differences between the two groups in terms of how they envisioned their futures and in their preferences for different stages of life. Although the investigators write as if their data support the distinction between modern and traditional schools, inspection of the results by and large suggests that the type of school attended made for little difference in the child's self-view.

Thus, despite the investigators' contention that the outcomes of this study were broadly consistent with their expectations, the actual data appear more largely to support the conclusion that the type of school environment, as implemented and evaluated in this study, had minimal impact upon the child's cognitive processes, social attitudes, or views of his/herself (Wallach, 1971).

This study raises a number of questions. Is the type of school attended really unimportant? Or are the measuring instruments not sufficiently sensitive to uncover these differences? Are these two constructs too complex and heterogeneous to be viable? Are there certain commonalities in both traditional and progressive schools that offset any differences between them? Does good, high-quality teaching within either educational philosophy facilitate personal competence? Does the influence of the community and of child-rearing practices in the home override any impact that the different types of schools might have? These and other issues must be settled before we will know the psychological impact of various kinds of school experiences on primary prevention efforts.

The Role of Stress: Harmful or Helpful?

There are two divergent conceptions regarding the impact of stress on mental health. One, the traditional notion, views stress as something noxious and therefore to be avoided. The other regards stress as a force that can be used productively to build immunity to anxiety.

According to the traditional Freudian hypothesis, traumatic events during early life render the individual more susceptible to anxiety in adulthood. Proponents of the view that conceives of stress as undesirable typically oppose such practices as teaching early reading, the use of grading in assessment, and the emphasis on academic excellence. They express concern over the price of competition, the frantic pace in education, and the emotional risks associated with increased demands for scholastic accomplishment. They raise such questions as: Does exposure to anxiety-producing situations endanger pupil mental health? What happens to students when they are prized more for academic achievement than for any other reason? What are the consequences of prolonged exposure to moderate stress?

One common source of stress in educational settings centers around the curriculum. Subsumed under the general heading of stress-inducing curricular experiences are grouping policies, promotional policies, and evaluation policies (Ringness, 1968). Inadequate provision for individual differences also constitutes a major shortcoming. For students exposed to a curriculum that does not match their abilities, interests, and cultural backgrounds, school soon becomes like a prison. Less obvious but nonetheless quite real and pervasive sources of frustration have been identified by Jackson (1968) from his observations of life in the classroom. He discusses four unpublicized features of school that can irritate students: delay, denial, interruption, and social distraction. Students seem to spend a surprising amount of time waiting—to sharpen pencils, to empty full bladders, to go to recess, to have teachers check papers, and so on. Denial is experienced when questions are ignored and requests refused. Classroom discontinuity stems from student misbehavior, outside visitors, bells ending classes, and other petty distractions and interruptions. It is difficult to determine the impact of these four hidden aspects of school life. While the episodes, in and of themselves, appear trivial enough, their significance increases when they are considered cumulatively over a 12-year period.

Deterrents to Primary Prevention

The size and complexity of the problems in carrying out primary prevention programs have overwhelmed lay groups and behavioral scientists alike. Since maladjustment arises from such varied sources as faulty parent–child relations, poverty, racial discrimination, constitutional factors, and school failure, many workers believe that anything short of a major societal overhaul would prove inconsequential. The problem is so vast that few know where to begin. The ensuing emotional response to the frustrations associated with prevention is one of despair. Consequently, few are inclined to make any whole-hearted effort along this line. Because psychologists are not Renaissance types with the know-how to alter the numerous life conditions that affect mental health outcomes, they must sort out those variables with which they are competent to deal and strengthen collaborative working relations with people in other fields whose work bears on primary prevention (Cowen, 1977).

A second source of resistance to primary prevention centers around the invasion-of-privacy issue. Always a cherished right, the freedom to live one's own life continues to be publicly reinforced. In certain states, for example, the schools need permission to administer personality tests to students. To prevent malad-justment is to meddle in the private affairs of persons. The crux of the difficulty lies in finding a way of intervention acceptable to the public. The difficulty arises in that preventive approaches cannot use all of the information-gathering tech-niques and intervention strategies that informed consent permits in treatment endeavors. Because primary prevention focuses on potential problems, the neces-sity for information of this type and primary intervention is not readily apparent to those who must sanction it.

Another deterrent involves certain cultural values. Notable among these is the belief that by working hard, controlling impulses, and using intellect, a person will be successful and achieve virtue. Conversely, if one is not conscientious, if one follows the pleasure principle, and lets emotions override better judgment, then one will be unsuccessful, a failure, and regarded as evil. In short, it is believed that the individual derives from life what he/she deserves.

Still another barrier to the development of prevention programs resides within the professional community itself. Unfortunately, the majority of mental health professionals view their primary task as one of treatment, not of prevention. The preoccupation is more with mental illness than with mental health. Witness the fact that, until recently, there was no word in our language to describe an ego-enhancing experience, but there has long been a term (trauma) to indicate an ego-debilitating experience. An ever-expanding segment of mental health workers is becoming more prevention oriented, but it remains difficult to enlist the full-fledged support of those doing diagnosis and therapy in a one-to-one relationship. Preventive work is regarded as less concrete, less exciting, and less urgent than treatment that is geared toward the immediate, the tangible, and the already overt disturbance (Cruickshank, 1963).

A final problem involves specifying and evaluating the goals of prevention. Is the goal that of promoting emotional robustness? Or is it that of reducing pathol-ogy, for example, delinquency? Difficult as the task may be, it is essential to establish both operational definitions of objectives and evaluative baselines if any programs are to be implemented and assessed. The day of the "soft sell" may well be on the way out for the mental health fields; they will have to demonstrate their worth as helpers of humanity. Programs of primary prevention must demonstrate their efficacy in reducing the incidence of various disorders through long-term follow-up studies. Even such studies yield ambiguous evidence because of the multitude of factors other than the intervention that might influence outcomes over long periods of time. A partial solution lies in the use of *intermediate* criteria (Flanagan, 1971). Such yardsticks represent desirable outcomes in themselves as well as presumed indicators of later adjustment (e.g., social problem-solving skills such as generating alternative solutions and considering the consequences of one's actions). We must also bear in mind that whereas the terms "innovation" and "change" ordinarily have a positive air about them, "experimentation" and "re-search" engender public distrust and disfavor.

Secondary Prevention

Primary prevention seeks to enhance the psychological functioning of all children. Because it is aimed at the population in general, it represents the broadest level of intervention. Primary preventive activities are applied before any signs of maladjustment are evident. Secondary prevention, which represents a bonafide alternative to traditional treatment, has two basic components—early identification of psychological and educational difficulties, and growth-enhancing interventions aimed at reducing problems before they become more severe. Thus, secondary prevention focuses on children who are already experiencing visible problems that are presumed to be highly amenable to change. The goal is to intervene before the problems become firmly entrenched and debilitating. The following discussion will review some of the better known projects that have been carried out at preschool and elementary school levels.

The Preschool Period

Retrospective studies suggest the feasibility of identifying emotional disturbances at the preschool level. In one study, the investigators examined the histories of 60 youngsters seen at a child guidance clinic and found that more than half of them had noticeable problems prior to school entrance (Oppenheimer & Mandel, 1959). Similarly, Bolton (1955) noted that 75 of 100 children seen at a clinic had manifested observable symptoms prior to kindergarten entrance. The difficulty of retrospective studies with respect to early identification and prediction is that they do not reveal how many youngsters in the general population had shown similar symptoms and yet later made an adequate adjustment to school (false positives) or how many who had not displayed observable symptoms grew up to be maladjusted (false negatives).

The Summer Child Study Project

The Summer Child Study Project (Newton & Brown, 1967) is one of the better known examples of secondary prevention at the preschool level. The purposes of the project were twofold—to develop a psychological screening procedure to predict how the child would adjust to school entry and future school stress, and to develop appropriate interventions to augment the child's coping skills. Screening procedures 6 months prior to school entrance consisted of structured observations and testing of the child by a psychologist together with an interview by a social worker. Each child was then given a rating by the team. When the youngsters were divided into two groups—the adjusted and maladjusted—and compared against later performance criteria (number of reading requirements completed, absenteeism, initiative, curiosity, self-concept), it was found that there were significant differences between the two groups. The investigators also reported on the basis of their clinical observations that intervention efforts contributed to the children's adjustment, but hard data on this point will be needed to objectify the stated gains. The development of child find projects throughout the country offers an excellent opportunity to broaden the data base regarding the efficacy of secondary intervention efforts at the preschool level.

THE MILWAUKEE PROJECT

Heber's (1976) 10-year longitudinal program provides a dramatic example of an intervention approach with high-risk children whose mothers had IQs of 75 or less. Starting shortly after the children were born, the enrichment and skill training took place over the first 5 years of the child's life at a center where the children spent all day. In addition, a home teacher was assigned to each family. Mothers were instructed in positive ways of interaction with children, occupational education, remedial education in the 3 R's, and homemaking and child-care skills. Initially, the child-training focus was on perceptual and motor skills, followed later by linguistic–cognitive training, and then by socioemotional training. Upon entrance in school, the children were assigned to small classes of 10 to 12 students.

Follow-up of the experimental (Es) and control children (Cs) and their mothers revealed some impressive findings. By age 22 months, the Es were significantly ahead of the Cs on all learning tasks used. There was no overlap between the groups. These differences held up over time. At age 7, Es had an average IQ of 121 compared to 87 for Cs. Comparable differences appeared on language measures. The intellectual and linguistic superiority of the Es was still evident at age 9, the most recent testing point. There were few clear-cut group differences in the socioemotional realm. E mothers had far more successful histories as judged by the number of them employed and their higher wages.

The Elementary School Level

Elementary school teachers are able to render reasonably reliable appraisals of a child's current personal adjustment. For instance, with respect to emotional disturbance, Lambert and Bower (1961) reported that 90% of elementary school pupils labeled as disturbed by teachers were also adjudged disturbed by experienced clinicians following individual assessment. Teacher ratings are also as reliable a technique as any available for the prediction of juvenile delinquency.

EMOTIONAL PROBLEMS

One of the best known programs for early identification is the Primary Mental Health Project, which has been in existence for over a dozen years in the city of Rochester, New York. During that time, it has gone through several phases. One of the original objectives of this program was the early identification and prevention of emotional disorders. To achieve this end, the school social worker interviewed the mothers of all first graders, classroom observations were made of all children, and some psychological testing was done with first graders. A clinical judgment was made on each child on the basis of this information. Those already showing problems or apparently having great potential for future disturbance were called the red-tag (RT) group. About 30% of entering first graders were given this label. Those adjusting well and thought likely to continue this way were called the non red-tag (NRT) group. The overall quality of family life seemed to be the most significant factor in determining whether a child fell into the RT or NRT group. The RT children differed from the NRT group on a variety of school record measures (nurse referrals, attendance, grade-point average, achievement test scores) as well as on several adjustment measures (teachers' ratings, clinicians' ratings, anxiety measures, self-report, and peer perceptions).

The treatment part of the program was directed primarily toward school personnel and parents. The children were given direct service in an after-school program. These 1-hour sessions led by teachers who had a facility for working with maladjusted students ran for a period of 20 weeks. The mental health specialist's role was that of a consultant and resource person rather than that of a direct service giver. A follow-up study of the RT and NRT some 6 years later when they were in the seventh grade yielded no definitive conclusions. The two groups differed on 14 of the 46 comparisons, but the pattern of differences was not clear-cut. The RT children were found to have lower grades, were more apt to be underachievers, and had poorer attendance records than NRT children. On the other hand, as a group, they were less anxious and scored better on standard achievement tests than did NRT children.

Detailed evaluation of the revised form of the Rochester Primary Mental Health Program is not yet available but measures that do bear on its effectiveness suggest its promise. To wit, four of the original six aides are still with the program, referrals to aides have grown substantially, and the school system is now committed to hiring aides for several inner-city schools out of its own funds (Zax & Specter, 1974). The program also appears most appropriately suited to shy, anxious children but less well suited to the needs of acting-out and learning-problem students (Lorion, Cowen, & Caldwell, 1974). These investigators deserve credit for being one of the few groups willing to undertake evaluation of their school-based treatment program and to make changes on the basis of their findings.

LEARNING PROBLEMS

In recent years there has been an increasing interest in the early identification of children who will later become learning disability cases. Haring and Ridgeway (1967) screened 1200 youngsters from 48 kindergarten classes in Kansas. In their search for distinctive psychometric patterns, the investigators administered a battery of tests measuring language perception and motor skills to all high-risk children. No specific test patterns worthy of note were found. This negative finding is not surprising because of the heterogeneous nature of their group.

Ferinden and Jacobson (1970) sought to determine which tests were most effective in accurately predicting later reading difficulties. Four diagnostic scales—the Wide Range Achievement Test, the Evanston Early Identification Scale, the Bender Gestalt Visual Motor Test, and the Metropolitan Reading Readiness Test—were used to select kindergartners from 10 classrooms. The authors concluded that teachers were about 80% effective in identifying children with learning problems using merely their own subjective judgment. The scale that added the most to teacher judgment was the Metropolitan Reading Readiness Test, which is nationally the most commonly used screening measure (Maitland, Nadeau, & Nadeau, 1974). The combination of teacher judgment and this brief readiness test reportedly resulted in 90% accuracy in screening.

DeHirsch, Jansky, and Langford (1966) reported a successful attempt in predicting failure in reading by the end of the second grade. Giving a battery of 37 tests to 53 kindergartners who had average ability and no obvious problems, the investigators claimed a 91% success rate in prediction.

One team of investigators (Feshbach, Adelman, & Fuller, 1974, 1977) compared two alternative models (the de Hirsch Predictive Index of Reading Failure and teachers' ratings) used to identify kindergarten children with a high risk of reading failure. They found that both approaches were about 75% accurate in their predictions but that they differed markedly in the types of errors made. With the de Hirsch scales, there were almost twice as many false positives (youngsters predicted to become reading failures but who did achieve satisfactorily) as in the teachers' ratings. Whether the de Hirsch approach or teachers' ratings are differentially valuable in developing an intervention program is, of course, a separate issue. It is heartening to note that a kindergarten teachers' ratings can predict first-grade achievement at least as well as a psychometric battery designed for this purpose.

Some Unresolved Problems

Educators and mental health specialists have often expressed a desire for earlier identification and treatment of problems in children as a preventive step. Moreover, the research literature suggests that through a combination of approaches using teacher judgment, peer perceptions, and self-ratings, deviant youth can be identified during the early school years. Yet several factors militate against the identification of problems in the early years of childhood.

1. Screening and diagnosing emotional and learning disability problems during the preschool years and in kindergarten pose more difficulties than when attempted with somewhat older children. Even experienced professionals, when dealing with individual children, have no reliable means for distinguishing between problems of a transitory nature and those indicative of the probability of later, more serious pathology. An extensive study involving more than 2400 chil-

dren in a southwest farming county in Minnesota demonstrated the difficulty associated with prediction of later individual adjustment (Anderson, 1959). In 1950, the subjects (who were in grades 4 through 12) were given a series of inventories dealing with such factors as family attitudes, social responsibility, and psychoneurotic symptoms. A follow-up study conducted from 1954 to 1957 utilized personality inventories and teacher ratings. The major finding pertaining to prediction of individual behavior over a span of 5 to 7 years was essentially negative. In other words, it cannot be stated with certainty that a youngster who does poorly as measured by the available tests and rating scales will make a poor adjustment some years later. Changes within the person and changes in the demands made over time were regarded as two factors rendering prediction difficult. Curiously, it was easier to predict outstanding adjustment than poor adjustment. The present screening devices are not sufficiently discriminating to identify who will be emotionally disturbed in later life. A more recent study (Rubin, Balow, Dorle, & Rosen, 1976) also showed that far greater reliance could be placed upon the use of high readiness scores as predictors of good academic performance than upon the use of low readiness scores as predictors of poor performance. It is not yet fully understood what kinds of disturbed youngsters grow up to be disturbed adults (with the exception of severe delinquents and grossly disturbed children).

2. It is difficult to arouse parental concern when the child is young, since the pathology is apt to express itself in a mild form. Likewise, teachers are often inclined to give the young pupil additional time in which to rally before requesting professional help. By the primary grades or early elementary school years, however, teachers and parents become increasingly concerned about the child's maladjusted behavior and therefore seek assistance at that time.

3. It is often not until the middle elementary years that latent pathology becomes overt under the stresses and pressures for adjustment to the academic and behavioral demands of the classroom. Torrance (1962) points to a number of cultural discontinuities that typically occur in the lives of middle-class pupils in the fourth grade. Classroom activities become more formal and organized, children are expected to sit in orderly rows in the classroom and are given less motor freedom, and they are supposed to "get down to business."

4. Teachers and parents are quite able to tolerate the mild forms of overt pathology characteristic of young children, whereas they are less well equipped or prepared to cope with the acting-out behavior of older children.

5. As Bower (1969) notes, it is not known "how early is early" in the detection of childhood disorders. How soon must intervention procedures be implemented after the onset of a problem in order for the intervention to be economical and effective? For example, is identification at the third-grade level early enough for neurotic youth? for delinquent youth? for learning disability cases? At present, the notion that early detection leads to efficient and effective treatment, though seemingly logical, remains an assumption rather than a fact. This idea raises a related point. If large numbers of maladjusted youngsters are identified,

what is going to be done about them? Current treatment services are already overloaded. Few school administrators would care to have a large identifiable group of students whose educational and personal needs cannot be met. At the present time, there is no definite answer to such dilemmas.

6. Many youngsters appear to "outgrow" their childhood disorders and enter successfully the mainstream of American adult life. What impact would the identification and labeling of such youngsters as "emotionally disturbed" have upon their later adjustment? Would the identification of these youngsters result in a self-fulfilling prophecy? Again, this is a difficult question to which there is no conclusive reply.

7. Few, if any, of the studies on identification of emotional disturbance or learning disability have explored the usefulness of various cutoff points. In selecting a cutoff point, say between emotionally disturbed and normal children, one must balance between two kinds of errors. If the cutoff point is set too high, then one will label as emotionally disturbed many youngsters who, in reality, are normal. These cases are called false positives. On the other hand, if the cutoff point is set too low, then an increased number of emotionally disturbed children will be considered normal when, in fact, they are troubled. These cases are called false negatives.

One cannot change the cutoff point without changing the number of both false positives and false negatives. This issue has to be recognized as part of the problem of any screening effort (Gallagher & Bradley, 1972). Regretably, few studies on early identification of emotional disturbances or learning disabilities report data on the percentage of diagnostic misses, namely, those labeled as having the condition who, in fact, do not have it (false positives), and those labeled as free from the condition but who, in fact, have it (false negatives). It is usually the diagnostic "hits" or general accuracy that is reported and the reader is left in the dark as to the diagnostic misses. Information on both the diagnostic hits and misses is needed to evaluate the effectiveness of identification procedures.

8. There are serious difficulties associated with the concept of diagnosis that deserve consideration. First of all, it is often difficult to agree on what the problem is. Thus, the child who has a problem in school is diagnosed as aphasic by the speech therapist, as passive–aggressive by a psychodynamically oriented psychologist, and as a learning disability case by the learning disabilities teacher. Second, finding causes both within the child and in his/her external environment is a particularly thorny problem. For example, the following factors were found in the case of one learning disabled student: difficult birth, high fevers in infancy, sibling rivalry, a working mother, moderate tensions in the home situation, an auditory perceptual disability on the child's part, emphasis on phonics instruction in an open classroom setting, signs of hyperactivity, and borderline intelligence. It is virtually impossible to say which of these caused the learning disability.

Third, predicting the course that a given problem might follow is also extremely complicated. For example, perinatal complications like anoxia have more dire consequences among lower-class students than they have among middle-class students (Sameroff & Chandler, 1975). While we now have some prognostic data regarding groups suffering from certain conditions (e.g., phobias, hyperactivity, varying levels of mental retardation, autism, and juvenile delinquency), there is less certainty regarding the long-term outcomes of other conditions (e.g., learning disabilities and run-of-the-mill behavior disorders). Predictions regarding individuals are always hazardous. One fact is clear, however. There is a definite tendency to be overly pessimistic in our predictions about emotional problems.

Last of all, although the real advantage of diagnosis is to suggest the treatment of choice, there is an absence of evidence to indicate that present diagnostic systems enable us to make a direct correspondence between specific treatments and specific disabilities. For example, one investigator (Hansen, 1970) found that the majority of children in a special public school program for the educationally handicapped were placed with recommendations for individualized instruction in a small-class setting, perceptual training, and counseling. Thus, there was a remarkable similarity of remedial recommendations despite wide diversity of characteristics among the children in the sample. In many instances, the assistance one receives depends upon the orientation of the helping agent and only secondarily on the child's diagnosis. For a more extended discussion of these problems, see Clarizio and McCoy (1976).

Tertiary Prevention

The aim of tertiary prevention is to assist individuals who have moderate to severe emotional problems, often of a chronic nature. Although only 5% of the school psychologist's time is typically devoted to direct therapy with children (Michigan Department of Education, 1976), the school psychologist's role in providing therapy is less controversial now than it was in the 1950s. Nonetheless, many people still question whether providing direct therapy to students represents the best use of the school psychologist's time. Indeed, providing consultation (indirect service) now appears to hold greater professional prestige than providing therapy. Aside from the issue regarding the wisest use of one's time, there are ethical considerations. Certainly no psychologist should attempt to provide therapy unless his/her professional competencies are adequate to the task. There is evidence to suggest that therapists vary in their abilities to help others (Ricks, 1974). Of course the therapist must know more than therapeutic techniques. He or she must also understand the culture of the school, since one cannot be fully effective without taking into consideration institutional characteristics (Sarason, 1971). But despite the above cautions, there will always be children who do need therapy. In this section, we will discuss outcome studies of psychotherapy with children and sample three selected treatment approaches that are receiving noticeable attention among school psychologists. Topics such as the use of nonprofessionals and drug therapy have been omitted because of space limitations. The reader is referred to Clarizio and McCoy (1976) and Zax and Specter (1974) for extended discussions of therapeutic approaches in the schools.

Evaluation of Tertiary Prevention

Parents and educators often turn to mental health specialists when attempting to resolve the problems of their children or pupils. Today there are approximately 2000 outpatient clinics and more than 400 hospitals with psychiatric units offering mental health services (Bower, 1970). The question naturally arises, How effective is the treatment provided by these facilities? The author can recall numerous occasions when he sat in on case conferences with mental health specialists and school personnel and heard a sigh of relief from the participants once the child was recommended for psychotherapy.

How realistic is it to feel such a sense of relief? Generally speaking, results at termination of treatment do indicate that from two-thirds to three-fourths of children seen at child guidance centers show improvement. Typical of such findings was a large-scale national investigation of outpatient psychiatric clinics in 1959, conducted by Norman, Rosen, and Bahn (1962), who discovered an improvement rate of 72%. Follow-up studies, moreover, indicate that children treated on an outpatient basis maintain their improved status (Levitt, 1957). The results of psychotherapy with residential treatment cases yield similarly high improvement rates both at the time of termination of treatment (Reid & Hagen, 1952) and at the time of follow-up (Rubin, 1962). Hence, data obtained on outpatients and inpatients at the close of therapy and at the time of follow-up seem to suggest that the grounds for the sigh of relief alluded to earlier are based on reality.

There are, however, two disquieting aspects regarding the outcomes of psychotherapeutic treatment of children. First, of approximately 200,000 children seen in outpatient psychiatric clinics in 1959, only one-fourth were accepted for direct treatment of some kind, another fourth were terminated by the clinic as unsuitable for treatment, and one-half were terminated with the majority of such cases being referred to the originating agency (Norman, Rosen, & Bahn, 1962). As Redl (1966) notes, the model of "the holy trinity" (psychiatrist, psychologist, and social worker) is obsolescent, and the need for new modes of treatment to cope with the new mixtures of childhood disturbances is apparent. Schofield (1964), in a somewhat similar vein, points out that psychotherapists have not been trained to deal with some of the more common types of problems being referred to them, namely, difficulties symptomatic of social distress and discomfort.

Second, professional rejoicing over the high improvement rates for those accepted for treatment would have to be predicated upon the proposition that untreated disturbed youngsters do not improve. But an examination of the base rates for improvement without psychotherapy yields little support for such a proposition (Levitt, 1957–1963).

Because of the difficult methodological problems associated with research in this area (e.g., using adequate control groups, equating therapies and therapists, increasing the sensitivity of the measuring instruments, locating former clients for follow-up study, estimating how much time should elapse between treatment and follow-up, controlling for placebo effect, and spontaneous cures), conclusive findings are hard to come by. Levitt, in his reviews of traditional or psychoanalytically oriented treatment, is quick to point out that his findings do not prove that psychotherapy with children is ineffective or useless. It is conceivable that the measuring procedures were not sensitive enough to detect changes stemming from treatment. Moreover, it should be remembered that some diagnostic groups (e.g., children with specific problems) benefited more than other groups. It is also quite possible that some therapists are much more helpful than other therapists, as Ricks (1974) notes in his discussion of "super-shrink."

Nonetheless, Levitt's large-scale studies clearly indicate that we cannot live on our laurels. We must seek alternatives to traditional treatment approaches for children's problems. Some of the newer approaches focus largely on individuals or small groups, while others emphasize more of a social systems approach. Many of these approaches take place in the natural environment of the child. There is an increasing belief that change is best effected by working through adults who are in a position to deal with the child's problem when and where it occurs. With the exception of the behavior modification approach, the outcomes of the approaches to be presented in the next section have not been carefully researched.

Treatment Approaches

Behavior Therapy

Since modern psychology has been largely dominated by theories of learning, it is understandable that the most distinctive contribution made by psychologists to treatment efforts has come in the area of learning theory. In large measure the application of learning theory concepts to the modification of deviant behavior can be attributed to the increasing number of clinical psychologists since World War II, the emphasis on more sophisticated training in research methodology at the doctoral level, the questioning of the traditional methods of psychotherapy, and the growing dissatisfaction with the appropriateness of the medical model for extension to behavior disorders (Ullmann & Krasner, 1965). Through the efforts of Dollard and Miller (1950), Shoben (1949), and Mowrer (1950), psychodynamic views were recast in learning theory terms but, as Ullmann and Krasner (1965) assert, a new approach to *doing* therapy was not forthcoming; simply a new way of *talking about therapy* was developed. Of the various learning theory approaches to therapy, behavior therapy is attracting the most attention today and is probably the most relevant to the treatment of childhood disorders.

Basically, behavior therapy refers to the systematic application of learning theory principles to the rational modification of deviant behavior (Franks, 1965). The term *behavior therapy* embraces not a specific technique but a variety of methods stemming from learning theory and focusing on the modification of deviant behavior. As such, it represents a meeting point for experimental and clinical psychology, fields that traditionally have been widely divergent.

While the roots of modifying behavior date back to the early Greeks, systematic attempts to produce changes as a consequence of manipulated environmental contingencies are a relatively recent phenomenon. The early classic studies done by Watson and Raynor (1920) on Albert, those done by Jones (1924) on Peter, and those of Jersild and Holmes (1935) demonstrated how the emotional responses of young children can be learned and unlearned. But it was not until recent years that behavior therapy was applied to a wide variety of children's disorders. Various behavioral techniques have been used with students to treat neurotic-like conditions such as schoolphobia, test anxiety, and withdrawn behavior (Clarizio & McCoy, 1976), learning disabilities (Bryan & Bryan, 1975), acting-out and delinquent behavior (Kent & O'Leary, 1976; Cohen, Filipczak, Slavin, & Boren, 1971), and childhood psychoses (Lovaas, Koegel, Simmons, & Long, 1973; Koegel & Rincover, 1974). Among the more interesting extensions of behavior therapy are the use of group approaches (Rose, 1972), behavioral contracting (De Risi & Butz, 1975), modeling and role playing (Sarason & Sarason, 1974), self-management (Lovitt, 1973), and overcorrection procedures (Clarizio, 1976).

The behavioral approach seems to have many advantages: (*a*) it is consistent with the school's setting of objectives and changing of behavior; (*b*) it encourages the development of healthy behavior as well as the reduction of negative behavior; (*c*) it yields specific practical suggestions rather than general platitudes; (*d*) help can be delivered in the child's natural setting, for example, the classroom; (*e*) it offers a variety of techniques to cope with different kinds of problem behavior; (*f*) it seeks to accomplish modest goals in a systematic way; (*g*) it is consistent with the current emphasis on accountability; (*h*) it is a parsimonious approach in that only data essential to analysis and actual treatment of the problem are collected; (*i*) behavioral techniques can be readily communicated to many of the child's caregivers, such as teachers and parents, thereby broadening the therapeutice base; and (*j*) behavioral therapy readily lends itself to evaluation of outcomes through the use of systematic observations and baselines.

Behavior therapies hold considerable promise but additional evidence is needed before the extent of their therapeutic efficacy is clear. Further research dealing with the problem of generalization of treatment results over time, across settings, and across behaviors is necessary if gains made during treatment therapy are to be maintained or spread. Experimental validation, as opposed to the case-study approach, is also needed in order to demonstrate the benefits of behavior therapy with children. Moreover, there is a dearth of experimental research comparing the effectiveness of behavior therapy with other psychotherapeutic approaches involving children with different kinds of problems. Behavior therapists have also failed to deal adequately with problems of entry into social systems (Reppucci & Saunders, 1974). That is, they have not yet developed a systematic body of knowledge for altering social systems to achieve their goals. The above problems are not restricted to behavior therapy. What is distinctive about behavior therapy is its open and willing attempt to answer via research the problems confronting it.

REALITY THERAPY

One approach to therapy that has attracted wide attention from practitioners in the schools is that of William Glasser's reality therapy (1969). Reality therapy derives its name from its emphasis on behavior in the real world rather than a client's subjective interpretation of his or her feelings and thoughts (Barr, 1974).

Responsibility is a central concept in reality therapy. Responsible behavior leads to happiness. And persons are happy or unhappy because of their own decisions, not because of the conditions in which they find themselves. No one forced the person to steal money, to curse a teacher, to take drugs, or to neglect class assignments. The person chose these actions and only he/she can and must assume responsibility for those choices. Persons are accountable for their actions.

For Glasser, responsible behavior means that the individual meets two fundamental needs—a sense of involvement and a feeling of self-worth—in a way that does not hurt others. If persons feel involved, they also feel that others care, that they matter to others, and that they, in turn, care about others. The individual, in short, is able to love and be loved. People must do more than become involved with others, however. They must regard themselves as successful or they will experience unbearable pain. They must feel worthwhile to themselves and to others. Each person has to develop an identity in which he/she feels successful. Teacher involvement, an emphasis on behavior, encouragement of value judgments by the child, and a firm commitment to a plan are all notions central to the implementation of reality therapy.

Among the most innovative approaches advocated by Glasser is the use of class meetings led by the teacher to solve behavioral and educational problems. Glasser (1978) regards the class meetings as the most efficient and most effective technique for helping students feel accepted and worthwhile. Through the use of class meetings, students come to feel that they have more of a stake in the school and problem behavior drops precipitously. The students sit in a circle and each youngster has a turn to speak. If the student has nothing to say, he/she has the right to pass. If a student does not want to take part in the meetings, he/she can sit apart from the circle.

Reality therapy is a straightforward approach that has considerable appeal. Its stress on the development of personal responsibility, its concern with the child's problems in the real world, its teaching children to use their brains in the solution of social problems, its improvement of communications between teacher and child, and its reliance on logic and behavior rather than on insight will earn this approach high marks from practitioners. Like any approach, it is not without its limitations, however. Glasser's insistence on a firm commitment, for example, would seemingly limit the number of students with whom this approach can be used. Many of the troublesome students find their misbehavior very rewarding and are, therefore, not inclined to make a commitment to change their ways. Others have already "tuned out" because of early failure experiences. Commitment does not come easily for such youngsters, for they have reached the point where they no longer care.

As valuable as class meetings can be, many teachers feel uncomfortable in conducting class meetings. Some teachers are too authoritarian to use this approach effectively. Others simply lack the skills required in getting meetings underway and in keeping them going in meaningful ways. Still others are afraid that class meetings will give the students too much power and that they will then "take over" the class. Moreover, the absence of an overall formal curriculum plan and materials leaves teachers unsure of how and where to start (Elardo & Elardo, 1976). Thus, for a variety of reasons, teachers will need training and encouragement if they are to use class meetings to the best advantage, if at all.

Finally, in view of the widespread use of Glasser's approach, it is disconcerting to see that relatively little formal, systematic evaluation of its impact has been published in refereed journals. The evaluative studies conducted to date have not permitted any definitive conclusion regarding the effectiveness of reality therapy (Glick, 1968; Hawes, 1970; Cook, 1972; O'Keefe, 1973; Shearn & Randolph, 1978).

ADLERIAN APPROACHES

In recent years there has been a resurgence of interest in Adlerian psychology as a way to deal with classroom problems. Adlerian principles were popularized largely through the efforts of the late Rudolph Dreikurs, who espoused democratic child management procedures. The following tenets are central to the Adlerian position (Dinkmeyer & Dinkmeyer, 1976).

1. Behavior is goal directed and purposive. Dreikurs postulated four goals of disturbing behavior—attention-getting, the struggle for power, the desire to retaliate, and the display of disability. This teleoanalytic approach focuses on the "here and now" behavior and its goal. Reactions by teachers, peers, and parents to the troublesome behavior are also considered.

2. According to Adlerians, motivation is best understood in terms of striving for significance. There is less concern for what the child is doing and more for how the child is seeking to be known. For example, the child's refual to do school work, which results in penalties, makes sense if it enables him/her to receive recognition from peers as one who dares to defy the teacher.

3. All behavior has a social meaning. Because behavior is always to be interpreted in terms of its social context, the Adlerian therapist relies on the teacher's classroom observations and anecdotes in developing tentative hypotheses. The therapist may also observe the child in the classroom, interpreting behavior patterns within the teleoanalytic frame of reference. Particular attention is devoted to social rewards that encourage maladaptive behavior, since social striving is regarded as primary.

4. The person is understood in terms of his/her phenomenological field. In contrast to reality therapy, Adlerian psychology is not concerned with external reality but with the meaning of the events for the individual. That is, the therapist must understand the child's private logic; the therapist must "guess" what the child is thinking.

5. The child has the capacity to make decisions. According to the Adlerian position, the individual is more than a reactive creature. He/she is also an active person who decides how he/she will respond. Individual choice can be used as a therapeutic factor if the therapist and teacher are willing to allow the child to experience the natural and logical consequences of his/her actions.

6. Failure to perform relates to the dynamics of discouragement. Extremely discouraged children assume that they cannot function, that they will fail, or perhaps that it is not worth the effort to succeed. Such expectations and beliefs strongly influence behavior. But, rather than attacking such belief systems directly, Adlerians focus on changing specific actions of the child which, in turn, will elicit different feedback from significant others. Manipulating the environment may be required to change the individual's opinion of self.

7. The need to belong is basic. Human beings have a strong desire to be accepted, to feel a part of the group, to find their place. Many behavior problems arise because the child is not meaningfully involved in the educational process. Academic expectations may be unrealistic or irrelevant. And the teacher's focus is often on diagnosing weaknesses rather than encouraging desired behavior. Corrective procedures based on group meetings and sociometric tools are activities that the Adlerian therapist utilizes to promote a sense of belonging.

8. Adlerians are more concerned with how a person decides to use what abilities he/she has than with what abilities a person has. Adlerians believe that psychologists are overconcerned with testing. They believe that greater attention should be devoted to the motivations, attitudes, and beliefs of the child. Thus, such data as anecdotes, sentence completion forms, autobiographies, and other scales that permit access to one's private logic are given precedence over those instruments that assess abilities or personality traits. Understanding "what works" with the individual child is seen as basic to the therapeutic and educational process.

The Adlerian approach has wide appeal and it may be a useful tool for those caregivers who strongly espouse democratic values. To date, however, there has been no research-based evaluation of this approach. Hence, objective judgment regarding its effectiveness is not possible at present. Regretably, advocates of this approach are not inclined to conduct empirical studies of its outcomes.

Summary

Schools have become increasingly concerned about the emotional well-being of all students, not just those in need of psychological repair. Careful delineation of the pivotal competencies comprising mental health should facilitate the contribution that schools can make to effective adjustment. To ensure a comprehensive mental health program, a three-level model of intervention is needed. Primary prevention programs, which have as their focus psychologically healthy individuals, are now becoming a reality. Secondary prevention activities involving early identification and treatment are also coming into vogue. Tertiary prevention services, which seek to treat psychologically damaged students, continue to receive the most attention. At the present time, it is difficult to demonstrate the effectiveness of prevention programs. Hopefully, the promise contained in new approaches will be realized and the psychological health of children will be strengthened as a result of school encounters.

References

Albee, G. The relation of conceptual models to manpower needs. In E. L. Cowen, E. Gardner, & M. Zax (Eds.), *Emergent approaches to mental health problems.* New York: Appleton-Century-Crofts, 1967, 63–73.

Allen, G., Chinsky, J., Larcen, S., Lochman, J., & Selinger, H. *Community psychology and the schools: A behaviorally oriented multi-level preventive approach.* Hillsdale, New Jersey: Lawrence Erlbaum Associates, 1976.

Anderson, J. *A survey of children's adjustment over time: A report to the people of Nobles County.* Minneapolis: Institute of Child Development and Welfare, University of Minnesota, 1959.

Anderson, S., & Messick, S. Social competency in young children. *Developmental Psychology,* 1974, **10,** 282–293.

Barr, N. The responsible world of reality therapy. *Psychology Today,* 1974, **65,** 67–68.

Bernstein, M. E. Psychotherapy in the schools: Promise and perplexity. *Journal of School Psychology,* 1976, **14,** 314–321.

Bessell, H. *Methods in human development: Theory manual,* 1973 Revision. El Cajon, California: Human Development Training Institute, 1973.

Bessell, H., & Palomares, U. *Methods in human development: Theory manual and curriculum activity guide.* San Diego: Human Development Training Institute, 1970.

Bolton, A. A prophylactic approach to child psychiatry. *Journal of Mental Science,* 1955, **101,** 696–703.

Bower, E. M. *The early identification of emotionally handicapped children in school* (2nd ed.). Springfield, Illinois: Thomas, 1969.

Bower, E. M. Primary prevention of mental and emotional disorders. In N. Lambert (Ed.), *The protection and promotion of mental health in schools.* Washington, D.C.: U.S. Government Printing Office, 1964.

Bower, E. M. Mental health. In R. Ebel (Ed.), *Encyclopedia of educational research* (4th ed.). New York: Macmillan, 1970.

Bryan, T. H., & Bryan, J. H. *Understanding learning disabilities.* Port Washington, New York: Alfred, 1975.

Clarizio, H. *Toward positive classroom discipline.* New York: Wiley, 1976.

Clarizio, H., & McCoy, G. *Behavior disorders in children.* New York: Crowell, 1976.

Cohen, A., Filipczak, J., Slavin, J., & Boren, J. *Programming interpersonal curricula for adolescents.* Silver Springs, Maryland: Institute for Behavioral Research, 1971.

Commission to study the consolidation of children's services. *A plan to transfer psychiatric and related services for children to the Department of Children and Youth Services.* Hartford, Connecticut: Council on Human Services, 1975.

Cook, J. *The effects of small group counseling on the classroom behavior of sociometrically underchosen adolescents.* Unpublished doctoral dissertation, University of Georgia, 1972.

Cowen, E. Social and community interventions. *Annual Review of Psychology,* 1973, **24,** 423–471.

Cowen, E. Baby-steps toward primary prevention. *American Journal of Community Psychology,* 1977, **5,** 1–22.

Cowen, E., Gardner, E., & Zax, M. *Emergent approaches to mental health.* New York: Appleton-Century-Crofts, 1967.

Cruickshank, W. *Psychology of exceptional children and youth* (2nd ed.). Englewood Cliffs, New Jersey: Prentice-Hall, 1963.

DeHirsch, K., Jansky, J., & Langford, W. *Predicting reading failure.* New York: Harper & Row, 1966.

De Risi, W., & Butz, G. *Writing behavioral contracts.* Champaign, Illinois: Research Press, 1975.

Dinkmeyer, D., & Dinkmeyer, D. Contributions to adlerian psychology to school counseling. *Psychology in the Schools,* 1976, **13,** 32–38.

Dollard, J., & Miller, N. E. *Personality and psychotherapy.* New York: McGraw-Hill, 1950.

Dorr, D. An ounce of prevention. *Mental Hygiene,* 1972, **56,** 25–27.

American Guidance Service. *DUSO: Developing understanding of self and others manual.* Circle Pines, Minnesota: Author, 1970.

Elardo, P., & Elardo, R. A critical analysis of social development programs in elementary education. *Journal of School Psychology,* 1976, **14,** 118–130.

Eldridge, M., Barcikowski, R., & Witmer, J. Effects of DUSO on the self concepts of second grade students. *Elementary School Guidance & Counseling,* 1973, **7,** 256–260.

Fairweather, G. *Social change: The challenge to survival.* Morristown, New Jersey: General Learning Press, 1972.

Ferinden, W., & Jacobsen, S. Early identification of learning disabilities. *Journal of Learning Disabilities,* 1970, **3,** 589–593.

Feshbacti, S., Adelman, H., & Fuller, W. Prediction of reading and related academic problems. *Journal of Educational Psychology,* 1977, **69,** 299–308.

Flanagan, J. Evaluation and validation of research data in primary prevention. *American Journal of Orthopsychiatry,* 1971, **41,** 117–122.

Franks, C. Behavior therapy, psychology and the psychiatrist: Contributions, evaluation and overview. *American Journal of Orthopsychiatry,* 1965, **85,** 145–151.

Freud, A. *Psychoanalytic treatment of children.* London: Imago, 1946.

Gallagher, J., & Bradley, R. Early identification of developmental difficulties. In I. J. Gordon (Ed.), *Early childhood education. Yearbook of the national society for the study of education* (Part II). Chicago: University of Chicago Press, 1972.

Gesten, E. L. A health resources inventory: The development of a measure of the personal and social competence of primary-grade children. *Journal of Consulting and Clinical Psychology,* 1976, **44,** 775–786.

Gesten, E., Flores de Apodaca, R., Rains, M., Weissberg, R., & Cowen, E. Promoting peer related competence in school. In M. Kent & J. Rolf (Eds.) *The Primary prevention of psychopathology: Promoting social competence and coping in children* (Vol. 3). Hanover, New Hampshire: University Press of New England, 1978.

Ginott, H. *Group psychotherapy with children.* New York: McGraw-Hill, 1961.

Glasser, W. Disorders in our schools: Causes and remedies. *Phi Delta Kappan,* 1978, **59,** 331–333.

Glick, B. *The investigation of changes in self-concept, social self-esteem and academic self-responsibility of emotionally disturbed boys who participate in open-ended classroom meetings.* Unpublished doctoral dissertation, Syracuse University, 1968.

Goldstein, H., Jordan, L., & Moss, J. W. *Early school development of low IQ children: Study of special class placement.* Urbana, Illinois: Research Institute for Exceptional Children, 1962.

Hansen, P. *Educationally handicapped programs in selected school districts of Southern California.* Los Angeles: Author, 1970.

Haring, N. G., & Ridgeway, R. Early identification of children with learning disabilities. *Exceptional Children,* 1967, **33,** 387–395.

Hartup, W. Peer relations and the growth of social competence. In M. Kent & J. Rolf (Eds.), *The primary prevention of psychopathology: Promoting social competence and coping with children* (Vol. 3). Hanover, New Hampshire: University Press of New England, 1978.

Heber, R. *Research in prevention of sociocultural mental retardation.* Paper presented at the Vermont Conference on the Primary Prevention of Psychopathology, Burlington, 1976.

Hawes, R. *Reality therapy in the classroom.* Unpublished doctoral dissertation, University of the Pacific, 1970.

Jackson, P. *Life in classrooms.* New York: Holt, 1968.

Jones, M. C. A laboratory study of fear: The case of Peter. *Journal of Genetic Psychology,* 1924, **31,** 308–315.

Jersild, F., & Holmes, F. Methods of overcoming children's fears. *Journal of Psychology,* 1935, **1,** 75–104.

Kent, R., & O'Leary, K. A controlled evaluation of behavior modification with conduct problem children. *Journal of Consulting and Clinical Psychology,* 1976, **44,** 586–596.

Koegel, R., & Rincover, A. Treatment of psychotic children in a classroom environment: Learning in a large group. *Journal of Applied Behavior Analysis,* 1974, **7,** 1, 45–60.

Koppitz, E. *Children with learning disabilities: A five year follow-up study.* New York: Grune & Stratton, 1971.

Koval, C., & Hales, L. The effects of the DUSO guidance program on self-concepts of primary school children. *Child Study Journal,* 1972, **2,** 57–61.

Lambert, N., & Bower, E. *Technical report on in-school screening of emotionally handicapped children.* Princeton, New Jersey: Educational Testing Service, 1961.

Lanbert, N. *The protection and promotion of mental health in schools.* Washington, D.C.: U.S. Government Printing Office, 1964.

Lemle, R. Primary prevention of psychological disorders in elementary and intermediate schools. *Journal of Clinical Child Psychology,* 1976, **5,** 26–32.

Levitt, E. Results of psychotherapy with children: An evaluation. *Journal of Consulting Psychology,* 1957, **21,** 189–196.

Levitt, E. Psychotherapy with children: A further review. *Behavior Research and Therapy,* 1963, **1,** 45–51.

Lippmen, H. S. *Treatment of the child in emotional conflict* (2nd ed.). New York: McGraw-Hill, 1962.

Lorion, R., Cowen, E., & Caldwell, R. Problem types of children referred to a school-based mental health program: Identification and outcome. *Journal of Consulting and Clinical Psychology,* 1974, **42,** 491–496.

Lovaas, I., Koegel, R., Simmons, J., & Long, J. Some generalization and follow-up measures on autistic children in behavior therapy. *Journal of Applied Behavior Analysis,* 1975, **6,** 1, 131–65.

Lovitt, T. Self-management profects with children with behavioral disorders. *Journal of Learning Disabilities,* 1973, **6,** 138–150.

Maitland, S., Nadeau, J., & Nadeau, G. Early screening practices. *Journal of Learning Disabilities,* 1974, **7,** 55–59.

Medway, F., & Smith, R. An examination of contemporary elementary school affective education programs. *Psychology in the Schools*, 1978, **15,** 260–269.

Michigan Department of Education. *Summary report of school psychological services: 1974–1975.* Lansing: Author, 1976.

Minuchin, P., Biber, B., Shapiro, E., & Zimiles, E. *The psychological impact of school experience.* New York: Basic Books, 1969.

Moos, R. *Evaluating treatment environments: A social ecological approach.* New York: Wiley, 1974.

Morse, W. The mental health dilemma in public education. *American Journal of Orthopsychiatry*, 1961, **31,** 332–338.

Morse, W., Cutler, R., & Fink, A. *Public school classes for the emotionally handicapped: A research analysis.* Washington, D.C.: Council for Exceptional Children, 1964.

Mowrer, O. *Learning theory and personality dynamics.* New York: Ronald Press, 1950.

Minuchin, P., Biber, B., Shapiro, E., & Zimiles, E. *The psychological impact of school experience.* New York: Basic Books, 1969.

Myers, P., & Hammill, D. *Methods for learning disorders.* New York: Wiley, 1976.

Newton, R., & Brown, R. A preventive approach to developmental problems in school children. In E. Bower & W. Hollister (Eds.) *Behavioral science frontiers in education.* New York: Wiley, 1967, 499–528.

Norman, V., Rosen, B., & Bahn, A. Psychiatric clinic outpatients in the United States, 1959. *Mental Hygiene*, 1962, **46,** 321–343.

Office of Child Development. *Report on the conference on the use of stimulant drugs with behaviorally disturbed young school children.* Washington, D.C.: Department of Health, Education and Welfare, 1971.

Ojemann, R. Incorporating psychological concepts in the school curriculum. *Journal of School Psychology*, 1967, **5,** 195–204.

Oppenheimer, E., & Mandel, M. Behavior disturbances of school children in relation to the preschool period. *American Journal of Public Health*, 1959, **49,** 1537–1542.

O'Keefe, E. *A comparison of group counseling approaches with behavior-problem boys in an urban elementary school.* Unpublished doctoral dissertation, Boston University, 1973.

Pearson, G. *Emotional disorders of children.* New York: Norton, 1949.

Piaget, J. *Psychology of intelligence.* Patterson, New Jersey: Littlefield, Adams, 1960.

Platt, J., & Spivack, G. *Workbook for training in interpersonal problem solving thinking.* Philadelphia: Department of Mental Health Sciences, Hahnemann Community Mental Health/Mental Retardation Center, 1976.

Platt, J., Spivack, G., & Swift, M. *Problem solving therapy with maladjusted groups.* (Research and Evaluation Report No. 28) Philadelphia: Department of Mental Health Sciences, Hahnemann Medical College and Hospital, 1974.

Redl, F. *When we deal with children.* New York: Free Press, 1966.

Reid, J., & Hagen, H. *Residential treatment of emotionally disturbed children.* New York: Child Welfare League of America, 1952.

Report to the Congress. *Learning disabilities: The link to delinquency should be determined, but schools should do more now.* Washington, D.C.: The Controller General of the United States, 1977.

Report of the Joint Commission. *The mental health of children: Services, research and manpower.* New York: Harper & Row, 1973.

Repucci, N., & Saunders, J. Social psychology of behavior modification. *American Psychologist*, 1974, **29,** 649–660.

Ricks, D. Supershrink: Methods of a therapist judged successful on the basis of adult outcomes of adolescent patients. In D. Ricks, A. Thomas, & M. Roff (Eds.), *Life history research in psychopathology* (Vol. 3). Minneapolis: The University of Minnesota Press, 1974.

Ringness, T. *Mental health in the school.* New York: Random House, 1968.

Roen, S. The behavioral sciences in the primary grades. *American Psychologist*, 1965, **20,** 450–452.

Roen, S. Primary prevention in the classroom through a teaching program in the behavioral sciences. In E. Cowen, E. Gardner, & M. Zax (Eds.) *Emergent approaches to mental health problems.* New York: Appleton-Century-Crofts, 1967.

Rose, S. *Treating children in groups.* San Francisco: Jossey-Bass, 1972.

Rubin, E. Special education in a psychiatric hospital. *Exceptional Children,* 1962, **29,** 184–190.

Rubin, R., Balow, B., Dorle, J., & Rosen, M. *Accuracy of preschool identification of potential learning disabilities.* Paper presented at the annual meeting of the American Educational Research Association, San Francisco, April 1976.

Sameroff, A., & Chandler, M. Reproductive risk and the continuum of caretaking casualty. In F. Horowitz (Ed.), *Review of child development research* (Vol. 4). Chicago: University of Chicago Press.

Sarason, S. *The culture of the school and the problem of change.* Boston: Allyn & Bacon, 1971.

Sarason, S. Community psychology, networks, and Mr. Everyman. *American Psychologist,* 1976, **31,** 317–328.

Schofield, W. *Psychotherapy: The purchase of friendship.* Englewood Cliffs, New Jersey: Prentice-Hall, 1964.

Scott, W. Conception of normality. In E. Borgatta & W. Lambert (Eds.), *Handbook of personality theory and research.* Chicago: Rand McNally, 1968.

Shea, G. *The effects of reality therapy oriented group counseling with delinquent behavior-disordered students.* Unpublished doctoral dissertation, Fordham University, 1973.

Shearn, D. Effects of reality therapy methods applied in the classroom. *Psychology in the Schools,* 1978, **15,** 79–83.

Shepherd, M., Oppenheim, B., & Mitchell, S. *Childhood behavior and mental health.* New York: Grune & Stratton, 1966.

Shoben, E. Psychotherapy as a problem in learning theory. *Psychological Bulletin,* 1949, **46,** 366–392.

Shure, M. Real life problem solving for parents and children: An approach to social competence. In M. Kent & J. Rolf (Eds.), *The primary prevention of psychopathology: Promoting social competence and coping in children* (Vol. 3). Hanover, New Hampshire: University Press of New England, 1978.

Slavson, S. *Child psychotherapy.* New York: Columbia University Press, 1952.

Spivack, G., & Shure, M. *Social adjustment in young children.* San Francisco: Jossey Bass, 1974.

Spivack, G., Platt, J., & Shure, M. *The problem solving approach to adjustment.* San Francisco: Jossey-Bass, 1976.

Trickett, E., & Moos, R. Personal correlates of contrasting environments: student satisfaction in high school classrooms. *American Journal of Community Psychology,* 1974, **2,** 1–12.

Ullmann, L., & Krasner, L. *Case studies in behavior modification.* New York: Holt, 1965.

U. S. Department of Health, Education and Welfare. *Report on the conference on the use of stimulant drugs in the treatment of behaviorally disordered young school children: 1971.* Washington, D.C.: U.S.Government Printing Office, 1971.

Wallach, M. *Essay review on the psychological impact of school experience. Harvard Educational Review,* 1971, **41,** 2, 230–239.

White, M. Little red schoolhouse and little white clinic. *Teachers College Record,* 1965, **67,** 188–200.

White, R. Competence as an aspect of personal growth. In M. Kent & J. Rolf (Eds.), *The primary prevention of psychopathology: Promoting social competence and coping in children* (Vol. 3). Hanover, New Hampshire: University Press of New England, 1978.

Watson, R. *The clinical method in psychology.* New York: Harper & Row, 1951.

Watson, J., & Raynow, R. Conditioned emotional reactions. *Journal of Experimental Psychology,* 1920, **3,** 1–14.

White, R., & Wat, N. *The abnormal personality* (4th ed.). New York: Ronald Press, 1975.

Zax, M., & Specter, G. *An introduction to community psychology.* New York: Wiley, 1974.

Appendix:
Resources in School Psychology

Journals

The *Journal of School Psychology* is published quarterly. Information concerning subscriptions and back issues can be obtained by contacting Human Sciences Press, 72 Fifth Avenue, New York, N.Y. 10011. *Psychology in the Schools* is published quarterly by the Clinical Psychology Publishing Co., 4 Conant Square, Brandon, Vt. 05733. The *School Psychology Digest* is published quarterly by the National Association of School Psychologists. Information concerning subscriptions can be obtained by writing to the address for NASP listed in the following section.

Organizations

In addition to state school psychology associations and other national organizations that may be of interest to some school psychologists, such as the Council for Exceptional Children, Association for Children with Learning Disabilities, American Association on Mental Deficiency, and American Personnel and Guidance Association, we recommend affiliation with both the American Psychological Association and the National Association of School Psychologists. Information concerning the American Psychological Association and the Division of School Psychology (Division 16) can be obtained by writing to APA, 1200 Seventeenth St. N.W., Washington, D.C. 20036. Student membership in both Division 16 and APA is available. APA and Division 16 membership benefits include subscriptions to the *American Psychologist* and *APA Monitor* (published monthly) and the Division 16 newsletter *The School Psychologist*. Division 16 also publishes monographs occasionally. Information concerning the National Association of School Psychologists may be obtained by writing to NASP, 1511 K Street N.W., Suite 927, Washington, D.C. 20005. Student membership in NASP is available. NASP membership benefits include subscriptions to the *School Psychology Digest* and a newsletter, *NASP Communique,* published eight times per year.

Index

EDUCATIONAL PSYCHOLOGY

continued from page ii

António Simões (ed.). The Bilingual Child: Research and Analysis of Existing Educational Themes

Gilbert R. Austin. Early Childhood Education: An International Perspective

Vernon L. Allen (ed.). Children as Teachers: Theory and Research on Tutoring

Joel R. Levin and Vernon L. Allen (eds.). Cognitive Learning in Children: Theories and Strategies

Donald E. P. Smith and others. A Technology of Reading and Writing (in four volumes).

> *Vol. 1. Learning to Read and Write: A Task Analysis (by Donald E. P. Smith)*
> *Vol. 2. Criterion-Referenced Tests for Reading and Writing (by Judith M. Smith, Donald E. P. Smith, and James R. Brink)*
> *Vol. 3. The Adaptive Classroom (by Donald E. P. Smith)*
> *Vol. 4. Designing Instructional Tasks (by Judith M. Smith)*

Phillip S. Strain, Thomas P. Cooke, and Tony Apolloni. Teaching Exceptional Children: Assessing and Modifying Social Behavior